The Photoshop 5 Toolb

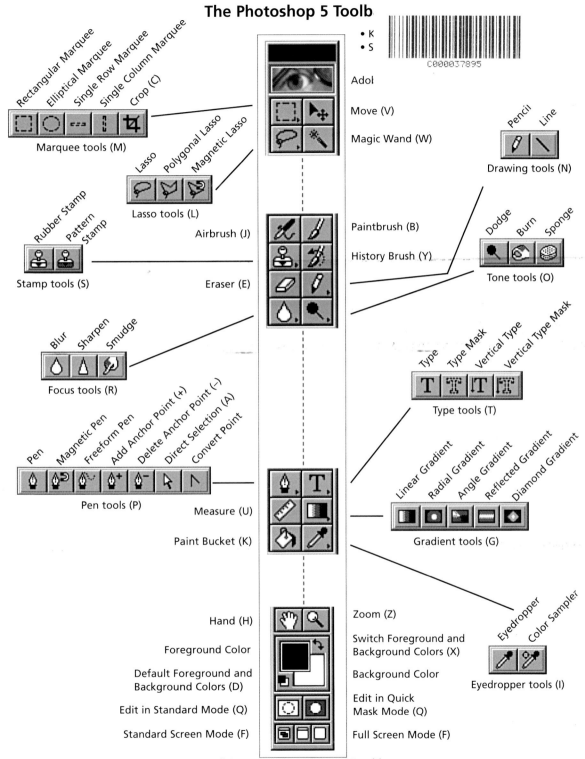

C000037895

Rectangular Marquee
Elliptical Marquee
Single Row Marquee
Single Column Marquee
Crop (C)

Marquee tools (M)

Lasso
Polygonal Lasso
Magnetic Lasso

Lasso tools (L)

Rubber Stamp
Pattern Stamp

Stamp tools (S)

Blur
Sharpen
Smudge

Focus tools (R)

Pen
Magnetic Pen
Freeform Pen
Add Anchor Point (+)
Delete Anchor Point (–)
Direct Selection (A)
Convert Point

Pen tools (P)

Pencil
Line

Drawing tools (N)

Dodge
Burn
Sponge

Tone tools (O)

Type
Type Mask
Vertical Type
Vertical Type Mask

Type tools (T)

Linear Gradient
Radial Gradient
Angle Gradient
Reflected Gradient
Diamond Gradient

Gradient tools (G)

Eyedropper
Color Sampler

Eyedropper tools (I)

• K
• S

Adol
Move (V)
Magic Wand (W)

Airbrush (J)
Paintbrush (B)
History Brush (Y)

Eraser (E)

Measure (U)
Paint Bucket (K)

Hand (H)
Zoom (Z)

Foreground Color
Switch Foreground and Background Colors (X)

Default Foreground and Background Colors (D)
Background Color

Edit in Standard Mode (Q)
Edit in Quick Mask Mode (Q)

Standard Screen Mode (F)
Full Screen Mode (F)

Full Screen Mode with Menu Bar (F)

Photoshop 5 Keyboard Shortcut Quick Reference

Top-level menus have keyboard mnemonics (accessed by pressing Alt+) for Windows users. Windows users should use the Control key instead of Command except where indicated.

FILE MENU

New	Cmd+N
Open	Cmd+O
Open As (Windows only)	Alt+Cmd+O
Close	Cmd+W
Save	Cmd+S
Save As	Shift+Cmd+S
Save a Copy	Option+Cmd+S
Page Setup	Shift+Cmd+P
Print	Cmd+P
Preferences->General	Cmd+K

EDIT MENU

Undo	Cmd+Z
Cut	Cmd+X
Copy	Cmd+C
Copy Merged	Shift+Cmd+C
Paste	Cmd+V
Past Into	Shift+Cmd+V
Free Transform	Cmd+T
Transform->Again	Shift+Cmd+T

IMAGE MENU

Adjust->Levels	Cmd+L
Adjust->Auto Levels	Shift+Cmd+L
Adjust->Curves	Cmd+M
Adjust->Color Balance	Cmd+B
Adjust->Hue/Saturation	Cmd+U
Adjust->Desaturate	Shift+Cmd+U
Adjust->Invert	Cmd+I

LAYER MENU

New->Layer	Shift+Cmd+N
New->Layer Via Copy	Cmd+J
New->Layer Via Cut	Shift+Cmd+J
Group with Previous	Cmd+G
Ungroup	Shift+Cmd+G
Arrange->Bring to Front	Shift+Cmd+]
Arrange->Bring Forward	Cmd+]
Arrange->Send Backward	Cmd+[
Arrange->Send to Back	Shift+Cmd+[
Merge Down	Cmd+E
Merge Visible	Shift+Cmd+E

SELECT MENU

All	Cmd+A
Deselect	Cmd+D
Reselect	Shift+Cmd+D
Inverse	Shift+Cmd+I
Feather	Alt+Ctrl+D (Windows)
	Shift+Cmd+D (Macintosh)

FILTER MENU

Last Filter	Cmd+F
Fade	Shift+Cmd+F

VIEW MENU

Preview->CMYK	Cmd+Y
Gamut Warning	Shift+Cmd+Y
Zoom In	Cmd++
Zoom Out	Cmd+-
Fit on Screen	Cmd+0 (zero)
Actual Pixels	Shift+Ctrl+0 (zero) (Windows)
	Alt+Cmd+0 (zero) (Macintosh)
Hide Edges	Cmd+H
Hide Path	Shift+Cmd+H
Show Rulers	Cmd+R
Hide Guides	Cmd+;
Snap To Guides	Shift+Cmd+;
Lock Guides	Alt+Cmd+;
Show Grid	Cmd+"
Snap To Grid	Shift+Cmd+"

HELP MENU (Windows only)

Contents	F1

OTHER SHORTCUTS

Move view up/down 1 screen	Page Up/Down (W)
	Opt+PageUp/Down (M)
Nudge view up/down	Shift+Page Up/Down (W)
	Opt+Shift+PageUp/Down (M)
Move view left/right 1 screen	Ctrl+Page Up/Down (W)
	Cmd+PageUp/Down (M)
Nudge view left/right	Shift+Ctrl+Page Up/Down (W)
	Cmd+Shift+PageUp/Down (M)
Previous History Entry	Ctrl+Shift+Z
Next History Entry	Ctrl+Alt+Z
Scroll through blending modes	Shift++ and Shift+-

Using

Adobe®

Photoshop® 5

Dan Giordan

Steven Moniz

que

A Division of Macmillan Computer Publishing, USA
201 W. 103rd Street
Indianapolis, Indiana 46290

Contents at a Glance

Using Adobe® Photoshop® 5

Copyright© 1998 by Que®

International Standard Book Number: 0-7897-1656-9

Library of Congress Catalog Card Number: 98-84418

Printed in the United States of America

First Printing: July, 1998

00 99 98 6 5 4 3 2 1

Trademarks

Executive Editor
Beth Millett

Acquisitions Editor
Karen Whitehouse

Development Editor
Bob Correll

Project Editor
Katie Purdum

Copy Editor
San Dee Phillips

Indexer
Greg Pearson

Technical Editor
Robert Stanley

Production
Marcia Deboy
Michael Dietsch
Jennifer Earhart
Cynthia Fields
Susan Geiselman

Contents

About the Authors

Steven Moniz is the Director of Training at Graphics Express in Boston and teaches regularly scheduled courses in everything from Macintosh Basics to Advanced Photoshop, QuarkXPress, HTML programming, and Web Design. On the cutting edge of Desktop Publishing and Electronic Prepress technology since its inception in the early '80s, Steve's background includes traditional offset printing, publishing, pre-press production, computer programming, and typesetting. Steve often lectures on Digital Prepress topics and provides customized training for corporate clients on both Macintosh and Windows platforms.

Steve is the author of *Photoshop Studio Skills* and co-authored *Photoshop 4 Complete*, both for Hayden books.

Steve wrote Chapters 1–7, 25–30, and contributed to Appendixes A and B.

Daniel Giordan is an artist, author, and lecturer who works in both digital and conventional artistic media. He is the author of *Dynamic Photoshop* (MIS Press, 1997), and a contributing author for *Using Macromedia Dreamweaver 1.2* (Que, 1998) and *The Whole Mac* (Hayden Books, 1996).

Dan wrote Chapters 11–13 and 15–20.

Carla Rose started her photography career at the age of 8 with a Brownie Hawkeye. A graduate of the School of the Museum of Fine Arts in Boston, she has been a TV news photographer and film editor, as well as an advertising copywriter and graphic artist, before discovering the Macintosh. Carla has written all or part of more than twenty computer books, including *Maclopedia, Teach Yourself Digital Photography in 14 Days, Sam's Teach Yourself Photoshop 4 in 24 Hours, Sams Teach Yourself Photoshop 5 in 24 Hours, Sam's Teach Yourself Photoshop in 14 Days, The Whole Mac, Managing the Windows NT Server, PageMaker 6.5 Complete, Mac Online, It's a Mad, Mad, Mad, Mad Mac, Turbocharge Your Mac,* and *Everything You Ever Wanted to Know About the Mac.* She lives near Boston, Massachusetts with her husband, audio guru Jay Rose, and a fluctuating number of cats. In her spare time, Carla plays computer games and enjoys cooking, swimming, and answering readers' questions. Write to `momcat@pinkcat.com`

Carla wrote Chapters 21–24.

Steve Banick is a network administrator and graphic designer (what a duo!) who is currently the client software developer for TELUS PLAnet Internet Services in Alberta, Canada. Life is nothing like a box of chocolates; however, it can offer you rich rewards. He has settled into a peaceful coexistence with his wife Christina and two dogs. Steve pursues (with vehemence) the cure to plague all that ails most modern individuals: cable television. Steve can be reached on the Web at http://www.banick.com and via email at steve@banick.com. Steve still remembers fondly the days of "Mule" and "Miner 2049er".

Steve wrote Appendixes A, B, and C.

Chris Denschikoff comes from a funny, little rumbly-tumbly town called Calgary, Alberta, where the sugar waterfalls and the peppermint forest enclose a forbidding fortress from which his evil minions issue. He writes a lot; he just wishes he got paid more. He also designs Web sites a lot for TELUS Advertising Services and wishes he got paid more. In his spare time he rocks out with the world's absolute worst band, Frank Slide (for which he doesn't get paid at all).

Chris is always willing to talk to all the interesting people who read his work and can be reached day or night at chris@banick.com. Finally, Chris really digs the latest release of Photoshop 5.0 but just wishes young people showed more respect.

Chris wrote Chapters 8–10.

Robert Stanley grew up in Lincoln Park, Michigan. At age 10, Robert was drawing caricatures for the city's charity. A self-taught artist, Robert's clients have included 20th Century Fox, Cigar Aficionado, Paper Moon Graphics, and the Firesign Theatre. Besides Photoshop, Robert is proficient in numerous other 2D and 3D graphics and animation programs.

Robert wrote Chapter 14 and contributed to Chapters 8–10.

About the Technical Editor

Robert Stanley grew up in Lincoln Park, Michigan. At age 10, Robert was drawing caricatures for the city's charity. A self-taught artist, Robert's clients have included 20th Century Fox, Cigar Aficionado, Paper Moon Graphics, and the Firesign Theatre. Besides Photoshop, Robert is proficient in numerous other 2D and 3D graphics and animation programs.

Acknowledgments

Special thanks to Karen Whitehouse, Bob Correll, Katie Purdum, and San Dee Phillips for their patience, guidance, and hard work on this title.

Tell Us What You Think

As the reader of this book, you are our most important critic and commentator. We value your opinion and want to know what we're doing right, what we could do better, what areas you'd like to see us publish in, and any other words of wisdom you're willing to pass our way.

As the Executive Editor for the Web Design and Graphics team at Macmillan Computer Publishing, I welcome your comments. You can fax, email, or write me directly to let me know what you did or didn't like about this book—as well as what we can do to make our books stronger.

Please note that I cannot help you with technical problems related to the topic of this book, and that due to the high volume of mail I receive, I might not be able to reply to every message.

When you write, please be sure to include this book's title and author as well as your name and phone or fax number. I will carefully review your comments and share them with the author and editors who worked on the book.

Fax: 317-817-7070

E-mail: desktop_pub@mcp.com

Mail: Beth Millett
Web Design and Graphics
Macmillan Computer Publishing
201 West 103rd Street
Indianapolis, IN 46290 USA

Tech Support

If you need assistance with the information in this book or you have feedback for us about the book, please contact Macmillan Technical Support by phone at **317-581-3833** or via email at support@mcp.com.

Orders, Catalogs, and Customer Service

To order other Que or Macmillan Computer Publishing books, catalogs, or products, please contact our Customer Service Department:

Phone: 1-800-428-5331

Fax: 1-800-835-3202

International Fax: 1-317-228-4400

Or visit our online bookstore:

htp://www.mcp.com/

Welcome to *Using Adobe Photoshop 5.0*, and thank you for selecting this book as your guide for exploration of Adobe Photoshop. This book has been written with one goal in mind: to provide you with the knowledge to freely create anything your mind's eye envisions using the tools within Photoshop 5.0. This new version of Photoshop refines old features and introduces useful, new additions to the Photoshop suite of tools, so a certain amount of relearning is required even for the most experienced of Photoshop users. Regardless of your level of expertise, we believe that you will find this book a valuable resource of information.

This book focuses on providing you with relevant information that you can use on an ongoing basis. It is not necessarily intended to be read cover to cover. Rather, it has been designed as a reference book that you can keep near your desk as you work. This introduction provides a brief overview of Adobe Photoshop, information on how this book is organized, and how to best use the information in this volume. Experienced users might want to immediately jump into subsequent sections of this book; however, everyone can benefit by familiarizing themselves with this book's layout.

Adobe Photoshop is arguably the de facto standard setter for image manipulation. Adobe calls Photoshop "the camera for your mind," and rightly so; if you can conceive an idea, Photoshop has the tools to execute it. Photoshop is a software package that enables graphic artists, designers, Webmasters, and photographers to create original artwork, retouch and correct images, manipulate scanned images, and prepare professional-quality output for both print and electronic media. Adobe originally created the Photoshop software as a tool for correcting photographs and scanned images. Today Photoshop is used as a tool for creating print images, photographic manipulation, and designing for CD-ROM and the World Wide Web.

Why This Book?

Have you ever purchased a Using book from Que? The Using books have proven invaluable to readers as both learning guides and as references for many years. The Using series is an industry leader and has practically become an industry standard. We encourage and receive feedback from readers all the time, and we consider and implement their suggestions whenever possible.

Using Adobe Photoshop 5 incorporates fresh new ideas and approaches to the Using series. This book is not a compiled authority on all the features of Photoshop. Instead, it is a streamlined, conversational approach for using Photoshop productively and efficiently. Here are the new features:

- *Improved index.* *To help you find information the first time you look!* What do you call tasks and features? Every possible name or description of a task was anticipated and cross-referenced in the index.

- *Real-life answers.* Throughout the book, you will find real-life examples and experiences. *How* to perform a task is only one question you might have, and perhaps the bigger questions are *why* and *what for?*

- *Relevant information written just for you!* The features and tasks have been carefully scrutinized; only those that apply to your everyday use of Photoshop have been included.

- *Reference or tutorial.* You can learn to quickly perform a task using step-by-step instructions, or you can investigate the why and wherefore of a task with discussions surrounding each task.

- *Wise investment.* Lastly, pay the right price for the right book. Don't waste your valuable bookshelf real estate with redundant or irrelevant material. You don't have to "know it all" to be productive. Here is what you need, when you need it, how you need it, with an appropriate price tag.

- *Easy to find procedures.* Every numbered step-by-step procedure in the book has a short title explaining exactly what it does. This saves you time by making it easier to find the exact steps you need to accomplish a task.

- *SideNote elements with quick-read headlines save you time.* Small tips or notes about how to make something work best are given here. Or perhaps you will find a caution or warning about a problem you might encounter. By giving these SideNotes precise titles that explain their topic and by placing them in the margins, each one is easy to skip if you don't need it and easy to find if you want to read it.

Who Should Use This Book

This book is focused on those who are relatively new to Adobe Photoshop and have no experience with Photoshop 5.0. Experience with previous versions of Photoshop is definitely an asset; however, previous experience is not a requirement. This book has been written to educate you on the basic principles on using Photoshop so that you can learn to explore this powerful, creative environment on your own. Using this book will enable you to safely step from novice to expert Photoshop user.

How This Book Is Organized

This book has been designed around five key sections of similar or related information, in addition to a series of appendixes. These sections each contain a number of chapters that directly relate to the topic or task being discussed:

- *Getting Started with Photoshop.* Section I of this book begins with the basics. This section is essentially a "Photoshop boot camp" that will get you up and running on the basics of the Photoshop interface and moving around inside the program. If you have no previous experience with Photoshop, this should be the first place you stop.

- *Using the Painting and Editing Tools.* Although the painting and editing tools in Photoshop share some common elements with other paint programs, Adobe has taken them to a more sophisticated level that is consistent with other tools within Photoshop and also make it easy for you to use their substantial power. Section II provides you with important information on using the editing tools in Photoshop to accomplish specific tasks.

- *Working with Select Areas of an Image.* Photoshop gives you a lot of power when working with regions of an image, especially when you use *masks*. The concepts of selections, masks, layers, and channels are covered in this section and are one of the keys of great success when working with Photoshop. Throughout your use of Photoshop, the skills you learn in section III will infuse your images with the power to achieve their fullest potential impact.

- *Using Filters and Creating Special Effects.* Most new users of Photoshop fall in love with the extensible effects in Photoshop found in filters. The power of these "add-ons" is astonishing and can be used to create incredible masterpieces. In addition to working with filters, section IV teaches you when to use them appropriately and how to create special image and type effects that are found very often in the advertising world.

- *Repairing, Retouching, and Enhancing Images.* Using Photoshop, you can take an existing image, such as a photograph, and repair or alter it to fit your needs. Section V explores the heady topics of corrective color management, colorizing images, working with light and shadows, and repairing damaged images. Additionally, this section gives you some useful information on creating montages and vignettes, and altering the images themselves.

- *Appendices*. These helpful resources cover installation, new features, and troubleshooting tips.

Throughout this book, you will find SideNote material to complement and extend the subject matter. These sidebars act as real-world references and examples for you. They include important information in understanding the nuances of the software and how to apply certain features to their best effect.

Conventions Used in This Book

Commands, directions, and explanations in this book are presented in the clearest format possible. You will encounter the following items:

- *Menu and dialog box commands and options*. You can easily find the onscreen menu and dialog box commands by looking for bold text like you see in this direction: From the **File** menu, choose **Save**.

- *Combination and shortcut keystrokes*. Text that directs you to hold down several keys simultaneously is connected with a plus sign (+), such as Ctrl+P. To differentiate Windows and Macintosh commands, Windows commands are contained within parentheses (Ctrl+P) and Macintosh commands are within brackets [Cmd+P].

- *Cross references*. If there's a related topic that is prerequisite to the section or steps you are reading, or a topic that builds further on what you are reading, you'll find the cross reference to it after the steps or at the end of the section like this:

SEE ALSO
➤ *To change the appearance of text in other ways, see page 261,435*

- *Glossary terms*. For all the terms that appear in the glossary, you'll find the first appearance of that term in the text in *italic* along with its definition.

- *Sidebars*. Information related to the task at hand, or "inside" information from the author is offset in sidebars as not to interfere with the task at hand and to make it easy to find this valuable information. Each of these sidebars has a short title to help you quickly identify the information you'll find there. You'll find the same kind of information in these sidebars that you might find in notes, tips, or warnings in other books but here the titles should be more informative.

Your screen might look slightly different from some of the examples in this book.

Getting Started with Photoshop

Exploring the Photoshop 5 Interface

Using the Toolbox

The Toolbox contains all the tools necessary to manipulate an image. Click the tools in the Toolbox to activate them or type the shortcut key indicated in Figure 1.1. Some of the cells in the Toolbox contain more than one tool. Click and hold the tools that have a tiny triangle in the lower-right corner to choose from the available tools (see Figure 1.2). If you used previous versions of Photoshop, notice that in Photoshop 5 some tools in the Toolbox appear in different positions and some tools have new shortcut keys.

Tool Palettes

Toggle through the available tool choices

(Alt)+click [Option]+click the tools to toggle through the hidden tools, or hold down the Shift key and type the shortcut key to change the tools. Double-clicking a tool displays that tool's Options palette.

With the exception of the **Type**, **Measure**, and **Hand** tools, each tool has a corresponding tool palette called the Options palette (see Figure 1.3). The information in the Options palette changes to reflect the available options for the selected tool. If the Options palette is not currently present, double-click a tool in the Toolbox. The Options palette contains two choices in its palette menu (see Figure 1.4). Click on the triangle in the upper-right corner of the Options palette to display the palette menu. Choose **Reset Tool** to restore the default settings for the tool. Choose **Reset All Tools** to restore the default settings for all tools in the Toolbox.

Palettes

Double-Click to change view

Double-click the **Hand** tool to change the view to fit on screen. Double-click the **Zoom** tool to change the view percentage to 100% (actual pixels). These same options are available under the **View** menu.

Aside from the Toolbox, Photoshop has eleven floating palettes arranged in four palette groups (see Figure 1.5). These palettes offer quick access for choosing color and brush shape and facilitate working with layers, channels, paths, and actions. All the palettes are available under the **Window** menu.

FIGURE 1.1

Type the highlighted letters to access a tool from the Toolbox.

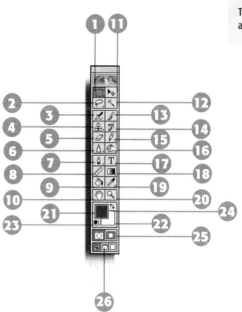

1 Marquee and Crop tools	**14** History Brush tool
2 Lasso tool	**15** Pencil and Line tools
3 Airbrush tool	**16** Toning tools (Dodge, Burn and Sponge)
4 Rubber Stamp tool	**17** Type tool
5 Eraser tool	**18** Gradient tool
6 Blur and Sharpen tools	**19** Eyedropper tool (i)
7 Pen tools & Direct Selection tool	**20** Zoom tool
8 Measure tool	**21** Foreground Color Swatch
9 Paint Bucket tool	**22** Background Color Swatch
10 Hand tool	**23** Default Foreground and Background Color
11 Move tool	**24** Swap Foreground and Background Color (x)
12 Magic Wand tool	**25** Quick Mask
13 Paintbrush tool	**26** Screen modes (f)

FIGURE 1.2

Click and hold on tools that have multiple options.

FIGURE 1.3

Double-click a tool to display the Options palette.

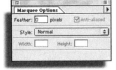

FIGURE 1.4

Click on the triangle in the upper-right corner of the Options palette to display the palette menu.

FIGURE 1.5

The eleven floating palettes available in Photoshop.

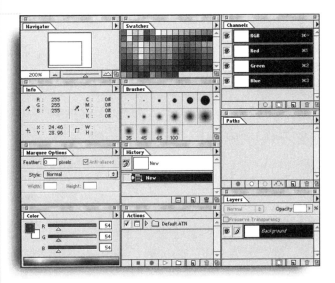

- The palettes can be grouped together or separated from their groups by dragging the tabs that contain the palette name.

- Double-click the palette tab to reduce the palette group to a bar that displays the tabs only. Double-click again on the tab to restore the full palette. Option+click the zoom box in the upper-right corner of the palette group to collapse the group on MacOS. Alt+click the minimize/maximize box in Windows to collapse a palette group.

- Click the (minimize/maximize box) [zoom box] in the upper-right corner of the palette group to reduce the palette to a minimum settings display. Click the (minimize/maximize box) [zoom box] again to restore the full palette.

- Reposition a palette group on the screen by clicking and dragging the title bar (gray bar at top of palette group).

- Resize the palette by dragging the size box in the lower-right corner (MacOS) or drag the lower-right corner (Windows). To return the palette to the default size, click the (minimize/maximize box) [zoom box].

- Close a palette group by clicking the close box in the upper-left corner (MacOS only) or choose the appropriate **Hide** option from the **Window** menu.

Using the Info Palette

The Info palette displays information about your file based on the location of the cursor and the state of your selections. The Info palette displays the color breakdown of pixels as you drag over them with the cursor, as well as the x and y coordinates of the cursor and the width and height of selections. The Info palette also displays up to four color samples taken with the Color Sampler tool (see Figure 1.7). Choose **Show Info** from the **Window** menu to display the Info palette (see Figure 1.6).

Hiding the palettes

To hide all the onscreen palettes, including the Toolbox, press Tab. Press Tab again to display the palettes. To hide all the palettes, except the Toolbox, press Shift+Tab. Press Shift+Tab again to display the palettes.

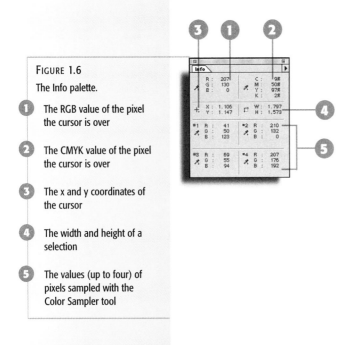

FIGURE 1.6

The Info palette.

1. The RGB value of the pixel the cursor is over

2. The CMYK value of the pixel the cursor is over

3. The x and y coordinates of the cursor

4. The width and height of a selection

5. The values (up to four) of pixels sampled with the Color Sampler tool

FIGURE 1.7

The Color Sampler tool.

- Two sections of the Info palette display color breakdowns, which means you can view the color breakdown of a pixel in two color modes, for example, *RGB* and *CMYK*. To change the color mode displayed, click the Eyedropper icon in the Info palette (see Figure 1.8). You can choose from any of Photoshop's available color modes, as well as *Total Ink* and Opacity. The Opacity choice displays the layer's Opacity (percentage of transparency); this option does not apply to the background layer.

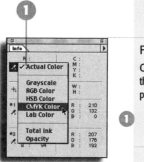

FIGURE 1.8

Click the Eyedropper icons in the Info palette to change display options.

1 Select from a list of color values.

- To change the units of measure used for the x and y coordinates, click the Crosshair icon in the Info palette and choose a measurement unit from the pull-down menu (see Figure 1.9).

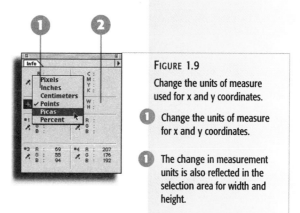

FIGURE 1.9

Change the units of measure used for x and y coordinates.

1 Change the units of measure for x and y coordinates.

1 The change in measurement units is also reflected in the selection area for width and height.

- When you click and drag a marquee selection on the image, the width and height of the selection area are displayed using the measurement units chosen for the x and y coordinates. When you create a marquee selection, the pixel value information in the upper-right area of the Info palette changes to reflect the x and y anchor points (where you started drawing the marquee) while you are dragging to create the selection (see Figure 1.10). When you release the mouse button, this information returns to its original color mode display.

FIGURE 1.10

When you create a selection, the Info palette information displays the anchor point, x and y coordinates of the cursor, and the width and height of the selection.

1 The anchor point is the x and y coordinates of where you started to create a selection marquee.

2 The width and height of the widest and longest area of your selection.

- When you use any of Photoshop's transformation tools (available under the **Edit** menu in the **Transform** submenu), such as **Rotate**, **Scale**, **Skew**, or **Distort**, the upper-right area of the Info palette displays the Width enlargement or reduction percentage, Height enlargement or reduction percentage, Angle of the rotation, and either the Horizontal or Vertical skew angle (see Figure 1.11).

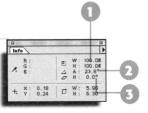

FIGURE 1.11

Transformation dimensions appear in the place of the color breakdown in the upper-right corner of the Info palette.

1 Percentage of enlargement or reduction

2 Angle of rotation

3 Skew angle

- When you use the **Move** tool to move an image on a layer or a selected area of the layer, or when you move a selection marquee, the Info palette displays information about the move in the upper-right corner of the Info palette (see Figure 1.12). The values displayed represent the Distance the selection is moved to the left or right, the distance the selection is moved up or down, the Angle the selection is moved in, and the total Distance the selection is moved.

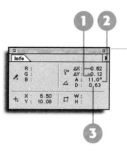

FIGURE 1.12

Information displayed when using the Move tool.

1 The distance moved up/down and left/right

2 The angle the move is offset from it's original position

3 The total distance of the move

Using the Color Palette

You use the Color palette to create the foreground and background colors. To change the foreground and background colors using the Color palette, choose **Show Color** from the **Window** menu to display the Color palette (see Figure 1.13).

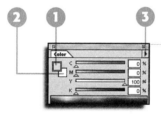

FIGURE 1.13
The Color palette.

1 Foreground color

2 Background color

3 Palette menu

Creating colors with the Color palette

1. The Color palette contains foreground and background swatches. If you click the active color swatch (outlined in black), the Color Picker dialog box appears. Click the inactive color swatch (not outlined in black) to make it active.

2. Select the *color model* for the Color palette by clicking the triangle in the upper-right corner of the Color palette and choosing an option from the palette menu (see Figure 1.14).

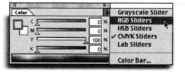

FIGURE 1.14

Choose a color model for the sliders in the Color palette.

3. The color bar at the bottom of the Color palette enables you to choose a color from the color model's spectrum. Click the triangle in the upper-right corner of the Color palette to display the palette menu choices and choose **Color Bar** to choose which color ramp displays at the bottom of the Color palette.

4. Drag the triangle sliders to mix a color.

Using the Swatches Palette

The Swatches palette enables you to save the foreground or background color into a palette of colors for use later. The colors in the Swatches palette can be chosen as the foreground or background color. You can create a Color palette from scratch, add to the palette displayed, save the Color palette, and load previously saved Color palettes. The default swatches contain the current palette. Choose **Show Swatches** from the **Window** menu to display the Swatches palette (see Figure 1.15).

FIGURE 1.15

The Swatches palette.

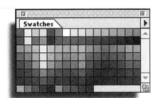

- Position your cursor over one of the color swatches in the Swatches palette. The cursor changes to an Eyedropper cursor.

- Click a swatch to load that color as the foreground color.

- Hold down (Alt) [Option] and click a color swatch to load that color as the background color.

- To add a color, position your cursor over an empty space in the Swatches palette. If no empty spaces are available, click and drag the lower-right corner of the Swatches palette to change the height and reveal empty spaces. The cursor changes to a paint bucket. Click the empty space to add the foreground color to the palette.

■ To replace a color in the Swatches palette, hold down the Shift key (the cursor changes to a paint bucket) and click the swatch to change the swatch color to the foreground color.

■ To insert a color swatch, position the cursor over a color swatch in the palette. Hold down (Shift+Alt)[Shift+Option] (the cursor changes to a paint bucket) and click the swatch to insert a new swatch in the foreground color.

■ To delete a color swatch in the Swatches palette, hold down (Ctrl) [Command]. When the cursor changes to the scissors, click a swatch to delete it.

■ To reset the Swatches palette to the default swatch colors, click the triangle in the upper-right corner of the Swatches palette to display the palette menu and choose Reset Swatches. A dialog box appears in which you can choose whether to replace all the current swatches with the default color swatches or append the default color swatches to the current swatches.

■ To save a custom set of color swatches, click the triangle in the upper-right corner of the Swatches palette and choose **Save Swatches** from the palette menu. Navigate to the folder or directory you want to save the swatches in and click the **Save** button. Save your swatches if you want to use them on another image at a later date. Opening an indexed color image or converting an image to indexed color replaces the custom Color palette with the indexed colors.

■ To replace the current swatches with swatches previously saved, click the triangle in the upper-right corner of the Swatches palette and choose **Replace Swatches** from the palette menu. Navigate to the folder or directory containing the saved swatches and click the **Open** button. The current swatches are replaced with this new set.

■ To append swatches previously saved, click the triangle in the upper-right corner of the Swatches palette and choose **Load Swatches** from the palette menu. Navigate to the folder or directory containing the saved swatches and click the **Open** button. The loaded swatches are appended to the current set.

■ To sample colors from your image to add to the Swatches palette, use the **Eyedropper** tool and click the image to load the colors of that pixel as the foreground color. Click an empty space in the Swatches palette to add it.

Using the Brushes Palette

All the painting tools in Photoshop use brushes with size and style defined and chosen from the Brushes palette. The default brushes are round brushes with hard or soft edges. The brush shape and size is entirely user-definable, enabling you to be as creative as you like when applying color to the image.

■ To choose a brush, choose **Show Brushes** from the **Window** menu to display the Brushes palette (see Figure 1.16) and click a brush to choose it.

■ The brush you choose is used for the particular tool that is active, which means you must choose a brush type for each tool you use.

■ The brushes in the Brushes palette appear in their actual size unless the brush is larger than the palette's cell size. In this case, the diameter of the brush in pixels is indicated below the brush, as is the case with the four brushes along the bottom row of the default Brushes palette.

FIGURE 1.16
The Brushes palette.

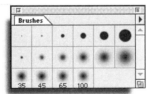

- To modify Brush options, double-click the brush in the Brushes palette or choose **Brush Options** from the palette menu. The Brush Options dialog box appears (see Figure 1.17), enabling you to specify the **Diameter**, **Hardness**, **Spacing**, **Angle**, and **Roundness** of the brush.

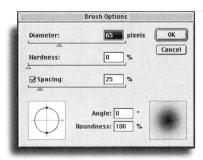

FIGURE 1.17
Modify the attributes of an existing brush or create a new brush.

- To create a new brush, click any of the empty spaces in the Brushes palette to display the New Brush dialog box or click the triangle in the upper-right corner of the Brushes palette to display the palette menu and choose **New Brush**. If you don't see any empty spaces, click and drag the lower-right corner of the Brushes palette to change the height and reveal the empty spaces. The Brush Options dialog box appears (see Figure 1.17), enabling you to specify the **Diameter**, **Hardness**, **Spacing**, **Angle**, and **Roundness** of the brush.

- To delete brushes, hold down the (Ctrl) [Command] key and position the cursor over the brush you want to delete to display the scissors cursor and click the brush to delete it. You can also choose the brush you want to delete and choose **Delete Brush** from the palette menu.

- To import and export brushes, choose **Save Brushes** from the palette menu of the Brushes palette to save the current set of brushes. Choose **Replace Brushes** from the palette menu to replace the current set of brushes with a previously saved set. Choose **Load Brushes** from the palette menu to append a saved set of brushes to the current set of brushes.

- To reset the brushes to the default brushes, choose **Reset Brushes** from the Brushes palette menu.

Using the Layers Palette

The Layers palette enables you to create or place images on separate transparent layers, juggle the layers around, and affect the way the layers interact with each other. The Layers palette can also contain adjustment layers, which enable you to make color adjustments that are nondestructive and overlay them with layers and other adjustment layers. Nondestructive means the original image and images on layers remain unchanged until the adjustment layer merges with the image layers. Most images in Photoshop start out with only one layer, the Background layer. The Background layer is always at the bottom of the layers and cannot be moved between other layers. The available options for the Layers palette are located in two places: in the pull-down palette menu and from the **Layer** menu in the menu bar. Choose **Show Layers** from the **Window** menu to display the Layers palette (see Figure 1.18).

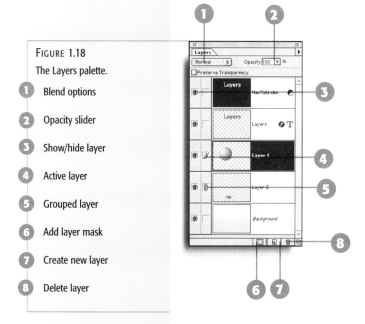

FIGURE 1.18

The Layers palette.

1. Blend options
2. Opacity slider
3. Show/hide layer
4. Active layer
5. Grouped layer
6. Add layer mask
7. Create new layer
8. Delete layer

- To create a new layer, click the **New Layer** icon in the Layers palette, choose **New Layer** from the Layers palette menu, or from the **Layer** menu choose **New**, and then select **Layer**.

- To delete a layer, select the layer you want to delete in the Layers palette and click the **Trash Can** icon in the lower-right corner of the Layers palette. You can also choose **Delete Layer** from the palette menu or from the **Layer** menu in the menu bar.

- To move a layer, drag any layer, except the Background layer, up or down in the Layers palette. When the dividing line between two layers is highlighted, release the mouse button to insert the layer you are moving between the two layers. You can also choose **Arrange** from the **Layer** menu and select **Send Backward**, **Bring Forward**, **Send to Back**, or **Bring to Front**.

- To hide or show layers, click the Eye icon to the left of the layer thumbnail to hide a layer; click the same spot again to make the layer visible. (Alt+click) [Option+click] the Eye icon to hide all layers except the one you clicked. (Alt+click) [Option+click] again to make all layers visible.

- To group layers together, select the first layer you want to group; the paintbrush icon indicates this is the active layer. Click between the Eye icon and the layer's thumbnail picture of another layer to group that layer with the active layer. The Linked-Chain icon indicates that the layer is now grouped with the active layer. When you group two or more layers, you can move them and transform them together as a unit.

- To choose a Blending mode for the current layer, click the **Blending Mode** pull-down menu in the upper-left corner of the Layers palette (see Figure 1.19). The Blending modes are explained in Chapter 4, "Understanding Layers."

Shortcuts to moving layers

To move layers using the keyboard, type (Ctrl+])
[Command+]] to move a layer up or (Ctrl+[) [Command+[to move a layer down. To move a layer to the top position, type (Ctrl+Shift+])[Command+ Shift+]].
To move a layer to the bottom position, type (Ctrl+Shift+[ )[Command+ Shift+[ ].

FIGURE 1.19

The Blending modes in the Layers palette.

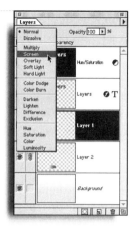

Specifying Opacity with the keyboard

You can quickly set the Opacity for the active layer by typing single digit numbers from 0 to 9. For example: typing **0** (zero) sets the Opacity to 100 percent; typing **5** sets the Opacity to 50 percent. To set the Opacity to a value other than increments of 10 percent, type a two-digit number quickly using the numeric keypad. For example: type **43** to set the Opacity to 43 percent. This same method works for any palette that contains the Opacity option.

- To set the Opacity for the current layer, click on the triangle to the right of the Opacity percentage and drag the slider. You can set an Opacity value from 1% to 100%.

- Turn on **Preserve Transparency** to protect the transparent pixels on the active layer from change. Changes you make to the image on the layer affect only the nontransparent pixels.

- Double-click the Background layer to make it a transparent layer like all the other layers. A dialog box appears in which you can enter a name for the layer. After you make the Background layer a transparent layer, you can move it between other layers.

- To add a layer mask, click the Add Layer Mask icon at the bottom of the Layers palette. The layer mask affects the Opacity of the pixels on the layer. You also can choose **Add Layer Mask** from the **Layer** menu, in which case you can choose **Reveal All** (100% Opacity) or **Hide All** (0% Opacity) for the initial mask. The layer mask thumbnail is added to the right of the layer thumbnail and is made active.

- To edit the layer mask: When the layer mask is active, the Layer Mask icon appears to the right of the Eye icon instead of the Paintbrush icon in the Layers palette, and the layer mask thumbnail is outlined in black. Paint over the image with 100 percent black to delete parts of the image (change the Opacity to 0 percent). Paint over the image with white to restore the image (100 percent Opacity). Paint with a percentage of black to change the image Opacity. For example: paint with 50 percent black to change the image Opacity to 50 percent in the painted areas; paint with 80 percent black to change the image Opacity to 20 percent in the painted areas.

- To view the layer mask, (Alt+click) [Option+click] the layer mask thumbnail in the Layers palette to toggle the layer mask view on and off.

- To view the layer mask in the Quick Mask color, (Shift+Alt+click) [Shift+Option+click] the layer mask thumbnail in the Layers palette. Double-click the Quick Mask icon at the bottom of the Toolbox to specify a color for the Quick Mask mode.

- To hide the layer mask, Shift+click the layer mask thumbnail in the Layers palette to toggle the layer mask on and off.

- To lock the layer mask to the layer so they cannot be moved independently, click between the layer thumbnail and the layer mask thumbnail in the Layers palette. The Link icon indicates that the layer and layer mask are locked.

- To apply or discard the layer mask, click the layer mask thumbnail to activate the layer mask. Click the Trash Can icon in the lower-right corner of the Layers palette and choose whether to apply or discard the mask from the dialog box that pops up. Applying the mask makes the changes to the layer permanent. You also can choose **Remove Layer Mask** from the **Layer** menu.

- Choose **Merge Visible** from the **Layer** menu to merge all visible layers into one layer. Choose **Merge Down** from the **Layer** menu or type (Ctrl+E) [Command+E] to merge the current layer with the layer under it. **Merge Down** and **Merge Visible** are also available in the Layers palette menu. When layers are linked together, **Merge Down** becomes **Merge Linked** in the **Layer** menu and **Layers** palette menu.

Merge a copy of the layer

Hold down the (Alt) [Option] key when choosing **Merge Down** to merge a copy of the layer with the layer under it. Hold down the (Alt) [Option] key when choosing **Merge Visible** to merge all visible layers onto the active layer. Hold down the (Alt) [Option] key when choosing **Merge Linked** to merge the linked layers onto the active layer.

■ To Flatten the image, choose **Flatten Image** from the **Layer** menu. This merges all layers together into a single Background layer. **Flatten Image** is also available in the **Layers** palette menu.

SEE ALSO

➤ *For more information on working with layers, see 141*

Using the Channels Palette

The Channels palette displays the individual channels for the particular color model you're working with along with a composite channel in the case of RGB, CMYK, and LAB color images. The Channels palette can contain mask channels called Alpha channels that are used to save and load selections. Choose **Show Channels** from the **Window** menu to display the Channels palette (see Figure 1.20).

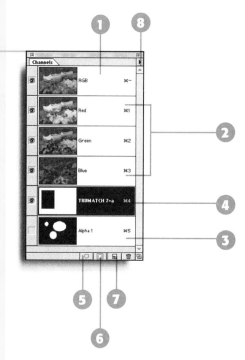

FIGURE 1.20

The Channels palette.

1 Composite channel

2 Color channels

3 Alpha channel

4 Spot Color channel

5 The Selection icon makes an Alpha channel into a selection.

6 The Mask icon makes a selection into an Alpha channel.

7 The New Channel icon creates new blank Alpha channels.

8 All options for the Channels palette are available from the palette menu.

- **To save a selection:** After you make a selection on your image, click the Mask icon at the bottom of the Channels palette to save the selection as an Alpha channel or choose **Save Selection** from the **Select** menu. A new channel that displays the mask for the selection is inserted after the last (see Figure 1.20).

- **To load a selection**, (Ctrl+click) [Command+click] an Alpha channel to load the channel as a selection or drag the Alpha channel onto the Selection icon at the bottom of the Channels palette.

- **To edit the Alpha channel**, click the channel name in the Channels palette to display the Alpha channel in the image window (see Figure 1.21). The selection area appears as white or percentages of black less than 100 percent. 100 percent black represents selected areas not selected. The mask channel is an 8-bit grayscale channel that can contain up to 256 levels of gray. Gray levels represent Opacity when the Alpha channel is used to make a selection. To go back to editing the color image, Shift+click the Alpha channel or click the composite color channel.

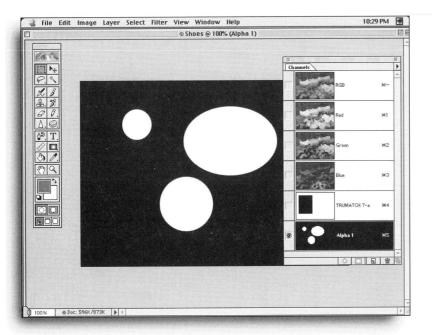

FIGURE 1.21
The mask channel can be edited in the image window.

- **To apply an Alpha channel to an image**, you must first load the Alpha channel as a selection, and then either copy/cut the selected area and paste it somewhere else or paste an image from the clipboard into the selected area (see Figure 1.22). To create a selection from an Alpha channel, choose **Load Selection** from the **Select** menu or (Ctrl+click) [Command+click] on the Alpha channel in the Channels palette.

FIGURE 1.22

The Alpha channel is loaded as a selection and the selected area is copied (Ctrl+C) [Command+C].

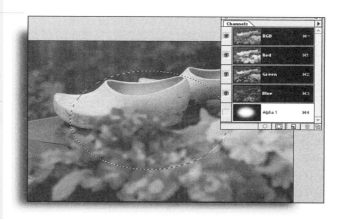

The copied image is pasted onto a white background to see the effect of the Alpha channel selection.

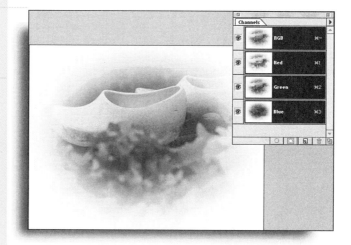

- The mask channel can be viewed with the image by clicking in the space to the left of the channel thumbnail to turn on the Eye icon. The mask is overlaid on the image in a mask color that you can specify; the default color is red at 50 percent Opacity.

- **To change the mask color**, double-click the mask layer to display the Channel Options dialog box and click the color swatch in the lower-left corner to change the mask color. Set the Opacity to a level that enables you to see the image through the mask; 50 percent works best in most cases.

- **To create a new blank channel**, click the New Channel icon at the bottom of the Channels palette or choose **New Channel** from the palette menu.

- **To duplicate a channel**, drag an existing channel onto the New Channel icon at the bottom of the Channels palette or choose **Duplicate Channel** from the palette menu.

- **To remove a channel**, drag the channel onto the Trash Can icon or choose **Delete Channel** from the palette menu. If the channel you want to delete is the active channel, click the Trash Can icon in the Channels palette to delete it.

Using the Paths Palette

The Paths palette works in concert with the path tools in the Toolbox. Using a **Pen** tool that creates vector curves and lines, you can create paths that can be stroked, filled, and saved as part of a Photoshop EPS file as a clipping path to create silhouettes. The Paths palette is empty until you create a path using the **Pen** tool. Drawing paths is covered extensively in Chapter 17, "Creating Paths to Define a Clipping Path." Choose **Show Paths** from the **Window** menu to display the Paths palette (see Figure 1.23).

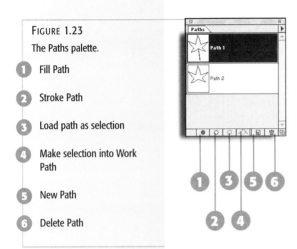

FIGURE 1.23

The Paths palette.

1 Fill Path

2 Stroke Path

3 Load path as selection

4 Make selection into Work Path

5 New Path

6 Delete Path

- When a path is first created using the **Pen** tool (located in the Toolbox, to the left of the **Type** tool), it is represented in the Paths palette as a work path. The work path is a temporary path that will not be saved with the file. Double-click the work path to define it as a path. You can name the paths anything you like to help keep track of paths when you have a lot of them.

- **To edit a path**, click a path in the Paths palette. Click the white space below the paths in the Path palette to hide all paths.

- **To create a new path**, click the New Path icon at the bottom of the Paths palette or draw with the **Pen** tool to create a new work path and double-click the work path.

- **To fill a path**, choose **Fill Path/Fill Subpath** from the palette menu the first time you fill a path to define the fill settings. The Fill Path dialog box appears, enabling you to set the fill options (see Figure 1.24). After you have defined the fill options, you can click the Fill Path icon at the bottom of the Paths palette to fill a path.

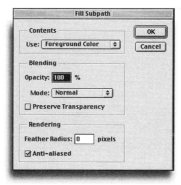

FIGURE 1.24
The Fill Subpath dialog box.

- **To stroke a path**, choose **Stroke Path/Stroke Subpath** from the palette menu. The Stroke Path dialog box appears, enabling you to choose the tool you want to use to stroke the path (see Figure 1.25). You should set up the tool options by double-clicking the tool in the Toolbox before choosing the tool as the Stroke Path tool. Select the appropriate brush size and foreground color when using painting tools such as the Paintbrush and Airbrush.

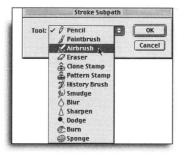

FIGURE 1.25
The Stroke Subpath dialog box offers a list of tools to choose from to stroke a path.

- **To convert a path to a selection**, (Ctrl)+click [Command]+click the path in the Paths palette or select the path in the palette and click the Selection icon at the bottom of the Paths palette or drag the Path onto the Selection icon. You can also choose **Make Selection** from the **Paths** palette menu to display a dialog box to control the way the selection is created (see Figure 1.26).

FIGURE 1.26
The Make Selection dialog box.

- **To convert a selection to a path:** When you have defined a selection marquee, click the Make Work Path icon at the bottom of the Paths palette. Choose **Make Work Path** from the palette menu to display the Make Work Path dialog box where you can set the tolerance level.

- **To duplicate a path**, drag the path onto the New Path icon at the bottom of the Paths palette or choose **Duplicate Path** from the palette menu to give the duplicate path a name while you create it.

- **To define the clipping path**, choose **Clipping Path** from the palette menu to choose which of the existing paths should be used as a clipping path when you save the file. The clipping path silhouettes the image when it is placed into a page layout application like QuarkXPress or PageMaker so only the area of the image within the path is displayed and printed.

- **To delete a path**, drag the path onto the Trash Can icon in the lower-right corner of the Paths palette or choose **Delete Path** from the palette menu.

Using the Actions Palette

The Actions palette enables you to record a series of actions, assign a name to them, and play them back. After actions are created they can be applied to a batch process that performs the actions on a folder or directory of files, as well as files that are input using a digital camera or scanner. Creating and playing actions is covered extensively in Chapter 6, "Automating Tasks with Actions." Choose **Show Actions** from the **Window** menu to display the Actions palette (see Figure 1.27).

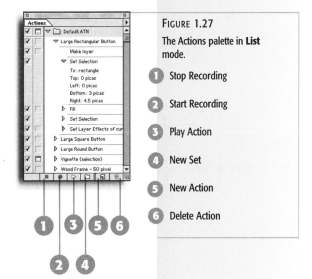

FIGURE 1.27

The Actions palette in **List** mode.

1 Stop Recording

2 Start Recording

3 Play Action

4 New Set

5 New Action

6 Delete Action

- The Actions palette has two display modes: **Button** mode and **List** mode. Choose **Button** mode from the **Actions** palette menu by clicking the triangle in the upper-right corner of the palette to display the actions as clickable buttons (see Figure 1.28). When in **Button** mode, creating new actions is disabled. To switch back to **List** mode, choose **Button** mode from the palette menu again.

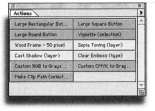

FIGURE 1.28

The Actions palette in **Button** mode.

- Before you can record an action, you must first create a **New Action** or choose an action in the Actions palette to record to. New actions are recorded in the selected Set. If you want to create a new set of actions, choose **New Set** from the **Actions** palette menu or click on the Folder icon at the bottom of the Actions palette.

- To create a New Action, choose **New Action** from the palette menu or click the New Action icon at the bottom of the Actions palette to display the New Action dialog box (see Figure 1.29). Type a name for the new action and choose a Function key and color. Click the **Record** button to begin recording the new action.

FIGURE 1.29

The New Action dialog box.

- **To stop recording**, click the Stop icon at the bottom of the Actions palette or choose Stop Recording from the palette menu.
- **To play an action**: When in **List** mode, click the action in the Actions palette and click the Play icon at the bottom of the Actions palette or choose one of the play options in the palette menu. When in **Button** mode, simply click the action in the Actions palette.
- **To record actions**, select an action in the Actions palette and click the Record icon at the bottom of the Actions palette, or choose **Start Recording** from the palette menu. To rerecord an action, choose **Record Again** from the palette menu.
- **To toggle actions on and off**, click in the check mark column in the Actions palette. When an action is toggled off, it cannot be played in either List mode or **Button** mode.
- **To toggle dialog boxes on and off**, click the column to the right of the check mark column. When dialogs are toggled on, the Action pauses at dialog boxes when running and require user input. If the Dialog icon is displayed in black, dialogs are turned on for all parts of the action. When the Dialog icon is red, it means that some parts of the action have dialogs turned on, whereas others do not.

- **To display the action parts,** click the triangles to the left of the action name to expand the list of commands used in the action. Click the triangles next to the commands to display the settings for the command. Note that you can turn the dialogs on or off for each command in the list.

Using the History Palette

The History palette records the state of your image at every step. You can set the History palette to record up to 100 states. The History palette also enables you to record snapshots of your image at any given time. After you make changes to your image, you can easily return to a previous state by clicking on it in the History palette. The History palette also facilitates the use of the History Brush in the Toolbox. Using the History Brush you can paint back portions of your image using a prior image state.

- **To set up the History palette options**: Choose **History Options** from the **History** palette menu to display the History Options dialog box (see Figure 1.30). Specify the maximum number of **History** items you want to store. When the maximum number of states is reached, the first states in the list are deleted to accommodate new ones. If you check the **Allow Non-Linear History** option, when you select a previous history state and perform a new operation, the selected state is duplicated at the bottom of the History palette along with the new change made. This enables you to preserve any changes made in case you want to return to them. I suggest leaving this option deselected until you're very comfortable with the History palette.

FIGURE 1.30
The History Options dialog box.

■ Snapshots are stored at the top of the History palette. If you checked the **Automatically Create First Snapshot** option in the History Options palette, a snapshot of the image prior to editing is stored in the History palette. Choose **New Snapshot** from the **History** palette menu to display the New Snapshot dialog box to create additional snapshots (see Figure 1.32). Click on the Page icon at the bottom of the History palette to take additional snapshots without displaying a dialog box (see Figure 1.31).

FIGURE 1.31

The History palette.

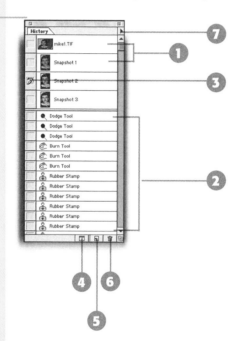

1 Snapshots are stored at the top of the History palette.

2 The previous image states are stored sequentially in the History palette.

3 Click in the embossed box to set the source for the History Brush.

4 Create a new document from the current state.

5 Take a new snapshot of your image.

6 Delete snapshots and states.

7 All the options for the History palette are contained in the palette menu.

■ To use the History Brush, you must first click on a point in the image history to select the source for painting. After you select a previous state to paint from, select an appropriate brush from the Brushes palette and begin painting on your image to restore it to the selected state in the History palette.

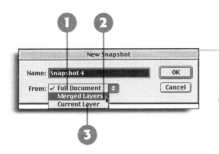

FIGURE 1.32

The New Snapshot dialog box.

1. Choose Full Document to take a snapshot of the entire document including hidden layers.

2. Choose Merged Layers to take a snapshot of the visible layers only.

3. Choose Current Layer to take a snapshot of the current layer only.

Using Context Menus

Context menus are floating menus that are available in various places in Photoshop. The context menus display choices for tools that are active or palettes that are displayed.

- **To display the context menu**: On the MacOS, hold down the Ctrl key and click the image to display the context menu for the active tool. In Windows, click the image with the right mouse button to display the context menu for the active tool (see Figure 1.33).

FIGURE 1.33

The context menu for the Paintbrush tool.

- Use the same technique to display the context menu for open palettes. (Right+click) [Ctrl+click] on the palette to display its context menu (see Figure 1.34). Not all palettes contain context menus.

FIGURE 1.34.

The context menu for the Layers palette.

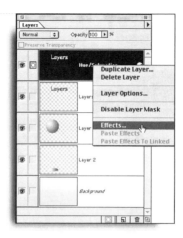

Selecting Layers with context menus

When working with multiple layers, be sure the **Move** tool is selected in the Toolbox and position the cursor over your image. (Right+click) [Ctrl+click] to display the context menu that displays all the layers occupying the place you clicked. Simply scroll to a layer in the list to switch to that layer.

SEE ALSO

➤ *For more information on working with layers, see 141*

Creating, Opening, and Closing Files

Creating files from scratch

Opening existing documents

Using Place and Import to bring in image data

Understanding the Window and Canvas area

Navigating around your image

How to find vital statistics for your image

Defining a New Document

To create a new document choose **New** from the **File** menu or type (Ctrl+N) [Command+N]. The New dialog box appears (see Figure 2.1). When you first open Photoshop, the default settings are 7 inches by 5 inches with a resolution of 72 pixels per inch and a color mode of RGB color. (**Transparent** is indicated as the contents of the new file and is the default setting.) When you change these values, your new settings will be in place the next time you create a new document. Photoshop can create an image that contains 900 million pixels at 72 pixels per inch, which equates to an image that is 30,000 by 30,000 pixels or 416×416 inches. The maximum size of the file comes down when the resolution is increased. A file of this size would be approximately 2.7 gigabytes in size and require an additional 9.5 gigabytes of disk space to even work on it. As you can see, Photoshop can accommodate any file size and resolution you're likely to require.

SEE ALSO

➤ *For more information on restoring default preferences, see page 182*

➤ *For more information on resolution, see page 70*

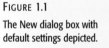

FIGURE 1.1

The New dialog box with default settings depicted.

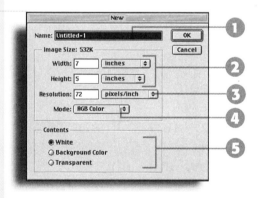

1️⃣ You can name your document at this point or wait until you save it.

2️⃣ Specify width and height in pixels, inches, cm, points, picas, or columns.

3️⃣ Specify a resolution in pixels per inch or pixels per centimeter.

4️⃣ Specify a color mode as **Bitmap, Grayscale, RGB Color, CMYK Color**, or **Lab Color**.

5️⃣ Indicate the contents of the new file.

Opening Existing Images

Photoshop can open a variety of file formats aside from the Photoshop proprietary format.

Opening files in Photoshop

1. To open an existing image choose **Open** from the **File** menu or type (Ctrl+O) [Command+O] to display the Open dialog box (see Figure 2.2).

2. Locate the file you want to open in the scrolling file window.

3. A thumbnail preview of the image appears at the bottom of the Open dialog box automatically on the Windows platform. If you use a MacOS, check the **Show Thumbnail** check box to display a thumbnail preview of the image if one exists. When a thumbnail preview exists, the button under the thumbnail image enables you to update the preview if it does not appear correct on the MacOS. When a thumbnail is not available, the **Update** button changes to a **Create** button, in which case Photoshop on the MacOS attempts to create a thumbnail from the image.

4. The format of the selected file and its size are indicated under the scrolling file window. When you check the **Show All Files** check box on the MacOS, every file in the current directory is listed along with a pull-down menu where you can specify the format of a file you want to open (see Figure 2.3). In the Windows version of Photoshop, choose **Open As** from the **File** menu to choose from all files in a particular directory.

Creating a new document from the Clipboard

When you have something cut or copied to the Clipboard, the New dialog box reflects the settings required to paste the Clipboard contents into a new file. For example: Open an RGB Color image that has a resolution of 300 pixels per inch and use the Marquee tool to select an area of the image that is 1 inch by 1 inch; then copy it (Ctrl+C) [Command+C] to the Clipboard. Type (Ctrl+N) [Command+N] to display the New dialog box. The width, height, resolution, and color mode match that of the Clipboard contents.

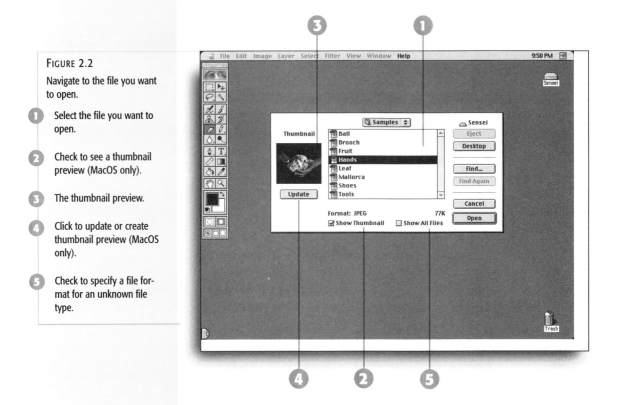

FIGURE 2.2

Navigate to the file you want to open.

1 Select the file you want to open.

2 Check to see a thumbnail preview (MacOS only).

3 The thumbnail preview.

4 Click to update or create thumbnail preview (MacOS only).

5 Check to specify a file format for an unknown file type.

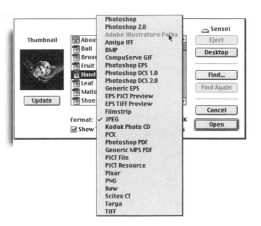

FIGURE 2.3

The available file formats when the **Show All Files** check box is selected.

SEE ALSO

➤ *For more information on file formats, see page 44*

Saving Files

Photoshop images can be saved in a variety of file formats including the most popular for desktop publishing and Web graphics. In most cases, the file format options are available in the **Save As** dialog box or in the **Export** submenu under the **File** menu. To save a file in the same format it was in when opened in Photoshop, choose **Save** from the **File** menu or type (Ctrl+S) [Command+S]. If the file you are working in has not yet been saved or if you want to save the file in a different format, choose **Save As** from the **File** menu or type (Ctrl+Shift+S) [Command+Shift+S] to display the Save As dialog box (see Figure 2.4). Navigate to the place you want to save the file and click the **Save** button. In some cases, an additional dialog box will pop up where you must specify additional settings to save the file.

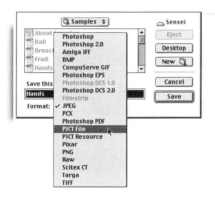

FIGURE 2.4

Choose a file format from the pull-down menu. Formats that are grayed out are not available for the particular file you are saving.

Using Save a Copy

When working in Photoshop, you probably will create alpha channels, paths, and layers at some point. When you need to save the file but continue working on the file with alpha channels, paths and layers intact, choose **Save a Copy** from the **File** menu or type (Ctrl+Alt+S) [Command+Option+S] to display the Save a Copy dialog box (see Figure 2.5).

FIGURE 2.5

The Save a Copy dialog box.

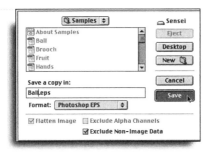

Painting from a saved image

Some tools in Photoshop, such as the **Rubber Stamp** and **Eraser** tools, enable you to paint your image using the last saved version of the file. The fill dialog boxes also offer an option to fill from a saved version of the file. Use **Save a Copy** to save your file at different stages in case you want to revert to a previous state in the image. The History palette gives you a way to go back to previous steps, but this method gives you a copy of the file on your hard disk.

- Check the **Flatten Image** check box to save the file with layers flattened.

- Check the **Exclude Alpha Channels** check box to save the file without alpha channels.

- When you check the **Exclude Non-Image Data** check box, nonimage data like paths, thumbnail preview, page setup information, and guides are not saved with the file.

- If you select a file format from the pull-down menu that does not support one or more of the check box items, the boxes are checked for you and the option grayed out.

File Formats

Each file format available in Photoshop has limitations to how the file can be used once saved and, in many cases, specific settings that must be set when saving the file to achieve a particular result. Each file format also has a corresponding three-character extension that is a necessary part of the filename for the Windows platform. Windows 95 supports large filenames, but you should conform to the DOS naming convention of an eight-character filename with three-character extension if you create files for use on platforms other than Macintosh.

SEE ALSO

➤ *For information on how to have Photoshop automatically append a three-character file extension, see page 184*

Photoshop

This is the native format for files created in the current version of Photoshop. These files can only be opened by the current version of Photoshop or higher. Save files in this format when you want to preserve all Layers and Channels for later modification. The **Erase to Saved** and **Fill from Saved** options can be used when the file is saved in this format.

Photoshop 2.0

This is the native format for files created in Adobe Photoshop 2.0. If you share files with other Photoshop users who have not upgraded to the latest version of Photoshop, this is the format they can open assuming they use version 2 or later.

Amiga IFF

The Amiga% Interchange File Format (IFF) is used on the Commodore Amiga computer system. Use this format if you are saving files for the Amiga's Video Toaster software. This is also the best format to save files for some IBM-compatible painting programs—most notably DeluxePaint from Electronic Arts.

BMP

Windows Bitmap Format is the native format for Microsoft Paint on the IBM PC and compatible platforms. Supported by a number of MS Windows and OS/2 software applications, this bitmapped file format can save up to 16 million colors. The BMP Options dialog box presents options for File Format and bit Depth as well as an option to use a *lossless* compression scheme called **Run-Length-Encoding (RLE)** (see Figure 2.6).

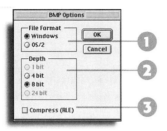

FIGURE 2.6

The BMP Options dialog box.

1 Choose the appropriate format.

2 Select a bit depth.

3 Check here to compress the file.

Compuserve GIF

Graphics Interchange Format was originally created by Compuserve (an online service) to save screen-oriented, low-file size graphics. The GIF file format is widely used today by Internet Web sites. The GIF format supports a maximum of 256 colors and must be in Indexed Color Mode, Grayscale, or Bitmap mode. Small file size and the capability to render on the screen using a method called *interlacing* makes this format highly portable and desirable for online services. The GIF Options dialog box offers two choices for **Row Order**: **Normal** and **Interlaced** (see Figure 2.7).

FIGURE 2.7

The Compuserve GIF Options dialog box.

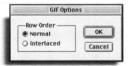

SEE ALSO

➤ *For more information on saving GIF files and the GIF89-a format, see page 47*

Photoshop EPS

The Encapsulated PostScript format can include both postscript data (vector graphics) and bitmap data. Because it can save postscript code, EPS is the format for files that contain *Clipping Paths*. All high-end desktop page layout programs such as QuarkXPress and PageMaker support the EPS format. When you save a bitmap (1-bit per pixel) image, you are given the choice to make the whites transparent. If you are exporting EPS images to be used for four-color printing, be sure the image is in CMYK mode before saving. The EPS Format dialog box offers format options before saving the file (see Figure 2.8). Choose a **Preview** option from the drop-down menu in the EPS Format dialog box. These settings determine how the image previews when placed in a page layout application:

- Choose TIFF (1 bit/pixel) to save a black-and-white preview that does not contain gray levels. This saves a smaller file, but it's rather difficult to work within the page layout application. Use TIFF previews for files saved for Windows.

- Choose TIFF (8 bits/pixel) when saving color images. This preview method saves a color preview. Use TIFF previews for files saved for Windows.

- Choose Macintosh (1 bit/pixel) to save a black-and-white preview that does not contain gray levels. Again, this saves a smaller file but creates a poor preview in the page layout application for anything but bitmap images. The Macintosh choice saves a PICT preview that cannot be read by Windows applications.

- Choose Macintosh (8 bits/pixel) when saving color images. This preview method saves a color preview. The Macintosh choice saves a PICT preview that cannot be read by Windows applications.

- Choose Macintosh (JPEG) to save a 24-bit *JPEG* preview using JPEG compression. You must have *QuickTime* installed on your Macintosh to take advantage of this option. Read about the JPEG file format to learn more about JPEG compression.

EPS Encoding Options

The **Encoding** options affect the actual image data sent to a printer, whereas the Preview options detailed above only affect the onscreen preview and have no bearing on output quality. The encoding option you select greatly affects the size of your file, as well as the quality of the printed piece.

- Choose *ASCII* to save the file in readable PostScript text that can be read in a word processor. This option is often necessary for files used on the Windows platform or for printing to printers using PostScript emulation.

- *Binary* encoding is the best choice for maximum quality and the smallest file size. The binary encoding that Photoshop uses, sometimes called Huffman encoding, compresses the data without sacrificing image quality.

- JPEG compression is a *lossy compression* scheme, which results in a degraded image quality when printed. JPEG compression is only good for printing to PostScript Level 2 or higher printing devices and should be avoided when high-quality output is desired. JPEG has four quality settings. The **low quality** setting results in higher compression, but a greater loss of color detail. Conversely, the **maximum quality** setting results in the least amount of compression, but a better image quality.

One of the advantages of the EPS file format is the ability to save printing attributes. You can specify a custom halftone screen in the Page Setup dialog box using the **Screen** button. Check the **Include Halftone Screen** check box to save the custom halftone screen settings with the EPS file. It's important to note here that custom halftone screens saved with EPS files override any halftone screen settings in layout applications (such as QuarkXPress and PageMaker). You can adjust the brightness and contrast of a printed image using the **Transfer** button in the Page Setup dialog box. Check the **Include Transfer Function** check box to save these settings in the EPS file. Check the **Postscript Color Management** check box to save the color profile information specified in the **Color Settings** under the **File** menu.

SEE ALSO

➤ *For more information on how to specify custom halftone screens and transfer function, see page 154*

➤ *For more information on specifying Color Settings, see page 115*

FIGURE 2.8
The EPS Format dialog box.

Photoshop DCS 1.0

The Desktop Color Separation (DCS) 1.0 file format is an extension of the Encapsulated Postscript File (EPS) format. When you save a CMYK image as **Photoshop DCS 1.0**, the DCS 1.0 Format dialog box appears (see Figure 2.9). A DCS 1.0 file creates five separate files that include a low-resolution controlling EPS composite file along with a separate file for Cyan, Magenta, Yellow, and Black. This format is supported only by applications that can perform four-color separations.

FIGURE 2.9
The DCS 1.0 Format dialog box.

- The **Preview** and **Encoding** options are the same as those previously described for the Photoshop EPS format.

- The **DCS** options determine how the low-res composite EPS file prints. Choose **Color Composite (72 pixel/inch)** to print to color printers. Choose **Grayscale Composite (72 pixel/inch)** to print to black-and-white laser printers. If you choose **No Composite Postscript** to save the DCS 1.0 file, the file will be saved without PostScript information for the printer. In most cases, the layout application will print the image using the Preview information for the file if you select **No Composite Postscript**.

Photoshop DCS 2.0

The Photoshop DCS 2.0 file format saves the Spot Channel information along with the Cyan, Magenta, Yellow, and Black information. Create Spot channels using the Channels palette. When you import the saved file into a page layout application that supports the DCS 2.0 file format, the spot colors are added to the application's color list and separate correctly when printed. The **DCS 2.0 Format** dialog box appears when you save a CMYK color file in the DCS 2.0 format (see Figure 2.10).

FIGURE 2.10

The DCS 2.0 Format dialog box.

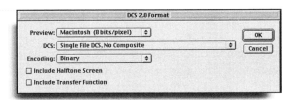

The **Preview** and **Encoding** options are the same as those previously described for the Photoshop EPS format.

- The **DCS** options describe the type of DCS file created and how the low-res composite EPS file prints. Choose whether the image will be saved as a single file or multiple file. If you choose the **Multiple File** options, a separate file will be created for each color used in the image along with the controlling EPS file. Choose **Color Composite (72 pixel/inch)** to print to color printers. Choose **Grayscale Composite (72 pixel/inch)** to print to black-and-white laser printers. If you choose **No Composite**, the file will be saved without PostScript information for the printer. In most cases, the layout application will print the image using the Preview information for the file if you select **No Composite**.

Generic EPS

The Generic EPS format is only available when opening files. The Generic EPS format is used to open EPS files generated by other programs such as Illustrator, Freehand, and QuarkXPress. When you open a Generic EPS file, the **Rasterize Generic EPS Format** dialog box appears (see Figure 2.11). Photoshop converts the vector information in the EPS file to bitmapped data (*rasterize*).

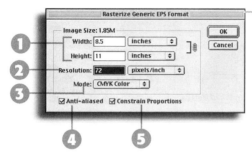

FIGURE 2.11

The Rasterize Generic EPS Format dialog box.

1. Specify a width and height. The width and height of the image appear here, but you can change them to anything you like.

2. Specify a resolution for the image.

3. Choose a color mode. The color mode of the EPS file is automatically selected.

4. Check the **Anti-aliased** check box to help curved areas of the image appear smooth.

5. Check the **Constrain Proportions** check box to keep the aspect ratio of the image correct.

EPS PICT Preview

This option is only available when opening files. The **EPS PICT Preview** option opens the 72 ppi preview of an existing EPS file as long as that file was saved with a PICT preview. When you save an EPS file out of Photoshop and choose either Macintosh (8 bits/pixel) or Macintosh (1 bit/pixel), the preview saved is a PICT preview. The preview is opened as an indexed color file mapped to the Macintosh System palette on the MacOS and the Windows System palette on Windows.

EPS TIFF Preview

This option is only available when opening files. The **EPS TIFF Preview** option opens the 72 ppi preview of an existing EPS file as long as that file was saved with a TIFF preview. When you save an EPS file for Windows, the preview saved is a TIFF preview. The preview is opened as an indexed color file mapped to the Macintosh System palette on the MacOS and the Windows System palette on Windows.

Filmstrip

The filmstrip format is generally first created by an application such as Adobe Premiere (a movie and QuickTime editing application) on the Macintosh. A filmstrip will more than likely include multiple frames from a segment of a movie. When modified in Photoshop, the movie can be saved back out as a Filmstrip format file and imported back into Premiere. The Filmstrip format file must not be cropped or resized in Photoshop. Refer to the Premiere Users Manual for information on saving filmstrip files.

JPEG

The Joint Photographic Experts Group (JPEG) format is most commonly used to display images on Web pages and is available when saving grayscale, RGB, and CMYK images. JPEG is a *lossy* compression scheme, which means it permanently removes essential color data from the image to conserve disk space. When you open a JPEG file and then save it again in the JPEG format, an additional amount of data is sacrificed. The JPEG Options dialog box enables you to choose a quality level to determine how much the image is compressed, and therefore how much the image quality is affected (see Figure 2.12).

SEE ALSO

➤ *For more information on saving JPEG files, see page 62*

Kodak Photo CD

The **Kodak Photo CD** format is available when opening files and supports Eastman Kodak's Photo CD and Pro Photo CD formats. The Photo CD format uses the YCC color model that is a variation of the CIE (Commission Internationale de l'Eclairage) color space. Photo CDs are typically created from 35mm film and slides, though the Pro Photo CD scanners can support 70mm film and 4X5-inch transparencies and negatives. When you open a Photo CD image (.PCD), you are offered six size choices (see Figure 2.13). The sizes are indicated in pixel dimensions based on a 72-pixel-per-inch image resolution. The first five sizes are available for the standard Photo CD format whereas the sixth size (4096×6144) is only available for the Pro Photo CD format. The standard Photo CD contains 100 images typically, but the Pro Photo CD only contains up to 25 to support the larger file size.

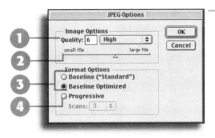

FIGURE 2.12

The JPEG Options dialog box.

1 Choose a **Quality** setting from the pull-down menu or type a value from 0–10.

2 A low-quality setting results in a small file size and a high- or maximum-quality setting results in a larger file (less compression).

3 **Baseline Optimized** provides better compression than **Baseline ("Standard")** and results in smaller file sizes.

4 Choose **Progressive** to create JPEG files that will build in stages on Web pages. The number of scans determines how many passes it takes to render the image on the Web page.

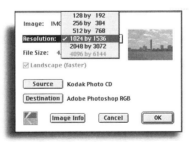

FIGURE 2.13

The Kodak Photo CD options dialog box.

■ Click on the **Source** button to display the source dialog box (see Figure 2.14). Choose the source of the original photograph from the choices offered. This plays a big part in how the image will be translated to the Photoshop format. If you're not sure what the source of the original is, click on the **Image Info** button.

FIGURE 2.14

The Source dialog box for the Kodak Photo CD format.

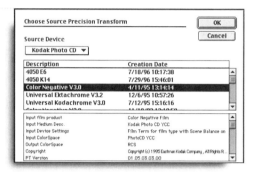

■ Click on the **Destination** button to display a dialog box where you can choose the target display format (see Figure 2.15). Photoshop ships with two preset destination choices: **Adobe Photoshop RGB** and **Adobe Photoshop CIELAB**. The RGB choice converts the YCC data into Photoshop RGB data and displays the image in RGB mode. The CIELAB choice converts the YCC data into Photoshop LAB data and displays the image in LAB mode.

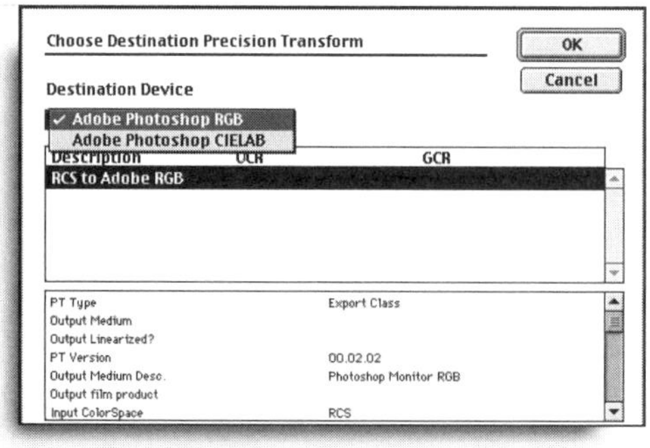

FIGURE 2.15

The Destination dialog box for the Kodak Photo CD format.

PCX

Paintbrush Color eXchange format. This is developed by Zsoft
for PC Paintbrush, an IBM DOS and MS Windows application.
Photoshop can open and save PCX files that contain up to 16
million colors (32 bits per pixel). The PCX format is only available for grayscale, bitmap, and RGB images. Most IBM PC
applications that support importing graphics support version 5 of
the PCX format. The PCX format does not offer a dialog box
when saving the file.

Photoshop PDF

The **Photoshop PDF** format enables you to save and open
Portable Document Format (PDF) files originally created with
Photoshop (see Figure 2.16). The PDF format is used by Adobe
Acrobat®, a format for electronic publishing created by Adobe.
An Acrobat format file can be read on Macintosh, Windows,
UNIX®, and DOS platforms using the Acrobat Reader software
available from Adobe Systems and included on the CD-ROM
that Photoshop comes on. See the Electronic Publishing Guide
on the Photoshop Tutorial CD-ROM for more information
about the PDF format.

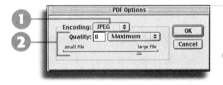

Generic MPS PDF

The **Generic MPS PDF** format is available when opening files
and opens PDF files created in applications other than
Photoshop. This format enables you to open multiple page PDF
files one page at a time (see Figure 2.17). Photoshop converts
the PDF data to rasterized bitmapped data and offers a dialog
box to specify the dimensions, resolution, and color space for the
PDF file (see Figure 2.18).

Using a CMYK profile for Kodak CD

You can purchase a profile to
convert the Kodak YCC format
into the Photoshop CMYK color
mode directly from Kodak.
Some stock photography hous-
es also provide CMYK profiles
and profiles for their specific
scanning equipment. These can
be added to the list of destination profiles available when
opening a Photo CD image in
Photoshop. If you don't have a
CMYK profile available to you
but want to end up with a
CMYK image, choose the
Photoshop **CIELAB** choice
from the destination profiles to
open Photo CD images in LAB
mode; then convert to CMYK
mode.

FIGURE 2.16
The PDF Options dialog box.

① Choose either **JPEG** or **ZIP**
for compression encoding.
Use ZIP for files that are to
be read on the Windows or
DOS platform only.

② Select a **Quality** setting
when using JPEG encoding.

FIGURE 2.17
You can only open one page
of a PDF file at a time.

FIGURE 2.18
You decide how to rasterize
the PDF file.

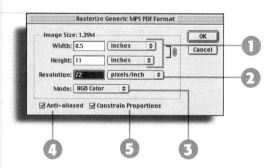

1 Specify a width and height.
The width and height of the
image appear here, but you
can change them to any-
thing you like.

2 Specify a resolution for the
image.

3 Choose a color mode. The
originating color mode of
the PDF file is automatically
selected.

4 Check the **Anti-aliased**
check box to help curved
areas of the image appear
smooth.

5 Check the **Constrain
Proportions** check box to
keep the aspect ratio of the
image correct.

PICT File

The PICTure file format is the Macintosh computer System's
native graphics format. The PICT format supports every bit
depth, size, and resolution. The PICT file format is most often
used for onscreen presentations and multimedia authoring software and is the format of MacOS screen captures. When saving
an RGB image, the PICT format offers either a 16-bit or 32-bit
per pixel resolution (see Figure 2.19). When saving grayscale
images, you can choose from 2, 4, or 8 bits per pixel. The compression options depicted in Figure 2.19 are only available if you
have QuickTime installed on your Macintosh.

PICT Resource

Resource files are used exclusively by the Macintosh computer to
display icons and pictures within applications. You can open
these hidden PICT resources in Photoshop by choosing **Import**
from the **File** menu and then selecting **PICT Resource**. The
PICT Resource file format is most often used to save
StartupScreen files on the Macintosh. When a file is saved as a

PICT Resource, named **StartupScreen** and placed in the
System Folder; the picture appears on the screen at startup time.
The PICT Resource Options dialog box requires an ID number
for the resources and a name. Specify resolution and compres-
sion settings by clicking on the appropriate radio buttons (see
Figure 2.20).

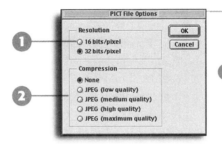

FIGURE 2.19

The PICT File Options dialog
box.

1 Choose whether to save 16
or 32 bits of data for each
pixel of an RGB image.
Choose between 2, 4, or 8
bits per pixel for Grayscale
images. Bitmap images are
automatically saved as 1 bit
per pixel images.

2 Choose a compression
method or select **None** to
save the PICT file without
compression. There are no
compression options for
bitmap 1 bit per pixel
images.

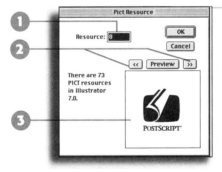

FIGURE 2.20

The PICT Resource Options
dialog box.

1 A single MacOS application
file can contain many PICT
resources, each assigned a
unique number.

2 Click the arrows to cycle
through the PICT resources.

3 A preview of the PICT
resource appears here.

PIXAR

This format is used exclusively by 3D rendering applications manufactured by the Pixar Corporation. The PIXAR format supports RGB Color and Grayscale images and offers no options when saving the file.

PNG

The Portable Network Graphics (PNG) format (pronounced "ping") was designed to replace the GIF format for some applications. The PNG format has three distinct advantages over the more common GIF format. The compression method is lossless, like the GIF file, so compressing and decompressing will not degrade the image. In Photoshop, you can choose from five different filters that prepare the file for compression: **Sub**, **Up**, **Average**, **Paeth,** and **Adaptive** (see Figure 2.21). The best way to choose the correct method of compression is to experiment with these five schemes, though the difference in the resulting file size is negligible. The interlace method used for PNG files is called Adam7 and differs somewhat from the way a GIF file is interlaced. When Adam 7 interlacing is turned on, the image builds on the screen in seven successive steps, each one making the image clearer and sharper. As of this writing, the most popular browser applications have only begun to support the PNG format and most Web page design applications such as Pagemill and Claris HomePage do not as yet support the PNG format.

FIGURE 2.21
The PNG dialog box.

SEE ALSO
➤ *For more information on saving PNG files, see page 62*

RAW

This format is a flexible file format for transferring documents between applications and computer systems. The RAW format consists of a stream of bytes describing the color information in the file. Unless you work with image scientists inventing new file formats or need to create a file for use on a mainframe system, you will likely never use this format. You must have a firm grip on file formats and file specifications to use this format. Please consult the Photoshop documentation for a rather lengthy explanation of each of the parameters that must be set to use this format properly.

Scitex CT

Scitex Continuous Tone format is most often used by Scitex Color Workstations and peripherals. No options are available for this format in Photoshop and files can be in either Grayscale, RGB or CMYK mode. Scitex CT is the default and proprietary format that the Scitex drum scanners create. The Scitex CT format is also the interim format created for output on other Scitex devices such as the Iris inkjet printer.

Targa

This format is most often used to combine Macintosh graphics with Live Video. This format was developed by TrueVision Corp. to facilitate the use of 32-bit images that contain an 8-bit Alpha channel to display the live video and can only be used by systems that include a Truevision® video card. The format is often supported by MS-DOS color applications. Grayscale, Indexed color, and RGB color files can be saved in the Targa format. When you save an RGB image in this format, you can choose the resolution from the Targa Options dialog box (see Figure 2.22).

FIGURE 2.22

The Targa Options dialog box when saving an RGB image.

TIFF

The Tagged Image File Format (TIFF) cannot save vector graphics. The TIFF file format can save raster data (the image bitmap), so most Photoshop files can dependably be saved in this format. If you have created Alpha channels for an image, they will be saved with the TIFF format as well as the default Photoshop format. Macintosh and PC-compatible computers use different "bit orders" for the TIFF file. You can specify the correct bit order for the TIFF file by clicking on the check boxes for either **MAC** or **IBM** when saving the file (see Figure 2.23). The LZW Compression option is a lossless compression scheme that does not throw data away when compressing. Adobe Photoshop reads and saves captions in TIFF files, used primarily by the Associated Press Picture Desk System. To enter caption information, choose **File Info** from the **File** menu.

FIGURE 2.23

Select the **Byte Order** for the computer platform the TIFF will be used on.

Saving Images for the Web

Web graphics have some very specific requirements as far as resolution and color depth go. Web graphics are generally rendered at 72 pixels per inch on Web pages designed in HTML (Hypertext Markup Language), and are indexed color images that can contain a maximum of 256 colors. Because Web pages are viewed on a variety of platforms, most notably Macintosh and Windows, the specification of color for Web graphics is very important. There are 40 colors of the 256 colors that do not display the same on both the Macintosh and Windows platforms. For this reason, Photoshop now supports a 216-color Web palette when converting color images to indexed color. At this writing, the most popular file formats for Web graphics are the GIF (Graphics Interchange Format) file and JPEG (Joint Photographic Experts Group) file, though I expect the relatively new PNG (Portable Network Graphics) format will continue to gain popularity and acceptance.

The GIF89a Format

The GIF file format was originally developed by Compuserve as a platform independent graphic format. GIF files are compressed using LZW compression, a lossless compression scheme. This means the GIF file can be compressed, decompressed, and recompressed any number of times without loss of image quality. GIF images are indexed color images that should be indexed to the lowest possible number of colors to a maximum of 256 colors. Photoshop comes with the GIF89a plug-in, enabling you to export indexed color images to the GIF format.

The GIF89a format supports a single transparency color that you define when saving the file and has the option of creating an interlaced GIF file. Interlaced GIFs are rendered on the screen in stages, enabling the person browsing a Web page that contains the GIF to see the full image right away so they can decide whether to wait for the graphic to complete (see Figure 2.24). GIF files are primarily used as design elements on Web pages and can also be used as hypertext links, which when clicked display another part of the Web page, another URL address, or a higher resolution JPEG file of the same image. The latest craze amongst Web designers is animated GIF files. Animated GIF files are simply GIF files that contain multiple frames of an image that when viewed in quick succession create animated effects, much like the nickelodeons of the '20s and '30s. A third-party application is necessary to create animated GIF files and a number of them are available as shareware on the Web.

FIGURE 2.24

Interlacing renders the image on the screen in stages, each successive stage making the image clearer and sharper.

JPEG Files

JPEG files are used on Web pages when high-resolution full-color images are needed because they are RGB images that can contain millions of colors, though JPEG files can also be grayscale. JPEG files are compressed using a *lossy* compression scheme that deletes color data from the file. Most software packages that generate JPEG files, Photoshop included, provide a method to specify the amount of compression to use based on the image quality desired. When the compression setting is set too high, the image quality suffers (see Figure 2.25). Because JPEG files are 24-bit RGB color images, they lend themselves well to transference over the Internet and across platforms. The drawback to JPEG is the type of compression used, because after the color data is thrown away to compress the file, decompressing the file does not restore the data.

FIGURE 2.25

The image on the left is the original image with no compression applied; the image on the right is a JPEG image with the maximum compression applied.

PNG Files

The Portable Network Graphics (PNG) format is continually gaining popularity, especially among software developers. The specifications for PNG reside in the public domain and are freely available to software developers to incorporate the format into their programs free of charge—as opposed to the GIF format that imposes large licensing fees on anyone incorporating the format into their programs. As of this writing the implementation of the PNG format is fairly limited, though eventually, a fully functional PNG file will provide three distinct advantages over the GIF format. Here are the advantages of the PNG Format:

- The PNG format supports Alpha channels and is capable of saving images with variable transparency such as vignettes and fades.

- The PNG format contains algorithms for gamma correction so images appear properly on different platforms.

- The PNG format supports two-dimensional interlacing to progressively display color images.

The PNG format also contains code that detects some forms of file corruption and performs data integrity checking to help the image display properly on the viewing computer platform.

The Image Window

When you open a document in Photoshop, it appears in a window that Photoshop refers to as the Canvas area. The Canvas window contains scrollbars on the right and the bottom to help navigate when the image is larger than the window (see Figure 2.26). The name of the file, as well as the view percentage, appears in the top bar of the image window. The view percentage also appears in the lower-left corner of the image window where you can click and enter a new view percentage. Statistics about the image appear to the right of the view percentage box in the lower-left corner. Click on the triangle to the right of the image statistics to display a menu where you can choose which statistics to display. There are five choices for image statistics:

- **Document Sizes**. This choice displays the document sizes in *kilobytes* (k) or *megabytes* (M). Two values are displayed separated by a slash. The first value, to the left of the slash, represents the size of the flattened file. Photoshop calculates

---

Resolution and dimensions for Web graphics

When designing a Web page, it is best to design for the lowest common denominator in regards to monitor size. The rule of thumb is to design for a 13-inch monitor (640×480 pixels) and a resolution of 72 pixels per inch. Keep in mind that the *browser* software takes up some of the space, so you probably want to keep the width approximately 600 pixels and the height approximately 400 pixels. When choosing color schemes or photographic images, it helps to remember that some folks on the Web only have a grayscale monitor. There isn't anything we can do about the people with non-graphical monochrome monitors, though alternate (ALT) text is usually provided by the Web designer to substitute for the lack of graphics in this case.

When creating graphics for Web pages in Photoshop, change the measurement units to pixels and work in the 100% view to see an accurate representation of the graphics you're creating. You should also keep in mind that many users connect to the Internet at less than optimum speed, some as slow as 2,400bps. Keeping the graphic elements small (approximately 150–200 pixels on a side) greatly reduces the amount of time a browser takes to draw a Web page compared to a graphic that covers half or more of the screen area.

this value by multiplying the width of the image in pixels by the height of the image in pixels, and then multiplying by the number of color channels the image contains. This result is then divided by 1,024 because there are 1,024 bytes in one kilobyte, and 1,024K in one megabyte. The number to the right of the slash represents the file size when layers are added.

- **Scratch Sizes**. The **Scratch Sizes** choice displays the amount of memory Photoshop is currently using to work on your file. The number to the right of the slash indicates the total amount of memory currently available to Photoshop. When the number on the left is larger than the number on the right, Photoshop is using your hard disk to swap information, and performance will decline because the reading and writing to disk takes significantly longer than working in memory.

- **Efficiency**. The **Efficiency** setting tells you what percentage of Photoshop operations are being performed in memory. If the number is less than 100%, Photoshop is using scratch disk space for some operations. If you notice this number consistently falling below 100%, assign more memory to Photoshop or install more memory in your computer if necessary; then assign more memory to Photoshop.

- **Timing**. This setting displays the amount of time it took to perform the last operation. This setting is handy for benchmarking purposes or to evaluate project time for large projects.

- **Current Tool.** The **Current Tool** option displays the tool currently selected from the Toolbox.

The backdrop color (the area around the canvas) is set to a neutral gray color by default. Color images are best viewed on a neutral gray background. However, if you want to change the color of the backdrop:

Changing the backdrop color

1. Click on the Foreground color swatch and select a new color for the backdrop.

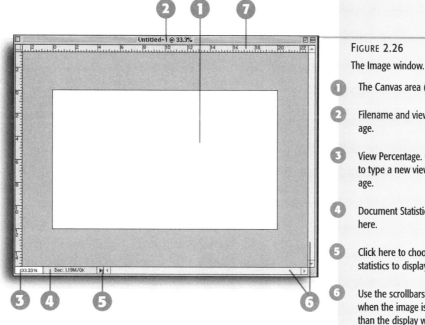

FIGURE 2.26
The Image window.

1 The Canvas area (live area).

2 Filename and view percentage.

3 View Percentage. Click here to type a new view percentage.

4 Document Statistics appears here.

5 Click here to choose which statistics to display.

6 Use the scrollbars to navigate when the image is larger than the display window.

7 Choose **Show Rulers** from the **View** menu or type (Ctrl+R) [Command+R].

8 Click here to close the document, choose **Close** from the **File** menu or type (Ctrl+W) [Command+W].

2. Select the **Paintbucket** tool from the Toolbox.

3. Hold down the **Shift** key and click on the backdrop area.

Navigating

Photoshop provides an array of methods to navigate around your image inside the image window, aside from the scroll bars on the right and bottom of the image window.

Using the Zoom Tool

The **Zoom** tool is used to zoom in closer, enlarging the image in the image window or to zoom out, reducing the size of the image in the image window.

Using the Zoom tool

1. Open any file to try the following functions.

2. Select the **Zoom** tool in the Toolbox.

If you change you mind

If you want to change the color back to a neutral gray, you need to perform the same steps using a gray color instead. You can always delete the preferences file, which restores all the default settings for Photoshop.

3. **To Zoom In:** Position the cursor over your image and click once to zoom in to the next preset percentage. You can also choose **Zoom In** from the **View** menu or type (Ctrl +) [Command +].

4. **To Zoom Out:** With the **Zoom** tool selected, position the cursor over the image and (Alt-click) [Option-click] on the image to zoom out. You can also choose **Zoom Out** from the **View** menu or type (Ctrl -)[Command -].

Here are some other Zoom features:

- To enlarge a specific area of your image, click and drag with the **Zoom** tool to select a rectangular area.

- When you have a tool other than the **Zoom** tool selected, hold down (Ctrl-Spacebar) [Command-Spacebar] to temporarily access the **Zoom** tool; then click in the image window to zoom in.

- Press (Ctrl-0 "zero") [Command-0 "zero"] to fit the image to the screen or choose **Fit on Screen** from the **View** menu.

- Press (Ctrl-Alt-0 "zero") [Command-Option-0 "zero"] to display the image at 100% or choose **Actual Pixels** from the **View** menu.

- Double-click the **Zoom** tool in the Toolbox to display the image at 100%.

- Double-click the **Hand** tool in the Toolbox to fit the image to the screen.

- Display the **Zoom Tool Options** palette by choosing **Show Options** from the **Window** menu and click on the **Resize Windows to Fit** button to make the image and image window resize to fit your screen when you Zoom in and out.

- When you have a tool other than the **Zoom** tool selected, hold down (Ctrl-Alt-Spacebar) [Command-Option-Spacebar] to temporarily access the **Zoom** tool and click in the image window to zoom out.

Using the Hand Tool

The **Hand** tool is used to move the image around inside the image window when you are zoomed in and the image is magnified larger than the image window. The **Hand** tool works like putting your hand down on a piece of paper and moving the piece of paper around by dragging.

Moving around with the Hand tool

1. Zoom in so the image is larger than the image window.

2. Select the **Hand** tool from the Toolbox.

3. Position the cursor over the image and click and drag with the **Hand** tool to position the image in the image window.

4. When you have any tool beside the **Hand** tool selected, hold down the Spacebar to temporarily access the **Hand** tool.

5. Double-click on the **Hand** tool to fit the image and image window to a dimension that fits your screen.

Using the Navigator Palette

The Navigator palette (Figure 2.27) displays a proxy preview of the image with a colored square indicating the part of the image currently displayed in the image window.

SEE ALSO

➤ *For more information on restoring default preferences, see page 182*

➤ *For more information on resolution, see page 70*

➤ *For more information on file formats, see page 44*

➤ *For information on how to have Photoshop automatically append a three-character file extension, see page 185*

➤ *For more information on saving GIF files and the GIF89-a format, see page 61*

➤ *For more information on how to specify custom halftone screens and transfer function, see page 154*

➤ *For more information on specifying Color Settings, see page 115*

➤ *For more information on saving JPEG files, see page 62*

➤ *For more information on saving PNG files, see page 62*

Change that percentage value again!

After you type a magnification value in the percentage box in the lower-left corner of the Navigator palette, hold down the Shift key when pressing Return or Enter to keep the percentage box highlighted. This enables you to change the percentage again.

FIGURE 2.27

The Navigator palette.

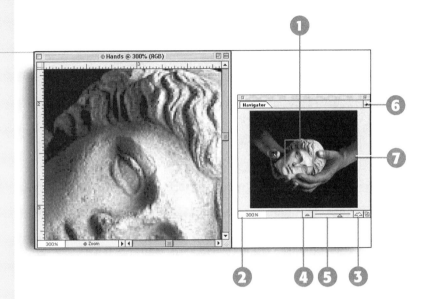

1. Click inside the colored box and drag to move the image inside the image window.

2. Click in the lower-left corner of the Navigator palette to type a magnification value. Choose Return or Enter after entering a value to change the magnification.

3. Clicking here is like clicking on the image with the **Zoom** tool.

4. Clicking here is like (Alt-clicking) [Option-clicking] with the **Zoom** tool.

5. Drag the triangle slider to the right to zoom in, and to the left to zoom out.

6. Choose Palette Options from the palette menu to change the color of the view box in the Navigator palette.

7. If you click outside the view box in the Navigator palette, but still on the image, the View Box moves to the area you click on. Hold down the (Ctrl) [Command] key and drag inside the Navigator palette's proxy image to change the size of the view box and zoom in or out on a particular area of the image.

Changing Canvas Size, Color Mode, and Resolution

Understanding resolution and bitmaps

Working in the various color modes

Changing the Image and Canvas size

Defining the correct color settings

Creating Monotones, Duotones, Tritones, and Quadtones

Understanding Resolution

In order to work effectively in Photoshop, you need to understand and adhere to some basic principles. Photoshop is an application that works on bitmapped images made up of pixels. The number of pixels in an image determines its resolution. The resolution of an image is important because it directly affects the quality of the printed image and, in the case of screen images for presentations and Web pages, the quality of the display.

Image resolution is primarily decided when the original image is created. The majority of Photoshop images are created by digital scanners, which capture image data at varying resolutions depending on the capability of the scanner. Scanners have their own resolution, also referred to as **DPI**, which determines the maximum image resolution (ppi). A scanner must have a resolution (dpi) that is equal to or larger than the desired image resolution when the image is scanned at 100%. If the resolution of the scanner is too low, the scanned image lacks detail, appears flat, and displays poor overall quality. Aside from scanning your own images on a flatbed scanner, you can purchase high-resolution scans from color prepress companies, service bureaus, and printers.

In the last few years, *digital cameras* and *video capture boards* have become widely popular as a means to capture digital image data. Digital cameras capture digitized images at varying resolutions and quality depending on the particular camera. Video frames are captured by importing video footage into a computer program such as Adobe Premiere or Avid VideoShop. The video editing program converts analog video, VHS or Beta for example, into individual digitized frames. Photoshop is capable of editing a single video frame or a Filmstrip, which is a series of video frames. Video captures are relatively low in resolution and size, so their uses are limited. Screen captures are image files created by taking a snapshot of the computer screen using specialized software or, in the case of the Macintosh, a built-in system function [Command+Shift+3]. Windows users can press the **Print Screen** key to capture the screen to the Clipboard and then paste into a new image file. The screen captures in this chapter, for example, were created using Snapz Pro by Ambrosia Software, Inc. Screen captures are generated at the monitor resolution, which is 72ppi for Macintosh and 96ppi for Windows typically.

You can also create an image of any size and resolution directly in Photoshop and create your own graphics using the painting and selection tools.

LPI, PPI, and DPI

The resolution of a Photoshop file is described in Pixels Per Inch (PPI). You might have heard image resolution referred to as dpi (dots per inch), but you'll see a little further on why this terminology is not quite correct. The resolution of the Photoshop image depends solely on where you intend to use the image. For example, the resolution for graphics used on Web pages and in presentation graphics programs such as Freelance Graphics and Microsoft Powerpoint is 72 pixels per inch; the resolution for images to be offset printed is significantly larger, usually twice the line screen.

Target resolution for an image that will ultimately be offset printed is determined by the size of the halftone dot. Halftone dots break down the gray levels of the image into dots of varying sizes, so the printing press can print the grayscale using a single solid ink color (see Figure 3.1). The size of the halftone dot is determined by the **LPI** —number of lines of halftone dots in an inch—and is often referred to as the screen frequency. The line screen (screen frequency) is determined by the printer, the person with the printing press. The paper, pressroom conditions, and the particular printing press are some of the factors that determine the optimum screen frequency. No magic number applies to all printing projects, so communication with the printer is necessary to learn the screen frequency.

FIGURE 3.1

Continuous tone images are broken down into halftone dots to be printed with solid inks.

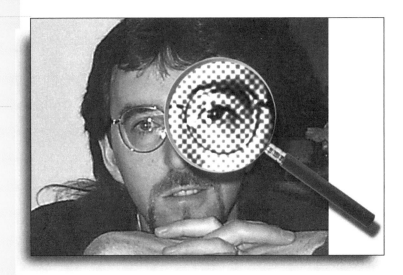

Screening methods without halftone dots

Some laser printers and color output devices such as the Iris inkjet printer use screening methods other than halftoning. For example, the Iris inkjet printer only requires a 150ppi resolution image to achieve optimum quality. Talk to your service bureau or printer before scanning images for use on these devices—most require a relatively low pixel-per-inch ratio compared to offset printing requirements.

The **DPI** is the resolution of the output device, such as a laser printer or high-resolution imagesetter. The laser printer or imagesetter prints your pages using an array of dots with a size determined by the printer's resolution. Halftone dots are also created using these dots, so the roundness of the halftone dot depends on the size of the laser printer or imagesetter dots used to create it (see Figure 3.2). Most desktop laser printers are either 300 or 600dpi, whereas an imagesetter can print at 1,200dpi, 2,400dpi, and higher. Because the size of the printer's dot affects the roundness of the halftone dot, high-screen rulings, 85lpi and higher, reproduce better on higher resolution printers.

Determining Resolution

In order to determine the correct resolution for your Photoshop image, you must decide on how the image will be used. In some cases, a target ppi is already determined for the output device or computer program. In the case of preparing files for offset printing, a simple formula determines the target resolution of the Photoshop image.

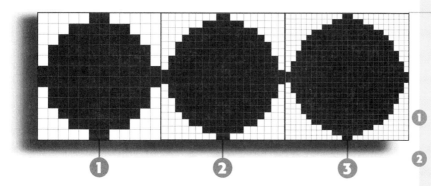

FIGURE 3.2

The halftone dots are created by the laser printer or image-setter using spot sizes determined by the laser printer's or imagesetter's resolution.

1 133LPI 50% Dot
300dpi Laser Printer

2 133LPI 50% Dot
1,200dpi Laser Printer

3 133LPI 50% Dot
2,400dpi Imagesetter

Line Art Images

Line Art is original artwork that contains only solid black and solid white areas (no grays). A high resolution is required for line art because a curved area appears jagged without gray pixels to help smooth it out. Line art can be colorized when it is scanned in and placed in a page layout application such as QuarkXPress or PageMaker; this is desirable because the white areas can be made transparent or colorized separately in the page layout application. The file size of a line art image is significantly smaller than that of a grayscale image, and line art images can be compressed to a remarkably small size using compression software such as Stuffit on the Macintosh or PKZip in Windows. When scanning line art or type, a resolution of 600ppi or higher is recommended. The best resolution would actually be the same as the printer resolution; when scanning line art to print on a 1,200dpi imagesetter, a resolution of 1,200ppi produces optimal quality. Scanning at the printer resolution can produce very large file sizes, however, and 600ppi is sufficient for most artwork (see Figure 3.3).

Grayscale Images

Grayscale images are images that contain a full range of grays to closely approximate continuous tone black and white photographs. In Photoshop, grayscale images can contain up to 256

FIGURE 3.3

An example of Line Art, scanned at 600ppi on the top and 72ppi on the bottom.

levels of gray. Each pixel in a grayscale image contains 8 binary bits of data to describe the pixel's brightness value. The individual gray levels are numbered 0 (zero) to 255; zero is inclusive. Think of the pixels in your grayscale image as representing different intensities of light. Black pixels have a value of 0 (zero) representing no light, and white pixels have a value of 255 representing maximum light. When a grayscale image is in Photoshop, the pixel's gray level, as well as the ink percentage (0% to 100%), can be viewed using the Info palette. The optimum resolution for grayscale images is two times the halftone screen frequency (line screen). For example, if an image is to be printed with a 133lpi screen frequency, it must be scanned at 266 pixels per inch (see Figure 3.4).

FIGURE **3.4**

The same image printed at 133 line screen.

1 133lpi/72ppi

2 133lpi/200ppi

RGB Color Images

RGB Color images are full color images that are created in three separate color channels: Red, Green, and Blue. RGB color images are created using colored light at varying intensities. All digital scanners use RGB to capture color images because a scanner must use light to capture the data. The same is true for computer monitors. Computer monitors display color by illuminating the individual pixels with varying intensities of red, green, and blue light. For this reason, RGB images are used for screen presentation in multimedia programs such as Macromedia Director and QuarkImmedia, presentation programs such as Harvard Graphics and Powerpoint, and for some Web formats such as JPEG and PNG. Some specialized output devices such as color slide/transparency imagesetters also require RGB data because they image color film using red, green, and blue light. The optimum resolution for RGB images that will ultimately be output to a printer or imagesetting device for offset printing is two times the line screen (lpi).

RGB images cannot be color separated to imagesetters and printers. However, because the scanner captures the image data in RGB, the RGB file is used to generate a CMYK image that will eventually be color separated to a printer or imagesetter. RGB images that are to be used in presentation programs such as those previously mentioned only require enough resolution to display optimally on the screen and should be 72ppi for both Macintosh and Windows. The same applies to RGB images for use on Web pages. Screen resolution is all that is needed if the image is for display purposes only.

In Photoshop, RGB images are represented by three individual grayscale channels for each of the colors—red, green, and blue and one composite channel to display the composite image on the screen. Because each of the three color channels is an 8-bit grayscale channel, each pixel in an RGB image can be one of 256 levels of gray for each color: 256 red, 256 green, and 256 blue. If you calculate every combination of the 256 possibilities for each color (256^3), the resulting number of possible colors is 16.7

million. When the red, green, and blue values are equal, the result is a gray level.

CMYK Color Images

CMYK Color images are used to print full color on an offset printing press using the four process color inks: cyan, magenta, yellow, and black. Some color scanners claim to scan in CMYK, but what is actually happening is the scanner scans the image data in RGB and converts the RGB data to CMYK using built-in Color Lookup Tables (CLUTs). When a scanned image is brought into Photoshop as RGB color, Photoshop is used to convert the RGB data to CMYK color data using a CLUT built into Photoshop. The optimum resolution for CMYK images to be printed to color separated plates for offset printing is two times the line screen (lpi). In Photoshop, the CMYK image is represented on four 8-bit grayscale channels—one for each of the process colors: cyan, magenta, yellow, and black. A fifth composite channel is used to display the four color channels combined but is not output when the file is printed (see Figure 3.5).

FIGURE 3.5

For offset printing, four colors are combined to create a full color picture.

1 Cyan

2 Magenta

3 Yellow

4 Black

4 Printed color image

Indexed Color Resolution

Indexed Color images are primarily used for screen display and are single channel images that can contain up to 256 separate and distinct colors. The colors in an indexed color file can be limited to only the colors used in the image, making for a much smaller color file for use on Web pages and in presentation/multimedia programs. When a color image contains more than 256 individual colors, the image can be optionally dithered using 256 colors or less to create the illusion of more colors.

Photoshop generates indexed color images from RGB color images and applies a color table that you specify. For example, if you scan a color picture that contains only black, degrees of gray, and degrees of red, you can convert the image to an indexed color file that contains only the colors used in the picture—256 colors maximum. Indexed color images are used to create GIF files as Web graphics. When creating a GIF file, some of the indexed colors can be assigned as transparency. Because indexed color images are used for screen display, the optimum resolution is 72ppi.

TABLE 3.1   Target resolutions for Photoshop images

Image Use	Image Format	Resolution
Line Art Printing	1-bit black and white	600ppi
Grayscale Printing	8-bit Grayscale	2×lpi
Presentation Graphics	Powerpoint, Director, and so on	72ppi
Web Graphics	GIF, PNG, JPEG, PDF	72ppi
Color Printing	CMYK color separations	2×lpi

Changing the Canvas Size

The image area in a Photoshop file is referred to as the Canvas area. New Canvas area is created in the current background color, so you need to specify the background color first. In order to increase the amount of canvas available for the image without modifying resolution, choose **Canvas Size** from the **Image** menu to display the Canvas Size dialog box (see Figure 3.6). Choose a new width and height for your canvas and click inside the grid to position the existing image.

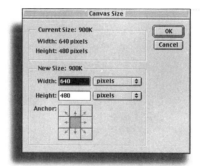

Changing the Size of an Image

Because resolution plays such an important part in the ultimate quality of a Photoshop image, enlarging or reducing the image when it is created can adversely affect that quality. Photoshop images must contain enough image data to accurately render the image; the amount of data necessary is solely dependent on the intended use of the image. You might think that "more is better" when it comes to resolution, but this isn't the case. Aside from creating unnecessarily large images, too much image data results in an output device like a printer throwing away data that it can't use. Although not entirely arbitrary, letting the output device determine which data to throw away and which data to keep often produces undesirable results. Get the resolution right in Photoshop and you won't have to worry about what the output device is going to do to your image.

Enlarging in Photoshop

Enlarging an image in Photoshop, although preferable to enlarging in the page layout application, has its limitations. In Photoshop, you can modify the image size as well as the resolution. Called resampling, Photoshop creates the needed pixels to increase the resolution based on the existing pixels. The method Photoshop uses to enlarge an image while retaining its resolution is called **interpolation**. There are three quality levels of interpolation that can be specified as the default method in the **General Preferences:** *Nearest Neighbor,* *Bilinear,* and *Bicubic.*

The Image Size dialog box contains a pull-down menu enabling you to select the method of interpolation when resizing. To resize the image and maintain the resolution, select **Image Size** from the **Image** menu. Check the **Constrain Proportions** check box to maintain the aspect ratio of the image. Check the **Resample Image** check box to maintain the resolution while resizing (see Figure 3.7).

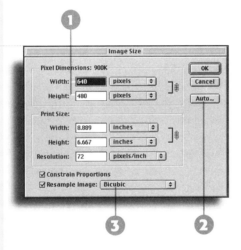

FIGURE 3.7

You can set the interpolation method in the Image Size dialog box independent of the default settings.

1 Specify the new image size in pixel dimensions or by percentage.

2 Click the **Auto** button to set the image resolution based on halftone screen frequency.

3 Select a method of interpolation; **Bicubic** is best.

SEE ALSO

➤ *For more information on interpolation, see page 182*

Reducing Image Size in Photoshop

Down-sampling in Photoshop is achieved by discarding the proper number of pixels to arrive at a target size and resolution. There is no interpolation involved here because Photoshop has to decide which pixels to throw away. To resize the image and maintain the resolution, select **Image Size** from the **Image** menu. Check the **Constrain Proportions** check box to maintain the aspect ratio of the image. Check the **Resample Image** check box to maintain the resolution while resizing. The quality of the resulting image is largely dependent on how high the resolution is to begin with. A 5×5-inch, 300ppi image, for example, resampled down to 3×3-inch at 300ppi only subtly affects the image quality, whereas a 5×5-inch, 72ppi image resampled down to 3×3-inch at 72ppi displays an apparent loss of quality. It's important to remember that Photoshop uses logic-based algorithms to determine which pixels to throw away, so sampling down too much can cause undesired results. The Unsharp Mask filter can help improve quality after resampling, though I suggest examining the pixel structure before and after to observe the effect resampling has on the image.

Photoshop's Image Modes

Photoshop can convert images between eight different image modes: Bitmap, Grayscale, Duotone, Indexed Color, RGB Color, CMYK Color, Lab Color, and Multichannel. The mode you select for your image is largely dependent on the intended use of the image and, in some cases, on the capabilities of a particular software application that will be used to import the image.

Bitmap Mode

Bitmap images, also called 1-bit images, are made up of pixels that contain one of two color values: black or white. For this reason, bitmap images require the least amount of memory and disk space. Line art is often scanned as a bitmap to preserve the sharpness of the lines. Because page layout applications such as PageMaker and QuarkXpress can make the white pixels of a Bitmap image transparent, grayscale images are sometimes converted to bitmap images with a halftone screen or dithered pattern applied. Many image editing options are disabled in Bitmap

Unsharp mask to fix interpolation effect

Resampling an image using interpolation can result in some blurring of the image. Applying the Unsharp Mask filter after resampling an image helps to improve overall sharpness.

When to rescan your image

The thing to remember about image quality is that it's all based on resolution—the number of pixels in the image. Although Photoshop can certainly resize and resample your image, there are times when the desired change in size and resolution is so great that the only sensible thing to do is rescan the image at the correct size and resolution. I've heard from many people how they routinely resize their images in Photoshop and get good results. My argument to this is always that quality is measured by comparison, and if you never see the image at its optimum quality (scanned at the right size and resolution), how do you know what you're getting when the resize in Photoshop is the best quality possible? It usually isn't, but it might be good enough quality for your particular project, a decision you must make based on the project at hand.

mode, making it necessary to edit these images in Grayscale mode before converting back to Bitmap mode.

In order to convert to Bitmap mode, the image mode must first be set to Grayscale. After you have converted color images to Grayscale mode, the **Bitmap** mode option is available under the **Mode** menu.

Convert to Bitmap mode

1. Choose **Mode** from the **Image** menu and then select **Bitmap** to display the Bitmap dialog box (see Figure 3.8).

FIGURE 3.8
The Bitmap dialog box.

2. Select the units of measure from the pull-down menu.
3. Enter the **Output** resolution. This will be the resolution of the resulting bitmap image. The current resolution is displayed automatically for output resolution.
4. Select one of the five options for the bitmap conversion method.
   - **50% Threshold** converts all gray pixels at or above 128 (50% black) to white and all gray values below 128 to black (see Figure 3.9).
   - **Pattern Dither** generates a dithered pattern of black and white pixels to represent the grayscale image. Bitmap images created using this method often print better than they appear onscreen (see Figure 3.10).

FIGURE 3.9
50% Threshold.

FIGURE 3.10
Pattern Dither.

- **Diffusion Dither** is the best choice for generating grayscale images at 1 bit per pixel for display on computer screens. The diffused pattern creates the illusion of gray values using only black and white pixels (see Figure 3.11).

FIGURE **3.11**
Diffusion Dither.

- **Halftone Screen** emulates the process of applying a halftone screen to a grayscale image. The resulting image is broken up into dots of various sizes to represent the grayscale (see Figure 3.12).

- **Custom Pattern** enables you to apply another image as the pattern to create the bitmap image. You can create special screens (wood grain, mezzotint, or stipple pattern, for example) and apply them to the bitmap image. The pattern should be the same size or larger than the image because smaller patterns are tiled to create the screen. Custom patterns capture more of the detail in the grayscale image when they contain gray areas. If you want to apply a pattern that is already bitmapped, convert it to grayscale first and apply the Gaussian Blur or Blur More filter to create some gray values. Keep in mind that patterns that are too tight might not print as you expect due to ink spread on press (see Figure 3.13).

FIGURE 3.12
Halftone Screen.

If you select Halftone Screen as the method to create the Bitmap image, a dialog box appears (see Figure 3.14).

Creating a bitmap from the Halftone Screen

1. Select the units of measure from the pull-down menu.

2. Enter a **Screen Frequency** value. The screen frequency is the "line screen" and ranges from 1 to 999 lines per inch or 0.400 to 400 lines per centimeter (lines per inch is the US standard). Decimal values are allowed here to accommodate matching advanced screening methods. Screen frequency for newspapers and circulars is usually between 65 and 85 lines per inch; magazines are usually between 120 and 150 lines per inch, but check with your printer before indicating a screen frequency because only the printer can tell you the best line screen for your project.

FIGURE 3.13
Custom Pattern.

FIGURE 3.14
The Halftone Screen dialog box.

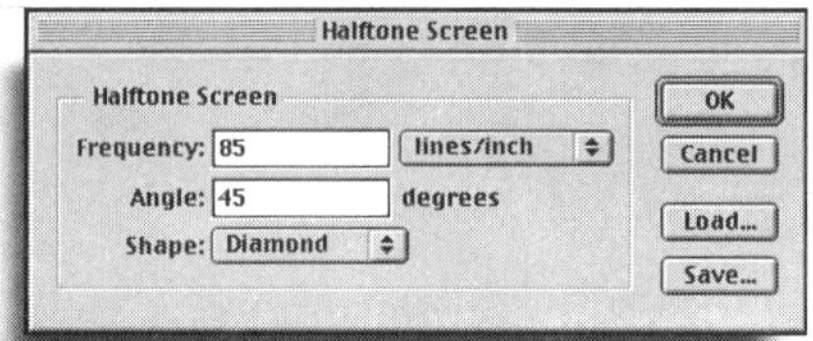

3. Enter the screen **Angle**. The screen angle can range from -180° to +180°. The printer or service bureau can also tell you what to use here, though images that are going to print in black ink or one color are generally at a 45° angle.

4. Choose a dot shape from the **Shape** pull-down menu. Most halftone screens are created using either elliptical or diamond-shaped dots.

5. Click **OK** to accept these settings and generate the bitmap image. Converting grayscale images to bitmap images using the Halftone Screen option enables you to override the halftone screen that is applied when the film is generated. The three images in Figure 3.15 were created using the Halftone Screen option to facilitate the use of multiple screen frequencies on the same page. You can save your halftone screen settings to a file by clicking on the **Save** button in the Halftone Screen dialog box and reload the settings by clicking on the **Load** button.

Grayscale Mode

Grayscale images are represented by up to 256 shades or levels of gray. Each pixel in a grayscale image contains 8 bits of data to describe the pixel's brightness value. Gray levels range from 0 (black) to 255 (white). The pixels in a grayscale image are also represented as percentage of black where 0% is white and 100% is black. Bitmap and color images (RGB, Lab, or CMYK) can be converted to Grayscale mode. When converting from color to grayscale, Photoshop discards all color information and generates the grayscale image from the luminosity values of the color image. When you convert grayscale images to RGB or CMYK, the gray pixel values are converted to their comparable values in the respective color space. In RGB for example, grays are represented by combining equal parts of Red, Green, and Blue such as 230 Red, 230 Green, and 230 Blue to represent 10% grayscale. In CMYK, the gray values are created using varied combinations of Cyan, Magenta, Yellow, and Black: 45% Cyan, 32% Magenta, 32% Yellow, 10% Black to create 50% grayscale for example.

FIGURE 3.15

The Halftone Screen breaks the grayscale image up into dots. Examine the dots with a loupe to see the dot structure.

1. 25 LPI

2. 65 LPI

3. 85 LPI

③

Converting Bitmap to Grayscale

Bitmap images are usually converted to grayscale to facilitate editing the image because many editing tools are not available in Bitmap mode. The resulting grayscale image contains just two gray levels — black (0) and white (255).

Convert bitmap to Grayscale

1. Choose **Mode** from the **Image** menu and then select Grayscale to display the Grayscale dialog box (see Figure 3.16).

2. Enter a **Size Ratio** for the conversion. A ratio of 1 creates a grayscale image of the same size. A number higher than 1 creates a smaller sized image. For example, a ratio of 2 generates a grayscale image at 50% of the size; Photoshop averages two pixels to create 1 pixel in the grayscale image in this case. Choosing a ratio value less than 1 might cause the

FIGURE 3.16
The Grayscale dialog box.

image to fall apart because Photoshop has to invent the needed data based on the existing bitmap.

Converting Color to Grayscale

When converting from RGB, CMYK, Lab, or Multichannel to Grayscale mode, Photoshop uses the luminance values of the pixels to generate the grayscale image.

Convert color to Grayscale

1. Open any RGB, CMYK, Lab, or Multichannel image.

2. Choose **Mode** from the **Image** menu and then select **Grayscale**.

3. A dialog box appears asking if you want to discard the colors. Click on **OK** to discard the color information. Note that after you discard the color information, converting back to RGB from Grayscale will not restore the color information.

Converting Grayscale to Color

You can convert a grayscale image directly into any of the available color modes, enabling you to add color or colorize a grayscale image. You can also create a "4-color halftone" or Quadtone by converting grayscale directly to CMYK mode because converting a grayscale image to CMYK mode does not put the image data on only the black plate.

Convert Grayscale to color

1. Open any grayscale image.

2. Choose **Mode** from the **Image** menu and then select **RGB Color.** You can select CMYK or Lab as color modes, as well.

RGB Mode

The RGB mode in Photoshop uses the RGB color model and represents color by using varying degrees of light intensity in each of the red, green, and blue channels (see Figure 3.17). The values for each color channel are created using 8 bits of data per pixel per color; therefore, each pixel in the RGB image contains a value from 0 to 255 for red, 0 to 255 for green, and 0 to 255 for blue. When all three color values are 255, the pixel displays as white. When all three color values are zero (0), the pixel displays as black. Equal proportions of the three colors result in a shade of gray. Because computer monitors are RGB devices, you should become familiar with and work in the RGB mode to edit color images. Because the RGB gamut is significantly larger than the CMYK gamut, editing color images in RGB mode offers more flexibility.

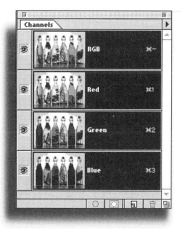

FIGURE 3.17
The RGB Channels.

CMYK Mode

CMYK images are used to produce the four process color plates used in four-color printing. For the most part, CMYK images are generated by Photoshop and programs like it from RGB

RGB mode to apply filter effects

Many special effects filters available under the **Filter** menu work only on an RGB image. Be sure to consider this fact before converting the RGB image into CMYK mode, because going back and forth between these modes causes color shifts.

images. In CMYK mode, each pixel of the color image is assigned a value that represents percentages of cyan, magenta, yellow, and black ink. Light colors have low percentages of color; dark colors contain high percentages of ink. In CMYK mode, the lack of ink percentage is equivalent to the paper color (white for proofing). Black is often represented by a high percentage of black combined with some percentage of the other three process colors.

When RGB images are converted to CMYK mode, the resulting color separation is generated using parameters in Photoshop's separation table. The separation table is generated to the specific settings in the Printing Inks Setup and Separation Setup dialog boxes. When the original image starts out in RGB mode, make color and retouching adjustments in RGB before converting to CMYK. You can use the **CMYK Preview** command available under the **Preview** submenu of the **View** menu to view the image in CMYK while working in RGB. If the images are already in CMYK mode when you receive them (from a service bureau, for example), edit the color images in CMYK mode. Converting to RGB from CMYK and then back again can cause some undesirable color shifts. CMYK mode contains four color channels for each of the four process colors and one composite channel (see Figure 3.18).

FIGURE 3.18
The CMYK Channels.

Converting to CMYK

A significant amount of preliminary work must be done in Photoshop before converting images to CMYK mode. Photoshop takes many factors into account when creating the separation table necessary to generate a CMYK image. When Photoshop converts a RGB image to CMYK, it first converts the image to Lab mode (internally; you don't see this). Photoshop uses the settings in **RGB Setup** to perform this interim conversion, so calibrating the monitor and entering the **RGB Setup** information is necessary. Refer to your Photoshop user manual for information on calibrating the monitor. The image is then converted from Lab mode to CMYK mode. During this step, Photoshop uses the settings in **CMYK Setup** to generate the separation table (see "Defining Color Settings" later in this chapter).

Convert to CMYK

1. Open any Grayscale, RGB color, or Lab color image.

2. Choose **Mode** from the **Image** menu and then select **CMYK Color**.

Lab Mode

Lab mode uses the L*a*b color model to represent the color of pixels. Each of the three color channels in Lab mode contains 8 bits of data for each pixel, for a total of 24 bits (see Figure 3.19). "L" is the lightness component of the image; each pixel has a value in the range of zero (0) to 100. The "a" value (green to red) and the "b" value (blue to yellow) range from +120 to -120. Because the color specifications in the L*a*b color model are device-independent, Lab mode is the best mode to use when transferring images from one system to another. Adobe recommends using Lab color to print to Postscript Level 2 devices, but check with your service bureau if they are doing the output. The Lab mode is the hardest to understand until you experiment with editing the lightness and color values separately.

FIGURE 3.19
The Lab Channels.

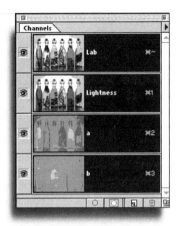

Converting to Lab Mode

Grayscale, RGB, Duotone and Indexed color images can be converted to Lab mode. You can adjust the "L" (lightness) value in Lab mode to adjust the brightness of the image or parts of the image without affecting the color. The image can then be converted back to RGB or Indexed color without affecting the color values. Lab images can also be converted to CMYK for process color printing. Converting between Lab mode and other color modes or vice versa does not affect the original colors of the image in any way unless you adjust the "a" or "b" values in Lab mode.

Convert to Lab mode

1. Open any Grayscale, RGB, CMYK, Duotone, or Multichannel image. Bitmap images cannot be converted to Lab mode because Lab mode requires at least 8 bits of information per pixel; convert the bitmap image to grayscale first.

2. Choose **Mode** from the **Image** menu and then select **Lab Color**.

Duotone Mode

When you choose **Duotone** from the **Mode** menu, the Duotone Options dialog box appears. A drop-down menu in this dialog box displays the four available modes: **Monotone**, **Duotone**, **Tritone**, and **Quadtone**. Monotones are 8-bit-per-pixel, grayscale images printed with a specific ink. Duotones are grayscale images printed with two colors, usually black and a spot color. Tritones and Quadtones are grayscale images printed with three and four colors respectively. Printing presses are generally capable of printing up to 50 levels of gray for one color, a lot less than the 256 gray levels generated by Photoshop. Duotones, Tritones, and Quadtones are often used to extend the gray levels of the printing process. When creating a Duotone, Tritone, or Quadtone, the gray values of the grayscale image are actually designated to the colors chosen, so the image is still an 8-bit-per-pixel image with the gray values mapped to two, three, or four colors. Unlike the RGB, CMYK, and Lab modes, the colors used in Duotones, Tritones, and Quadtones are contained in a single 8-bit channel and are only adjustable using the curves in the Duotone Options dialog box.

Creating a Duotone

To create a Duotone, start with a grayscale image. If you use a color image, you have to convert it to Grayscale mode before continuing.

Creating a Duotone

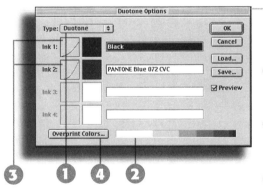

FIGURE 3.20

The Duotone Options dialog box.

1. Select **Monotone**, **Duotone**, **Tritone**, or **Quadtone** from the pull-down menu.

2. Click on the color swatches to select a color from Photoshop Color Picker

3. Click on the Curves graphic to display the Curves dialog box.

4. Click **Overprint Colors** to specify the way overprinting colors display onscreen.

1. Open any Grayscale image and choose **Mode** from the **Image** menu. Then select **Duotone** to display the Duotone Options dialog box (see Figure 3.20).

2. Select **Duotone** from the **Type** pull-down menu.

3. Select the colors for your Duotone by clicking on the color box to the left of the color name. When the Photoshop Custom Color Picker appears, you can use any of the Custom Color models to select a color for your Duotone or click on the **Picker** button to specify a color mix in one of Photoshop's color spaces. If you choose a Custom spot color, be sure the color is named exactly as the color name in your page layout application (upper- and lowercase count as well).

SEE ALSO
➤ *For more information on selecting colors, see page 216*

4. To modify the Duotone curve, click on the curve box to the left of the ink swatch in the Duotone Options dialog box to display the Duotone Curve dialog box (see Figure 3.21). The default Duotone curve is a straight diagonal line across the entire grid. The default Duotone curve maps the printing ink percentages exactly to the grayscale values in the

FIGURE **3.21**

The Duotone Curve dialog box.

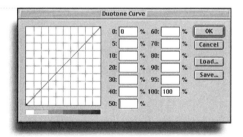

image; a 10% highlight pixel in the image prints with a 10% dot of the ink color and a 60% midtone value prints with a 60% dot of the ink color, for example.

5. You can adjust the Duotone curve for each of the ink colors by dragging points on the graph or by entering values for the printing ink percentages to correspond with the grayscale values in the image. Check the **Preview** check box to see the changes you make reflected in your image.

- Another sub bullet to show an example

- Click on the diagonal line in the center of the graph and drag to the right to adjust the ink percentages toward the shadow areas. Drag the point down until the value in the 50% box becomes 30% (see Figure 3.22). With this setting, the 50% grayscale values in the image will be printed with a 30% printing ink dot. The values between 0% and 30% and the values between 30% and 100% are automatically recalculated by Photoshop, even though the numbers are not inserted in the corresponding boxes. This ink color will map the grayscale values in the image that are between 0% and 50% to print with the color ink between 0% and 30%, so the ink coverage will be light in these areas. The ink coverage will be highest for the midtone, 3/4 tone, and shadow areas because the largest proportion of ink percentage is distributed between the 50% and 100 grayscale values in the image. Here are some more things you can do in the Duotone Curve dialog box.

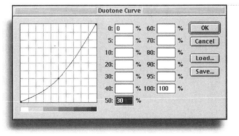

FIGURE 3.22
The Duotone Curve dialog box with the 50% grayscale pixel mapped to a 30% printing dot.

- Click on the diagonal line in the center of the graph and drag to the left to adjust the ink percentages toward the highlight areas. Drag the point up until the value in the 50% box becomes 70% (see Figure 3.23). With this setting, the 50% grayscale values in the image will be printed with a 70% printing ink dot. The values between 0% and 70% and the values between 70% and 100% are automatically recalculated by Photoshop, even though the numbers are not inserted in the corresponding boxes. This ink color will map the grayscale values in the image that are between 0% and 50% to print with the color ink between 0% and 70%, so the ink coverage will be heavy in the highlight and 1/4 tones. The ink coverage will be lowest for the midtone, 3/4 tone, and shadow areas because the smallest proportion of ink percentage is distributed between the 50% and 100 grayscale values in the image.

FIGURE 3.23

The Duotone Curve dialog box with the 50% grayscale pixel mapped to a 70% printing dot.

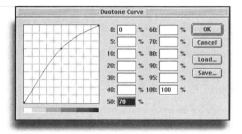

- You can click on the diagonal line in the graph and add up to 13 points to set the values for the 13 boxes (see Figure 3.24). Note that the end points of the diagonal line can also be adjusted to set the 0% and 100% values. Photoshop calculates any intermediate ink percentages automatically.

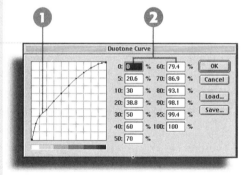

FIGURE 3.24

The Duotone Curve dialog box with all 13 values mapped on the diagonal line.

1 Click along the curve line to add anchor points.

2 The anchor point values are reflected here. You can enter a value to adjust the curve as well.

- Click and drag the points off the grid to remove them.
- Click on the **Save** button in the Duotone Curve dialog box to save a particular curve setting.
- Click on the **Load** button in the Duotone Curve dialog box to load a previously saved curve setting.

6. After you adjust the Duotone curves, click **OK** in the Duotone Options dialog box. Duotones created with both colors having the same curve produce a Duotone that prints one ink entirely over the other, so make sure you change the curve for at least one of the colors. If you want to readjust the color settings for your Duotone, choose **Mode** from the **Image** menu and then select **Duotone** again.

7. Save the file in **Photoshop EPS** format if you want to import the Duotone into a page layout application such as QuarkXPress or PageMaker.

Setting Duotone Overprint Colors

When two or more unscreened colors overlap in a Duotone, Tritone, or Quadtone, the overlapping colors create a new color (for example, red and yellow produce orange). You can adjust how these colors display onscreen only, which is helpful if you want to calibrate your screen display to accurately display the colors that will print in Duotone mode. Adjusting the colors for overprint does not affect the overall monitor RGB setup and only applies to the specific image you're working with.

Set Duotone overprint colors

1. Choose **Mode** from the **Image** menu and then select **Duotone** to display the Duotone Options dialog box. You can do this even if you're already in Duotone mode.

2. Click on the **Overprint Colors** button to display the Overprint Colors dialog box (Figure 3.25). The combinations that will result when colors overprint are indicated here.

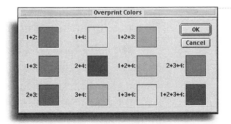

FIGURE 3.25

The possible color combinations are highlighted in the Overprint Colors dialog box.

3. Click on the color swatch over the combination you want to adjust to display the Photoshop Color Picker.

4. Select the color you want for this combination and then click **OK**.

5. Perform steps 3 and 4 for all the color combinations you want to change before clicking **OK** in the Overprint Colors dialog box.

Loading and Saving Duotone Curves

You can save the Duotone curve information in a file for later retrieval. Click on the **Save** button in the Duotone Options dialog box and give the file a name that reflects the colors used. To load saved Duotone presets, click on the **Load** button in the Duotone Options dialog box. There are a number of Duotones presets included with your Photoshop package in the Goodies directory.

Creating a Monotone

Creating a Monotone is a simple process. Monotone images are grayscale images that have a color specification assigned to them. If you specify a Custom Color (PANTONE 156, for example) and save the file in EPS format, the file can be imported into a page layout application such as QuarkXPress or PageMaker where it will separate out to a color plate called PANTONE 156. To create a Monotone image, start out with a grayscale image.

Create a Monotone

1. Choose **Mode** from the **Image** menu and then select **Duotone** to display the Duotone Options dialog box.

2. Select **Monotone** from the **Type** pull-down menu.

3. Select the color for your Monotone by clicking on the color box to the left of the color name. When the Photoshop Custom Color Picker appears, you can use any of the Custom Color models to select a color for your Monotone or click on the **Picker** button to specify a color mix in one

of Photoshop's color spaces. If you choose a Custom spot color, be sure the color is named exactly as the color name in your page layout application (upper- and lowercase count as well).

4. Click on the Duotone Curve diagram to display the Monotone Curve dialog box. If you want a Monotone image that represents the grayscale with a color, leave the Duotone curve linear (a straight line from the bottom left to the top right).

5. Click **OK**. If you want to readjust the color settings for your Monotone, perform steps 1 through 4 again.

6. Save the file in **Photoshop EPS** format if you want to import the Monotone into a page layout application.

Creating a Tritone or Quadtone

Follow the previous steps for creating a Duotone but specify three colors to create a Tritone or four colors for a Quadtone image. Custom presets for Tritones and Quadtones are contained in the Goodies directory (Windows) or the Goodies folder (Macintosh) in the Photoshop application's directory. The best way to get a feel for what settings to use for Duotones, Tritones, and Quadtones is to experiment and examine some of the presets provided with Photoshop.

Setting Screen Angles for Duotones

A Duotone, Tritone, or Quadtone creates overlapping areas of the grayscale image when it is created. In order for the halftone screens to print properly, the halftone screen angles for the color plates should be at least 30° apart. For four-color process separations, black is usually set to a 45° angle with magenta and cyan 30° away from that on either side (15° and 75°). Setting the angles 30° apart ensures that an overlapping of the halftone dots does not create a *moiré pattern*. For CMYK printing, the yellow plate is printed at 90° (only 15° away from the nearest color). Yellow is chosen as the color that must overlap because it is the least dominant of the four colors. Use this same setup for

Duotones, Tritones, and Quadtones. For Quadtones, keep in mind that with four inks, one of them must overlap in the halftone dot area. Choose the lightest of the four colors to be set at the "yellow" angle.

Before you set the screen angles for your *Duotone*, *Tritone*, or *Quadtone* images in Photoshop, consult your printer or service bureau. Many screening algorithms are in use today, such as Agfa's Balanced Screening and Linotype Hell's Diamond Screening, plus advanced screening technologies for Stochastic Screening, sometimes called FM (frequency modulation) screening. It might cause more harm than good to set the screen angles independently for the image in Photoshop because service bureaus and printers might be using improved screening techniques that they can set up for your file during output. You can set up the screen frequencies and angles.

Setting screen angles

1. Open a Duotone image and choose **Page Setup** from the **File** menu to display the Page Setup dialog box (see Figure 3.26).

FIGURE 3.26
The Page Setup dialog box.

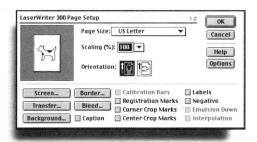

2. Click on the **Screen** button to display the Halftone Screens dialog box (see Figure 3.27).

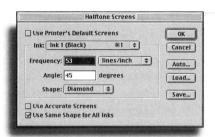

FIGURE 3.27
The Halftone Screens dialog box.

3. Remove the check from **Use Printer's Default Screens** and select the **Ink** color from the pull-down menu (see Figure 3.28). Note that the ink color list is composed of the colors used in your Duotone, Tritone, or Quadtone.

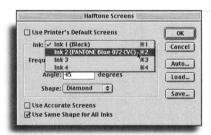

FIGURE 3.28
The colors used in your Duotone, Tritone, or Quadtone are listed under the Ink pull-down menu.

4. Enter a Screen **Frequency** and **Angle** for the color. Black should be at 45° with other colors 30° apart at either 15° or 75°. Talk to your printer for suggested angles.

5. Choose a dot **Shape** from the pull-down list. For standard halftone screens, use a **Diamond** dot here. If you want all plates to have the same dot shape, click on the **Use Same Shape for All Inks** check box.

6. Click on the **Use Accurate Screens** check box if your file will be printed to an output device using PostScript Level 2 or an Emerald controller or Emerald RIP (Raster Image Processor). If you check this box and do not print to one of these devices, the accurate screens setting has no effect.

7. Specify the screen information for each color in your image.

8. You can save your settings to reload for subsequent images

by clicking on the **Save** button in the Halftone Screens dialog box. Click on the **Load** button to reload the settings previously saved. Click **OK** if you're done.

9. In order for the screens you just set up to be used for the image when it is saved as a Photoshop EPS file, you must click on the **Include Halftone Screen** check box when saving the file in **Photoshop EPS** format (see Figure 3.29).

FIGURE **3.29**
The EPS Options dialog box.

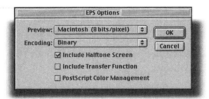

Indexed Color Mode

Indexed color images are images that contain a specific Color palette of up to 256 colors. An indexed color image can contain just the colors used in the image (if 256 or less), facilitating smaller file sizes and faster display in multimedia applications and Web pages. When you convert a color image from one of the other color modes to indexed color, Photoshop creates a color lookup table (CLUT) to store the color values for the image. If the image contains more than 256 distinct colors, Photoshop finds the closest matches and builds an indexed color table with 256 colors. The color table generated for indexed color images can also be edited to reduce the number of colors used.

Converting to Indexed Color

Choose **Mode** from the **Image** menu and then select **Indexed Color** to display the Indexed Color dialog box (see Figure 3.30). There are various options for generating an indexed color image.

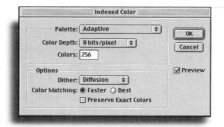

FIGURE 3.30
The Indexed Color dialog box.

Convert to indexed color

1. Open a RGB image and choose **Mode** from the **Image** menu; then select **Indexed Color**.

2. Choose a **Palette**. There are five palette choices to convert to indexed color in the **Palette** pull-down menu. You can view the color table that is generated by choosing **Mode** from the **Image** menu and then selecting **Color Table** by displaying the **Swatches** palette.

   - The **Exact palette** is created with the exact same colors used in the RGB file, assuming the RGB file contains 256 colors or less. If the RGB contains more than 256 distinct colors, the Exact option will be grayed out.

   - The **System (Macintosh) palette** uses the Macintosh default Color palette. This palette contains an even sampling of the colors in the RGB color space. Note that the Macintosh Color palette and Windows Color palette might contain some of the same colors, but they are organized in a different order. So choose a System (Macintosh) Color palette only when you're sure the image will be used on a Macintosh only.

   - The **System (Windows) palette** uses the Windows default Color palette. This palette contains an even sampling of the colors in the RGB color space. Note that the Windows Color palette and Macintosh Color palette might contain some of the same colors, but they are organized in a different order. So choose a System (Windows) Color palette only when you're sure the image will be used on a Windows computer only.

- The **Web palette** uses a palette of the 216 colors recognized by Web browser applications. If you create graphics to be exported to GIF89a format, choose Web when converting to Indexed color for the best results on both Macintosh and PC-Windows platforms. The Web palette works best for images that contain a limited number of colors or that were created using the Web-safe 216 colors. Full color images generally reproduce better on multiple platforms if you use the Adaptive palette.

- The **Uniform palette** uses a uniform sampling of the colors in the RGB image's gamut of colors. The Uniform palette's colors are generated based on the Color Depth specified. Specify dithering for Uniform indexed colors less than 8-bits-per-pixel color depth.

- The **Adaptive palette** samples the colors used in the image and builds a color table based on the most common occurrences, which can be helpful for images that are weighted in specific color areas. You can also base the color table on a selected portion of the image. Select the portion of the image you want to base the indexed color table on before converting to Indexed mode. Photoshop uses the selected area of the image to weigh the color choices made for the Color palette.

- The **Custom palette** is used to build your own color table of up to 256 colors. When you choose this option, the Color Table dialog box appears. See the section on "Modifying the Color Table" later in this chapter for information on how to enter the colors for the color table.

- The **Previous** choice is only available if you chose the Custom or Adaptive options the last time you converted to Indexed Color. The **Previous** option uses the Color palette from the previously generated Custom or Adaptive Color palette, even if you didn't save the palette.

3. Select a **Color Depth**. The **Color Depth** option is available only when you choose **Uniform** or **Adaptive** from the **Palette** drop-down list in the Indexed Color dialog box.

Photoshop uses the **Color Depth** information to generate the Indexed Color file. The maximum setting is 8 bits per pixel here because 8 bits per pixel generates 256 colors. Choosing a number less than 8 bits per pixel results in fewer colors, though the Indexed color image is still going to be an 8-bit-per-pixel image. When you choose **Other** as the **Color Depth** option, you can specify the exact number of colors desired.

4. Select a **Dithering** Option. When the color table generated by converting to Indexed Color mode does not contain the exact 256 colors used in the RGB image, the resulting image appears posterized to some extent, unless some form of dithering is applied to the image. When dithering is used, the missing colors in the image are simulated by the application of a pattern. If you use the Exact palette, the Dithering options will be grayed out (unavailable) because the image contains all the color values needed. Here are the dithering options:

- When **None** is selected and the RGB image contains more than 256 colors, posterization can become apparent because Photoshop fills in the blanks with the closest color in the palette.

- The **Pattern** method of dithering creates patterns of pixels to simulate the missing colors. You must be using one of the System palette options to apply a Pattern dither.

- **Diffusion** offsets pixels to avoid an obvious pattern when dithering and is the most common choice for dithering, when dithering is necessary.

Making Color Table Choices

There are six predefined color tables available at the top of the Color Table dialog box (see Figure 3.31). You can apply any of these color tables to your indexed color image.

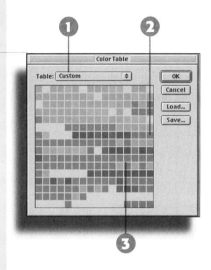

FIGURE 3.31

Display the Color Table dialog box by choosing **Mode** from the **Image** menu and then select **Color Table**.

1. The Custom color table displays the colors in the indexed color image. To remap the colors, select a color **Table** from the pull-down menu.

2. Click on a color cell to display the Photoshop Color Picker and specify a color.

3. Click and drag through the table to select a range of colors. When the Color Picker appears, select the first color in the range and click **OK**. When the Color Picker reappears, select the last color in the range.

- **Custom** represents any color table that is not a Photoshop built-in color table.

- **Black Body** is based on the colors a black body radiator radiates when heating up. The colors range from black to red, orange, yellow and then white.

- If you select **Grayscale**, the image is rebuilt using 256 levels of gray.

- The **Macintosh System** color table displays the Macintosh 256 Color palette.

- The **Spectrum** palette contains transitions between the primary hues: violet, blue, green, yellow, orange, and red.

- The **Windows System** color table displays the Windows 256 Color palette.

Saving and Loading Color Tables

You can save the displayed color table by clicking on the **Save** button in the *Color Table* dialog box. To load a previously saved color table, click on the **Load** button in the Color Table dialog box. You can also load the saved color tables into the Swatches palette. To load a color table into the Swatches palette, choose **Load Swatches** or **Replace Swatches** from the Swatches palette menu. Locate a previously saved Swatch file or *CLUT file* and click on the **Open** button.

Modifying the Color Table

The color table contains all the colors (up to 256 of them) that are contained in your indexed color image. You might want to modify the colors that make up your indexed color image to combine similar colors into one flat color or to change the values of individual colors for effect.

Modify the color table

1. Choose **Mode** from the **Image** menu and then select **Color Table** to display the Color Table dialog box.

2. Click on a color to modify an individual color *or* click and drag through a range of colors.

3. The Photoshop Color Picker appears. If you clicked on just one color tag, choose a new color and click **OK**. If you selected a range of colors, choose the first new color for the range and click **OK**. The Color Picker reappears, so you can select the last color in the range. The first color you pick also appears in the color picker the second time it appears, so simply clicking **OK** without entering a color changes the whole range of colors to the one color.

4. Click **OK** in the Color Table dialog box to apply the changes. If you click on the **Cancel** button, the Color palette is restored.

Multichannel Mode

When color images are converted to Multichannel mode, the color plates are recreated as 8-bit-per-pixel grayscale channels named for the process ink colors (see Figure 3.32). Converting an RGB image to Multichannel mode, for example, results in three channels named Cyan, Magenta, and Yellow representing the red, green, and blue channels of the RGB file. Converting a CMYK image to Multichannel mode creates four channels named Cyan, Magenta, Yellow, and Black to represent the cyan,

Saving indexed colors from the Swatches palette

When you have converted an RGB image to Indexed Color mode, display the Swatches palette to see the colors in the Color Table. From the Swatches palette menu choose **Save Swatches** to save the colors from the table in a file to be used later. This method can be helpful when designing for multimedia presentations to maintain a uniform Color palette for created graphics or added text.

magenta, yellow, and black plates respectively.

Multichannel mode is not an option for Grayscale, Bitmap, and Indexed Color images because these contain only one channel to begin with. After you convert to Multichannel mode, you can convert back to the original color mode or Lab mode. Multichannel mode lends itself well to breaking out particular color channels to create specialized printing effects, such as bump plates where a fifth color is included to enhance a particular color value in the printed piece. Choose **Split Channels** from the Channels palette menu to split the channels of a Multichannel image into individual grayscale files. Choose **Merge Channels** from the Channels palette menu to merge individual files into a single Multichannel, RGB, Lab, or CMYK file. When you choose to merge channels, dialog boxes appear, prompting you to select which file goes on which channel.

FIGURE 3.32

The Multichannel mode creates numbered grayscale channels.

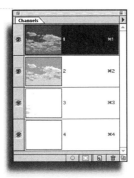

Color Gamut

The range of colors available in a specific color model is that model's color gamut. The visible spectrum (colors you can see with your eyes) is significantly larger than any of the available color model's color gamut. In Photoshop, Lab mode encompasses the largest color gamut including all the colors in the RGB and CMYK gamut. The RGB gamut contains all the colors that can be generated on the computer monitor, as well as on television screens. The CMYK gamut, the smallest of all the color gamut's in Photoshop, contains all the colors that can be printed using the cyan, magenta, yellow, and black process color inks. Because the RGB gamut is quite a bit larger than the CMYK gamut, it stands to reason that there are colors that can be displayed on the monitor that cannot be represented by process color inks.

When colors displayed on the monitor are outside the range (gamut) of colors that can be produced using process color inks, these colors are considered to be "*out-of-gamut.*" In Photoshop, the colors that are indicated as out-of-gamut reflect the settings in the CMYK Setup preference. Before using any of Photoshop's methods to bring colors into gamut, be sure these preferences are set correctly.

Identifying Out-of-Gamut Colors

Photoshop has a few methods to help you identify the colors outside the printable CMYK gamut. When working in RGB or HSB mode, choose **Gamut Warning** from the **View** menu. You might have to wait a few seconds for Photoshop to calculate the out-of-gamut colors. A gray mask appears over your image indicating the areas of the image that contain out-of-gamut colors (see Figure 3.33). Activating the gamut warning in this way enables you to make specific modifications to the colors in your image to bring them into gamut.

You can usually adjust the saturation of the color to bring it into gamut. If you convert a RGB image that contains out-of-gamut colors to CMYK, Photoshop adjusts the display of those colors to more closely match the colors that are printed—in effect bringing those colors into gamut. After you select **Gamut Warning** from the **View** menu, it remains active until you select it again to deactivate it. The performance of Photoshop is not affected when you have **Gamut Warning** turned on.

Photoshop displays an exclamation point (!) inside a triangle to indicate out-of-gamut colors in the Photoshop Color Picker (see Figure 3.34), as well as the Color palette (see Figure 3.35). When in RGB or HSB mode, drag the cursor over the image pixels with the Picker palette on the screen. When the cursor is

Changing the out-of-gamut color

If your image contains colors similar to the gamut warning color, you might want to change the color of the out-of-gamut mask. To change the gamut warning color to something other than the default gray, choose **Preferences** from the **File** menu and then select **Transparency & Gamut**. Select a new color by clicking on the color square and select a color from the Photoshop Color Picker. Set the desired **Opacity** and click **OK**.

over an out-of-gamut color, the gamut warning symbol appears next to a color swatch that shows the closest color within the CMYK gamut in the lower-left corner of the Picker palette. Clicking on the gamut warning symbol in either the Color Picker or Color palette adjusts the out-of-gamut color to the closest color within the CMYK gamut.

FIGURE 3.33

Photoshop displays a mask over your image to indicate out-of-gamut colors.

FIGURE 3.34

The Photoshop Color Picker displays the out-of-gamut warning under a color swatch representing the closest match within the CMYK gamut.

1 The out-of-gamut warning

2 Click this swatch to adjust the out-of-gamut color to the nearest color that is in the CMYK color gamut.

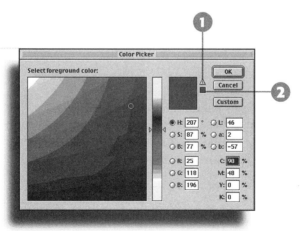

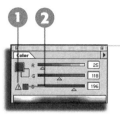

Choose **CMYK Preview** from the **View** menu to display an RGB image the way it converted to CMYK using the current separation table. Choosing **CMYK Preview** reflects the settings in the Printing Inks and Separation Setup dialog boxes. The **CMYK Preview** command gives you a picture of what the RGB image looks like in CMYK.

Defining Color Settings

Color Settings are available under the **File** menu in the **Color Settings** submenu. Using the color settings options in Photoshop, you can specify precisely the printing conditions and conditions for viewing on the monitor in your office or room. Before you adjust any of the color settings, calibrate your monitor using the supplied software that comes with Photoshop, or a third-party product that supports your color monitor. Most calibration tools enable you to adjust the gamma, color balance, and white-and-black points for your monitor. Calibrating your monitor eliminates color casts, balances the grays and neutrals, and even helps you standardize how you view color images on different monitors. Calibrating your monitor in no way guarantees that the four-color process printing you do will be accurate and match your screen. In fact, a computer monitor always displays RGB data and cannot display exact CMYK colors. However, because we humans are highly dependent on visual input, having a calibrated monitor certainly helps you spot obvious color problems.

Photoshop comes with a separate control panel for the Macintosh to adjust the color monitor settings. PCs running Windows have the calibration software installed as part of the

Creating a New View window

TIP: The best way to utilize the **CMYK Preview** command is to create a new window for your image by choosing **New View** from the **View** menu. Turn on **CMYK Preview** for one of the windows and work in the other window with **Gamut Warning** turned on. When you make color adjustments to the image, the changes are also reflected in the second window with **CMYK Preview** turned on.

Photoshop program. If you want to use a third-party product, such as the Radius Calibrator, follow the directions for that device; otherwise use the software supplied with Photoshop and follow the directions for calibrating your monitor in the Photoshop user's manual. Use one method or the other, but not both.

Specifying RGB Setup

The information you enter in the RGB Setup dialog box determines how Photoshop displays color information. On the MacOS, the information displayed in the RGB Setup dialog box reflects the settings of Apple's Colorsync control panel. For windows 95/98/NT, this information comes from the settings specified in the Adobe Gamma control panel. If you use the Adobe Gamma control panel to calibrate your monitor on the MacOS, the profile settings you save will also update Colorsync profile specified in the Colorsync control panel. Choose **Color Settings** from the **File** menu and then select **RGB Setup** to display the RGB Setup dialog box (see Figure 3.36).

- Choose a monitor profile from the **RGB** pull-down menu. If you have already calibrated your monitor using the Adobe Gamma control panel, or in the case of the MacOS, selected a Colorsync profile, the pull-down menu will display a choice for **RGB Monitor**. Select this option to use the settings you described when calibrating the monitor.

- If you choose one of the monitor profiles in the pull-down menu, the **Gamma**, **White Points** and **Primaries** will be set for that profile. Changing any one of these three values changes the RGB monitor profile to **Custom**.

- Check the **Display Using Monitor Compensation** to apply the **Brightness** and **Contrast** settings from your monitor profile if you calibrated your monitor.

Specifying CMYK Setup

The CMYK Setup dialog box is where you set up the separation preferences to control ink, paper stock, dot gain, and generation of the color plates (see Figure 3.37). The information needed to make the choices for the CMYK Setup's dialog box are available from your printer, though some standard settings return good results. Photoshop uses the information in the CMYK Setup dialog box to convert color values between modes. If you change the settings in the CMYK Setup dialog box after you convert an image from RGB to CMYK, the changes affect only the screen representation, leaving the data unchanged. Converting back and forth between RGB and CMYK is not a good idea because Photoshop has to recalculate the color values each time and causes a slight shift in color each time.

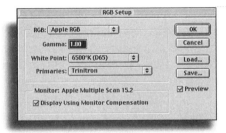

FIGURE 3.36
The RGB Setup dialog box.

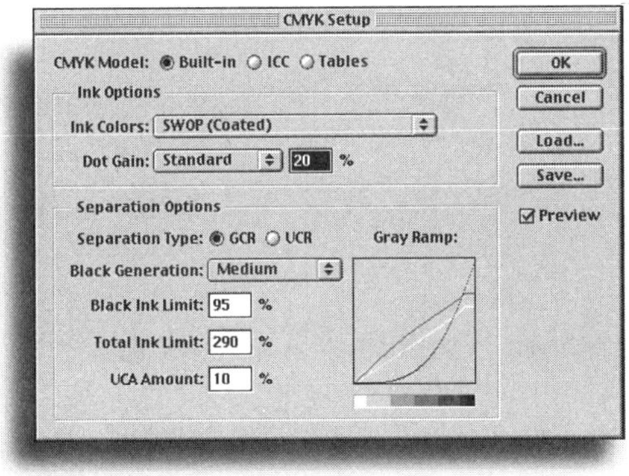

FIGURE 3.37
The CMYK Setup dialog box.

CMYK setup

1. Choose **Color Settings** from the **File** menu and then select **CMYK Setup** to display the CMYK Setup dialog box (see Figure 3.37).

2. You can specify the CMYK Setup information in one of three ways: **Built-in**, **ICC,** or **Tables**—radio buttons at the top of the CMYK Setup dialog box.

- Choose **Built-in** to specify the traditional information required to create color separations (see Figure 3.37). This choice enables you to specify **Ink Color** sets, **Dot Gain** compensation, and a **Separation Type**, along with the specific information required for the **Separation Type**.

- Choose **ICC** to select a color profile created using the Colorsync or Gamma control panel on the MacOS or the Gamma control panel on Windows 95/98/NT. Photoshop provides color profiles for a variety of color output devices including SWOP and Pantone (see Figure 3.38). These color profiles can be created within Photoshop using the **Built-in** option, using the Colorsync control panel on the MacOS, or using the Kodak Colorsync 2.0-compatible Color Management Module. Choose the **Engine** used to create the color profile from the **Engine** pull-down menu. Choose the type of image you plan on converting to CMYK from the **Intent** pull-down menu.

FIGURE 3.38

The CMYK Setup dialog box with the **ICC** radio button selected.

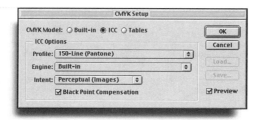

- Choose **Tables** to load previously used separation tables. In order to load a separation table, you must first save one by converting to CMYK mode and then clicking the **Save** button. After you have saved a separation table, it can be loaded at a later date by clicking on the **Load** button (see Figure 3.39). You can also set up color separation tables with device profiles for color printers defined by the Apple Colorsync Manager

(MacOS) or the Kodak ICC Color Management System (Windows). Refer to the Photoshop documentation and the documentation of your particular color management system for specific details on how to use this function.

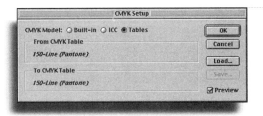

FIGURE 3.39
The CMYK Setup dialog box with the **Tables** radio button selected.

3. Select the **Ink Colors** profile from the pull-down list. The default setting here is **SWOP (Coated)**. SWOP stands for Specifications for Web Offset Publications and is the industry standard for color separation in the United States. The most common ink color specifications are available in this pull-down menu; choose the one that best describes your printing needs (see Figure 3.40). This color profile adjusts the color display of your file to represent the type of paper and printing ink set specified here. If you choose **Custom** from this list, the Ink Colors dialog box displays (see Figure 3.41). To enter color values in the Ink Colors dialog box, you need specific numbers acquired from a reflective densitometer's readings off of a color proof or printed piece.

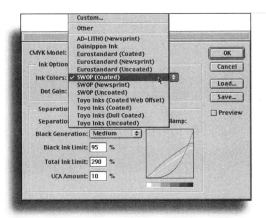

FIGURE 3.40
Choose SWOP (Coated) for high-quality printing if you are not sure.

FIGURE **3.41**
The Ink Colors dialog box.

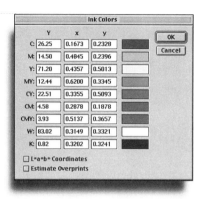

4. The **Dot Gain** field has a value in it if you chose a **Standard** profile from the **Ink Colors** setting. Don't change this value unless you have already seen a proof and talked to the printer. The **Dot Gain** percentage indicated here represents compensation in the halftone dot size for press conditions that cause the halftone dot to grow during printing. A 20% setting in the **Dot Gain** field means that when the CMYK file is generated, a 50% dot will be adjusted down to a 30% dot, so when the file is printed on press and the dot gains in size by 20%, it will be at the correct size (50%). Although dot gain can be identified on the proof, (assuming the proofing system is calibrated to emulate dot gain), always talk to the Printer before specifying any dot gain compensation. Select either **Standard** or **Curves** to indicate how you want to specify dot gain compensation. When you select **Standard**, you simply have to input a percentage in the field to the right of the pull-down menu. When you select **Curves,** a dialog box appears enabling you to specify dot gain on a contrast curve (see Figure 3.42).

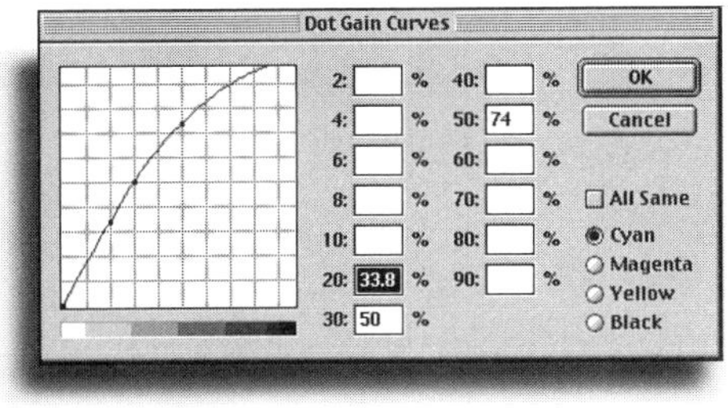

FIGURE 3.42
The Dot Gain Curves dialog
box.

5. The **Separation Options** indicate the method used to generate the black printing plate as well as some important
information about total ink density and black ink limit.

- **UCR** (Undercolor Removal) and **GCR** (Gray
  Component Replacement) are settings used to determine how the black plate will be generated when converting from RGB to CMYK mode. When **GCR** is
  selected, the black plate will contain a wide range of
  grays and is usually used for images that contain dark
  saturated areas. Internally, the image data is evaluated
  to locate the areas of the image where combinations of
  all the colors contain a gray component that can be
  represented with black ink instead of a CMY combination. Undercolor Removal (UCR), however, leaves the
  gray components of the colors in tact, generating a
  "skeleton" black plate that is concentrated in the shadows and detail areas of the image. Paper and press conditions are ultimately the deciding factors in choosing
  which method to use for black generation. Printers are
  quite familiar with these terms and can help you decide
  which method to use.

- There are six choices available for **Black Generation**:
  Light, Medium, Heavy, Maximum, Custom, and
  None. **Medium** is the default setting in Photoshop and
  is the correct choice for most separation types. The
  Light setting creates a black plate that is only slightly
  lighter than the medium setting. Use the Light setting
  if you think the overall darkness of the image is too
  high. The **Heavy** setting creates a black plate that is
  darker than that created with the Medium setting, but
  again, only to a small degree. Use heavy if the image

seems flat or too even in the darker areas. **Maximum** puts all the gray areas on the black plate and is most useful for high-contrast images that contain light backgrounds. Screen captures from a computer monitor or images that contain black text as part of the image are some examples. **Custom** is used to create a setting not represented in the Black Generation list. Selecting custom displays a curve dialog box that contains a curve representative of the last setting for black generation before you selected **Custom**. A setting of **None** generates an empty black plate; all the image detail will be represented by CMY only.

- The default setting for **Black Ink Limit** is 100%, though this value is typically set slightly lower. This setting affects the generation of the black plate in concert with the black generation method you chose previously. The black ink limit is also part of the **Total Ink Limit**.

- The **Total Ink Limit** is the maximum ink density supported by the printing press that the color separation is going to print on. The default for Total Ink Limit is 300%, a value that works well for most high-quality print jobs. Note that when you change the **Black Ink Limit** or **Total Ink Limit** the change is reflected in the composite curve diagram in this dialog box. Check with your printer before deciding on **Total Ink Limit** and **Black Ink Limit**.

- The **UCA** (undercolor addition) **Amount** option is a choice only when you choose **GCR** as the separation type. **UCA** adds back some of the CMY color in the shadow areas, where **GCR** removed the gray component to the black plate. **UCA** is a value between 1% and 100%; the default is 0% (no UCA). For the majority of printing conditions, leave this value at 0%. Your printer can tell you what value to plug in here.

- Saving your settings can save you many future phone calls to your printer. If you use the same printer frequently for the same types of projects, ask the printer if you can use these same settings for future projects as well. Saving your settings is a good habit to get into and is especially important if you have created your

own dot gain compensation and black generation by
adjusting the curve. Click on the **Save** button in the
CMYK Setup dialog box and give your file a name that
will make sense in the future. Load saved settings by
clicking on the **Load** button in the CMYK Setup dialog
box.

Specifying Grayscale Setup

The **Grayscale Setup** color setting enables you to preview a
grayscale image on the screen as it will appear when printed on
white paper. Typically, the RGB values used to generate the
grayscale image are increased to create a lighter appearing
image. The actual black ink percentage that will be used to print
the image remains unchanged, regardless of which of the two
choices you select. Choose **Color Settings** from the **File** menu
and then select **Grayscale Setup** to display the Grayscale Setup
dialog box (see Figure 3.43). When you select **RGB** as the
grayscale behavior, the gray values of the image are treated as
opaque values resulting in a darker image on screen than actually
print. When you select **Black Ink**, the RGB values in the image
are adjusted to more closely approximate the transparency of
black printing inks with dot gain compensation taken into
account. In short, the RGB values of the image are adjusted for
display purposes only, whereas the black ink percentages remain
constant.

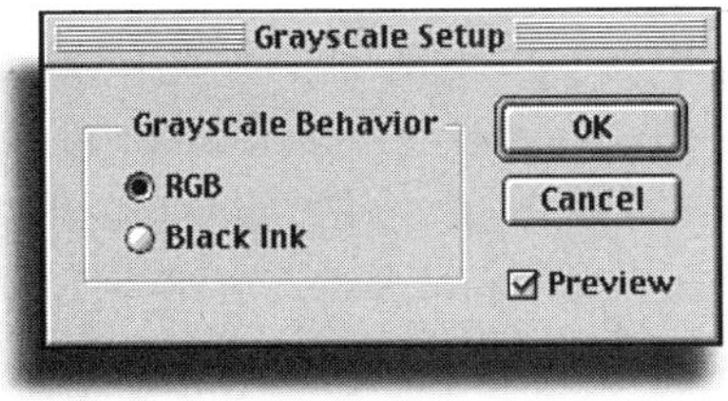

FIGURE 3.43

Select the way you want
grayscale images to behave in
Photoshop by clicking the corresponding radio buttons.

Specifying Profile Setup

The **Profile Setup** color setting enables you to specify the ICC
Profiles you want saved with your image and to handle opening
files that have ICC Profiles attached to them. If you're not
familiar with ICC color profiles, you might want to turn off
these options until you have a chance to learn more about how
they affect your images. Choose **Color Settings** from the **File**

menu and then select **Profile Setup** to display the Profile Setup dialog box (see Figure 3.44).

FIGURE 3.44
The Profile Setup dialog box.

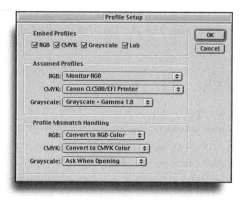

- **Embed Profiles:** Check the radio button next to the color modes to save ICC Profile information with your file. Saving profile information with your file enables Photoshop to set up the correct environment for the image when it is opened again in the future. This color profile information comes from the **RGB Setup**, **CMYK Setup**, and **Grayscale Setup**. Keep in mind that the color profile information is saved in its entirety with the file and will add to the size of the file, though the addition to the size of the file is negligible in most cases.

- **Assumed Profiles—RGB:** Use these settings to make assumptions about the embedded profiles in images you plan to open but not to indicate color profiles to be saved with your images when the profiles are embedded. Click on the pull-down menu next to **RGB** to select the profile you want to use to display your image on screen. If you select **None** here, the **RGB Setup** specifications will be used. Select **Ask When Opening** if you want to be prompted about these settings when you open a file that contains an embedded profile. If you used the **Adobe Gamma** control panel to create a custom profile for your monitor, it will be listed in the pull-down menu along with all other installed monitor profiles.

- **Assumed Profiles—CMYK:** The CMYK profiles listed in the pull-down menu are typically profiles for color printers and color separation setups. These profiles enable Photoshop to create a close approximation (on the monitor) of the color values that will be printed. If you select **Ask When Opening**, you will be prompted via a dialog box to select the appropriate profile for you image when opening it (see Figure 3.45).

- **Assumed Profiles—Grayscale:** The Grayscale profiles listed in the pull-down menu reflect the monitor gamma to be used for grayscale images. If you went through the trouble of calibrating your monitor gamma using the Adobe Gamma control panel or a third-party application, select **None** here to use those settings. Select **Ask When Opening** to choose a gamma setting when opening grayscale images (see Figure 3.45).

- **Profile Mismatch Handing:** Determine how you want Photoshop to handle opening images that contain different color profiles from the ones you select in the **Assumed Profiles** section. You can choose whether to automatically convert to a specific profile, in which case you will not be prompted or informed of a conversion taking place. If you choose **Ignore**, the color profile information embedded in the file will be used automatically and the current profile settings ignored. Your best bet here is to choose **Ask When Opening** so you will know when there is a mismatch and have the opportunity to make a decision about how to handle it (see Figure 3.45).

SEE ALSO

➤ *For more information on interpolation, see page 182*

➤ *For more information on selecting colors, see page 216*

FIGURE 3.45

When a profile mismatch occurs, the Profile Mismatch dialog box appears, enabling you to make choices about how to open the image.

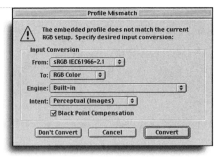

Understanding Layers

The Layers Palette

In order to use Photoshop effectively and productively, you must become familiar with layers. The paradigm of layers is one that relates closely to the traditional method of overlaying transparent sheets of acetate on a layout to combine elements and affect the way each layer interacts with the underlying layers. When working with layers, you must use the **Move** tool located in the upper-right corner of the Toolbox. In Photoshop, we have a Layers palette that enables us to build images on layers and modify those layers independently of others. Many of the corresponding layer commands are found under the **Layer** menu in the menu bar at the top of your screen, as well as in the Layers palette menu. The thumbnail previews in the Layers palette provide a visual key to what is contained on the layer, as well as the layer effects that are present on that layer at the time. Choose **Show Layers** from the **Window** menu to display the Layers palette. When you have an image that contains layers open, the layers appear in the Layers palette (see Figure 4.1).

FIGURE 4.1

The Layers palette.

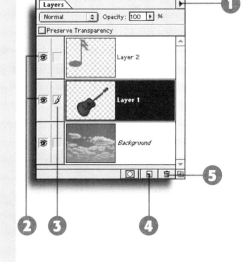

1 Options for layers are available under the palette menu.

2 The Eye icons enable you to make layers visible and invisible.

3 The Paintbrush icon indicates the active layer. Other icons appear here when you add layer masks or link layers together.

4 Click the Page icon to create a new layer. Drag a layer on the Page icon to duplicate that layer.

5 Click the Trash Can icon to delete the current active layer or drag layers onto the Trash Can icon to delete them.

Transparent Backgrounds

When you create a new document, you have the option to create the new file with a transparent background. All layers, with the exception of the Background layer, also contain a transparent background. The transparency is indicated in Photoshop as a gray checkerboard by default, though you can change this to suit your tastes (see Figure 4.2). To change the way transparency is represented on the screen, choose **Preferences** from the **File** menu and then select **Transparency & Gamut** to display the Transparency & Gamut dialog box.

SEE ALSO

➤ *For more information on setting transparency options, see page 188*

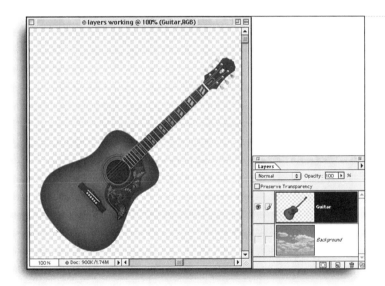

FIGURE 4.2

Transparency is represented on the screen and in the Layers palette.

Moving, Linking, and Transforming Layers

When you have multiple layers in your document, you can rearrange the layers simply by clicking and dragging the layer in the Layers palette. If a Background layer is present, it resides as the very bottom-most layer in the Layers palette. The Background layer is always at the bottom of the layer list and

Viewing one layer at a time

To view one layer while making all the other layers invisible, (Alt+click) [Option+click] the Eye icon to the left of the layer's thumbnail preview. (Alt+click) [Option+click] on the Eye icon again to make all layers visible. The checkerboard pattern that represents transparency appears only with your image when the Background layer is made invisible.

transparent layers cannot be moved below it, nor can the Background layer be moved up in the list by clicking and dragging. You can also rearrange the layers by selecting the options for bringing the layers forward or sending them backward. Choose **Arrange** from the **Layers** menu to select the option for moving the layer.

Rearranging the layers

1. Type (Ctrl+]) [Command+]] to bring a layer forward, moving it up in the Layers palette.

2. Type (Ctrl+[) [Command+[] to send a layer backward, moving it down in the Layers palette.

3. Type (Ctrl+Shift+]) [Command+Shift+]] to bring a layer to the front, moving it to the top of the Layers palette.

4. Type (Ctrl+Shift+]) [Command+Shift+]] to send a layer to the back, moving it to the bottom of the Layers palette. If a Background layer is present, this action moves the layer to the one above the Background layer.

Linking Layers

Setting the Background layer free

Double-click the Background layer to make it a transparent layer like all the other layers. A dialog box appears in which you can enter a name for the layer. After you make the Background layer a transparent layer, you can move it between other layers. The Background layer automatically becomes a transparent layer if you click and drag on it with the **Move** tool. This can also happen accidentally sometimes when you have the **Move** tool selected and type one of the arrow keys.

Link layers together when you want to affect multiple layers at the same time or modify the contents of linked layers at one time. When layers are linked together, you can perform transformations, color adjustments, and filter effects to all the linked layers at once and move the contents of these layers together as a group. To link layers together, start by selecting one of the layers you want to link in the Layers palette. Click in the embossed box to the left of another layer's thumbnail preview to link that layer to the active layer (see Figure 4.3). Do this for any additional layers you want to include in the linked group. Click and drag inside the image window with the **Move** tool and notice that all linked layers move simultaneously. To unlink the layers, click on the Link icon to the left of the thumbnail preview again. Linked layers can be merged together to form a single layer by selecting **Merge Linked** from the **Layers** menu or by typing (Ctrl+E) [Command+E]. This option is also available in the Layers palette menu.

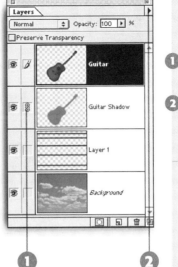

FIGURE 4.3

Linked layers can be manipulated together.

1 Click here to link this layer to the active layer above it.

2 Choose **Merge Linked** from the Layers palette menu to merge the linked layers into one layer.

Aligning and Distributing Linked Layers

The contents of layers that are linked together can be aligned vertically and horizontally, as well as distributed equally so that the space between the objects is equidistant. Link two or more layers together and choose **Align Linked** from the **Layer** menu to select from the available alignment options (see Figure 4.4). The contents of the linked layers will be aligned with the contents of the active layer, so be sure you have the layer selected that you want to use as the anchor for the alignment. Choose **Align Vertical Center** followed by **Align Horizontal Center** to center the objects.

Choose **Distribute Linked** from the **Layer** menu to select the way you want the space between the objects on your linked layers to be distributed (see Figure 4.5). You must have more than two layers linked together for this option to be available. The space will be distributed evenly between the objects on the layers, but not within the image area itself.

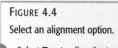

FIGURE 4.4

Select an alignment option.

1 Select **Top** to align the top edges of the objects on the linked layers.

2 Select **Vertical Center** to align the vertical centers of the objects on the linked layers.

3 Select **Bottom** to align the bottom edges of the objects on the linked layers.

4 Select **Left** to align the left edges of the objects on the linked layers.

5 Select **Horizontal Center** to align the horizontal centers of the objects on the linked layers.

6 Select **Right** to align the right edges of the objects on the linked layers.

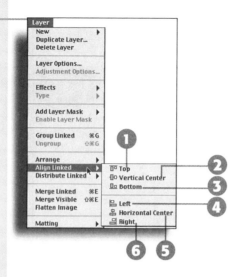

Transforming Objects on Layers

Using Photoshop's transformation commands, you can transform selected objects, the contents of individual layers, the contents of linked layers, and entire images when layers are not present. Because this chapter deals with layers, we will concentrate on performing transformations on the contents of layers. Choose **Transform** from the **Edit** menu to select from the available transformation options.

- Choose **Scale** to enlarge or reduce the size of the layer contents. When you select this option, the image area of the layer is enclosed in a rectangle with points at each corner and in the center of each side (see Figure 4.6). Click and drag these points to resize the image. It is important that you hold down the **Shift** key when scaling and drag the corner points if you want to maintain the aspect ration of the image. Keep in mind that resizing your layer contents might adversely affect the quality of the image, especially when enlarging. **Double-click** inside the rectangle, press the Return key or the Enter key to accept your modifications or press the Esc key to leave the image unchanged. Selecting another tool in the Toolbox also ends the transformation without making changes.

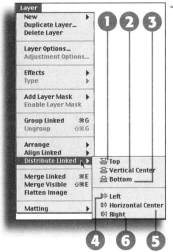

FIGURE 4.5

Select an option to distribute the space between the items on the linked layers.

1 Select **Top** to distribute the space vertically based on the tops of the objects on linked layers.

2 Select **Vertical Center** to distribute the space vertically based on the vertical centers of the objects on linked layers.

3 Select **Bottom** to distribute the space vertically based on the bottoms of the objects on linked layers.

4 Select **Left** to distribute the space horizontally based on the left edges of the objects on linked layers.

5 Select **Horizontal Center** to distribute the space horizontally based on the horizontal centers of the objects on linked layers.

6 Select **Right** to distribute the space horizontally between the right edges of the objects on linked layers.

- Choose **Rotate** to rotate the layer contents around the center axis (see Figure 4.7). Hold down the Shift key to constrain the rotation to 45-degree increments. You can relocate the center axis point by dragging the crosshair from the center of the selection. When you drag it back, close to the true center, the crosshair snaps to the center again. Think of this crosshair as an anchor; wherever you place it, the image rotates around that anchor point.

- Choose **Skew** to skew the contents of the layer, an effect often used to create the illusion of depth. Click and drag the corners to adjust the two sides connected to that corner. Click on the points between the corner points to adjust three sides of the image at once (see Figure 4.8).

FIGURE 4.6

Click and drag the points of
the transformation rectangle to
modify the image.

Moving while transforming

When using the transformation
tools, you can move the layer contents surrounded by the transformation rectangle by simply clicking and
dragging in the center of the rectangle. Use the up, down, left, and
right arrows on your keyboard to
move the contents in one-pixel
increments. Hold down the Shift key
and use the arrow keys to move the
object in ten-pixel increments.

FIGURE 4.7

The Rotate transformation.

FIGURE 4.8
The Skew transformation.

- Choose **Distort** to adjust the individual sides of the rectangle, unlike the Skew option which always changes at least two sides (see Figure 4.9).

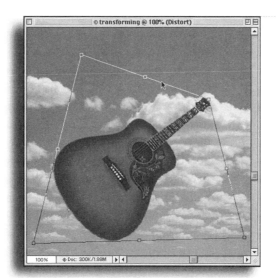

FIGURE 4.9
The Distort transformation.

■ Choose **Perspective** to create the illusion of different perspectives for the contents of the layer. Click and drag the corner points to draw the sides toward the center point. Click and drag the center points to adjust three sides of the image at once (see Figure 4.10).

■ Choose **Numeric** to transform the image numerically by entering values in the **Numeric Transform** dialog box (see Figure 4.11). Type x and y coordinates when the **Position** check box is selected to move the contents of the layer. You can use negative values here to move left and up and positive values to move right and down. When the **Relative** check box is checked, the contents will be moved in relation to where it is in the image window. When Relative is not checked, you can specify the exact x and y coordinates based on the zero point of the ruler, the upper-left corner of the image by default. Choose the options for **Scale**, **Skew**, and **Rotate** and then click **OK** to perform the transformation.

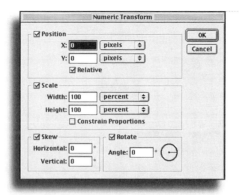

FIGURE 4.11
The Numeric Transform
dialog box.

- To perform the last transformation again, type
  (Ctrl+Shift+T) [Command+Shift+T].

Specifying Blending Mode and Opacity

At the top of the Layers palette, you can specify an opacity setting for layers as well as a Blending mode that determines how a
layer interacts with underlying layers. Type an opacity value into
the **Opacity** box at the top of the Layers palette or click on the
small triangle and drag to select an opacity for the layer (see
Figure 4.12). Opacity values range from 1% to 100%. Select a
Blending mode from the pull-down menu at the top of the
Layers palette (see Figure 4.13).

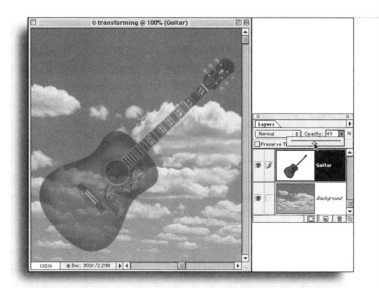

FIGURE 4.12
Type a value for opacity or
click and drag the opacity
slider at the top of the Layers
palette.

FIGURE 4.13

Select a Blending mode from
the pull-down menu.

Changing the opacity from the keyboard

You can quickly set the opacity for the active layer by typing single digit numbers from 0 to 9. For example: typing **0** (zero) sets the opacity to 100 percent; typing **5** sets the opacity to 50 percent. To set the opacity to a value other than increments of 10 percent, type a two-digit number quickly using the numeric keypad. For example, type **43** to set the opacity to 43 percent.

Blending Modes

The Blending modes are available in many palettes in Photoshop, including all the Painting tool palettes. The Blending modes affect the way the color you paint with interacts with the underlying image. In the case of layers, the Blending modes affect the way the colors on one layer interact with the colors of underlying layers. The Blending modes are available whenever you add color to the Photoshop image, regardless of the technique used.

- The **Normal** Blending mode is the default mode in Photoshop. Normal mode replaces the values of the painted pixels with foreground color. The Normal mode is called **Threshold** when you work in Bitmap mode.

- The **Dissolve** Blending mode replaces the values of the pixels randomly, based on the **Opacity** setting in the Layers palette. Set the opacity to something less than 100% to view the effect of this mode.

- The **Behind** Blending mode works only when painting on transparent layers using one of the Painting tools. The transparent pixels are exclusively affected with this blending option. This means that when you paint, only the transparent part of the layer is affected, leaving the original image intact. The Paintbrush Options palette has its own pull-down menu for blending options that affect painting.

- The **Clear** Blending mode is available only when you use the **Line** tool, **Paint Bucket** tool, **Fill** command, or **Stroke** command and only when you work on a transparent layer. Each of these has its own pull-down menu to select a Blending mode. This option replaces the values of the pixels with the transparent value. In other words, the image part of the layer is removed leaving the affected part of the image transparent.

- The **Multiply** Blending mode multiplies the color values of the image on the active layer with the color values of the underlying values to create a darker complementary color. The Multiply Blending mode is quite effective for creating shadow effects. If the underlying color is black or white, the Multiply Blending mode yields no effect.

- The **Screen** Blending mode produces a bleaching effect making the composite area lighter depending on the colors of the active layer and the underlying layer. Lighter colors on the active layer have a stronger effect than dark colors; therefore, darker colors create a subtler effect.

- The **Overlay** Blending mode combines the color value of the active layer with the colors of the underlying layers while preserving the highlight and shadow values of the image. This mode is effective when colorizing a color image with the painting tools or compositing images on layers.

- The **Soft Light** Blending mode darkens or lightens the image based on the color being used. A lighter color with a gray value less than 50% lightens the image creating a dodged effect. A darker color with a gray value greater than 50% darkens the image creating a burn effect.

- The **Hard Light** Blending mode combines the effects of the Screen mode and the Multiply mode. When you paint with a color that has a gray value less than 50%, the effect is like that of the Screen mode described earlier. When you paint with a color that has a gray value greater than 50%, the effect is like that of the Multiply mode described earlier.

- The **Color Dodge** Blending mode lightens the color of the image pixels to reflect the lightness value of the selected color. Dark colors produce a subtler change than light, bright colors. Painting with black yields no effect, whereas painting with white results in an overexposed blown-out effect.

- The **Color Burn** Blending mode darkens the color of the image pixels based on the selected painting color or color on the active layer. Light, bright colors produce a more subtle effect than dark colors. Painting with white yields no effect.

- The **Darken** Blending mode changes the color of the pixels that contain values that are lighter than those of the active layer. If the underlying pixels are darker than the active layer pixels, they are left unchanged.

- The **Lighten** Blending mode changes the color of the pixels that contain values that are darker than those of the active layer. If the underlying pixels are lighter than the active layer pixels, they are left unchanged.

- The **Difference** Blending mode evaluates the brightness values of the colors in each channel and compares these values with the comparable values in the image color. The color with the lightest brightness value is subtracted from the color with the darkest brightness value resulting in the value for the image pixel. Dark colors produce a subtler effect than light, bright colors. Painting with white results in an inverse image, much like a color negative.

- The **Exclusion** Blending mode produces an effect similar to the Difference mode, but with a softer effect.

- The **Hue** Blending mode replaces only the hue value of the image pixels, leaving the saturation and luminance values intact.

- The **Saturation** Blending mode replaces the saturation value of the underlying pixels with the saturation value of the pixels on the active layer.

- The **Color** Blending mode replaces both the hue and saturation values of the image pixels with the hue and saturation values of the pixels on the active layer. Use this mode to paint in local color changes without affecting the grayscale portion of the image.

- The **Luminosity** Blending mode maintains the hue and saturation of the image pixels, but it changes the luminance value to that of the foreground color or layer colors when compositing layers.

Using Preserve Transparency

Turn on **Preserve Transparency** to protect the transparent pixels on the active layer from change. Changes you make to the image on the layer affect only the nontransparent pixels. This, in effect, masks the transparent parts of the image protecting them from change. If you have the **Preserve Transparency** check box checked and try to modify the image in a way that causes it to grow (such as using any of the Blur filters), the change cannot take place with **Preserve Transparency** activated. The **Preserve Transparency** option also appears in the Fill dialog box when you select **Fill** or **Stroke** from the **Edit** menu.

Working with Layer Masks

Adding a layer mask to a layer is like adding a dynamic Alpha channel to your image. The layer mask is a grayscale mask that affects the opacity of the image on the layer. To add a layer mask, click the Add Layer Mask icon at the bottom of the Layers palette or choose **Add Layer Mask** from the **Layer** menu. If you choose **Add Layer Mask** from the **Layer** menu, you can select **Reveal All** (100% Opacity) or **Hide All** (0% Opacity) for the initial mask. The layer mask thumbnail is added to the right of the layer thumbnail and is made active.

Editing the Layer Mask

When the layer mask is active, the Layer Mask icon appears to the right of the Eye icon instead of the Paintbrush icon in the Layers palette, and the layer mask thumbnail is outlined in black.

Selecting Blending modes from the context menu

The Blending mode options are available under the context menu of the painting tools, such as **Airbrush** and **Paintbrush**. Hold down the Control key and click anywhere in the Canvas area to display the context menu on the MacOS; click in the Canvas area with the right mouse button in Windows.

Create an inverted layer mask

To create an inverted new layer mask (Hide All), (Alt+click) [Option+click] the Add Layer Mask icon at the bottom of the Layers palette.

Select one of the Painting tools from the Toolbox, such as the Paintbrush. Paint over the image with 100 percent black to delete parts of the image (change the **Opacity** to 0 percent). Paint over the image with white to restore the image (100 percent **Opacity**). Paint with a percentage of black to change the image opacity. For example, paint with 50 percent black to change the image **Opacity** to 50 percent in the painted areas; paint with 80 percent black to change the image **Opacity** to 20 percent in the painted areas (see Figure 4.14).

FIGURE 4.14

Changes made to the Layer mask affect the image immediately. Paint with white as the foreground color to restore the image.

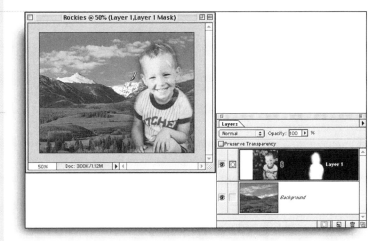

Working with the layer mask

1. To view the layer mask, (Alt+click) [Option+click] the layer mask thumbnail in the Layers palette to toggle the layer mask view on and off (see Figure 4.15).

FIGURE 4.15

The layer mask view.

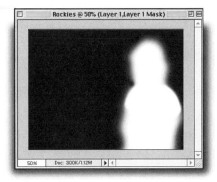

2. To hide the effects of the layer mask, Shift+click the layer mask thumbnail in the Layers palette to toggle the layer mask on and off. A large red X will appear over the layer mask thumbnail. You can also choose **Disable Layer Mask** from the **Layer** menu.

3. (Ctrl+click) [Command+click] the layer thumbnail to load the layer's transparency mask or (Ctrl+click) [Command+click] the layer mask thumbnail to load the layer mask's transparency mask. When you load the transparency mask, a selection is created in the shape of the nontransparent pixels.

4. The layer and the layer mask are automatically linked together when you create a layer mask. This means that if you use the **Move** tool to move the layer contents, the layer mask moves with it and vice versa. To unlink the layer and layer mask, click on the Link icon between the layer thumbnail and the layer mask thumbnail. The layer mask can now be moved independently of the layer contents.

5. To **Apply** or **Discard** the layer mask, click the layer mask thumbnail to activate the layer mask. Click the Trash Can icon in the lower-right corner of the Layers palette or drag the layer onto the Trash Can icon. When a dialog box appears, choose whether to apply or discard the layer mask. Applying the mask makes the changes to the layer permanent. You also can choose **Remove Layer Mask** from the **Layer** menu.

Merging Layers

You will from time to time want to merge layers together to create a single layer. Choose **Merge Visible** from the **Layer** menu or the Layers palette menu to merge all visible layers into one layer. Choose **Merge Down** from the **Layer** menu or the Layers palette menu, or type (Ctrl+E) [Command+E] to merge the current layer with the layer under it. When layers are linked together, **Merge Down** becomes **Merge Linked** in the **Layer** menu and Layers palette menu.

Tips for merging layers

Hold down (Alt) [Option] when choosing **Merge Down** to merge a copy of the layer with the layer under it. Hold down (Alt) [Option] when choosing **Merge Visible** to merge all visible layers onto the active layer. Hold down (Alt) [Option] when choosing **Merge Linked** to merge the linked layers onto the active layer.

Flattening the Image

Flattening the image is the final step before saving a file in a format such as TIFF or EPS that can be read by page layout applications such as QuarkXPress and Pagemaker. When you flatten the image, all the layers are flattened into one Background layer. You might want to save your image with all the layers intact in case you have to make edits in the future. Save the image in Photoshop format to preserve the layers. You can also choose **Save a Copy** from the **File** menu and choose a format to save your file. If you choose a format that does not support layers, a copy of the image will be flattened when saved, leaving the working file untouched. Choose **Flatten Image** from the **File** menu or from the Layers palette menu to flatten the image leaving only a Background layer.

Using Adjustment Layers

Adjustment layers are used to make nondestructive color changes to your image. This means that you can perform color adjustments on their own layers and affect underlying layers without actually changing the pixel values of the underlying layers. Using Adjustment layers enables you to apply many of the choices commonly found when choosing **Adjust** from the **Image** menu to a transparent layer so that the image adjustments affect the layers below the adjustment layer.

Creating Adjustment layers

1. Choose **New Adjustment Layer** from the Layers palette menu, the **Layer** menu in the menu bar, or (Ctrl+click) (Command+click) on the **New Layer** button at the bottom of the Layers palette.

2. When the New Adjustment Layer dialog box appears, select the type of color adjustment you want to make (see Figure 4.16).

3. To choose an adjustment type, click the **Type** pull-down menu in the New Adjustment Layer dialog box and choose the type of color adjustment you want to make (see Figure 4.17). Click **OK** to display the dialog box that corresponds

to the choice you made for type. Make adjustments and click **OK**.

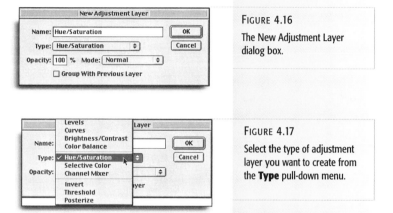

FIGURE 4.16

The New Adjustment Layer dialog box.

FIGURE 4.17

Select the type of adjustment layer you want to create from the **Type** pull-down menu.

4. The Adjustment Layer is inserted in the Layers palette above the active layer and only affects the layers beneath it (see Figure 4.18).

FIGURE 4.18

The Adjustment layer affects only the layers beneath it.

5. You can stack Adjustment layers on top of each other in the Layers palette to combine the effects of the adjustments. Create additional Adjustment layers to combine the effects they produce.

6. Choose an **Opacity** setting by dragging the opacity triangle slider in the Layers palette or by typing an opacity percentage on the numeric keypad to reduce or increase the overall effect of the adjustment.

7. The Adjustment layer is actually a mask that you can paint to isolate the adjustment to parts of the underlying layer images and is indicated by the Layer Mask icon to the left of the layer thumbnail (see Figure 4.19). Paint with 100 percent black to mask areas. Paint with white to open the mask and apply the Adjustment layer to the underlying layers. Use percentages of black to decrease the overall effect of the Adjustment layer in specific areas.

FIGURE 4.19

The Adjustment layer is a mask layer that you can paint to control the application of the adjustment.

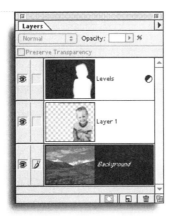

8. Treat the Adjustment layer like any other layer in your image. You can apply the Blending mode choices to this layer, move the adjustment layer up or down in the Layers palette, and merge the Adjustment layer with underlying layers.

9. To view the Adjustment layer's mask, (Alt+click) [Option+click] the layer thumbnail.

10. To force Photoshop to ignore the layer's built-in mask and apply the Adjustment layer's effects to the whole image, Shift-click the layer thumbnail. A red X appears over the Adjustment layer's thumbnail preview. The adjustment is still applied, but the mask is ignored.

11. To turn off the Adjustment layer's effect, click the Eye icon next to the layer thumbnail.

Make a selection before creating an Adjustment layer

If you make a selection using the selection tools before you create an Adjustment layer, the selection creates the mask for the Adjustment layer. Remember, you can (Ctrl+click) [Command+click] on a layer or layer mask thumbnail to make a selection based on the transparent pixels.

Using Group with Previous Layer

The **Group with Previous Layer** option in the Layers palette enables you to use a layer such as a cookie cutter, capturing other layer information in the shape of a single layer. On the

MacOS, double-click on a layer to display the Layer Options palette and click the **Group with Previous Layer** check box to group that layer with the layer directly beneath it in the Layers palette. Windows users must choose **Group with Previous** from the **Layer** menu to group the selected layer with the one directly beneath it. The "previous layer," the layer directly beneath the active layer, is the cookie cutter. You can group additional layers the same way. All the layers that have **Group with Previous Layer** turned on will be contained in the shape of the image on the layer directly below the bottom-most layer (see Figure 4.20).

A shortcut to Group with Previous Layer

Hold down (Alt) [Option] and point at the dividing line between two layers with your mouse pointer. When the cursor changes to two interlocked circles, click to group the layer above the divider line with the layer beneath it. Perform this step again with other layers or on the same layers to ungroup them.

FIGURE 4.20

The underlined layer is the cookie cutter for the layers separated by the dotted lines that have **Group with Previous Layer** turned on.

Creating Text Layers

When you create text in Photoshop, a Text layer is added to the Layers palette, inserted above the active layer. The Text layer enables you to edit the text on the layer as many times as necessary before rendering the text as a bitmap, which you will ultimately have to do. There are four tools in the Toolbox used to create type: the **Horizontal Type** tool, **Vertical Type** tool, **Horizontal Type Mask** tool and the **Vertical Type Mask** tool. Use the **Type Mask** tool when you want to create a selection in the shape of the text but not a new text layer.

Click somewhere in the image window with the **Type** tool to display the Type Tool dialog box (see Figure 4.21). Check the **Preview** check box to view the text on the image as you spec it in the Type Tool dialog box. Notice that the **Move** tool is automatically selected when the Type Tool dialog box appears. This enables you to move the text on the image while the dialog box displays.

FIGURE 4.21
The Type Tool dialog box.

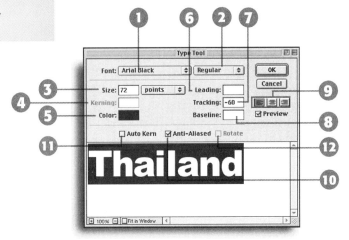

1 Select a type face from the pull-down menu.

2 Select a type style from the pull-down menu.

3 Indicate the size of the type in either points or pixels.

4 Position the cursor between a pair of characters and type a value here. A negative value brings them closer together, whereas a positive value separates them.

5 Click on the color swatch to display the Color Picker and choose a color for your text.

6 If you are entering multiple lines of text indicate a **Leading** value for the space between the lines (baseline to baseline).

7 When you have a range of text selected, type a **Tracking** value to reduce or increase the space between all characters.

8 Select individual characters, words, or groups of words and enter a value for **Baseline** shift here. A positive value shifts the text up whereas a negative value shifts the text down.

9 Indicate the alignment of the text here if you have multiple lines of text. This does affect the way the text aligns within the image area.

10 Check the **Anti-Aliased** check box if you are compositing this text with other imagery to create a smooth transition without harsh edges.

11 Check the **Auto Kern** check box to kern characters based on logical rules built into the typeface. You must deselect this box to input your own *kerning* and *tracking* values.

12 The **Rotate** option is only available when you create text with the Vertical Type tool, enabling you to rotate the text from a column to text on its side.

When you click **OK** in the Type Tool dialog box, a new layer is inserted in the Layers palette (see Figure 4.22). The letter T appears to the right of layer thumbnail to indicate a text layer. Double-click on the Text layer in the Layers palette to redisplay the Type Tool dialog box and make changes to your text.

FIGURE 4.22
New Type layer.

- Choose **Type** from the **Layer** menu and then select **Render** to convert the outline text into a pixel bitmap. When you do this, you cannot edit the text on this layer using the Type Tool dialog box. The text will now be treated as an image and can be manipulated as such. When you flatten the image, the Type layers will automatically be rendered as bitmaps before being combined with other layers onto the Background layer.

- Choose **Type** from the **Layer** menu and then select **Horizontal** or **Vertical** to change the way the text appears on the image. This does not affect your ability to edit the text using the Type Tool dialog box.

Adding Layer Effects

Creating effects such as drop shadows, glows, bevels, and embossing couldn't be easier using the layer effects available in Photoshop. Layer effects can be applied to any layer, including Text layers and can even be separated out to their own layers for further manipulation. Choose **Effects** from the **Layer** menu and then select an effect from the group at the top of the submenu to display the **Effects** dialog box (see Figure 4.23).

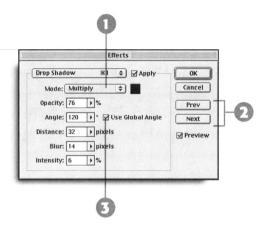

FIGURE 4.23

FIGURE 4.23

The Effects dialog box depicting the Drop Shadow settings.

1 Select an effect from the pull-down menu and then check the **Apply** check box to apply that effect to the layer.

2 Cycle through the five available effects by clicking the **Prev** and **Next** buttons.

3 The **Use Global Angle** check box refers to a global angle you can set in the **Effects** submenu under the **Layer** menu.

After you click **OK** in the Effects dialog box, the effect is applied to the active layer and is indicated by an icon (the letter **f** in a circle). Double-click on this icon to display the **Effects** dialog box and edit the effects applied to that layer.

Exploring layer effects

1. Choose **Effects** from the **Layer** menu and then select **Copy Effects** to use the same effect on another layer. Go to another layer and choose **Paste Effects** to apply the copied effects to that layer.

2. Choose **Effects** from the **Layer** menu and then select **Paste Effects To Linked** to paste copied effects to the active layer and all layers linked to it.

3. Choose **Effects** from the **Layer** menu and then select **Global Angle** to display the Global Angle dialog box. Indicate an angle to be used whenever the **Use Global Angle** check box is checked in an Effects dialog box.

4. Choose **Effects** from the **Layer** menu and then select **Create Layer** to create a new layer that contains the effects of the active layer. This results in the effect being removed from the active layer and placed on its own layer where it can be modified.

5. Choose **Effects** from the **Layer** menu and then select **Hide All Effects** to make all the effects invisible. Choose **Show**

All **Effects** from the same place to turn the effects back on. Effects that have been placed on their own layers are not affected by this command.

Using Layer Via Cut and Layer Via Copy

The **Layer Via Cut** and **Layer Via Copy** commands enable you to cut or copy a selected part of a layer and paste it onto a new layer in exactly the same place.

Cutting and copying to layers

1. Make a selection of part of an image on a layer using one of the selection tools such as the **Marquee** tool or **Lasso** tool.

2. Choose **New** from the **Layer** menu and then select **Layer Via Cut** (Ctrl+Shift+J) [Command+Shift+J] or **Layer Via Copy** (Ctrl+J) [Command+J].

3. If you selected **Layer Via Cut**, the selected area was cut from the active layer and pasted onto a new layer in exactly the same place.

4. If you selected **Layer Via Copy**, the selected area was copied from the active layer and pasted onto a new layer in exactly the same place. The copied area resides on the new layer as well as the original layer.

➤ *For more information on setting transparency options, see page 188*

Using context menu to display the Effects dialog box

On the MacOS, hold down Control and click on a layer in the Layers palette to display the context menu; then select **Effects**. If you use Windows, click on a layer in the Layers palette with the right mouse button and then select **Effects**.

Printing Your Results

For the majority of us, printing from Photoshop usually involves printing to a desktop laser printer or color printer. Photoshop can print to any output device as long as its *printer driver* resides on your computer system. Like most desktop publishing software, printing in Photoshop is set up through the Page Setup and Print dialog boxes. Before printing your document, be sure to check the size and resolution of your image using the **Image Size** dialog box.

SEE ALSO

➤ *For more information on image resolution, see page 70*

Specifying Page Setup

The Page Setup dialog box is where you specify the paper size, orientation, and scaling percentage for the printed file. Choose **Page Setup** from the **File** menu to display the Page Setup dialog box (see Figure 5.1). The printer driver you have installed on your computer determines the paper size choices, as well as the options available when you click the **Options** button.

FIGURE 5.1

The Page Setup dialog box.

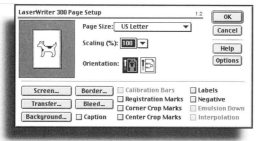

Specifying Halftone Screens

Click the **Screens** button in the Page Setup dialog box to specify the Halftone Screen information for your image (see Figure 5.2). You should always check with your service bureau or printer before specifying your halftone screen information.

Setting Halftone Screens

1. If you are printing to a PostScript Level 1 printer, check the Use Printer's Default Screens check box.

2. If you are printing to a PostScript Level 2 printer, check the Use Accurate Screens check box.

3. Click the **Auto** button to display the Auto Screens dialog box where you can specify a printer resolution and halftone screen frequency to set the screen angles automatically in the Halftone Screens dialog box (see Figure 5.3).

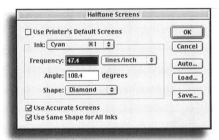

FIGURE 5.2
The Halftone Screens dialog box.

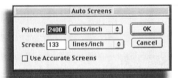

FIGURE 5.3
The Auto Screens dialog box.

Adjusting Transfer Functions

Click the **Transfer** button in the **Page Setup** dialog box to display the Transfer Functions dialog box (see Figure 5.4). You can use the Transfer Functions dialog box to correct for a printer's calibration errors. Before you can enter any values in the Transfer Functions dialog box, you must perform some printed tests using calibration bars and a color densitometer. Enter the values from the color densitometer in the corresponding slots in the Transfer Functions dialog box to compensate for calibration problems. Most color printers come with calibration software or have ways to set the calibration on the device itself, so it's unlikely you will specify Transfer Functions in Photoshop.

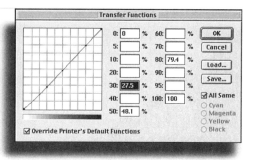

Setting Background Color and Border

Click the **Background** button in the Page Setup dialog box to specify a background color using the Color Picker. When you select a background color, the rest of the page area outside the image area fills with the background color. This option is useful if you are printing slides to a film recorder, for example, because you can fill the background of the slide with black or another dark color. If you would like your image to print with a black border, click the **Border** button in the Page Setup dialog box to display the Border dialog box and specify a width for the border in points, millimeters, or inches.

Setting the Bleed Option

Click the **Bleed** button in the Page Setup dialog box to display the Bleed dialog box; enter a width for the bleed in inches, millimeters, or points. The bleed amount insets the crop marks by the amount specified to trim your image. The image size does not increase to accommodate the bleed amount.

Printing a Caption with the File

Check the **Caption** check box in the Page Setup dialog box to print the caption you specified in the File Info dialog box. Choose **Info** from the **File** menu to display the File Info dialog box to enter the caption text before choosing Page Setup (see Figure 5.5). When printing CMYK color separations, the caption text is printed on the black plate.

When to Specify a Bleed

The only time you'll have to specify a bleed in Photoshop is when the image is printed directly from Photoshop. A bleed is necessary when an image goes right to the edge of a printed page to accommodate trimming and binding after the page is printed. For example, if you create an image that is to cover an entire 8.5 × 11-inch page when printed, you must create the image larger to facilitate a bleed on all sides (typically 1/8 inch). This means the Photoshop image will be 8.75 × 11.25 inch with a .125 inch bleed specified in the Page Setup dialog box. When the page is printed and ready to be trimmed, the person cutting the page down to size uses the inset crop marks to trim the page to its correct size of 8.5 ×11 inches.

FIGURE 5.5
The File Info dialog box.

Printing Registration Marks

Check the appropriate boxes to print registration marks with your image. If you are printing to a film imagesetting device, check **Negative** to print negative film and select the emulsion setting (usually **Emulsion Down** for offset printing). Use the **Interpolation** check box when printing to a PostScript Level 2 printer that supports interpolation to resample a low resolution image while printing (see Figure 5.6). The registration options available are as follows:

- **Registration Marks:** Photoshop prints bull's-eye registration marks on all four sides of the image to help when registering color plates for proofing and offset printing.

- **Corner Crop Marks:** Photoshop inserts crop marks at the four corners of the image.

- **Center Crop Marks:** Photoshop centers crop marks on each side of the image to indicate the center point of the image.

- **Calibration Bars:** When the printer driver supports this feature, you can print calibration bars to check the dot percentages and density of the image using a densitometer.

- Click the **Labels** check box to print the name of the file centered above the image as well as the names of the color plates when printing separations.

FIGURE 5.6
Registration marks.

1 Corner Crop Marks

2 Center Crop Marks

3 Label

4 Registration Marks

5 Caption

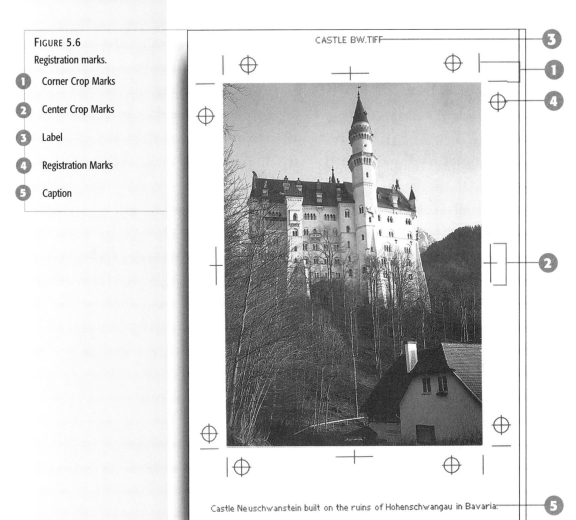

Castle Neuschwanstein built on the ruins of Hohenschwangau in Bavaria.

Printing the Image

Before you print your image, click and hold on **Document Statistics** in the lower-left corner of the Image window on MacOS or along the bottom-left of the screen in Windows to preview how the image fits the specified paper size you selected in the Page Setup dialog box (see Figure 5.7). You should make sure that the image area fits on the page. Choose File>Print to display the Print dialog box (see Figure 5.8).

FIGURE 5.7
A preview image of how the file prints with the current page setup.

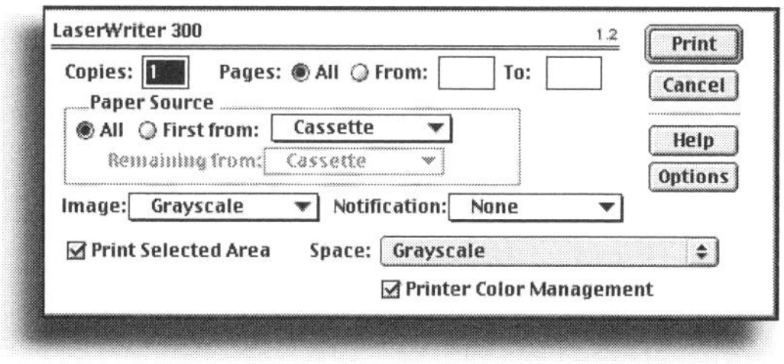

FIGURE 5.8
The Print dialog box.

If you are printing color separations of a CMYK file, click the **Print Separations** check box. You can select a section of your image using the selection tools, and then print just the selected area by checking the **Print Selected Area** check box in the Print dialog box on the MacOS or the **Selection** radio button in

Windows. Your particular printer may include other options not mentioned here, although the basic options remain the same from one printer to the next. If you're working with a lot of small images and do not need crop marks for each image, you can save paper and printing time by placing the images in a page layout application like QuarkXPress or Pagemaker and printing them ganged up on pages. Consult your printer manual for the specifics about your particular printing device.

Printing a Contact Sheet

When you need to print a contact sheet of all the images in a particular folder or directory, you can instruct Photoshop to build a contact sheet and specify how many images appear on each page. All images in the specified folder are opened, scaled, and placed on a new page with a transparent background. These pages can then be printed following the above instructions for printing from Photoshop. To create a contact sheet, choose **Automate** from the **File** menu, and then select **Contact Sheet** to display the Contact Sheet dialog box (see Figure 5.9).

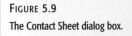

FIGURE 5.9

The Contact Sheet dialog box.

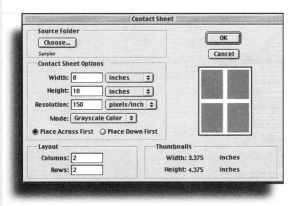

Automating Tasks with Actions

Learning about actions

Recording and playing actions

Batch processing with actions

Saving and loading actions

Learning the Actions Interface

Using the Actions palette, you can record processes you perform in Photoshop and then play them back later in the same file or other files. Although it would be nice to record everything you do in Photoshop, this isn't necessarily the case with actions. You can access all the menu commands, but you can't record some of them; you must add them to an Action script using the **Insert Menu Command** option, explained later in this chapter. Choosing Page Setup while recording and specifying Page Setup parameters are not recordable, although you can use the **Insert Menu Item** command to add the **Page Setup** command to an action.

In the toolbox, some tools are fully actionable, while others can only be selected. You can specify foreground and background colors, swap the foreground and background colors, and reset them to the default colors. The good news is that a majority of the functions you perform in Photoshop is recordable via the Actions palette. You can divide the actions you record into sets, represented by a Folder icon in the Actions palette. Photoshop comes with a set of actions called "Default Actions," which are worth checking out, especially if you're new to using the Actions palette. Choose **Show Actions** from the **Window** menu to display the Actions palette (see Figure 6.1).

The Default Actions Set

A number of actions are already defined for you in the **Default Actions** set located in the Actions palette. If you're relatively new to the way actions work, try some of these Default Actions.

Using the Default Actions

1. Click the triangle to the left of the **Default Actions** set in the Actions palette to display the contents of the Default Actions set.

2. Click the triangle to the left of the individual action to expand and view the contents of that action.

FIGURE 6.1
The Actions palette.

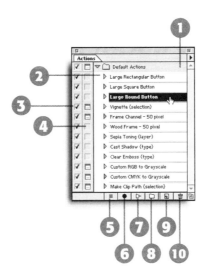

1. Action sets are depicted as folders in the Actions palette menu.

2. Click the triangles next to the actions to expand the details of the action.

3. Check this box to enable this action in Button Mode. If this box is unchecked, the action appears as a button in Button mode but is deactivated.

4. Click in this space to turn on dialog boxes for the steps in the action that contain dialog boxes. When the icon is black, all the steps that have dialog boxes stop and wait for input when the action is playing. When the icon is red, it means that only some of the steps in the action have dialog boxes turned on.

5. Stop playing/recording an action.

6. The record button is black until you start recording. This button appears red while recording is taking place.

7. Click the Play button to play a selected action.

8. Click the Folder icon to create and name a new set.

9. Click the Page icon to create a new action and begin recording that action.

10. Select an action in the Actions palette and click the Trash icon to delete the action, or drag an action onto the trash can to delete it.

3. Click once on one of the actions listed under the Default Actions, "Large Round Button," for example. Click the triangle to the left of this action to expand it so you can watch the progress of the action as you play it.

4. Choose **Play** from the Actions palette menu or click the Play button at the bottom of the Actions palette. Watch the results of the playing action in the image window while monitoring the progress of the action in the Actions palette.

5. You can click the Stop button at the bottom of the Actions palette or choose **Stop** from the Actions palette menu at any time to stop the playback of an action.

6. Choose **Button Mode** from the Actions palette menu to display the Actions palette in Button mode, in which case you can simply click a button to play an action (see Figure 6.2). Choose **Button Mode** again to return to the Script mode of the Actions palette. Note that you cannot record actions while in Button mode.

FIGURE 6.2

The Actions palette in Button mode.

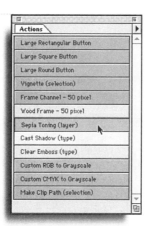

Understanding the Default Actions

All of the Default Actions provided with your Photoshop package perform actions that require the existence of an open file. In some cases, you must have some conditions set up before playing the action, like creating text or making a selection. The following is a brief description of what you can expect to happen when you play the Default Actions.

- When you play the **Large Rectangular Button** action, a 0.5-inch X 0.75-inch embossed box is created in the foreground color and positioned in the upper-left corner of your file (see Figure 6.3). The button is created on its own layer so you can reposition it with the **Move** tool.

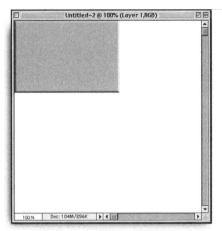

FIGURE 6.3

An embossed button is created on a layer when you play the Large Rectangular Button action in the Actions palette.

- When you play the **Large Square Button** action, a 0.5-inch X 0.5-inch embossed box is created in the foreground color and positioned in the upper-left corner of your file. The button is created on its own layer so you can reposition it with the **Move** tool (see Figure 6.4).

- When you play the **Large Round Button** action, a 0.5-inch X 0.5-inch embossed circle is created in the foreground color and positioned in the upper-left corner of your file. The button is created on its own layer so you can reposition it with the **Move** tool (see Figure 6.4).

- When you play the **Vignette (selection)** action, a vignette is created, based on the shape of a selection you make using one of the selection tools. The action stops at the Feather dialog box so you can input the feather radius. The areas of the image that are not selected are painted white in the process (see Figure 6.5).

FIGURE 6.4

Use the Move tool to reposition the buttons after first selecting their respective layers in the Layers palette.

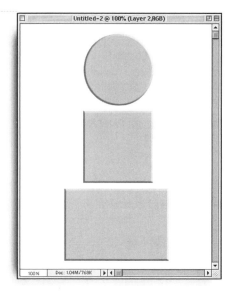

FIGURE 6.5

Create a selection with the selection tools before playing the Vignette (selection) action.

- When you play the **Frame Channel - 50 pixel** action, a 50-pixel selection is created around your image to enable you to apply Frame effects (see Figure 6.6). This action creates alpha channels in the Channels palette as part of the process.

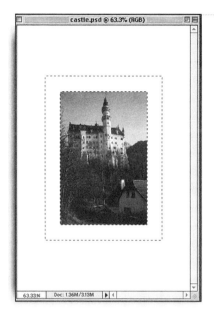

FIGURE 6.6

A Selection marquee is created so you can apply some of your own frame effects when you play the Frame Channel action.

- When you play the **Wood Frame - 50 pixel** action, a 50-pixel wood frame is rendered and placed around your image (see Figure 6.7). A combination of selections and Filter effects is applied to achieve the wood grain look. Examine the steps in this action to learn how the wood grain is created.

- When you play the **Sepia Toning (layer)** action, a grayscale version of your image is created on a separate layer and an adjustment layer is added to change the hues to sepia tones. The original image still exists in the Layers palette beneath the new layers that are created.

- When you play the **Cast Shadow (type)** action, a cast shadow is created on a separate layer (see Figure 6.8). This action works best on layers that contain text and rasterizes text layers in the process.

FIGURE 6.7

A wood grain is created using some of Photoshop's built-in filters and is applied to a 50-pixel embossed frame.

FIGURE 6.8

The effect created using the Cast Shadow action.

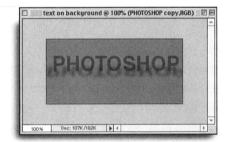

- When you play the **Clear Emboss (type)** action, a raised lettering effect is created when a layer that contains rasterized type is selected (see Figure 6.9). This action will work on other layer types, though the effect is most often used on text.

- When you play the **Custom RGB to Grayscale** action, the image is converted to grayscale and you're given the chance via the **Channel Mixer** dialog box to specify how the source colors (RGB in this case) are converted to grayscale (see Figure 6.10). Check the Preview check box to see the results of your adjustments previewed in the image window.

FIGURE 6.9

The Clear Emboss action does a nice job of creating raised text.

FIGURE 6.9

The Clear Emboss action does a nice job of creating raised text.

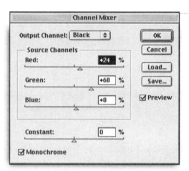

FIGURE 6.10

This action stops and displays the Channel Mixer dialog box so you can adjust the RGB values of the image before the conversion to grayscale.

■ When you play the **Custom CMYK to Grayscale** action, the image is converted to grayscale and you're given the chance via the **Channel Mixer** dialog box to specify how the source colors (CMYK in this case) are converted to grayscale (see Figure 6.11). Check the Preview check box to see the results of your adjustments previewed in the image window.

FIGURE 6.11

This action stops and displays the Channel Mixer dialog box, so you can adjust the CMYK values of the image before the conversion to grayscale.

■ When you play the **Make Clip Path (selection)** action, a
clipping path is created and added to the Paths palette based
on the current selection. This means you have to have a
selection created before playing this action. This action will
stop, prompt you for a path name, and then prompt you to
choose a clipping path to save with the file. Keep in mind
that this method of creating a clipping path generates many
more anchor points than you would use to create the path
using the Path tools (see Figure 6.12). Too many anchor
points can lead to problems outputting the file to an imagesetter or laser printer, so I recommend taking the time to
create your paths with the Path tools.

FIGURE 6.12

The Make Clip Path action creates a large number of anchor
points to create the path.

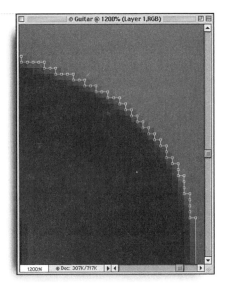

The Default Actions are a good place to start to understand how
the Actions palette works. In the following sections, you discover
methods to modify parts of an action. You can use the Default
Actions as a starting point to customize your own actions, based
on the structure already provided.

Recording Actions

Recording actions is a relatively simple procedure. The Actions
palette contains some VCR-like buttons at the bottom of the

palette to facilitate recording. The Record button is represented by a solid black circle, the Stop button a solid square, and the Play button a right-pointing white triangle.

Before you click the Record button to begin recording an action, you must first create a new action and give it a name. If you do not create a new set, the new action is inserted into the selected set of actions. In the following example, we will create an action that prepares color images for placement on Web pages.

Example Action to Create Web Graphics

1. Open any RGB in Photoshop to use as a model in creating our action. The process of opening an image can be recorded as part of an action, though you may want to avoid this in most cases, because the action always opens the same file unless you turn on the dialog box for the Open command.

2. Choose **Show Actions** from the **Window** menu to display the Actions palette, which contains the Default Actions that come with Photoshop. If you want to start out with an empty Actions palette, drag the Default Actions onto the Trash icon at the bottom of the Actions palette. You can always restore the Default Actions by choosing **Reset Actions** from the Actions palette menu.

3. Click the triangle in the upper right-hand corner of the Actions palette to display the Actions palette menu and make sure that you have not selected (or checked) Button Mode.

4. Choose **New Set** from the **Actions Palette Menu** or click the Folder icon at the bottom of the Actions palette to create a new set. A dialog box appears prompting you for a name for the new set. Let's call this set "Web Actions." Click **OK** to make a new set in the Actions palette.

5. Make sure you have the new set you created in the previous step selected in the Actions palette. Choose **New Action** from the **Actions Palette menu** or click the New Action icon at the bottom of the Actions palette to display the New Action dialog box (see Figure 6.13).

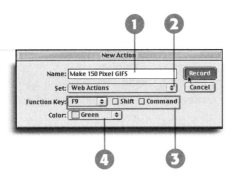

FIGURE 6.13.

The New Action dialog box.

1 Give your new action a unique name that is descriptive.

2 Select the Set that contains the new action.

3 You can assign a Function key to this action. Combine the Shift and Command keys along with a Function key by clicking the check boxes.

4 Select a color for this action's button when in Button Mode.

6. When giving your action a name, try to make it descriptive and unique so you know what it does without having to examine the content. In our example, we are going to create some GIF files that are 150 pixels wide. Name this action "Make 150 Pixel GIFs" and choose a Function key and color. (The Function key and color choices are optional.) If you assign a color to this action, the action displays as a colored button in the Actions palette when it's set to Button mode. If you do not have the correct set selected in the Actions palette, you can select the set for this action in this dialog box.

7. Click the Record button to begin recording this action. Note that the Record button at the bottom of the Actions palette turns red to indicate recording mode. Photoshop adds the new action you defined to the bottom of the Actions list within the specified set.

8. Choose **Image Size** from the **Image** menu to display the Image Size dialog box (see Figure 6.14).

9. Make sure that you have checked the **Constrain Proportions** and **Resample Image** (Bicubic) check boxes. Change the Resolution to 72 pixels/inch. For purposes of this example, limit your Web graphics to no more than 150 pixels in width. Enter 150 in the Width text box. Click OK to resize the image.

10. Choose **Mode** from the **Image** menu; then select **Indexed Color** to display the Indexed Color dialog box (see Figure 6.15).

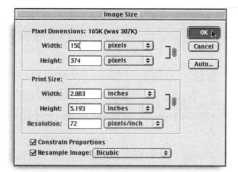

FIGURE 6.14
The Image Size dialog box.

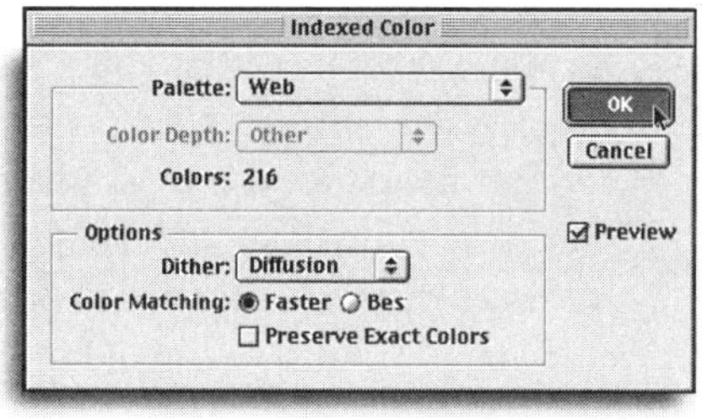

FIGURE 6.15
The Indexed Color dialog box.

11. Choose **Web** as the palette type from the **Palette** drop-down menu. The Color Depth and Colors values automatically change to Other and 216 respectively. Choose **Diffusion** as the Dither type if it's not already selected. Click **OK** to convert the RGB image to Indexed Color.

SEE ALSO

➤ *For more information on Indexed Color, see "Photoshop's Image Modes" page 83*

➤ *For more information in changing image size, see "Changing the Size of an Image" page 81*

12. Choose **Save As** from the **File** menu to display the Save As dialog box. Navigate to your hard disk and select a location for the file you are saving. It's okay to create a new directory while saving the file because this part of the save process is not recorded in the action. Choose **Compuserve GIF** from the **Format** pull-down menu (see Figure 6.16). Click Save to display the GIF Options dialog box. Click the Interlaced radio button and then click **OK** to save the file as a GIF file.

Appending File Extensions on the MacOS

Choose **Preferences** from the **File** menu, select **Saving Files** to display the Preferences dialog box, and choose **Always** from the pull-down menu to the right of **Append File Extension**. Set this preference so a three-character file extension is appended to your file when saving. A three-character file extension is always appended to the file name in MS-Windows.

FIGURE 6.16
The Save As dialog box.

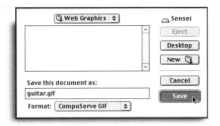

13. Click the Stop Recording icon at the bottom of the Actions palette, or choose **Stop Recording** from the **Actions palette menu**. Close the open file without saving changes.

Examine the new action you just recorded to see what information was actually recorded for each step. Run this action on another file to see if it works correctly. When you run this action on the new file, it should change the image size to 150 pixels wide, set the resolution to 72 pixels per inch, convert to indexed color mode, and save the file in GIF format.

SEE ALSO

➤ *For more information on the GIF file format, see "File Formats" page 44*

Batch Processing with Actions

Once you have recorded an action, you can apply that action to an entire directory or folder of files using the batch processing feature. Before performing a batch operation on a large number of files, I recommend testing the batch on a small sample group of files to be sure things turn out the way you expect. Batch processing is one of the automation features included in the **Automate** submenu under the **File** menu.

Creating a Batch

1. Choose **Automate** from the **File** menu; then select Batch from the Actions palette menu to display the Batch dialog box (see Figure 6.17).

2. Choose a **Set** and an **Action** from the set to play on the batch of files.

3. Choose **Folder** from the Source pull-down menu to select a

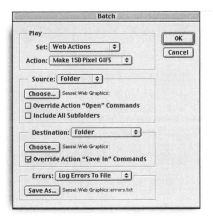

FIGURE 6.17
The Batch dialog box.

folder full of files to perform the batch on. Choose **Import** here if you want to perform the batch using one of the import options available when you choose **Import** from the **File** menu.

4. Click the **Choose** button to select a source folder. Navigate to the folder of files you want to perform the batch on and click the selection button under the window that displays the file list (see Figure 6.18).

5. Check the **Override Action "Open" Commands** if you

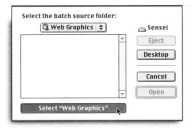

FIGURE 6.18
Select a source folder for the batch.

recorded the process of opening a file in your action. Check the **Include All Subfolders** check box to perform the batch on files that are located in folders within the selected folder.

6. Choose **Folder** from the Destination pull-down menu and click the Choose button to select the target directory for your batched files. If you choose **None** here, the files in the batch remain open in Photoshop after the action is performed. If you choose **Save and Close**, the files are saved over the original files and then closed.

7. Check the check box for **Override Action "Save In" Commands** to make sure that the files are saved in the directory you specified in the Batch dialog box, not the directory specified in the action.

8. Choose **Log Errors To File** and click the **Save As** button to specify a name for the error log if you want to record errors that happen during the batch in a text file.

9. Click **OK** to begin batch processing the files. Once the batch is complete, you will find the converted files in the destination folder you specified in the Batch dialog box.

Inserting Menu Items into Actions

All the menu choices in Photoshop can be included in your recorded actions, even if they cannot be recorded when recording the action. To insert a menu item into your action, click the step in the action you want the menu item inserted after, and then choose **Insert Menu Item** from the **Actions Palette menu** to display the Insert Menu Item dialog box (see Figure 6.19). Choose a menu item using the mouse or type a partial name and click the **Find** button. The selected menu item is inserted in the action after the selected step in the action. When you insert a menu item in your action, the settings for that menu item are ignored and a dialog box for the menu item is automatically displayed when the action is played.

Inserting and Rerecording Actions

If you want to insert an action step in an existing Action, click the step you want to insert it after and click the **Record** button at the bottom of the Actions palette. Click the **Stop** button when you're through recording the additional steps. The new steps you recorded are inserted after the step that was originally selected. To record a step in an Action, select the step, then choose **Record Again** from the Actions Palette menu.

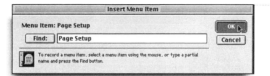

FIGURE 6.19
The Insert Menu Item dialog
box.

Inserting Stops

You can insert dialog boxes in your actions to halt the progress
of the action and provide the user with information or instructions. For example, you may want to alert the user to a destruc-
tive step in the action and give him the option to stop the action
or continue.

Inserting a Stop Action

1. Select the step in the action you want the Stop action to follow.

2. Choose **Insert Stop** from the **Actions Palette menu** and
specify the information you would like the Stop to convey in
the Record Stop dialog box (see Figure 6.20).

FIGURE 6.20
The Record Stop dialog box.

3. Click the **Allow Continue** check box if you want to include
a **Continue** button as part of the dialog box that is displayed
(see Figure 6.21). If you do not check this option, the user
must click the **Record** button again to continue playing the
action.

Inserting Paths

Paths can be used as stencils to record fill and stroke operations,
as well as to make selections. The **Insert Path** command enables
you to record an action using a path or selection, and then
include other paths for duplicate actions.

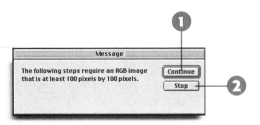

FIGURE 6.21

The Stop dialog box that is displayed when the action is played.

1 The Continue button enables the user to continue playing the action.

2 The Stop button stops playing the action but leaves the playhead in place, so the user can click the Play button to continue playing the action.

For example, let's say you have 10 files, each with their own paths, and you want to apply a particular sequence of fills and strokes to the path using the **Fill Path** and **Stroke Path** commands in the Paths palette. Record the action for one of the files using its defined path, then open the other files, and insert the correct path into the action. Choose **Show Paths** from the **Window** menu and click a path. Of course, you have to create a path if one doesn't exist for the file. **Choose Insert Path** from the **Actions Palette menu** to insert the selected path into the action.

Playback Options

Specify the way you would like your actions to play back using the **Playback Options** choice in the **Actions Palette menu** (see Figure 6.22). Choose **Accelerated** to play the action without displaying the steps in the Actions palette during playback. Choose **Step by Step** to see the progress of the action in the Actions palette as it is played. Choose **Pause for # seconds** to pause the playback at each step in the action—a good way to debug complex actions.

FIGURE 6.22.

The Playback Options dialog box.

Importing and Exporting Actions

You may want to save your sets of actions to keep the number of defined actions in the Actions palette down, especially if you record actions on a regular basis. It's also a good way to exchange actions with others. Actions are automatically saved in a separate preferences file in the Photoshop folder and remain in the Actions palette unless this file is deleted or moved. It may become necessary at some point to dispose of this preferences file, especially if some sort of file corruption takes place. Saving your actions ensures that you can retrieve them at a later date.

- Click a **Set** in the Actions palette and choose **Save Actions** from the **Actions Palette menu.** When the dialog box appears, select a location for the file and click **OK.** Individual actions within sets cannot be saved individually.

- Choose **Load Actions** from the **Actions Palette menu** to append saved action sets to the Actions palette. The imported action set is added to the Actions palette, even if it already exists there, so be careful when naming your sets because multiple sets with the same name can co-exist in the Actions palette.

- Choose **Replace Actions** from the **Actions Palette menu** to replace all sets with the imported set. If you use this option and have unsaved actions, they will be lost.

- Choose **Reset Actions** to restore the Default Actions set. A dialog box appears asking whether you want to replace all the sets with the default set or simply append the default set to the existing ones.

- Choose **Clear Actions** to delete all the sets in the Actions palette. A dialog box appears to ensure that you really want to delete all the actions in the Actions palette.

Other Actions Included with Photoshop

A plethora of useful actions are also included in the **Extras** folder in the **Photoshop** folder. Choose **Load Actions** or

Replace Actions from the **Actions Palette Menu** and navigate to the Extras folder in the Photoshop folder. The extra actions included with Photoshop provide a great way to learn how to create some special effects and are a good source for ideas when designing a project of your own:

- The **Buttons** action set contains actions to create a large variety of buttons, including buttons created from a selection on an image.

- The **Commands** action set contains actions for some of the most often needed Photoshop commands. Double-click these actions to assign Function keys (F-keys) to the actions to increase productivity.

- The **Frames** action set contains actions that create a wide variety of frame effects on existing imagery. There are some really neat frame effects here and you can learn a lot about creating dimension by examining these actions.

- The **Image Effects** action set contains actions that create some stunning image effects by combining a variety of filters's image editing techniques.

- The **Production** action set contains actions that help to increase productivity. Assign Function keys to these actions or run the Actions palette in Button mode.

- The **Text Effects** action set contains actions for some of the most popular text effects and some new ones I haven't seen before.

- The **Textures** action set contains actions to create paper textures, wood textures, and a variety of others.

Setting Preferences

Deleting the preferences file

There are a few reasons why you might want to delete the Photoshop preferences file to restore the factory default settings. If Photoshop starts to act up, chances are that the preferences file on your hard disk is corrupt. Deleting the preferences file in this case will more than likely remedy the problems you're encountering.

When you delete the preferences file from your hard disk, Photoshop creates a brand new preferences file with all the factory default settings in place. You should also back up the preferences file on your hard disk when Photoshop is working smoothly, so you can restore them if you have to delete the preferences file in the future.

The preferences settings on MacOS are stored in the file named "Adobe Photoshop 5.0 Prefs," located in the **Adobe Photoshop Settings** folder within the **Adobe Photoshop** folder. On the Windows 95/NT platform the preferences are saved in the **Adobe Photoshop 5.0 prefs.psp** file located in the **Adobe Photoshop Settings** folder within the **Adobe Photoshop** folder.

The Default Preferences

When you first launch Photoshop, all the preferences are set to what is referred to as the default preferences. Photoshop maintains a preferences file on your hard drive that records changes you make to the preferences, so that they are set the same way when you quit and relaunch Photoshop.

Setting the General Preferences

The General Preferences is where you set some general information about how you want things to work in Photoshop. Choose **Preferences** from the **File** menu; then select **General** or type (**Ctrl-K**) [**Command-K**) to display the Preferences dialog box (see Figure 7.1).

Color Picker

Choose the Color Picker you want to use to specify color. On the MacOS, you can choose from Photoshop or Apple; in Windows, the choices are Photoshop or Windows. In most cases, the Photoshop Color Picker is the best choice, although you may be more comfortable using the Color Picker for your particular system.

Interpolation

When Photoshop has to invent new pixels to enlarge a file, it uses a method called interpolation to accomplish this. The three choices for interpolation are Bicubic, Bilinear, and Nearest Neighbor. For best results, choose Bicubic; for the fastest interpolation times, choose Nearest Neighbor.

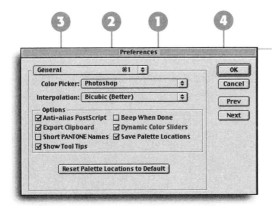

FIGURE 7.1
The General preferences.

1 Choose the Color Picker that is displayed when you specify color using the foreground and background color swatches.

2 Choose a method of interpolation; Bicubic is recommended.

3 Choose from the list of available preferences.

4 Go to the next Preferences Settings dialog box.

Options

- Select **Anti-alias PostScript** when you want to remove jagged edges from a pasted or placed element created in a PostScript drawing program such as Illustrator. If you are pasting or placing line art, this option should be off to preserve the sharp lines.

- Select **Export Clipboard** to save the contents of the Clipboard when quitting Photoshop on the Macintosh. Export Clipboard displays a prompt when quitting Photoshop in Windows, asking you whether you want to make the contents of the Clipboard available to other applications. When the Clipboard is exported, you can open another application and paste something you copied or cut in Photoshop.

- Select **Short Pantone Names** so the names assigned to the Pantone inks in Photoshop conform with the naming conventions in programs such as Adobe Illustrator, Adobe PageMaker, and QuarkXPress.

- Select **Show Tool Tips** to display information about the Tools and Palette options when you position the cursor over them.

- Select **Beep When Done** if you want Photoshop to beep every time it completes a command or function.

- Select **Dynamic Color Sliders** to make the sliders in the Color palette display the colors in the Foreground or Background swatch as you drag.

- Select **Save Palette Locations** if you want the palettes to be in the same place they were the last time you used Photoshop.

- Click the **Reset Palette Locations to Default** to return the palettes to their original palette groups and display position.

Setting the Saving Files Preferences

The Saving Files preferences enable you to specify details about how you want your files to be saved, and whether you want them to have certain properties that may affect the file size. Choose **Preferences** from the **File** menu and select **Saving Files** to display the Preferences dialog box (see Figure 7.2).

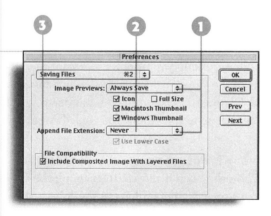

FIGURE 7.2

The Saving Files preferences.

1. The Image Previews determine whether a preview is saved with the file. These choices add to your file size.

2. If you're working on the Mac and sharing files with Windows users, file extensions are necessary.

3. Check here if you want to open files that contain layers in programs that don't support layers.

Image Previews

The Image Preview options often add size to your file and take longer to save in the case of large files.

- There are three choices in the Image Preview pull-down list: **Always Save**, **Never Save**, and **Ask When Saving**. Choose **Always Save** to save the preview options you checked with every file. Choose **Never Save** to ignore the checked preview options and never save an image preview. Check **Ask When Saving** to have Photoshop prompt you to save the file with the checked preview options.

- MacOS users can check the **Icon** button to save a Preview icon that appears on the file when viewed on the desktop.

- MacOS users can save a full-sized PICT resource with the file. Check the **Full Size** button to save a full-size PICT resource with the file. This PICT resource is used by some older programs to preview the image when importing on the MacOS. The resource can also be manipulated using ResEdit™ or by choosing **Import** from the **File** menu in Photoshop and then selecting **PICT Resource**.

- MacOS users can check the **Macintosh Thumbnail** button to save a thumbnail preview with the file. This thumbnail preview enables other MacOS programs to preview the image while importing.

- MacOS users can check the **Windows Thumbnail** button to save a thumbnail preview with the file. This thumbnail preview enables other Windows programs to preview the image while importing. Note that you can check both **Windows Thumbnail** and **Macintosh Thumbnail** to provide a preview for both platforms in the same file.

Append File Extension

MacOS users can choose to append a three-character file extension that adheres to DOS naming conventions so that the files are recognized by Windows applications. Windows always appends a three-character file extension; so the only choice here is whether to make that three-character extension lower or uppercase:

- Choose **Never** to never append file name extensions.
- Choose **Always** to always append a three-character file name extension.
- Choose **Ask When Saving** to be prompted when saving the file to add a file name extension.
- MacOS users can check the **Use Lower Case** check box to save files with a lowercase extension. Windows users have the option of saving with lowercase or uppercase extensions.

File Compatibility

Check the **Include Composited Image With Layered Files** check box to save a flattened composite version of a file that contains layers. This enables other image editing programs that do not support layers or Photoshop version 2.5 or earlier to open Photoshop files that contain layers, but only in composite form.

Setting Display & Cursors Preferences

The Display and Cursors preferences affect the way certain processes are displayed in Photoshop and enable you to set the type of cursors to use for painting and editing tools. Choose **Preferences** from the **File** menu, then select **Display & Cursors** to display the Preferences dialog box (see Figure 7.3).

FIGURE 7.3

The Display & Cursors preferences.

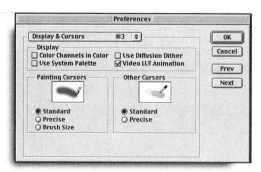

Display

- Select **Color Channels in Color** to display the individual color channels in their respective colors.

- Select **Use System Palette** if you want all colors to be displayed using your systems 8-bit Color palette. This option affords a maximum of only 256 colors and should be left unchecked unless you are using an 8-bit color or grayscale monitor. If you are using an 8-bit color monitor and you select **Use Diffusion Dither**, Photoshop smoothes the appearance of the color on the screen by dithering.

- Select **Video LUT** (lookup table) **Animation** to see the changes you make when adjusting color on the whole screen. Selecting this option speeds up the process of updating the color on the screen when you are making color adjustments. If you check the Preview check box in the dialog boxes used for color adjustment when adjusting a selected area of the image, the Video LUT Animation is temporarily turned off and the color changes are reflected in the selected area only.

Painting Cursors

The painting cursors affect the way the cursor appears for the Painting tools such as the Paintbrush, Pencil, and Airbrush:

- Select **Standard** if you want the cursor to display the Tool icon as the cursor icon.

- Select **Precise** to display the cursor as a crosshair.

- Select **Brush Size** to display the cursor in the shape and size of the active brush.

Other Cursors

To change the way the cursor appears for tools other than the Painting tools, choose **Standard** to display the tool icon as the cursor icon or **Precise** to display the tool as a crosshair icon.

Color Table Animation

In Windows, color table animation only works when the monitor is set to 256 colors. To achieve color table animation in 24-bit mode with Windows, you must install a third-party extension in the PLUGINS directory. Contact your video card manufacturer to see if an extension is available. Turn off Video LUT Animation when in 24-bit mode if you do not have the proper extension installed. For the MacOS, some 24-bit and 32-bit video cards may cause problems when Video LUT Animation is turned on. Turn off Video LUT Animation if you experience problems and contact the video card manufacturer for possible solutions.

Setting the Transparency & Gamut Preferences

The **Transparency & Gamut** preferences are used to set the way the transparent layers are displayed and are used to choose a color and opacity for out-of-gamut colors when the **Gamut Warning** is turned on. The Gamut Warning is used by Photoshop to help the user identify colors that are outside the range of colors (the gamut) available for CMYK printing when working in other color modes. Choose **Preferences** from the **File** menu; then select **Transparency & Gamut** to display the preferences dialog box (see Figure 7.4).

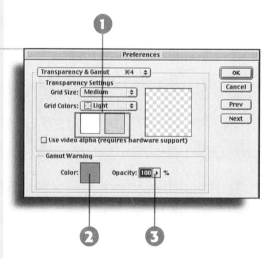

FIGURE 7.4

The Transparency & Gamut preferences.

1 Click the two color swatches to change the colors used for the checkerboard pattern of the transparency grid.

2 Click this color swatch to change the color used to depict out-of-gamut colors.

3 An opacity setting of less than 100% enables you to see the image underneath the out-of-gamut mask.

Transparency Settings

The transparency settings are located in the top half of the Transparency & Gamut preferences dialog box.

- Choose a **Grid Size** and **Color** from the pull-down menus to set how transparency is indicated on layers when they are viewed alone. You can click the color swatches to set the colors of the checkerboard if you can't find a suitable color in the pull-down menu. Choose **None** from the **Grid Size** pull-down menu to display a white background where transparency exists. The transparency settings also affect the way transparency is indicated in the **Gradient Options** palette.

- The **Use video alpha** option requires that you have the proper hardware installed. Do not select this option unless you have a 32-bit graphics card installed, such as the TrueVision NuVista or Raster-Ops ProVideo32.

Gamut Warning

The **Gamut Warning** is the way Photoshop informs you that colors specified in RGB, LAB, or HSB cannot be converted accurately to CMYK for printing. When you turn on **Gamut Warning** in the **View** menu, a color mask is overlaid on the image to indicate where colors are out-of-gamut.

- Click the **Color** to choose a color for this overlay mask. Try to choose an unusual color that stands out on your images.

- Choose an opacity that is around 50% so you can see the image underneath.

Setting the Units & Rulers Preferences

The **Units & Rulers** preferences are simply the preferences that define what ruler units to use. The **Column Size** options refer to the **Columns** choice in the **Image Size** and **Canvas Size** dialog boxes. If you are going to be printing to a PostScript imaging device, choose **PostScript (72 points/inch)** when working with picas and points. Use the **Traditional (72,27 points/inch)** only if you are trying to match something that was created outside the realm of electronic publishing where a pica gauge was used. Choose **Preferences** from the **File** menu and then select **Units & Rulers** to display the preferences dialog box (see Figure 7.5).

FIGURE 7.5

The Units & Rulers
preferences.

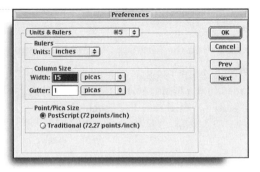

Setting the Guides & Grid Preferences

Choose a **Color** and **Style** for the guides and grid and specify
the size of the grid. You can click the color swatches to choose a
color using the Color Picker. You can select from **Lines** or
Dashed Lines in the **Style** pull-down menu for **Guides.** The
Grid can be depicted as **Lines, Dashed Lines,** or **Dots.**
Choose Preferences from the **File** menu, and then select
Guides & Grids to display the preferences dialog box (see
Figure 7.6).

FIGURE 7.6.

The Guides & Grids
preferences.

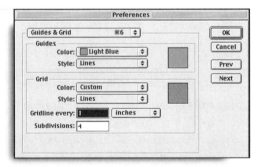

Setting the Plug-ins & Scratch Disks Preferences

The **Plug-Ins folder** is where Photoshop's plug-ins are stored
on the hard disk. Plug-Ins are used to expand the functionality
of Photoshop by adding commands to the menus and
import/export filters. In order for Photoshop to find installed

plug-ins, you must specify the location of the Plug-Ins folder by clicking the **Choose** button and navigating to the folder or directory. **Scratch Disks** is hard drive space that Photoshop uses to perform processing operations when it runs out of RAM (memory) space. You can choose up to four separate hard disks for scratch disk space. If you want to use a removable drive like a Bernoulli, Zip, or Syquest drive, keep in mind that the performance of Photoshop is greatly hindered because removable drives have much slower access times than a hard disk. You must quit Photoshop and restart for any changes made in this dialog box to take effect. Choose **Preferences** from the **File** menu, and then select **Plug-Ins & Scratch Disk** to display the Preferences dialog box (see Figure 7.7).

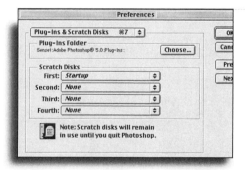

FIGURE 7.7
The Plug-Ins & Scratch Disks preferences.

Setting the Memory & Image Cache Preferences

The **Image Cache** preferences determine how Photoshop caches the images it uses for screen display when performing certain functions. The higher the cache level, the faster Photoshop displays changes. You can choose a Cache level between 1 and 8. If you choose **Use cache for histograms**, Photoshop displays the histograms in **Levels and Histogram** faster but less accurately. You must quit and restart Photoshop for these changes to take effect. The **Memory** setting is only available on the Windows platform and is where you set the amount of Random Access Memory (RAM) assigned to the

Photoshop application. MacOS users set application memory at the desktop level by choosing Get Info from the Desktop File menu. For the MacOS, choose **Preferences** from the **File** menu, and then select **Image Cache** to display the preferences dialog box (see Figure 7.8). For Windows, choose **Preferences** from the **File** menu; then select **Memory & Image Cache** to display the preferences dialog box (see Figure 7.9).

FIGURE 7.8

The Image Cache (Macintosh) preferences.

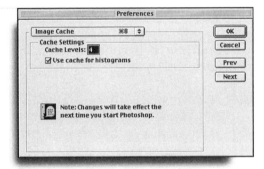

FIGURE 7.9

The Memory and Image Cache (Windows) preferences.

Using the Painting and Editing Tools

Selecting Areas

Create selections using the various Marquee tools

How to generate freeform selections

Discover the Magic Wand's capability to select unique areas

Use the Selection menu to uniquely tailor your selections, including growing, contracting, and saving

Selection Using the Marquee Tool

Photoshop 5.0 is composed of a series of incredibly powerful tools, but these tools cannot be applied universally. If you apply all the Photoshop filters to the same image, you'd likely end up with a muddy mess. However, if you applied said filters to certain selectively applied segments of an image, then you'd probably end with a much more artful effect. This is true of any effect or Photoshop tool; they generally require an area to act upon.

These areas are known as *selections*, a series of pixels within an image that are chosen specifically to be acted upon. You know when an area has been selected because it is surrounded by a slowly rotating and blinking border. If you, for example, wanted to paint with the Paintbrush tool and had an area selected, you could only paint within that selected area. That said, it's about time you learned how to make your own selections.

Rectangular Marquee Selection

One of the most basic and common methods of selection is the Marquee tool, found in the topmost left-hand corner of the toolbar. By default, it is the Rectangular Selection tool. You can select simple, four-sided selections using the Rectangular Marquee Selection tool by following these instructions:

Select the Rectangular Marquee Selection tool from the toolbar, or if it isn't currently selected, press 'M.'

Make certain that you're on the correct layer that you want to manipulate and that the layer's **Preserve Transparency** check box is not checked.

Drag-click a rectangle that encapsulates the area you wish to select.

Modify the selected area using the rest of the Photoshop tools, as shown in Figure 8.1.

You can control how the Selection Marquee behaves depending on what key you have depressed at the time of selection. Table 8.1 lists some of the more common behaviors:

TABLE 8.1   **Universal modifiers to the Marquee Select command.**

Key Depressed	Effect
Shift Select	If creating a new selection, this constrains a selection to a square. If a selection exists, this adds a shape to that selection.
Alt [Command] Select	If creating a new selection, this draws a selection from the center instead of the corner edge. If a selection exists, this subtracts a shape from that selection.
Control Select	This allows you to move the selected area around the layer. If no area is selected, it moves the entire layer.

The Marquee Select is a powerful tool within its own boundaries. For example, it's ideal for easily delineated spaces that need either filling or deleting. For more complex structures, you can add or subtract shapes from the selection using the Shift and Alt keys.

Even with these options, the **Rectangular Marquee** is something of an inflexible tool. However, you can configure it further by using the Options palette, pictured in Figure 8.2.

FIGURE 8.2

You can determine how the marquee is drawn using the Options palette.

From the Marquee Options palette, you can set several settings:

- **Feather**—Determines how many pixels a selection is *feathered*. A feathered selection has a fringe or haze of pixels around its defined border. The higher this number, the less defined your selection edges will be.

- **Style**—This picklist determines how the Marquee tool actually draws. The **Normal** option lets you drag and pull marquee shapes as you normally would. **Constrained Aspect Ratio** makes the marquee expand at a set ratio, which you fill in below the pick list. If both the height and width fields are set to 1, then you'll only be able to select perfect squares. If height is set to 2 and width to 1, for every one pixel wide your selection is, it will also be two pixels tall. Finally, you can choose a **Fixed Size** for your selection, which is handy when you need to produce identically-sized images.

Elliptical Marquee Selection

If you need to select an area that is not rectangular in shape (a common occurrence), then perhaps the Elliptical Selection Marquee will fulfill your needs. Essentially it's the round equivalent to the Rectangular Marquee. Instead of defining squares or rectangles, you're selecting ovals and circles.

First of all, you need to determine how to choose the Elliptical Selection tool. By default, the Rectangular Marquee is always selected until you decide otherwise. There are two ways to change which marquee you're using. The first is a simple mouse click away. Click the Marquee tool while holding down the mouse button, and then mouse slightly to the right of the button. A small extended list should appear. Mouse over the oval selection and let go of the mouse button. You should now have the Elliptical Marquee tool chosen.

Selecting an Elliptical Marquee is identical to the Rectangular Marquee mentioned previously, up to and including the use of Control to move, Alt (Command) to subtract, and Shift to add to your selection. You can also set identical parameters from the Options palette, including the feather depth, style, width, and height. An option unavailable in the Rectangular Marquee Options palette, the **Anti-Aliased** check box becomes active for the Elliptical Marquee. This check box controls how "jaggy" a selection looks, especially if it's been feathered. This option is meant specifically for cut, copy, and paste operations.

If you want to copy and then paste an oval selection to another layer, or even another document, you may want to have the **Anti-Aliased** check box on or off, depending on what your eventual goal is. If you want the copied selection to have a very smooth, fuzzy feel around the edges, then leave **Anti-Aliasing** on. If you want a sharp, clearly-delineated cut, then you'd turn the **Anti-Aliased** option off.

Single Row and Column Marquee Selection

The single row and column Marquee Selection tools are essentially short cuts for the Rectangular Marquee. If you want a selection that is only one pixel wide or one pixel tall, then these two tools are the ones for you. The single row and column tools create a line that stretches the entire width or height or your document but are only one pixel tall or wide.

Scrolling through options

If you don't want to mess about with all that clicking and dragging, you can just press the 'M' key several times while holding down the Shift key to scroll through the four **Marquee** options.

For example, if you select the single row Marquee tool and click somewhere within your document, you'll get a selection that covers the entire width of the image and is only one pixel tall. The reverse is true if you use the single column Marquee tool. You can still use the Shift key to add to a selection, the Alt (Command) key to subtract from a selection, and the Control key to move a selection, but unlike the other Marquee commands there are no options to modify.

The question then remains, when would you use such a tool? By itself, not very often. It's rare that you need just a one-pixel line stretching from side to side of an image. However, when used in combination with other Selection tools, the single column and row Marquee tools become more practical. If you have an elliptical selection that has a line or series of lines radiating from it, you can use a column or row to add to it. The single column and row Marquee tools are meant more for generating shapes than selecting existing ones.

Mass Selecting Using the Crop Tool

Cropping tip

If you already have an area of the image selected, clicking with the Crop tool deselects it. You'll have to click again to enter Cropping mode.

Although not specifically one of the Marquee tools, the Crop tool is grouped alongside them because it uses a similar method for selection. Imagine the Crop tool as a variable-sized box that you drop on your picture. Everything inside the box stays; everything outside gets discarded.

Crop an Image

1. Select the Crop tool by either pressing "C" or holding down the mouse button over the **Marquee** button. Then mouse slightly to the right and select the Crop tool from the resulting expanded list (it's the last one on the right).

2. Draw a rectangle using the Crop tool to define which area stays in your image. Don't forget that you can resize, rotate, or change the rotation center of the cropping area by manipulating the handles on each side of the box, shown in Figure 8.3.

3. Press Enter to confirm that the area you've selected is what you want to crop to. Conversely, if you want to get out of Cropping mode without changing the image, press Escape.

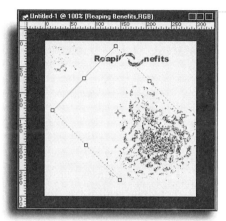

FIGURE 8.3

By changing the center of rotation, you can cause the cropping box to move around a different point.

When in Cropping mode, you can influence the cropping box in several ways. First, if you move the pointer around *outside* the cropped area, you have the ability to rotate the cropping box around a central axis, with the addition of the Shift key constraining the rotation to 15 degree increments. If you mouse *inside* the cropping box, you'll have the ability to move that central axis, with the addition of the Shift key constraining along 45 degree vectors. Finally, if you move the handles on the edges of the cropping area, you can scale the amount of image you wish to retain, with the addition of the Shift key constraining the scaling effect to a perfect square.

Cropping and rotating

If you rotate the crop area to a non-perpendicular angle, you'll still end up with a right-angle "square" image. The crop process simply rotates the canvas to suit your new angle.

Like the Rectangular Marquee, the Crop tool has a powerful set of options associated with it for sizing an image. The Crop Options palette is shown in Figure 8.4.

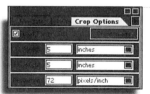

FIGURE 8.4

You can enter an exact size when cropping, instead of just eyeballing like the old days.

The Crop Options palette deals with getting an exact figure on how much image you wish to retain and how much you wish to discard. The options break down as follows:

- **Fixed Target Size**—Without this check box being active, you can't access any of the other **Crop** options.
- **Height, Width,** and **Resolution**—These three values determine the eventual size and resolution of the cropped image. You can select from a variety of units.
- **Front Image**—This option automatically inserts the values (height, width, resolution) from the selected layer into the Option palette, setting the values for the new image.

It's important to note that the Height, Width, and Resolution fields do not in any way influence the size of the cropping area. Instead, Photoshop takes the area you crop and jams it into the defined area. For example, if you define an area five inches wide by five inches tall, and the area you select is only three inches wide by three inches high, then you'll end up with a 5 x 5 image that looks like it's been slightly enlarged. Photoshop takes the 3 x 3 information and maps it to your predefined 5 x 5 area.

Selection Using the Lasso Tool

You've already learned that the Marquee tool can be an incredible boon to the selection-hungry user. However, there are still some limitations to it. First of all, Marquee Select really only works well with primitive geometric shapes such as squares, ovals, and single-pixel lines. Secondly, it's possible to create a complex, non-linear selection, but it takes a lot of time and Shift-selecting and Alt-Selecting. If you have a more complex shape, sometimes it's more efficient to trace it out than to block it out using a combination of several shapes.

The Freehand Lasso Tool

Some shapes you can only draw yourself, regardless of how powerful Selection tools ever get. In those cases, you'll want to use the Freehand Lasso tool. If you're faced with a complex selection that resides in one layer (a flattened image from a client for example), you'll probably need something like the Lasso tool to trace out a convoluted outline. In order to do so, you must:

Selecting with the Freehand Lasso tool

1. Choose the layer you wish to make a selection from.

2. Select the Lasso tool.

3. Trace around the shape you wish to select, keeping the mouse button depressed.

4. When you're done, release the mouse button. You should get an irregular shape as shown in Figure 8.5.

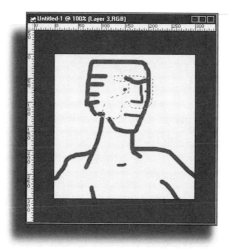

FIGURE 8.5

The **Lasso tool** can be as selective as any line drawing. It can be especially exact with the help of a tablet.

Once again, you can influence the selection by pressing Shift to add to it, Alt [Opt] to subtract from it, or Control to move it. The Lasso tool's Options palette is much simpler than any of the Marquee Selection tools, consisting solely of the capability to control feathering or to turn anti-aliasing on or off.

Lasso autocomplete

If you don't join up the ends of your lassoed selection, Photoshop automatically completes whatever shape you are drawing. This usually has adverse effects, because all Photoshop does is draw a straight line from the beginning point to your end point, sometimes cutting off the very areas you wanted to select.

The Polygonal Lasso Tool

The Polygonal Lasso tool draws your selection as a series of straight lines. Every time you click the mouse you create a point that you can use to change the direction of the line that makes up your selection. In order to close a Polygonal Lasso selection, you must pull the cursor close enough to the start of the selection that a small "o" appears near the Polygonal tool icon. If you press the Alt [Opt] key while creating a selection with the Polygonal Lasso tool, it converts to the Freehand Lasso tool for the time that you hold the key down. By the same token, if you use the Freehand Lasso and hold down Alt [Opt], the tool becomes the Polygonal Lasso tool.

The Magnetic Lasso Tool

The Magnetic Lasso tool starts getting into a different area than the traditional Lasso tool. The annoying thing about either Lasso tool is the fact that Photoshop could care less if you stuck inside the lines or not. Generally if you're selecting something with the Lasso tool, it's very important that you stay within the lines. The Magnetic Lasso tool lets you do so automatically.

You set it up like any other Lasso, except in this case the selection path tends to "stick" to something that's been drawn in that layer. For example, if you draw the Magnetic Lasso nearby an existing line, the selection line snaps to that line. The power of this is obvious; it allows you to make exacting, complex selections by mousing in the same general area of the image you want outlined. The only thing you have to remember is that you have to press Enter to register your selection or else you'll just keep on outlining selection areas 'till you're blue in the hand.

Much like the other Selection methods, the Magnetic Lasso has its own **Options** panel, pictured in Figure 8.6. Because the Magnetic Lasso tool is so powerful, it also has some unique configurability to make it even more helpful.

FIGURE 8.6

The Magnetic Lasso only picks up paths that are beyond a certain contrast threshold when compared to the image's background.

- **Feather** and **Anti-Alias**—These familiar options control the amount of feathering around a selection, and whether or not the selection edges are anti-aliased, respectively.

- **Lasso Width**—This setting controls how "important" a detected edge is versus your actual mouse path. If the option is set at 10 pixels, and you're drawing a lasso 11 pixels away from an existing line, the selection is along the line you draw. If your lasso is nine pixels away from that line, the selection "sticks" to it.

- **Frequency**—This option controls how often the Magnetic Lasso automatically inserts points along its selection line. The more points, the finer things like curves and soft edges will be. More points also gives the Magnetic Lasso less leeway to "backtrack" when you move off of a graphic.

- **Edge Contrast**—This percentage tells the Magnetic Lasso how to decide what's a line and what's a background. If you have this option set at 50%, then lines that are 49% saturated and lighter won't be "sticky," whereas lines 50% and greater will be stuck to by the Magnetic Lasso.

Like the Freehand Lasso, the Magnetic Lasso completes incomplete shapes for you, often causing you to cut out parts of a selection that you meant to keep. When using the Lasso tools, try to keep an "open edge" where you can go off to the side of a selection and make sure that the ends match up, creating a complete shape.

Using the mouse and Magnetic Lasso

It's important to note that you don't have to hold down the mouse button to draw an extended shape like you do with the Freehand Lasso. The Magnetic Lasso continues to draw and seek out existing lines until you either press Enter or Escape. This lets you add another state to button clicks and keyboard combinations.

Finally, the Magnetic Lasso has some added keyboard functionality. While the familiar Shift to add to selection, Alt to subtract from selection, and Control to move selection is still in force, there are two other uses for the Shift and Alt keys.

- Shift constrains the Lasso line to polygonal increments when held down while the mouse button is up.
- Alt forces a selection point to be added wherever you click the mouse and hold down the key.

The reason selection points are important to the Magnetic Lasso is simple; they indicate the last place that a change can take place along the lasso line. If you play around with the Magnetic Lasso, you'll note that it jerks around and sticks to various lines depending on how close your mouse is to those lines. This can make sticking to a definite path difficult, especially if you're equidistant between two different graphics. If you want to guarantee that earlier portions of your lasso line stay intact, you need to define selection points along that path. You can do so either by inserting a high frequency value into the Options palette or by using the Alt-click shortcut to add a selection point to the current location.

Selection Using the Magic Wand

The Magic Wand is quite another tool entirely when compared with the other Selection tools out there. There's no shape for you to draw, no predefined selection area. Like the Magnetic Lasso, the Magic Wand's selections are based entirely upon the image you use it on.

The Magic Wand's operation is quite simple; you click it on an area and the Wand does the rest, seeking out similar pixels that are adjacent to one another. Unlike the Magnetic Lasso, which operates on the principle of non-background colored images, the Magic Wand seeks out any and all pixels nearby the one you selected that happen to share the same color.

Only three real options can modify the Magic Wand tool, all of which are found in the Options palette. First there's the familiar old **Anti-Aliased** check box. Second comes the **Tolerance**, which controls how sensitive the Magic Wand is. The higher the tolerance, the greater the amount of pixels is selected. The lower, the less. Finally comes the **Use All Layers** check box, which determines whether the Magic Wand should make its selection based on the contents of the current layer, or all visible layers.

Experienced users should note that you can hold down Shift while selecting to add to a Magic Wand selection, Alt to subtract from a selection, and Control to move the selected area or layer around.

Utilizing the Select Menu

All of the **Selection** options you've learned about thus far have been visual in nature. That is, you've had to draw a shape or visually define a path around whatever section of an image you want to select. Starting now, that all changes. The **Select** menu contains a variety of options designed to help you regardless of what your selection looks like, big or small. The menu itself is pictured in Figure 8.7.

FIGURE 8.7

Many people overlook the **Select** menu, thinking it only contains an overview of the existing tools they already know. Those people would be wrong.

Selecting non-transparent areas

You can also select all the non-transparent material within a layer by pressing Control + A/Command + A, and then Control/Command and one of the arrow keys. This selects everything that isn't transparent space in that layer.

Global Select Functions

The first four options in the menu deal with **Global Select** options. These options are either on or off, and it's pretty hard for one of them to be used in conjugate with another. Their use and definitions are:

- **Select All** (Control + A/Command + A)—This option does exactly what it says, selects the entire contents of a layer. This is exactly the same as if you had taken the Rectangular Marquee tool and made a selection encompassing the entire visible area of an image.

- **Deselect** (Control + D/Command + D)—This option is the reverse of **Select All** above; it deselects everything. This is exactly the same as single-clicking once with one of the Marquee tools without selecting anything; it resets the selection.

- **Reselect** (Shift + Control + D/Shift + Command + D)— This option is like an **Undo** button for selections exclusively; it reselects the last selected area, even if you've made changed to the image itself since deselection.

- **Inverse** (Shift + Control + I/Shift + Command + I)—This option is invaluable when dealing with complex selections designed to exclude certain parts. Thanks to the **Inverse** menu item, you change selection philosophies. Instead of agonizing to select what segments of an image you want, you can just select what you *don't* want, and then inverse the selection.

Selection by Color Range

Next on the menu comes Color Range, a powerful Selection tool in and of itself. If the Magic Wand selects based on similar colors and pixel adjacency, then the Color Range function picks based solely on colors. It ignores adjacency, instead selecting all pixels within a certain color range within a document. This can be very useful for tasks like trimming out flat-colored backgrounds, modifying certain hues, or even just getting rid of a

color you don't like. The most important tool to use with the
Color Range option is the Color Range picker dialog box, pictured in Figure 8.8.

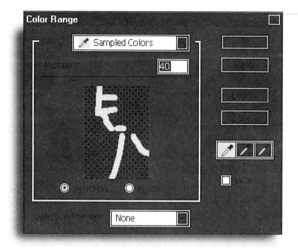

FIGURE 8.8

The Color Range picker can
also select ranges of color in
two ways, by either using a
median based on one color, or
by selecting multiple colors that
are added to a list.

The procedure is simple. You select **Color Range** from the
selection menu, and from there, pick your color either through
the Color Picker or by using the Eyedropper tool on the existing
image. The functionality of the color range Color Picker breaks
down like so:

- **Select**—This drop-down list determines what base range
  you'll be selecting colors from. The default value, Sampled
  Colors, is whatever color(s) you select using the Eyedropper
  tool. The rest of the values are essentially broad ranges of
  color, such as all Reds, Blues, and Greens, or even Shadows,
  Highlights, and Midtones. Use these options if you know
  your color(s) fall within their ranges, but with photographic
  images things are rarely so simple.

Save and load color selections

You can also load and save color selections if you're going to be applying them to more than one document, or even if they're just very complex.

Changing the selection border

There's another handy selection command you can use to get rid of that annoying checkered/flashing border around every selection you make. Press Control [Cmd] + H/Command + H (H is for Hide) to make them go away. Press it again to make them come back.

- **Fuzziness**—This sliding rule determines how "fuzzy" Photoshop's discrimination of your color is. The lower the fuzziness, the more exact Photoshop is in selecting color(s) from the image. The higher the fuzziness, the larger the selection of colors. This option is ideal for cases when you want to select many colors within an associated hue but don't want to pick them out one by one. However, you should be careful; a high fuzziness often selects more than you really want selected.

- **Selection** and **Image** preview methods—These two radio buttons simply toggle between which preview method is used, one based on the colors you've selected, or one simply displaying the affected area of the image.

- **Selection Preview**—This pick list determines which preview method is used on the actual image to show you which pixels and colors have been selected and which have not. You can choose from None, Grayscale, Black Matte, White Matte, and Quick Mask.

- **Eyedropper Tools**—These three options determine how you pick color. The first eyedropper is like the standard Photoshop tool; it selects one color. The second or additive eyedropper selects a color *in addition* to any color you previously had selected. The third or subtractive eyedropper subtracts a color from the list you can build by using the additive eyedropper. Remember that the Fuzziness value influences all the colors you select, not just the current one.

- **Invert**—This check box is similar to the **Invert** menu selection, except in this case it inverts the selected colors.

Modifying Selections

You can already modify selections on a gross scale by using the other Selection tools to add and subtract from a selection. However, you can get more subtle effects by the simple application of some of the **Select** menu's modification functions. These four menu options are explained following:

- **Feather** (Alt[Opt] + Control [Cmd] + D)—This is just like the familiar **Feather** option found on most selection Option palettes. It lets you define a haze around the selection of variable size.

- **Modify**—This option reveals a small subset of modification choices. From here you can cause a selection to expand or contract by a certain amount (measured in pixels). You can also create a border selection or smooth out the rough edges on a jagged selection.

- **Grow**—The **Grow** option causes the selection to grow to the next logical stage. Think of it as the Magic Wand tool that builds upon its previous efforts. Each time you select the **Grow** option it's like adding to the selection with the Magic Wand.

- **Similar**—The **Similar** option is close to Grow in operation but is defined differently. Instead of expanding from a central point, **Similar** seeks out parts of an image that are like one another.

Transforming Selections

New to Photoshop 5.0 is the capability to manipulate selections and *not* the area they represent. This new addition to the **Select** menu operates almost identically to the bounding box found on the Crop tool, explained earlier in this chapter. Once again, the corner and side handles represent the capability to scale the selection. If you click outside the selection, you can rotate it around a central axis, and if you click within the selection, you have the ability to change that axis's position. When you're finally done manipulating the selection, you can either press Enter to accept your changes or Escape to annul them.

It's important to note that these modifications affect only the selection. Your base image remains the same until you make changes to it directly. At this point, you have only changed your selection criteria and not the selection itself.

Loading and Saving Selections

Many of your selections will be complex procedures that you don't want to duplicate again. Thankfully, Photoshop has the capability to save and retrieve your selections by storing them as channels.

SEE ALSO

➢ *For more information about channels, see Chapter 20, "Manipulating Color and Mask Channels" on p. 370*

All you have to is make your selection and then choose Save Selection from the **Select** menu. There you fill in the channel name, and voilá, suddenly it appears in your channel display, as shown in Figure 8.9.

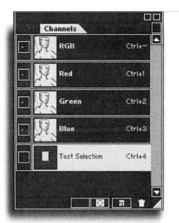

FIGURE 8.9

Color channels can do much
more than store selections. For
example, you can make transparent .GIFs for the Web using
channels.

Loading a selection is just as easy. You go to Load Selection from the
select menu and choose your channel name from those presented.
Click **OK** and voilá, suddenly your selection is back again. This
process is especially handy for difficult selections such as keylines,
Magnetic Lasso selections, and so on.

SEE ALSO

➤   *For more information about channels, see Chapter 20, "Manipulating Color and
    Mask Channels" on p. 370*

Picking and Selecting Color

Use the flexible Color Picker tool

Selecting colors by moving your document

Selecting colors using the Eyedropper

Using The Color Picker

Without color, Photoshop isn't a very useful program. Fortunately, Adobe has included several different methods of selecting and determining color. The most basic, and what will become the most familiar, is the Color Picker. In order to access it, you need only to click the foreground color/background color patches found in the toolbar.

Depending on your configuration, you can use either your operating system's Color Picker or Photoshop 5's. For the sake of efficiency, in this book we'll assume that you're using the default Photoshop Color Picker.

Change or restore the Color Picker

1. Click on the **File** menu, then **Preferences**, and then General.

2. In the resulting dialog, choose your preferred Color Picker from the **Color Pick** drop-down list box. You should be able to choose either Apple (for Macintoshes), Windows (for Windows 95/NT), or any third-party plug-ins that replace the Color Picker.

3. Press **OK** to apply your choice.

The Color Picker is an incredibly flexible tool that lets you select colors in a variety of ways.

Figure 9.1 illustrates the primary Color Picker dialog.

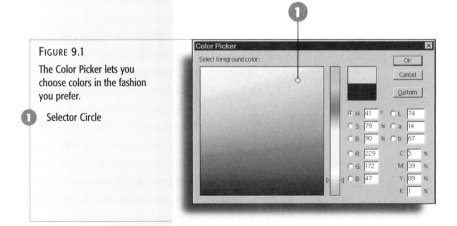

FIGURE 9.1

The Color Picker lets you choose colors in the fashion you prefer.

1 Selector Circle

There are four basic methods of selecting color within the Color Picker dialog. The default system is based around Hue, Saturation, and Brightness.

Figure 9.1 determines which attribute a color is selected by. If the Hue radio button is selected (as is the default), then the slider control located to the right of the color window controls the Hue of the selected color. If Saturation is selected, then moving the slider up or down adjusts the amount of saturation applied to the color. This is true for Hue, Saturation, Brightness, Red, Green, Blue, and LAB (also known as CIELAB).

CMYK Colors are treated differently because they are created expressly for print purposes. Generally you don't work with CMYK as a selection or definition tool; rather you convert an RGB document to the CMYK standard for print output. Because CMYK represents an approximation of ink values, the numbers are represented as percentages and generally don't translate to computer monitors very accurately.

You'll notice that you can enter numbers into the text boxes next to each color attribute descriptor. This allows you to enter exact values when you need to ensure an exact value should be used.

All these acronyms can be confusing and you're probably not sure which system to use. Table 9.1 gives you a little background on each system and why you'd want to use one over another, depending on the situation.

TABLE 9.1   **Color Selection modes and their uses**

Color Mode	Why Use It
HSB	Fast and Convenient, uses familiar "color wheel" methodology
RGB	Internet electronic color standard, exact
LAB	Device-independent, exact
CMYK	Print industry standard, used for universal color reference

The reason all these color systems are incorporated into Photoshop is variety. Different people work with different systems. A Web designer or photo-retoucher may operate exclusively in RGB or HSB color, but a print-based graphic artist may operate exclusively in CMYK. HSB color is used for picking out colors visually, when you know you want a red and can 'see' it in the back of your mind. RGB color is used primarily for common color definitions, because colors can be easily and conveniently represented in hexadecimal notation. CMYK color is used for rendering colors to print. Lastly, LAB color is used when it's imperative that a color be a certain value, independent of whatever device its being displayed on, be it a monitor or printer. Because color and its measurement are so relative, pure mathematics models like LAB color are required in some instances.

Finally, you can also use a series of predefined colors designed primarily for print purposes. The power behind these custom colors is that they're generally "agreed" upon as a standard by various print industry parties. Monitor resolutions and color depths vary so much it's impossible to have a consistent color across every system. On one computer a color appears red, and on another it looks orange. Not only that, but what appears on your screen rarely looks that way on paper.

Essentially, the custom colors are designed to let you use a standard color that most printers are confident they can reproduce. You might struggle to describe "Rose Red" to your local printer, but you know for certain he'll understand what "PANTONE 123-1 Process" means. In order to select from a predefined list of custom colors you must:

Selecting custom colors

1. Bring up the Color Picker by clicking the foreground or background color swatch.

2. Bring up the custom colors dialog by clicking the <u>C</u>ustom button (as shown in Figure 9.2).

3. From there, select whichever CMYK color you want, from one of the color books included with Photoshop 5 (ANPA Color Guide, DIC Color Guide, FOCOLTONE, PANTONE, TOYO, and TRUMATCH).

   Click **OK** to choose the selected color *OR* click the **Picker** button to return to the standard Color Picker.

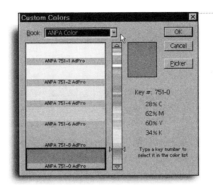

FIGURE 9.2

The Custom Colors dialog lets you choose colors that have already been defined and used by most print shops.

Color Selection Using the Eyedropper Tool

The Color Picker is fine if you already know what color to use, but what if you're trying to match an existing color? You could place the Color Picker next to whatever color you're trying to define and simply plug away until you finally get the numbers right, or you could just use the Eyedropper tool.

What the Eyedropper tool does is take color information from an existing pixel and make that information current. If you click a red rose image using the Eyedropper tool, your foreground color becomes that exact shade of red. In order to select a color in this fashion you must:

Sampling with the Eyedropper tool

1. Either click the Eyedropper tool button in the button bar, or use the **I** hotkey to select the dropper.

2. Mouse over the area you want to get color from and left-click.

3. To set the background color, hold down the Alt key when clicking.

Using the Color Sampler Tool

New to Photoshop 5 is the Color Sampler tool, which takes the traditional role of the Eyedropper tool and turns it upside down. Instead of the usual method of mousing over a color and then

Sampling exactly what you want

The Eyedropper tool is very exact, which means it can be very frustrating. Be careful when mousing over very specific areas of color. Also keep in mind that the dropper reports only the color of the pixel it's currently pointing at, and at low Zoom levels it's hard to tell which pixel is which. In order to get around this, you can hold down the mouse button while mousing over colored areas. The foreground color will be updated for each pixel you pass over.

selecting it, the Color Sampler instead puts the dropper in a static point and forces you to move the image around. This is especially useful for small areas where you need an exact color. In order to select a color using the Color Sampler you must:

Taking multiple samples

1. Click the Eyedropper tool or press **I**.

2. Select an area that you wish to monitor the color in and then Shift-click.

In choosing the area you wish to sample, you can make a mistake or you can decide to monitor another area. If you press Ctrl [Cmd] while clicking a Color Sampler icon, you can move the Sampler to another area and its the icon changes to show it's being moved. To remove a Color Sampler icon, press Shift + Alt [Opt] while clicking the offending icon; scissors appear to indicate the icon is being cut.

Now look at the Info palette and see how it's expanded to accommodate a new field that describes the color wherever you placed the Color Sampler points (as shown in Figure 9.3). If you do not see the Info palette displayed, go to Window on the menu and choose Show Info.

3. Press the Ctrl [Cmd] key and press the direction arrows on the keyboard. This moves the image in the direction of the arrow you choose in one-pixel increments each time you press the key.

After you've moved the image around to get your readings, *don't* forget to move the image back!

4. Note the Info palette. The values change each time the image moves. When you have the color values you need, write them down (for example: R: 256, G: 256, B: 256).

5. Next open the Color Picker by clicking the foreground color swatch. In order to select the color described in the Color Sampler, you need to enter the exact RGB/HSB/LAB/CMYK values into the Color Picker.

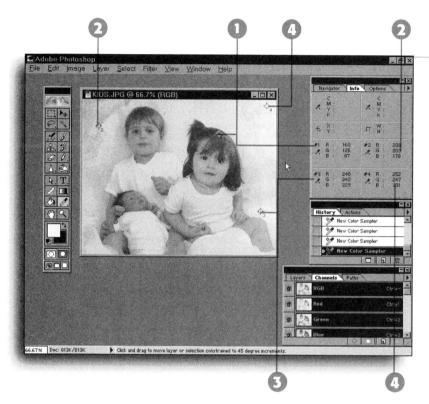

FIGURE 9.3.

You can have up to four Color
Samplers before running out of
room on the Info palette.

1 Color 1

2 Color 2

3 Color 3

4 Color 4

Painting and Drawing

Learn about some of the basic tools you'll be using and their decidedly complex natures

Learn how to configure brushes to the sizes and characteristics you want

Create your own tools, and learn how to save and load them

Set up your tablet

Tools of the Trade

You have a variety of tools at your disposal when using Photoshop to create images. This rogue's gallery of functions can be your best friend, or your most inscrutable barrier. Learning to use these tools if vital. Now let's try a simple run through.

Testing out the Airbrush, Paintbrush, Pencil, and Line tools

1. Open a new document by choosing the File menu and selecting **New**. Enter a **Width** of 5 inches, a **Height** of 7 inches, and a **Resolution** of 72 pixels/in. Press **OK**.

2. Choose the Airbrush tool from the Toolbox or press the J key.

3. Select any brush from the middle row. If the Brushes palette is not displayed, choose the **Windows** menu and select **Show Brushes**.

4. Press the D key to bring up the **Default** colors, **Black** and **White**.

5. Start airbrushing! Make a couple of start and stop movements, and hold the Airbrush tool in one spot while still spraying to see what happens.

Photoshop's Airbrush tool is nearly as good as the real thing when it comes to airbrushes—all the resolution and none of the smelly clean up of the real thing. Use the **Airbrush** tool to create highlights and shadows, or to add emphasis to already existing areas of flat color.

6. Press the B key or choose the Paintbrush tool from the Toolbox. Select the largest brush in the top row of brushes; it's on the far right.

7. Paint with the Paintbrush. Make zigs and zags and anything you can think of, but leave some space! You're about to move on.

The Paintbrush is your general all-purpose tool for filling areas. You can paint huge swatches of solid color or experiment with water-coloresque settings.

8. Choose the Pencil tool from the toolbar (or press N); if the Line tool is displayed, choose the Pencil by activating the rollout. Place the cursor in the Toolbox cell and gently slide it until the rollout appears.

9. Select the same size brush as you used for the **Paintbrush**.

10. Draw! Draw! Draw! Note how the edge of the Pencil is harder than the Paintbrush. You're not through yet!

Lacking the soft edges of the Paintbrush, the Pencil creates hard-edged, non anti-aliased lines.

11. Choose the Line tool from the Toolbox. Open the Options palette by double-clicking on the Line tool in the Toolbox. Enter a **Line Weight** of 6 pixels.

12. Make wacky lines.

The **Line** tool had a cell all to its own in previous versions of Photoshop, but its new home is a smart place. It's a tool you might not need much of the time, but sometimes you'll have a job that only the Line tool can handle.

Painting Tool Options Palette

All of the previous items have been lumped together because they all operate under the same general principles within Photoshop. All of the attributes for the Airbrush, Paintbrush, and Pencil are controlled from one simple dialog box, the Tool Options, shown in Figure 10.1.

The first setting is the **Mode** drop-down list, which by default is set to **Normal**. Table 10.1 shows a brief description of each mode and what it does.

FIGURE 10.1

By using the Options palette of a tool, you can wildly vary the look and feel of your document.

TABLE 10.1   **Breakdown of brush modes**

Mode	Description
Normal	"Normal" paint mode, like any other program.
Dissolve	Adds a diffuse, frayed edge to the area painted.
Behind	Paints "behind" current layer, filling only transparent areas.
Multiply	Uses color additively, by multiplying their color values. When painting over other colors, the two combine and always produce a darker color.
Screen	Like painting with a universal lightener, **Screen** applies a slightly brighter color to whatever color its painting over.
Overlay	Applies color only over existing colors, as if a transparent gel had been placed between the light source and the canvas.
Soft Light and **Hard Light**	Duplicates the effect of differing intensity light sources while painting. Soft light darkens or lightens, depending on your chosen color. Hard light multiplies.

Mode	Description
Color Dodge	Emulates a "dodging" effect in terms of color intensity, resulting in lighter colors (depending on the color you paint with).
Color Burn	Simulates "burning" a photographic image, resulting in darker colors (depending on what you paint with).
Darken	Only paints in areas where your chosen color is darker than the background color on that layer.
Lighten	Only paints in areas where your chosen color is lighter than the background color on that layer.
Difference	Takes the difference between the color you're painting with and the color you're painting over and applies that difference to the painted area.
Exclusion	Very similar to **Difference**, yet a smoother color transition. When painted on white, the color reverses.
Hue	Resulting color has the same luminance and saturation as the original but the hue of your chosen color.
Saturation	Resulting area has the luminosity and hue of the original but the saturation of your chosen color.
Color	Resulting color has the luminosity of the original but the hue and saturation of your chosen color.
Luminosity	Resulting color has the hue and saturation as the original but the luminosity of your chosen color.

You can apply all of these paint modes to any of the drawing tools mentioned in this chapter—and in several other places. It's important to note though, that you don't have to memorize each and every mode, because you can achieve the same affects through other methods. There is no one best way to do things in Photoshop.

The brush **Opacity** setting controls how transparent or "see-through" the brush is while you paint with it. It operates on a sliding scale between 0 and 100 per cent.

Next comes the **Fade** options. A Fade is when you start out with your selected color and slowly fade to either transparent or the background color. Fading effects can be especially useful for shading, quick gradients, and even highlights. The first area

Using Fade from the Options palette with the Painting and drawing tools

If you use the **Fade** option, remember that after the brush has "faded" it stays transparent until you let go of the mouse button and begin a new stroke.

defines how many steps are in a complete fade. This determines how "smooth" your transition is from one state to the next. If you have several steps, your transition from color to transparent or background will be almost unnoticeable in the short run. If you have two steps, the transition will be readily apparent. Below that is the drop-down list that determines whether the color fades to transparent or your currently selected background color. Lastly, you see the **Wet Edges** check box, which only appears on the Paintbrush options palette. This controls whether you paint with a wet or dry medium. With wet edges turned on, you can duplicate a variety of watercolor paint effects, as well as paint additively.

Turn Back Time with the History Brush

In terms of actual brush size and configuration, the History Brush is nearly identical to the traditional Paintbrush tool. Where it differs is that the History Brush doesn't actually paint any new pixels; it paints pixels from a past iteration of that image. Notice a new feature to Photoshop 5.0 in the palette containing the Actions tab; the History tab is shown in Figure 10.2.

FIGURE 10.2

The **History** option finally grants a multiple undo functionality that Photoshop users have been wanting for years.

The first and most obvious use of the **History** tab is that you can undo your mistakes for several generations, but in this case, it's the application of the **History Brush** that you're concerned with. The **History Brush** paints pixels from a previous version of your image onto the contemporary version. However, you need to tell Photoshop which previous version of the document to paint from.

Testing the History Brush

1. Select the **History** tab, either by clicking on it or by using the **Windows** menu and selecting the **Show History** option.

2. Click in the small empty box directly left of an existing History item. If you haven't done anything in this document, there won't be any history items to modify. When you properly select a History item, the **History Brush** icon appears next to the History item.

3. Select the **History Brush** tool by clicking on the appropriate button or by pressing the Y key.

4. Paint whatever you like from your previous image's incarnation onto the contemporary document.

Unique to the **History Brush** is the **Impressionist** check box. This option takes whatever source color is picked up by the **History Brush** and uses it to create quasi-impressionist effects such as rapid color cycles or smears. The effect is very similar to using the **Smudge** tool.

The **History Brush** is an incredible update to Photoshop's already impressive arsenal of functionality, keep the following in mind when using it:

- **Layers.** Each layer can only contain its own history. That means a change made to a layer in the past can only be "recaptured" using the **History Brush** *on that layer*. Unfortunately, each layer doesn't have its own unique history, so you have to be very careful when deciding which History item to base your painting on.

- **History Items.** The History queue doesn't stretch on forever, so if you're going to do something with the **History Brush,** it's best if you do it on a reasonable time scale. This is also true when you're using the History tab to rollback to previous versions of your image.

- **Painting History.** You can paint history on anything in the History queue, which includes **History Brush** operations themselves! This creates some interesting opportunities for artistic expression and Dada-esque constructions.

Repetition Using the Rubber Stamp and Pattern Stamp

Like the **History Brush**, the Rubber Stamp doesn't actually create new content in your document but rather obtains it from somewhere else. In this case, the "somewhere else" is within your current document. The time frame is constant; unlike the **History Brush**, you can move the actual position of the source pixels.

To define and paint with the Rubber Stamp you have to do the following.

Using the Rubber Stamp tool

1. Select the Rubber Stamp tool either by clicking on in from the main toolbar or pressing the S key.

2. Hold down the Alt/Option key and click within the area you want to duplicate.

3. Paint in the area you want to fill with duplicated material just as you would with the **History Brush**. Note that you have two cursors, one to indicate where you're painting, and another to indicate where you're painting *from*.

There are two options you can set from the **Rubber Stamp Options** tab. The first is the **Use All Layers** check box. This option lets you sample from all visible layers instead of just one. The second is the **Align** check box, which orients the source cursor depending upon which direction you start painting in. For example, if you start painting horizontally from left to right, the source cursor appears below the destination cursor, but still at the same distance you originally sampled it at.

Grouped with the Rubber Stamp tool is a subtool, the Pattern Stamp. The idea is the same, except in this case, the Pattern Stamp uses a predefined pattern as opposed to an existing section of your image. However, in order to use the **Pattern Brush,** you first need to define a pattern.

Be careful!

The Rubber Stamp tool can transcend layers. It's possible to use one layer as a source for the Rubber Stamp and paint on another entirely, if you have the **Use All Layers** box checked in the **Options** palette. It's also possible to forget that this is possible and confuse yourself entirely when you keep on painting from the wrong layer. Always remember which layer you're working on and which you're working from.

Trying the Pattern Brush

1. Marquee select a rectangular area to define as a pattern.

2. Choose the **Edit** menu and select **Define Pattern**.

Some tips to keep in mind when defining patterns: Make sure the pattern can be repeated without looking ugly. Most patterns are simply geometric shapes. Size can also be a consideration, although only on lower-end systems. The pattern occupies RAM space until purged, so if you're carrying around a 32-bit color, 1024×768 pixel pattern, you might notice a difference. You can purge pattern information from the **Edit** menu.

Now that you have defined a pattern, you are ready to paint with one:

3. Select the Pattern Stamp tool by clicking on the Rubber Stamp tool in the main toolbar and then pulling to the right.

4. Paint your pattern.

Other than the definition phase, the Pattern Stamp is almost identical to the Rubber Stamp. The only difference being that the Pattern Stamp doesn't support the **Use All Layers** option because its sample area is predefined.

Controlling Brush Size and Attributes

You've already learned how to control brush behavior and how to apply different brush types. Now you need to get a handle actually modifying brush sizes and attributes. These instructions can be applied to *all* tools that use brushes. This includes every tool covered in this chapter and some that aren't.

Changing Brush Size

The first thing to determine is size. All of your brush manipulation will take place from one point, the Brushes tab pictured in Figure 10.3.

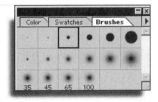

FIGURE 10.3
The **Brushes** tab enables you to control sizes, and even load and save your own brushes.

Different brush settings

Each tool has a different brush setting, so it's easy to get confused. The Paintbrush can have a different brush size than the **History Brush,** and the Rubber Stamp brush can be different than the Pattern Stamp brush. Always make sure you know which brush you're using with which tool. This is also true of the paint modes such as **Normal, Dissolve**, and so on.

If you want to change the size of a brush, you simply click on one of the brush "dots" pictured in Figure 10.3. The harder brushes are mostly for the Paintbrush tool, whereas the brushes with the diffuse halo around them are "softer" and meant for airbrush applications. This isn't to say that you can only use one kind of brush with one kind of tool, but you'll be more effective by using Airbrush brushes with the Airbrush, and so on. Note that if you have the Pencil selected, all the brushes turn "hard" and anti-aliased. This is because the Pencil tool leaves no trailing edges whatsoever and therefore can't duplicate either paintbrush or airbrush effects.

Creating, Saving, Editing, and Loading Brushes

Changing brush size is certainly a powerful ability, but what if you want to define your own brushes? Or change an existing brush to suit your needs? That's where the Brush Options dialog box comes into play.

There are several ways to summon the Brush Options dialog box, depending on what you want to do to a brush. To create a new brush, double-click in the open gray area in the Brushes palette. To modify an existing brush, double-click on the brush you want to change.

Creating your own brush

1. First, choose the Airbrush tool by pressing the J key.

2. Open the Brush options by double-clicking inside the gray area on the Brushes palette.

3. Start by sliding the **Diameter** bar back and forth a couple of times. Now enter a value of 100 pixels in the **Box** next to the bar.

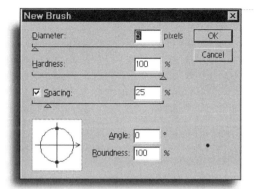

4. Move down to the **Hardness** bar and slide that around, just to see how it effects the brush. Type a **Hardness** value of 42%.

5. Type in a value of 25% in **Spacing** and make sure the box is checked next to the slider. You can play with the slider, but you won't see anything happen.

6. In the lower-left area is a representation outline of the brush you're making. Click on a black dot in the image and slide it up and down. Make the brush as narrow as you can.

7. Grab the arrow indicator with your cursor and spin the brush around. Make the arrow point straight up.

8. Click **OK** and try out the new brush you just made.

9. Open up the Brush Options dialog box again by clicking on the icon of the brush you made in the Brushes palette.

10. Deselect the **Spacing** button and click **OK**. Try your brush now. Do you like this better? You can keep going back until you find what you like.

Another way to access Brush Options is to click on the triangle on the upper-right corner of the Brushes palette, which opens the **Brushes** menu, where you may choose Brush Options.

FIGURE 10.5

Some of the functions found on the **Brushes** menu can be accessed only from this point.

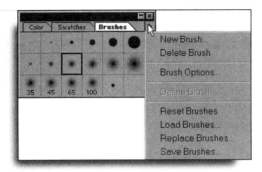

This menu is central brush control for you, as it lets you load, delete, create, and save brushes. Table 10.2 explains the functions.

TABLE 10.2   Breakdown of Brush menu functions

Function	Description
New Brush	Opens the Brush Options dialog box to create a new brush.
Delete Brush	Deletes the brush from that set.
Brush Options	Opens the **Brush Options** menu for the selected brush.
Define Brush	Converts a grayscale image to a brush. You must first select the area you want to use as a brush with a marquee or lasso for this option to become active.
Reset Brushes	Returns brushes to their default state.
Load Brushes	Loads up an additional set of brushes.
Replace Brushes	Replaces current brush sets with what you load.
Save Brushes	Saves current brush set.

When it comes to loading and saving, the lowest common denominator for brushes is the set. You can't load up a single brush (unless you deleted the rest of the set, which would be wasteful). Photoshop 5.0 includes a few standard brush sets, including square brushes, shaded brushes, and a miscellaneous grab bag. You should note the difference between loading brushes and replacing brushes. Loading brushes appends them to the end of the existing brushes list. Replacing them removes all the existing brushes (saved or not) and puts the new set in by itself.

Enabling Tablet Support

If you're lucky enough to have a tablet installed on your system, it's quite easy to get it working in Photoshop. You may notice certain settings at the bottom of some of the Tool Option palettes such as Stylus: Pressure, like those shown (grayed out) in Figure 10.6.

FIGURE **10.6**

The stylus settings are easy and intuitive and can be set on a tool-to-tool level.

The following table lists all of these stylus options, where they're found, and what they influence.

TABLE 10.3   **Breakdown of stylus options**

Option	Description	Where You Find It
Size	Tablet pressure determines brush size	**Paintbrush, Stamp, History Brush, Eraser, Pencil, Blur, Dodge**
Opacity	Tablet pressure determines brush opacity	**Paintbrush, Stamp, History Brush, Eraser, Pencil**
Color	Tablet pressure determine color (between background and foreground)	**Paintbrush, Airbrush, Pencil**
Pressure	Tablet pressure determines tool intensity	**Airbrush, Blur, Dodge**
Exposure	Tablet pressure determines amount of light exposure	**Dodge, Burn**

Warning!

While it's easy to set up tablet settings within Photoshop, sometimes it's hard to go back to using the mouse again. If you have the tablet settings on and then start using the mouse, you'll get some strange results. Always remember to turn off tablet sensitivity when you stop using it.

Each of these options is simply set as you use the tool, and the power granted by using them is considerable. If you want to, you can only have one attribute of a paintbrush controlled by tablet pressure, and the rest can be at a "default" solid mouse state, which makes illustration and line drawing much simpler.

Creating Text

Text and Photoshop

The idea of using text in Photoshop has always been a compromise at best—and a disaster at worst. In the pre 3.0 days before there were layers, placing text in a document had the effect of casting it in stone, in that it became immovable and absolute. You couldn't change the size, changing the color was a project, and heaven help you if you misspelled anything.

It wasn't Photoshop's fault or anything; it was simply behaving like a bitmap program was supposed to behave. The good news is that Adobe didn't rest on convention, and it set out to overcome the shortcomings imposed by working within a bitmap environment. They created layers in 3.0, which addressed the problem with overwriting the material beneath it, as it allowed the blocks of type to be repositioned.

Although this was a step in the right direction, things were still problematic. You couldn't control leading and tracking at all, kerning was a project, and correcting a misspelling meant trashing the text and starting over. Photoshop just wasn't delivering the text controls that designers were used to in all the other applications. Much of that goes away in version 5.0.

The 5.0 Changes

We all knew that Adobe understood which text controls were needed. After all, they gave us outstanding text capabilities in Illustrator and PageMaker. Photoshop 5 begins to catch up with its siblings with the capability to control text in a number of different ways. Although this chapter explores all these changes in great detail, the next paragraph or two summarizes what's new in the Photoshop 5 type tools.

Adobe added three new type tools, offering a type masking tool, a vertical type tool, and a vertical type masking tool. In addition, Adobe offers enhanced formatting controls in the type dialog box, and the box itself has been redesigned to be easier to use.

One of the biggest additions to the 5.0 type features is the ability to preview text formatting before you exit the type dialog box. Type in the box and the text appears in your image. Change the color, size, or font, and the changes update in the image in real-time. You can even move your cursor into the image area with the type dialog box open, and click and drag to move the type. In addition, Photoshop creates the type in a special type layer that remains editable at all times. All this is a far cry from the days when placing type in an image was considered risky business.

Creating Text in Photoshop

This section progresses from simple to complex type creation— adding text, reformatting and repositioning the type as we go. I outline all this using the standard Horizontal Type tool, and we'll touch on the Vertical tool afterward. All the formatting and preview options apply to the vertical as well as the horizontal.

Horizontal Type Placement

I'm going to walk through the creation of a poster that requires various type treatments to get its message across. In the process, we look at the various formatting and editing options within the Photoshop type controls. I'm going to use an image with strong contrasts and solid areas of color that support type elements, allowing them to display and read clearly. Start by getting some text into the image.

Adding type to an image

1. Select the Horizontal Type tool from the Toolbox and click in the middle of the image.

2. In the Type Tool dialog box that appears, type the words `Interiors, an photography exhibit by Bill Smith` (see Figure 11.1) Notice that the type appears in the window as you type.

3. If the type is too large or too small for the image, drag your cursor over it in the dialog box to select it and add a larger or smaller type size in the **Size** window.

4. If the type fits in the image, but not in the dialog box, check the **Fit in Window** check box to shrink it to fit.

5. Click **OK** to apply the effect.

When you add type to an image, Photoshop automatically adds a new layer, with the same name as the text that is entered. In this case, the Interiors layer appears above the background layer, as shown in Figure 11.2. Although it's nice to have text on the screen, we obviously have some changes to make; we need to move it and resize it.

Moving text in an image

1. In the Layers palette, select the type layer to be moved. In this case, select the **Interiors** type layer.

2. Select the Move tool.

3. Click on the type in the image and drag it to the upper-left corner (see Figure 11.3).

Now that the text is where we need it, the next task it to change its size so that it fills the space. We will go in and edit the text layer we just created in order to refine the type effect.

FIGURE 11.2
The basic text entry.

FIGURE 11.3
Drag the text into position.

1. Double-click the **Interiors** layer to reopen the dialog box. Notice that the settings remain exactly as we left them when we closed the box (see Figure 11.4).

FIGURE 11.4

Double-click the type layer to relaunch the Type tool dialog box.

2. Select the word Interiors, in the dialog box to highlight it.

3. Increase the font size in the **Size** box, experimenting with different sizes until it looks right on screen.

4. Move your cursor into the image and click and drag the type into position, relative to the image (see Figure 11.5).

5. Now we need to move the remainder of the text to the next line so that it functions as a subhead. To do this, click to place your cursor after the word Interiors, and press Return. Click **OK** to apply the changes.

FIGURE 11.5
Move the cursor into the image
and reposition the type.

By Photoshop standards, we have a lot with type, but we're not finished yet. The subhead is a bit too close to the word Interiors, and the line is a bit short. It would be nice to stretch it out to fill under the entire headline. We can do these actions using **Leading** (pronounced "leh-ding") and **Tracking**. Leading controls the spacing between lines of text, and tracking is the spacing on an entire line, expressed as the spaces between the words. Both of these controls use points as a unit of measure.

Setting leading and tracking

1. Double-click the **Interiors** layer, reopening the Type Tool dialog box.

2. Highlight the subhead text by clicking and dragging your cursor over the words.

3. Click your cursor inside the **Leading** box and enter a value relative to the point size of the font. Typically, look for the leading to be 20%–30% more than the type size, depending

on the font to be used. In this case, I entered a leading value of 45 for a font size of 20 points, but you can experiment with different values until the spacing looks right.

4. With the subhead still highlighted, click in the **Tracking** box and enter a tracking value. In this case, 50 points gives me the word spacing I need to align with the upper word.

5. As a final tweak for this session, place you cursor after the comma and delete it (Figure 11.6). Click **OK** to apply the corrections.

FIGURE 11.6

The results of setting the leading and tracking.

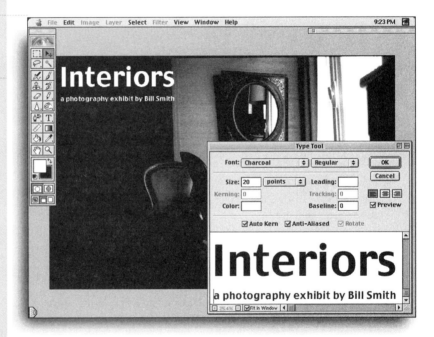

Additional controls you should be aware of in the Type Tool dialog box are **Kerning**, **Baseline**, and **Color**. These controls are explained next, rounding out the details for the Type Tool dialog box.

The *baseline* value shifts the position of the baseline for the text up or down depending on whether you enter a positive or negative number. A positive number moves the baseline up, and a negative number moves it down. At first glance, baseline appears to do the same thing as leading, but with some subtle differences. The main one is that leading always applies itself to the entire line of text, whereas baseline can be applied to a word, or even a character. This extends even further in that leading always affects the lines that follow. For example, if you open up the leading on one line, the lines beneath it move down as well, maintaining some consistency. Baseline moves the line or word independently, without moving the surrounding lines or words.

In the same way that tracking controls the spacing between words, kerning controls the spacing between letters. Again, positive or negative values move letters further apart or closer together. To apply kerning, click the cursor between the two letters you want to modify and enter the value in the **Kerning** box. Kerning can get pretty tricky, and if you're not careful, you can have text and letters going in all directions. If you're not comfortable with kerning, try selecting the **Auto Kern** check box, which creates a degree of even spacing throughout the text.

You also need to leave the **Anti-Aliased** box checked for smooth text edges, and you usually want to leave the left text alignment where it is. Now that you can reposition type so freely, the alignment controls are less of an issue—at least for small blocks of text. Although the preceding examples didn't touch directly on color changes, don't forget about them. Clicking the **Color** box opens the Photoshop Color Picker, letting you select the colors you want using a real-time preview in the image.

As a final note, don't forget to exploit the new font controls. The Font Selection pop-up menu at the top of the dialog box allows you to use any font on your system for new or selected text. This means that you can select a letter at a time and apply a different font or formatting change.

Vertical Type Placement

Adobe added a Vertical Type tool to the toolset with Photoshop 5. This tool does pretty much what you expect: you type text and its arranged vertically up the image rather than across it.

The Auto Kern default

Photoshop checks the **Auto Kern** box by default. This box disables the standard kerning control, which shows as being grayed out. To enter custom kerning values, be sure to deselect the **Auto Kern** check box and click your cursor between the appropriate letters.

Generally speaking, you will find that vertical type takes up much more room that horizontal, given that most type is taller than it is wide. This means that you might have to reduce the size of the font, even though you're filling a vertical space that's twice as large.

In addition, you should probably stay away from sentences and paragraphs that run up and down. Anything more that a headline is just too hard to read. To show what I mean, I reset the type used in the first set of examples in a vertical space. Notice how difficult it is to read the second line, although the word Interiors remains legible.

Setting vertical type

1. Select the Vertical Type tool. If it is not visible in the Toolbox, click and hold on the Type tool and select it from the pop-out menu that appears (see Figure 11.7).

FIGURE 11.7

Select the Vertical Type tool from the Type Tool pop-out menu.

2. Click in the image to set the starting point for the text and to open the Type Tool dialog box.

3. If you want the baseline for each letter to run vertically, select the Rotate check box, as shown in Figure 11.8.

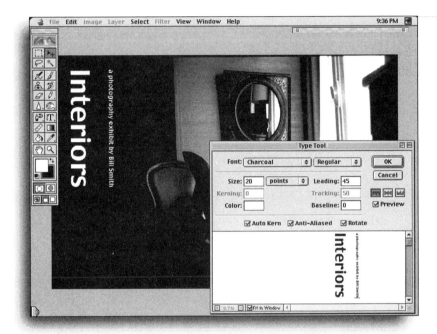

4. Set the type parameters as desired and click **OK**.

Creating Text Masks

Adobe has added a Type Masking tool for both the Vertical and Horizontal Type tools. These tools generate an active type-based selection within the current layer. This works well as an alternative to making a standard selection and selecting the type with some tool, having the edges roughen due to anti-alias artifacts, and spending a considerable amount of time making things look right.

With the Type Mask tools, you simply select the tool, enter the text, and press **OK**. A perfect selection awaits you as soon as the dialog box disappears.

Applying a Gradient

Apply gradients to a layer or an image

Create a single or multicolored gradient

Add transparency to a gradient

Edit an existing gradient or gradient preset

The Gradient Mystique

Gradients are synonymous with computer graphics, right up there with chrome spheres, drop shadows, and checkerboards. In the old days, people couldn't get enough of these objects, which were served up as hearty examples of how the computer could make "art." Although most of us have had our fill of chrome and checkerboards, the gradient and the drop shadow (really just a gradient) are still going strong. In this chapter, we'll take a close look at the right way and the wrong way to put these components to work.

When you think about it, it should come as no surprise that the gradient was so popular with computer imaging. After all, computers follow a certain linear logic as they process data, and gradients are linear mathematical equations, describing the smooth transition from one color or tonality to another. Computers can render gradients fast and easy, and they offer a lot of control along the way. In taking things just a bit further, drop shadows are simply gradients positioned behind an object. Using drop shadows for text is a time-honored tradition, and now that Web design is popular, the drop shadow is making a comeback with the HTML crowd.

What Is a Gradient?

Let me start by giving a simple and direct answer, modifying it into a more complex definition as we go. Gradients are smooth transitions between two colors, where one color fades out and another gradually replaces it. The two colors might also be black and white, shades of gray, or even tonality and transparency. In addition, other colors, tones, or opacities can also be interspersed within the spectrum. This means that you can fade from black to green to transparent and back to white again, creating a banded effect, as shown in Figure 12.1.

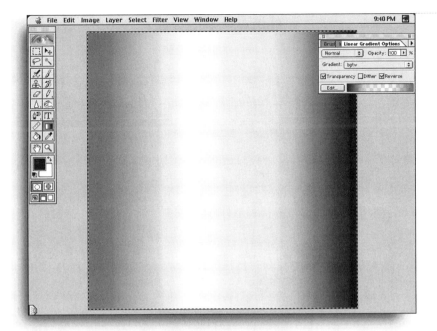

FIGURE 12.1
A gradient can transition between multiple colors and opacities.

A gradient can be either linear or *radial*, in the way the transitions take place. A linear gradient creates straight transitions, moving out in whatever direction is specified. Typical is a horizontal gradient, with tonalities that blend from top to bottom (see Figure 12.2). A radial gradient creates a circular pattern similar to a sunburst, with the transitions emanating out from the center point, as shown in Figure 12.3.

In addition to straight linear and radial patterns, you can also create gradients that are cone shaped, diamond shaped, and that repeat themselves, creating a mirror image effect (see Figure 12.4).

Gradient flexibility

Gradients can be applied to an entire image, inside a selection, behind an object or inside text. Like layers, they can be applied using transparency, and you can apply gradients with apply modes for an even wider range of effects.

FIGURE 12.2

A linear, horizontal gradient. Gradients can also run vertical or at any angle.

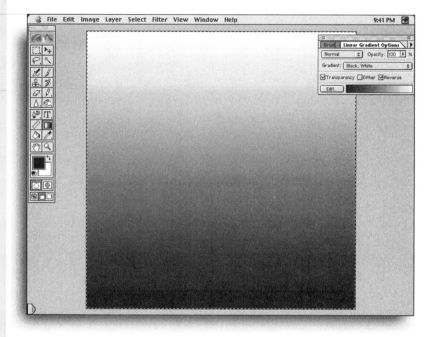

FIGURE 12.3

A radial gradient.

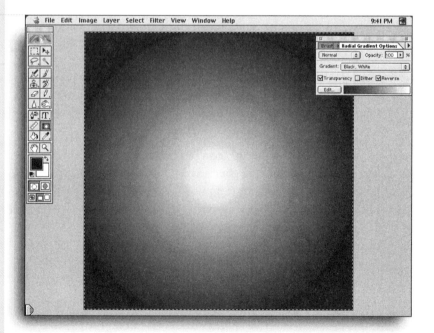

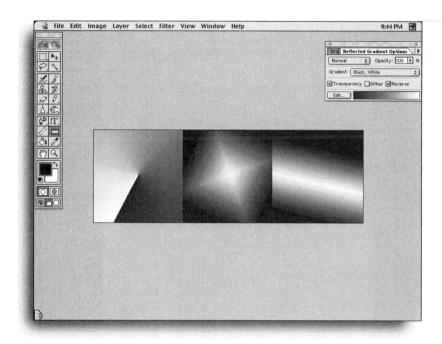

FIGURE 12.4
Cone, diamond, and mirror
gradients.

The Gradient Controls

With a better understanding of the definition of gradients, the
next step is to understand the controls used to create them. You
can find the gradient controls in the Tool palette and the
Gradient Tool Options palette. The variables under your
control are as follows:

- The gradient pattern
- The gradient color presets
- The gradient color editing tools
- The opacity of the gradient
- The dither of the color pattern
- The direction of the gradient color set
- The apply mode used for the gradient

For now, we will touch on each of the variables mentioned, clari-
fying the role each of the controls play in the process.

The Gradient Pattern

The first thing to decide is what pattern the gradient should have. Options are linear, radial, angled, mirrored, and diamond shaped. To select the desired pattern, click and hold on the gradient tool in the Toolbox and select the pattern from the pop-out options that appear (see Figure 12.5).

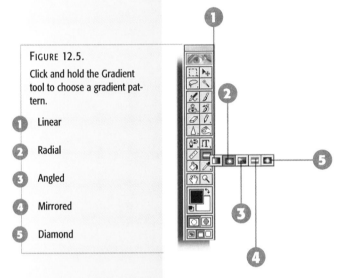

FIGURE 12.5.

Click and hold the Gradient tool to choose a gradient pattern.

1 Linear

2 Radial

3 Angled

4 Mirrored

5 Diamond

A comment on presets

The gradient presets that ship with Photoshop are pretty lame, featuring harsh colors and a complete lack of subtlety. You can avoid using these presets by creating your own, as described in the pages that follow. When created, all your custom presets also appear in the gradient pop-up menu.

The Gradient Color Presets

When you understand the pattern, you need to decide what color/tonal/transparency variables will cycle through the gradient. The default setting is black and white, but you can choose from a set of predesigned options in the Gradient Options palette. Click and hold on the gradient pop-up menu and select the desired preset. A sample of the preset appears at the bottom of the Options palette when it's selected (see Figure 12.6).

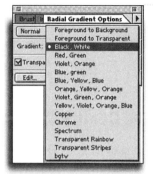

FIGURE 12.6
The gradient preset pop-up list.

The Gradient Color Editing Tools

The tools to modify a gradient color set are accessed by selecting the **Edit** button at the bottom of the Options palette (see Figure 12.7). This launches the Gradient Editor, which shows the current gradient presets, along with a full set of color and transparency controls (see Figure 12.8).

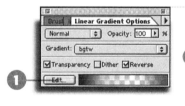

FIGURE 12.7
The Gradient Options palette.

1 Clicking on the **Edit** button brings up the Gradient Editor.

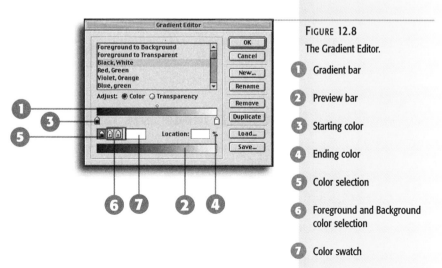

FIGURE 12.8
The Gradient Editor.

1 Gradient bar

2 Preview bar

3 Starting color

4 Ending color

5 Color selection

6 Foreground and Background color selection

7 Color swatch

From this point, you have two options: you can create a new gradient from scratch or you can modify an existing preset by selecting it from the scrolling window. A main gradient bar controls color transitions and transparency, either of which is activated by the radio buttons in the **Adjust** section.

The Opacity of the Gradient

Found in the Options palette (Figure 12.9), this Opacity slider should be familiar to the most casual Photoshop user. Lower the opacity to create transparency throughout the entire gradient.

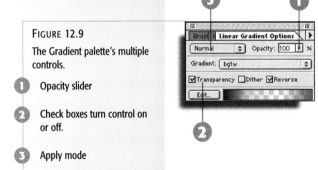

FIGURE 12.9

The Gradient palette's multiple controls.

1 Opacity slider

2 Check boxes turn control on or off.

3 Apply mode

Transparency, Dither, and Reverse Controls

These check boxes in the Options (see Figure 12.9) palette turn transparency and dithering capabilities on and off. The **Reverse** check box changes the direction of the right to left progression of the colors.

The Apply Mode Used for the Gradient

Clicking the Apply mode pop-up menu (see Figure 12.9) in the Options palette shows the standard Photoshop set of apply modes, allowing you to apply one as the gradient is created.

Applying a Gradient

To apply a gradient, select the gradient tool of your choice and then click and drag to apply the effect. The starting point reflects the left color in the color set, progressing through the other colors to the right. The colors move in a linear fashion for the Linear and Mirror tools and in a radial fashion for the Radial, Angle, and Diamond tools. Dragging a short distance compresses the gradient, and a long drag spreads the gradient transition along the entire stroke.

Creating a basic gradient

1. Select the desired gradient tool from the Toolbox.
2. Set the Options palette controls as desired, making sure to choose a gradient preset and opacity.
3. Click and drag in the image to apply the effect. With nothing else selected, the gradient expands to fill the screen.
4. If the gradient isn't exactly where you want it, check that the apply mode is set to **Normal** and repeat step 3. This overwrites the previous attempt, enabling you to fine-tune the placement.

Editing Gradients

Given that Adobe ships only the most basic of preset gradients, it won't be long before you decide that you want to create your own. The basic process is to define which colors, tones, or transparencies will be used as variables and then control how they transition from one to one another.

You have three options when editing gradients: create a new gradient, edit an existing preset gradient, or duplicate an existing preset gradient for further editing.

When editing gradients, click to select the right or left color swatch to change its color. The triangle above it turns black to show that it is active and editable. The midpoint diamond at the top of the gradient controls the break between two colors. Click and drag it to extend or contract the transition between them.

Creating a new gradient

1. Open the Gradient Options palette by double-clicking the gradient tool.

2. Select the **Edit** button, launching the Gradient Editor dialog box.

3. Click **New** and name the new gradient in the pop-up menu that appears.

4. Set the **Adjust** radio button to **Color**, and double-click the lower-left color swatch pointer, launching the Color Picker. Select the desired color and click **OK**. The gradient now shows the color you selected, fading to white (see Figure 12.10).

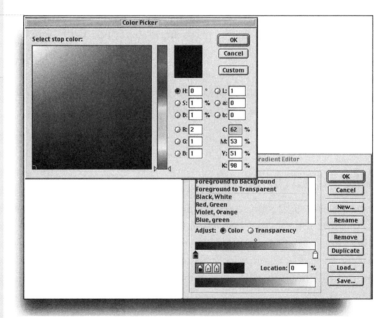

FIGURE 12.10

Select a color for the color swatch pointer.

5. Double-click the right color swatch pointer, select a color for the right side, and click **OK**.

6. Move the Midpoint diamond right or left as desired to control the break between the two colors. Click **OK** to create the gradient.

In the next example, we will edit an existing gradient, adding additional colors to make it more complex.

Editing existing gradient presets

1. Open the gradient Options palette and select the **Edit** button to launch the Gradient Editor dialog box. Check to make sure the **Color** radio button is selected.

2. Select a gradient preset, scrolling if necessary to find one that works for you. When selected, the gradient is represented in the adjust section along with its relative color swatch and midpoint controls. It also appears as a preview at the bottom of the dialog box.

3. Double-click a swatch pointer to launch the Color Picker and change the color associated with that section of the gradient.

4. To add an additional color swatch pointer, click below the gradient in the spot where you want the pointer to appear. An additional midpoint control automatically appears between any two pointers.

5. Modify the midpoint sliders as desired and click **OK**.

In addition to adding multiple colors across a gradient, you can also add transparent areas that let the image below show through. This option has many uses. One is to create a color gradient that gradually fades into an image. Another use is to create a series of linear or concentric bands that alternately fade between color areas and the image below.

Creating transparent gradients

1. Select **Edit** in the Gradient Options dialog box to launch the Gradient Editor.

2. Determine whether you want to create a new gradient or edit an existing one, either selecting **New** in the Gradient Editor or selecting a preset to edit from the list at the top of the dialog box.

3. Select **Transparency** in the **Adjust** section. This changes the color swatch pointers to all black indicating that no transparency is present. Photoshop looks at transparency in

Duplicating gradients

Given that the previous example edited an existing preset, you might want to save the result as a separate gradient, preserving the original gradient you started with. To do this, select the **Duplicate** button in the Gradient Editor dialog box, renaming the new gradient in the screen that follows.

reference to grayscale values, with white indicating 100% transparency and black indicating 100% opacity. The midpoint diamond reverts to the center, and the gradient bar above the color swatch pointer shows all black, indicating an opaque gradient (Figure 12.11).

FIGURE 12.11

Setting the transparency levels in the gradient.

4. Click on a color swatch pointer to activate it. (The pointer section of it turns black, indicating it is selected.) Type a percentage number from 1 to 100 into the **Opacity** box. Photoshop represent the transparency as a grayscale value and shows the actual transparent fade in the gradient preview at the bottom of the Gradient Editor.

5. As always, click anywhere in the color swatch pointer section to create another pointer. Enter its transparency or opacity value in the **Opacity** box, just as you did in step 4. Click **OK** to create the gradient.

13

Resizing and Reshaping Images

Optimize image size for print, multimedia, and the Web

Adding additional work area with the Add Canvas command

Using the Transform commands to distort an image

Using keyboard shortcuts in the Free Transform mode

The Need for Flexible Image Resolution

Before the dawning of multimedia and the Internet, almost all digital images were destined to end up in print. In those days, all that was important was knowing that you had enough resolution to match up with the printer's *line screen*, keeping the image from pixelating. Things have come a long way since then.

We live in a multimedia culture that communicates via print, the Web, multimedia, and video. In many cases, the same images need to be repurposed across a wide spectrum of mediums and formats. This basic repurposing is what the first part of this chapter is all about.

In addition to the resizing aspect, we will also consider how Photoshop enables you to reshape an image. Reshaping within this context refers to a global distortion applied by a command rather than being locally applied by a tool.

Resizing Images

The central consideration in resizing images is *resolution*; specifically, does the image have enough detail to look good in print, onscreen, or wherever it's going? When you know that you have adequate detail in an image, you don't want wasted detail, which can result in an inflated file size. The ability to maximize image quality and minimize file size determines whether an image has been resized successfully.

An Introduction to Resolution

Resolution is initially expressed in terms of pixels when viewed onscreen and dots when printed or sent to film. The difference is one of context; pixels are what a monitor uses to render an image and dots are what printers and imagesetters use. These two options are expressed in terms of pixels per inch (PPI) or dots per inch (DPI). A third resolution increment is lines per inch (LPI), which refers to a printer's line screen used to create a halftone for offset printing. There are a number of good books on printing and prepress that explain these nuances in great detail—check them out for more details.

Whether it's PPI, LPI, or DPI, think of image resolution units as a grid of squares that make up the entire image. If the squares are large, the image will be coarse, whereas a fine grid results in more detail. When image resolution is too low, the grid becomes evident, and the image is said to be pixelated (see Figure 13.1). This pixelization is never a good thing, unless it's used intentionally for graphic effect. Generally it just means that you tried to blow up an image beyond the limits of the available detail. From this point on, I will keep the discussion to PPI, given that all digital images begin in that state, regardless of where they end up.

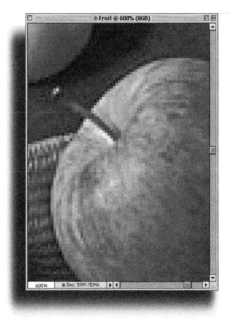

FIGURE 13.1

Enlarging this image to 600% shows the individual pixels that make up the image.

Image Capture Is Critical

The most important thing to remember about modifying image resolution is that if the detail isn't present when the image is captured, it's very hard to put it back later. Sometimes it's impossible. This means that when you capture an image with a scanner or digital camera, you need to make sure you have enough detail for the task at hand. If you think you might need more resolution later, make the effort to capture the detail upfront.

When you enlarge an image, also known as *sampling up*, Photoshop has to create pixels from scratch. Because it only sees the existing pixels as numeric values rather than a visual context, it doesn't know what values to assign the new ones. Its best guess, as explained next, is never up to the task of simulating a natural photographic image.

Conversely, *sampling down* an image is usually manageable, in that Photoshop is eliminating pixels and can be coached into eliminating the right ones to maintain image quality. The only place where this gets tricky is in sampling down an image for GIF files, where the Index color mode might require some difficult color choices.

Modifying Image Size

You can change an image's physical size by changing its height and width dimensions or by changing its resolution. It's best to determine the ultimate resolution requirements and then change the dimensions. Here are suggested resolutions:

- Offset printing, 150-line screen (commercial printing): 300 ppi
- Offset printing, 133-line screen (magazine): 250 ppi
- Offset printing, 80-line screen (newsprint): 150 ppi
- Web design/multimedia: 72 ppi

Resizing an image

1. From the **Image** menu, select **Image** and choose **Image Size**, which opens the Image Size dialog box. Make sure the **Resample Image** check box is not checked.

2. Determine the resolution value based on where the image will be used, and enter it in the **Resolution** field. The width and height fields change as the resolution value changes.

3. If you need to alter the width and height dimensions, check the **Resample Image** box and enter the appropriate width and height dimensions.

Increasing Canvas Size

Sometimes you will want more image area to work with, adding more canvas to an existing image. By adding canvas, you don't change the size or resolution of an existing image, you simply add more area around it.

Increasing image canvas size

1. In the **Image** menu, select **Image** and **Canvas Size**.

2. Enter the desired new dimensions in the **Width** and **Height** fields.

3. The shaded square in the matrix represents the current image. Click to place the square as needed, understanding that the new canvas will flow around it. Click **OK** to add the canvas, as shown in Figure 13.2.

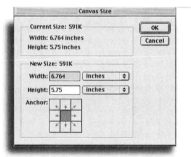

Cropping an Image

The opposite of adding canvas is cropping an image. Cropping involves defining a rectangular shape and cropping to delete all the image area outside of that rectangle.

Using the Cropping tool

1. Click and hold the Marquee tool, selecting the Cropping tool from the pop-out menu that appears (see Figure 13.3).

Image resampling options

When you resize an image, Photoshop gives you three options for how it inserts pixels: Bicubic, Bipolar, and Nearest Neighbor. For the best quality, use Bicubic, which is a process where Photoshop considers and averages the pixel values on all four sides of the pixel being added, averaging among all of them. Available but seldom used is Bipolar, which is faster than Bicubic, but not quite as accurate. The fact is that if you're going to use this one, you should just stick with Bicubic.

Nearest Neighbor duplicates the values to the right and left of the pixel to be added. This is sometimes useful, especially when resampling images with hard-edged, geometric patterns.

FIGURE 13.2

The shades square in the Canvas Size dialog box determines how the new canvas will flow around the existing image.

Canvas colors

When adding canvas to your image, remember that the new canvas will be the current background color. Select the desired background color before choosing the Canvas Size command.

FIGURE 13.3

Select the Cropping tool from
the Marquee pop-out menu.

2. Move the cursor into the image and draw a marquee to
define the crop.

3. Modify the handles that appear as necessary; click and drag
the center point to control how handles drag and move
(see Figure 13.4).

FIGURE 13.4

Adjust the handles around the
shape if necessary before
applying the final crop.

4. Double-click within the marquee to apply the crop.

Using Rotate Canvas

Another group of effects that you can apply to the entire image is the **Rotate Canvas** commands. These options rotate the image to any desired angle, either clockwise or counterclockwise (see Figure 13.5).

Cropping alternative

It is also possible to crop an image by drawing a rectangle with the Marquee tool and selecting Image and Crop. This has the same effect as using the Crop tool.

FIGURE 13.5
The **Rotate Canvas** menu options.

The presets are a useful component of this command that enable you to rotate the image 180 degrees or 90 degrees clockwise or counterclockwise. To apply these commands, from the **Image** menu, choose **Rotate** and **Canvas**; then choose either **180**, **90CW** (clockwise), or **90CCW** (counterclockwise). Photoshop automatically rotates the canvas as specified. These commands are very useful when scanning images, where an original might have been placed in the scanner with the wrong orientation.

Another command in the **Rotate Canvas** command set is the **Arbitrary** command. This launches a dialog box that enables you to rotate the canvas a specified number of degrees, clockwise or counterclockwise. Because anything other than a 90- or 180- degree angle results in a skewed rectangle, Photoshop enlarges the canvas to accommodate the angles, keeping the image horizontal and vertical as it fills the added area with the background color. Activate the **Arbitrary** command from the **Image** menu by choosing **Rotate Canvas** and **Arbitrary**.

One last set of commands in the **Rotate Canvas** set is **Flip Horizontal** and **Flip Vertical**. Rather that rotating the image around a center point, these commands flip the image over, transposing the content's mirror-image style around the vertical or horizontal pole. These commands appear at the bottom of the **Rotate Canvas** submenu. (From the **Image** menu, choose **Rotate Canvas** and **Flip Horizontal** or **Flip Vertical**.)

Applying Transformations to Layers and Selections

Similar to the **Rotate Canvas** commands are the **Transform** commands. Found in the **Edit** menu and the **Transform** submenu, these options enable you to rotate, twist, and skew your image (see Figure 13.6). The main difference between the **Rotate Canvas** option and the **Transform** option is that **Transform** options are applied only to individual layer information, whereas **Rotate Canvas** modifies the entire image as a single unit. In addition, the **Transform** commands can be applied to a selection as well as the entire layer.

FIGURE 13.6
The **Transform** menu options.

The various **Transform** options are listed here, along with a brief description of how they affect the image.

- **Scale**. Places corner and center handles around the layer, enabling you to scale the layer up and down around a movable center point. Drag any handle to resize the layer. Click and drag the center point to move it, which affects the way the layer is modified. Hold down the Shift key while dragging a handle to maintain the height and width proportions as you scale the image. Click any tool to apply the transformation.

- **Rotate**. Places corner and center handles around the layer, enabling you to rotate the layer up and down around a movable center point. Drag any handle to rotate the layer. Click and drag the center point to move the rotation axis, which affects the way the layer rotates. Click and drag within the Transform object to reposition the layer anywhere on the screen. Click any tool to apply the transformation.

- **Skew**. Places corner and center handles around the layer, allowing you to skew the layer at any angle around a movable center point. Drag any corner handle to create an angled effect for the corresponding layer. Moving the segment handles shifts the two connected corner handles in tandem, skewing that side of the image. Click and drag the center point to move the rotation axis, which affects the way the skew is applied. Click and drag within the Transform object to reposition the layer anywhere on the screen. Click any tool to apply the transformation.

- **Distort**. Places corner and center handles around the layer, enabling you to distort the layer around a movable center point. Drag any corner handle anywhere in the image, distorting the layer as desired. Click and drag the center point to move it, which affects the way the skew is applied. The main difference between **Distort** and **Skew** is that **Skew** restricts the handles that can be used to modify the layer, whereas **Distort** allows free placement of any handle in any area. Click and drag within the Transform object to reposition the layer anywhere on the screen. Click any tool to apply the transformation.

Transforming one-layer images

If your image consists only of the background layer, you cannot transform it in Photoshop. You have two ways to get around this. One is to double-click the Background layer in the Layers palette, name the layer in the dialog box that appears, and click OK. Photoshop considers this a standard layer, and all Transform options will be available. The other option is to make a selection on the Background layer, which can be distorted without changing the background status of the layer itself.

- **Perspective**. Places corner and center handles around the layer, enabling you to apply basic perspective effects. As you drag any corner handle, the opposite corner handle automatically moves in a mirror image. Click and drag the center point to move it, which affects the way the skew is applied. Click and drag within the Transform object to reposition the layer anywhere on the screen. Click any tool to apply the transformation.

The Rotate and Flip Options

Keyboard transform shortcuts

While working in any Transform mode, hold down the Control key to access a pop-up menu of all Transform options. This enables you to move from one Transform mode to another without accessing the menu or applying the transformation.

The **Transform** submenu also contains **Rotate** and **Flip** commands that perform the same functions as their **Rotate Canvas** counterparts. The only difference is that the **Rotate Canvas** is applied to the whole image rather than a single layer, as is the case with **Transform**.

Numeric Transform

The **Transform** commands provide an intuitive interaction between the application and the user. They let you click and drag the layer into whatever position looks right, without worrying about angle or pixel values.

Numeric Transform is for the times when you want numeric precision. If you rotate a series of images or layers, for example, you want to know exactly how much to rotate each image so that they all look consistent.

The Numeric Transform dialog box reduces all **Transform** options to numbers and values so that you can repeat the same moves just by entering values. It is located in the **Transform** pop-up menu and can be accessed from the **Edit** menu, by choosing **Transform** and **Numeric Transform**, as shown in Figure 13.7. Options available in the Numeric Transform dialog box are **Position**, **Scale**, **Skew**, and **Rotate**. Here's a brief description of these options:

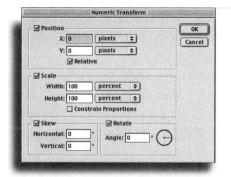

FIGURE 13.7
The Numeric Transform dialog box.

Position. Determines exactly where the layer aligns relative to the canvas as a whole, as well as any other layers. The dialog box enables you to specify the placement of the top-left corner of the active layer relative to the pixels of the canvas itself. The **X** value refers to the horizontal direction, and the **Y** refers to the vertical. Typing the coordinates of 5X and 3Y places the upper-left corner of the layer 5 pixel across from and 3 pixels down from the upper-left corner of the canvas itself.

Scale. Resizes the layer based on a percentage of its original size. You can resize each height or width value independently from the other, distorting the image in either direction. To avoid distortion, check the **Constrain Proportions** check box, which automatically enters the same value in each box, maintaining the height and width ratios.

Skew. Applies a skewed slant to the active layer along a horizontal or vertical axis. The degree of skew is measured numerically in degrees, which is entered in the **Horizontal** or **Vertical** box.

Rotate. This feature simply rotates the layer around a central axis. The layer control features a circular diagram with a horizontal line that represents the degree of rotation. By default, it is set to 0 degrees in the 3:00 position. To rotate to any other position, check the **Rotate** check box and click and drag the line. You can also enter the degree of rotation in the **Angle** field.

Free Transform

The idea behind the **Free Transform** option is that you can apply more than one kind of transformation at one time, without clicking **OK** and reselecting another option in between. At any given time, you can rotate, scale, and reposition the layer or selection, interactively dragging it into the desired position.

Using the Free Transform option

1. From the **Edit** menu, choose **Free Transform**. This creates handles around the image at the corners and in the center of each segment border. If a rectangular selection is active, the handles appear only around the selection.

2. Click and drag the center segments to resize linearly in a vertical or horizontal direction.

3. Without clicking to accept the transformation, click and drag the corner points to resize up or down diagonally.

4. To reposition the selection or image, move the cursor inside the active shape and drag the shape or layer into any position onscreen.

5. To rotate the image or selection, drag the cursor outside of the active shape, and it changes to a Rotation icon to show that it will rotate the image. Drag up or down while this icon is present to apply the effect.

In addition to these basic commands, Adobe includes additional keystroke modifiers that deliver even more control to the **Free Transform** command. The modifiers are dictated by the position of the cursor, whether scaling, rotating, or repositioning the object. The next list shows all the available options for the **Free Distort** command.

- **Shift Drag a Corner Point**. Resizes diagonally, maintaining a proportional aspect ratio.

- **Shift Drag Outside the Object**. Rotates in 15-degree increments.

- **Shift Drag Inside the Object**. Constrains repositioning to 45-degree increments.

- **(Option/Shift) or [Alt] Drag a Corner**. Resizes diagonally relative to the center point.

- **(Option) or [Alt] Drag a Center Segment.** Resizes both sides linearly in a mirrored effect.

- **(Option) or [Control] Drag a Corner.** Distorts freely in any direction.

- **(Command) or [Control] Drag a Center Segment**. Skews the shape freely in any direction.

- **(Option+Command) or [Control+Alt] Drag a Corner Point**. Distorts both diagonal corners at once with a mirrored effect.

- **(Option+Command) or [Control+Alt] Drag a Center Segment.** Skews freely relative to a center point.

- **(Option+Command+Shift) or [Control+Alt+Shift] Drag a Corner Point.** Create a perspective effect. Drag horizontally to pinch the opposite horizontal corner and drag vertically to pinch the opposite vertical corner.

- **(Option+Command+Shift) or [Control+Alt+Shift] Drag a Center Segment.** Skew the shape around a center point.

Manipulating Focus with Blur, Sharpen, and Smudge

Manipulating focus

Blurring for effect

Sharpening for emphasis

Smearing for excitement

Manipulating Focus

One of the things that separate professional photographers from amateurs is that professional photographers can control the focus of photographic images. Most people get upset when they look through a new batch of pictures only to find a fuzzy photo; they savor an image that's entirely in focus. This chapter shows you how to use the Focus tools to challenge the notion that a photo has to be 100% crystal clear to be attractive.

If you look at many current films, television commercials, magazine ads, MTV videos, Web pages, or any other image-dependent medium in the world, you might notice an interesting phenomenon. More and more, designers are incorporating blurring as a visual effect. Some advertising uses blurring in the extreme; you can hardly make out the subject in the image, and the blurring leads the eye around the ad toward the text. Blurring, if used with good compositional judgment, is soothing to the eye. More importantly, blurring a part of a scene draws the eye to the sharp portion of the image. Like a magician, you can manipulate your audience's attention to staring at what *you* choose as the center of interest and nothing else, through the skilled use of blurring.

At the same time, some of the same images that use blurring almost excessively also use the visual property of sharpness very carefully for emphasis. The subtle use of sharpness combined with selectively applied blurring can create quite an impact.

Blurring for Effect

When people buy Photoshop, they buy it for the great tools and features. Artists want the Rubber Stamp tool, the powerful compositing ability of layers, or one of the other many cool features. If polled, practically nobody would vote for the Blur tool as one of the most important features in Photoshop. Many people think their photos already have too much blur, so why add more? These folks bought Photoshop to *get rid* of the blur. Stamp out blur! Photoshopists want clearer images. *You* want clearer images…right?

So a lot of Photoshop owners use the Blur tool infrequently, if at all. The truth is, however, if used carefully, the Blur features in Photoshop can transform a poor-looking composite image into a completely believable piece of fictional or nonfictional imagery.

In the scheme of Adobe's construction of Photoshop 5, the Blur tool is a *local* way to blur the little things in an image. The **Blur** filters on the menu, however, were designed to add blur globally to an image or large selection area. At least that's what Adobe's concept is! Because there are more ways to control mistakes, many designers use the **Blur** filters for the little jobs, too.

The following concept applies to the Sharpness tool *and* the Toning tools—Dodge, Burn, and Sponge. After you read this chapter and perhaps think about it later, you'll see that the utility of the Focus tools is a lot more open ended than you imagined. The general concepts shown in this chapter apply to *any* tool. But in this chapter, we pay primary and much deserved attention to the unloved and little respected Blur tool.

Test Driving the Supercharged Blur Tool

With Photoshop 5, the Blur tool has a whole new life, a new set of purposes. You won't feel threatened by the inability to control it, as you might have in the past. Before version 5, the biggest drawback to using the Blur tool was that if you overused it, you would wind up with an out-of-focus mess. You could stroke anywhere you wanted, as much as you wanted, but whatever you did, you had to make sure that you did it in one pass. If you weren't extremely careful with your mouse clicks, your work would end up looking like a view through your grandmother's trifocals! Why? Because you could only undo the last editing move you made. So, if you made a very elaborate mouse move that you messed up at the very end, and then made a quick accidental second click, you had no way to undo the important, elaborate mistake. The workaround for those brave souls willing to use the Blur tool instead of a filter was to turn down the **Pressure** setting to a very low number. The **Pressure** setting controls the intensity of the effect that's being applied. By working with the Blur tool and very low **Pressure**, you have a safety

Handling pressure

Any traditional airbrush artist knows that air pressure controls the stream of paint out of the nozzle, but what's a **Pressure** setting for the Blur tool (or even the airbrush—we're in the digital world here) used for? **Pressure** is actually a way to control the tool's transparency. So if you see a setting of 95 for the **Pressure** for any tool in Photoshop 5, read this as 95% opacity.

Sample files

The images I'm using are from the Photoshop CD-ROM that ships with several samples. If you don't have access to them, you can follow along with any other image you want.

Using the Caps Lock key for precision

For more flexibility in your Photoshop work, it is recommended that you have the **Standard** cursor chosen in the box marked **Other Cursors**, found under **Preferences** (Ctrl+K)[@⌘+K]. If you select the **Precision** cursor, it's on all the time, and you might not want **Precision** cursors for all your work. By selecting the **Standard** cursor, you can identify which tool you're using, *and* when you need the **precision** cursor, you can activate it by pressing the Caps Lock key.

net, enabling you to make a number of passes and then stop when the effect is sufficiently apparent.

To get a better idea of one of the effective ways you can use Photoshop 5's Blur tool, let's walk through some steps using a stock image that you can find in the Goodies/Samples folder in the Photoshop directory on your hard disk.

Blurring your skull out with the Blur tool

1. Open Skull.tif located in the Goodies/Samples file of your Photoshop directory.

2. Click on **Background** in the Layers palette to make it the active layer. If the Layers palette isn't currently onscreen, press F7.

3. You want the image size to be at 100%. If the percentage is lower than 100% (you can see this on the title bar), double-click **Viewing Resolution**.

4. Choose the Blur tool from the Toolbox; double-click the **Blur** on the Hand tool on the Toolbox. Doing this brings the image to 100%; the 1:1 tool icon looks like a water drop. Or press Shift+R until you see the Blur tool depressed on the Toolbox.

5. Double drag the **Pressure** setting to 100. You want to see what the Blur tool will do at full strength; click on the Blur tool on the Toolbox to display the Options palette.

6. Press F5 to open the Brushes palette if it isn't currently onscreen. Click on the **100** pixel tip.

7. Press the Caps Lock key to activate **Precision** cursors.

8. Place the cursor in the middle of the image and make a circle motion over the skull, while releasing the mouse button and clicking at regular intervals. Approximately ten clicks is good. Do your best to really blur that skull out. Pretend you're working on the show "Cops" and this skull just knocked over a convenience store (see Figure 14.1).

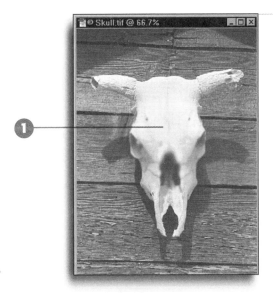

FIGURE 14.1

Bad cow. A product of environment or bad genes? Or: Make sure to click about ten times while blurring.

1 Blur area

You just *ruined* this picture! Onnnnly kidding; we're *experimenting* here to demonstrate an important new technique; remember, you're using the new *supercharged* Blur. It's the same Blur tool as you used (or didn't use) in previous versions of Photoshop, and (Ctrl+Z) [⌘+Z] still will only undo the last editing move you made. But wait! Do you remember how in Chemistry, if you mix two inert substances together you can end up with an explosive combination? Well, try out this formula: Blur + History = Cool technique with a capital "C."

9. Make the History palette active by clicking on the tab marked **History**; the tab will turn white to show it's activated. If you don't see the History palette at all in the workspace, choose **Window**, **Show History**.

10. Slide the scrollbar of the History palette up so that you can see the word **Open** in the window, but don't click on **Open**. Click on the bar below it that reads **Blur tool** and note what happens.

11. Now, all the titles below the one you just selected should be gray. Move the scrollbar down and pick another grayed out Blur tool title in the History palette and click on it. Note the changes in the image.

Where's the Sweet Spot?

Here's a *real insider's* tip about the **Precision** cursor. Notice the dot at the very center of the cursor's crosshairs? The cursor contains a "sweet spot" of just one pixel. Regardless of which brush size you use, the sweet spot remains a single pixel. Keep this in mind when you paint or edit.

12. Close the image and select **don't save any changes** when prompted by the attention box.

What conclusion can be drawn from the previous steps? Even though the tool itself has not changed, the Blur tool really *is* more powerful now by using it in combination with the new History palette. The Blur tool is up to the task of being used on assignments that would previously have gone to its sibling rival, the **Blur** filter. You can feel comfortable using the Blur tool, safe in the knowledge that you have a much better way of controlling mistakes than through **Pressure** settings alone. The History palette gives you the ability to freely experiment. Armed with this knowledge, let's discover some practical applications of the "new" Blur tool.

It should be noted that in this exercise you used *only* the Blur tool with the History palette.

SEE ALSO
➤ *To learn the History palette's features, see page 35*

Using Blur for Clarity

Professional photographers use an optical trick to generate money. They buy expensive telephoto lenses to shoot their subjects. (To be fair, a pro photographer's bag of tricks features many other techniques; *this* photographic trick simply relates to the Blur tool.) Telephoto lenses can blur out the background (and foreground, if desired) so that the eye is drawn to just the subject. The following technique shows you how to mimic the properties of a telephoto lens in order to draw attention to your subjects.

Let's pretend for a moment that you want to give your Uncle George a picture of himself and his daughter taken on her wedding day. You want to fix up the image beyond its present condition. The effect you're looking to create is to blur everything in the image outside of Uncle George and his daughter.

Here's how to start. First, you must choose an image. If you have access to a scanner and plenty of photos, choose any snapshot. If you don't have a way to bring your own personal pictures into

Photoshop, search through the Photoshop CD-ROM. The Photoshop CD-ROM contains a lot of stock photos.

If you can't find any photos with people, try to find an image with a strong central subject, such as a flower or an animal. The subject(s) should occupy at least 1/3 of the image. Try to find an image where the edges of the subject(s) are clearly visible in the photo, so you aren't hindered when you try to blur around them. Loose hair or a transparent scarf (anything you can see the background through) are items in an image to avoid, as they will create more work than is necessary for the following example. Now that you made your choice of images, let's go to work.

Applying Blur in increments

1. Before using the Blur tool, first perform any kind of image adjustments necessary to make the exposure of the photo correct. In this example image, some dodging and burning was performed, as well as some **Curves** adjustments.

2. Choose the Blur tool from the Toolbox.

3. Double-click the Blur tool icon or go to the menu and select **Show options** to activate the Options palette. Set the **Pressure** on the Options palette at 100%.

4. Open the Brushes palette by clicking on palette's tab, or in the **Window** menu, choose **Show Brushes**. Start with the 100 pixel brush, located in the bottom row of brushes, the last brush on the right. At this point, you need to cover as much of the background behind Uncle George and his daughter as you can. If you want, go into **Preferences** (Ctrl+K) [⌘+K] and under **Brush size** select **Cursors** so you can see where you are in the image.

5. Stroke the Blur tool along the outer edges of the photo at first, as shown in Figure 14.2. Try not to go over any one area more than another, or you'll create patches in the image that have more blur than others. You might find that it takes several complete passes to get the amount of blur you want.

Scanning the market

Thinking about buying a scanner? Like everything else that's computer related, the prices have dropped considerably. A scanner that might cost several hundred dollars today would have cost several thousand dollars just three years ago.

FIGURE 14.2

Using a large brush, blur the outer parts of the image first.

1 Large blur area

6. After you're satisfied that you can do no more with a larger brush, select a smaller brush from the Brushes palette. A smaller brush enables you to get closer to the subjects. For the image of Uncle George in the example image, I chose the second brush from the right on the second row of brushes.

7. To wrap this up, you need to use the smallest brushes on the Brushes palette. On the top row on the left are the hard-edged brushes; in the second row on the left are the soft-edged versions. You need these for tight coverage around the subject's edges and in tough spots such as under the arms.

   One other area that needs addressing is the bride's wedding train. The little girl that was carrying it is unimportant, so she is blurred out, but the train in her hand needs to be blurred also because it is on the same focal plane as she is, as shown in Figure 14.3.

8. A medium brush is chosen, the second brush from the right in the second row, and it is carefully passed around the little girl's hand so it looks as though the train gradually comes into focus. For the image you are working on, this step involves checking the details. Do the edges look natural? Is there anything that looks like it might need to be softened?

FIGURE 14.3

Some portions of the image will need to be blurred gradually.

1   Gradual blur area

Now that you have the image looking pretty good, we're going to take the enhancement a step further. As mentioned earlier, pro photographers have many items in their bag of tricks. Here's another trick. It's called *diffusion*. There are people who think diffusion means out of focus, but it's not the same. Diffusion creates a softened image, yet edge detail is still sharp; an out-of-focus image has no sharp edges. Diffusion is big among pro wedding photographers wanting to create a warm, romanticized mood.

The one flaw with the different diffusion techniques that many pro photographers use has to do with contrast. Generally, a photograph with diffusion has less contrast than a normal photograph. This is why the following technique is a good one. Photoshop keeps the contrast nice (you can have nice deep black areas in the image), and the colors stay saturated, which is also an impossibility in the traditional world of photography.

You might not care for the look of diffused images; if that's the case, save your file now. If you *do* like that look, let's go!

   9. Click on **Make Duplicate Layer** on the **Layers** menu, or press the **Menu Flyout** button on the right side of the Layers palette.

  10. The Blur tool should still be selected, so go to the Brushes palette and pick the 100 pixel brush. Now blur the subjects! Make everything nice and blurry.

11. Go back to the Layer palette and click on the **Opacity** fly-out to bring up the Opacity slider. Drag the Opacity slider to 50%. Alternatively, you can press 5 on the keyboard, as shown in Figure 14.4.

FIGURE 14.4

Uncle George with the diffu-sion technique applied.

Uncle George.JPG @ 66.7% (RGB)

Extra credit

For extra credit, after you finish the chapter, come back and open any image you choose. Perform steps 9 through 13, replacing the Blur tool with the Sharpen tool. Then try the Smudge tool with the same steps, just to see what kind of effect you might get.

That's it. If you made it completely through this exercise, pat yourself on the back; you deserve it! You've turned a simple snapshot into a professional-looking image.

Sharpening for Emphasis

On the road to final output, you can take several paths to end up with an image that is less than clear. If you use a scanner to turn your images into computer files, your images are probably not as sharp as you might think. Even in the hands of a skilled opera-tor, the output of a scan might not be at optimal sharpness. Even if you think the image looks sharp, believe it or not, you can probably do even better. Most scans can benefit from sharpening in one form or another. If you don't own a scanner and have your images scanned professionally, you might still have scans that are less than perfectly sharp. For an eye-opening experience, after you experiment a bit with the Sharpen tool, pull out any file that has been scanned. Pass the Sharpen tool over the image using a large brush to see what happens.

Lack of focus is not the sole mistake of a professional scanning your image, however. Resizing images and forcing Photoshop to interpolate new pixels for the image is another leading cause of image fuzziness. For years, I resized images and didn't realize that the image became out of focus as a result. As with scans, my images originally appeared to be sharp. The reason for the degrading of the image files? Every time you check the **Resample Image** box in the Image Size dialog box (the box that appears after choosing **Image**, **Image Size**), you transform (read: degrade) the image. Another unwanted way to destroy image focus on a single layer is to perform a transformation using **Scale**, **Distort**, **Skew**, or **Perspective**.

In all the preceding scenarios, the amount of degradation is not heavy, but it is there. To see this degradation and how the Sharpen tool works, perform this exercise.

Minimizing degradation using the Sharpen tool

1. Choose **File**, **New** or (Ctrl+N) [⌘+N]. Make the image 2 inches wide and 2 inches in height with a resolution of 72 pixels and choose RGB color as the mode. Click **OK**.

2. Double-click on the Hand tool on the Toolbox to make the image fill your screen.

3. Click on the Type icon to select the Type tool or press T.

4. Click the cursor in the center of the image; the Type Tool dialog box appears. Select any font; I chose **Arial**. Type 50 in the **Size** box and select **Points** in the box next to where you typed 50. Deselect the **Antialised** box. Type an uppercase s in the **Type** tool window. Press **OK**. Notice how sharp the edges appear.

5. Choose **Layer**, **Type**, **Render Layer**.

6. Select the Rectangular Marquee tool from the Toolbox and then drag a box around the letter **S** to select it.

7. On the menu, choose **Edit**, **Transform**, **Scale**. The Transform bounding box appears. Pull the handles to increase the size of the **S**.

8. Stretch the **S** out until it fills up the image area; then double-click inside the bounding box to apply the **Scale** transformation.

9. Click anywhere on the white part of the image to deselect the **S**.

You can see how the interpolation used in resizing affected the edges of the letter in Figure 14.5. You might not think this is too bad, but keep in mind this is a very simple image. Think about how much edge and texture detail makes up a normal photograph; it might all end up damaged.

FIGURE 14.5

There were no gray pixels before this image was resized.

10. Select the Sharpen tool from the Toolbox. Press 0 (zero) on the keyboard to make the pressure 100%.

11. Run the cursor over the **S** until you see the anti-aliasing artifacts start to disappear.

You can never completely restore the original sharpness, but you can still make an image look excellent.

The last exercise was in black and white to give you the ability to easily see image degradation. Unfortunately, you weren't able to see the biggest drawback of using the Sharpen tool, and that is noise. When using the Sharpen tool, it can be easy to introduce noise into the area in which you're working. A friend of mine uses this "drawback" to his advantage. He sometimes uses the Sharpen tool when he needs to match film grain in an image.

In the next example, we'll see how the Sharpen tool can enhance a resized image, and we'll examine what we can do about over-sharpening.

Recovering lost clarity using the Sharpen tool

1. Open the CMYKballoons.tif file from the Samples file in the Goodies folder located in the Photoshop directory.

2. Choose the Crop tool from the Toolbox. Double-click the Crop icon to open the Options palette.

3. Check the box marked **Fixed Target** and then press the **Front Image** button. This brings up the size of the full image. Change the second box in the **Width** and **Height** rows to **Pixels**. Type 300 in the **Width** row and 250 in the **Height**.

4. Drag a diagonal across the image and the **Cropping** bounding box appears.

5. Click inside the box near one of the corners to reposition the box in the area, as shown in Figure 14.6. Double-click inside the bounding box after you have the bounding box in place.

How sharp is too sharp?

How do you know when you oversharpen an image? When an image's edges start to look like a video and stop looking like a photograph, you over-sharpened the edges and details. If you have an area with little detail (such as the sky area of the CMYKbaloons image), watch for noise or colored pixels that might start to appear where none were before.

FIGURE 14.6
Move the bounding box over to this area.

6. Now, choose **Image**, **Image Size**. Check the **Constrain Proportions** and **Resample Image** boxes. Then type 600 Pixels in the **Width** row. Click on **OK**.

7. Select the Sharpen tool from the Toolbox. Press 5 on the keyboard for 50% Pressure.

8. Choose the **100 pixel** brush, located in the bottom row of brushes. It's the brush on the far right.

9. Drag the Sharpen tool over the giant balloons. It's time to emphasize them! See Figure 14.7.

FIGURE 14.7
Oversharpening in action.

1 This balloon has been oversharpened

See the arrow pointing at the balloon? Kick loose and just let the Sharpen tool sit on the balloon until the area is unrealistically sharpened, as shown in Figure 14.7. You'll do this plenty of times accidentally on odd occasions, so go ahead and do it one time on purpose.

10. Choose the Blur tool from the Toolbox. Press 5 on the keyboard for 50% Pressure.

11. Run the cursor over the offending area and you're done.

The Web is one place where it is acceptable to have oversharpened images. If you are going to have a thumbnail image of your art so that people can download a larger image, sharpen the thumbnail until it looks like a bad photocopy. You'll see that in context of the Web, where everything needs to be small (composed of very few pixels), the thumbnail will look great.

The Sharpening tool is useful for composite layers. Judicious use around some edges can mean the difference between a layer looking like it's sitting on top of an image, and a layer that looks like it's actually occupying the 3D space that it's supposed to in the image.

Smearing for Excitement

The Smudge tool is useful for great special effects. One friend swears by the Smudge tool for making seamless Web page backgrounds.

Perhaps the Smudge tool would be more appropriately titled if it were called the Blending tool. That's really what it does—it blends. Who wants to smudge up their image? Everybody wants a well-blended image. If you want to blend a composite, you might want to smudge it a little.

The following exercise is the solution to the problem of how to paint hair in Photoshop. I wanted to do a complicated composite using a 3D program and an existing photograph from a famous movie. I wanted to poke fun at the movie and amuse my friends at the same time (oddly, no one got the joke, so it must be them). The key to tying all the elements together would be the hair, so it had to be believable. Let's see how this problem was solved.

Creating a hair-raising experience with the Smudge tool

1. Press (Ctrl+N) [⌘+N]. Create a document that's 5 inches in **Width** and 7 inches in **Height** with a **Resolution** of 72 pixels/inch, in RGB Color mode. Press **OK** to create the new document.

2. Choose the **Airbrush** tool from the Toolbox, or press the J key. Press 5 on the keyboard to give the **Airbrush** a pressure of 50%.

3. Select the 65 pixel brush from the Brushes palette.

Creating seamless backgrounds using the Smudge tool

Here's a way to generate seamless backgrounds in Photoshop. Open a new image with a width and height of 256 pixels, with a resolution of 150 pixels/in. Paint a texture using any tools you choose; then choose Filter, Other, Offset. You see the Offset dialog box. In the Horizontal and Vertical pixel fields enter 100. In the Undefined Area field, click on the Wrap Around button. Make sure the preview button is checked. Smear the edges together with the Smudge tool. Save your new seamless background.

4. Press D to bring up Photoshop's default colors of **Black** in the **Foreground** and **White** in the **Background** in the Toolbox.

5. Paint a black sphere about 2 inches in diameter.

6. Select the Smudge tool from the Toolbox.

7. Select a medium sized brush to start. Select the third brush from the left in the middle row of brushes.

8. Place your cursor inside the black part of the image and stroke outward with a slight curving motion. Try to vary the brush sizes between the one you're using now and the next smaller brush, as you work.

If you want the hair strands to be longer, make the smaller strokes with the previously recommended brushes and then pick a much larger brush and make one or two quick strokes over the smaller strokes, as shown in Figure 14.8.

FIGURE 14.8

Notice how the strokes gently curve out.

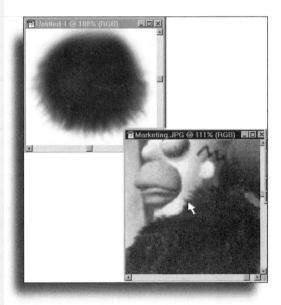

In Figure 14.8, you can see the image generated with this technique. In the exercise, we painted on the Background layer. If it were an image with a lot of other things going on behind the hair, such as the image in the figure, you should work on a duplicate layer, just to play it safe. Now, you have the great History palette, so you have several choices for the finished piece. As with everything in Photoshop, use whatever works best for you.

You can make smoke in Photoshop using any number of methods, and you can get some very believable results. I did some work for a big cigar magazine and developed a number of different techniques for creating smoke. I ended up spending more time on the technique in the steps to follow, not because it was hard, but because it's not. The fact is, it's just fun! When you start smearing with the Smudge tool, try to do it a little slowly. The smoke will swirl lazily, just like real smoke. The technique is so much fun, I had a hard time trying to stop playing with it—try it out now and see for yourself.

Learning to smoke with the Smudge tool

1. From the **Layers** menu, choose **New Layer**. This way, you can play to your heart's content without disturbing the pixels on the layer beneath.

2. Press the D key on the keyboard to specify **Default** colors.

3. Press the X key on the keyboard to switch **White** to the **Foreground** color.

4. Click on the **Paintbrush** tool on the Toolbox, or press the B key. Type 35 to change the **Opacity** for the Paintbrush.

5. Select a brush that has a size that is approximately the width that you want the smoke to be.

6. Make a couple of strokes with the paintbrush similar to those shown in Figure 14.9. The **White** color can be heavy and the stroke can even be a bit shaky.

7. From the **Window**, choose **Show Layers**. Click on the **Opacity** flyout and turn the **Opacity** down to 60%.

8. Click on the Smudge tool in the Toolbox. Press 5 on the keyboard to adjust the **Pressure** of the Smudge tool to 50%.

FIGURE 14.9

Don't worry—the smoke lines don't need to be perfect.

1 Initial smoke

FIGURE 14.9

Don't worry—the smoke lines don't need to be perfect.

1 Initial smoke

9. Try to select a brush that is about twice as large as the paint-brush you chose earlier.

Because you are using an image that you have chosen, the author can't recommend specific brush sizes. This will have to be a judgment call on your part. Don't get too wrapped up in the details in this exercise, anyway. Just try to have fun with the program and experiment a lot with the settings. You can only learn from it.

10. Push the **White** color around with Smudge tool. Give your computer a few seconds to update; it's doing some serious calculations behind the scenes. Note Figure 14.10.

You can repeat steps 6–10 on a new layer to build the effect up. If you like the effect that you have on a single layer but you feel it needs more punch, here's a simple, but effective, trick. Choose **Layers**, **Make Duplicate layer**. Cool, eh?

FIGURE 14.10
Playing with smoke.

1 Smudged smoke

Adjusting Tone with Dodge, Burn, and Sponge

Using the Dodge tool to lighten images

Darken images with the Burn tool

Control saturation with the Sponge tool

Contrast control in black-and-white images with the Sponge tool

An Introduction to Toning Images

The Photoshop manual devotes a whole two paragraphs to the toolset we look at in this chapter. The reason they can look at it in such brevity while we consider it in length is that the Dodge, Burn, and Saturation tools are very easy to use. A few paragraphs is all that is needed to understand the basics of how the tools work. Understanding when, where, and why to use them is a different story (see Figure 15.1).

FIGURE 15.1

The Dodge, Burn, and Sponge tools are located in a pop-out menu in the Toolbox.

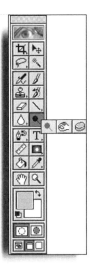

Using the Dodge/Burn Tools

The Dodge and Burn tools are based on the darkroom practice of dodging and burning photographs to control the amount of light, and hence the tonality of specific areas of an image. Although the enlarger allowed global changes to the entire image, photographers sometimes needed to lighten or darken specific areas or objects.

The same requirement exists in Photoshop, where it is sometimes necessary to modify an image locally rather than globally. The global commands such as **Curves**, **Levels**, or any other

Adjust commands don't give the local control necessary in many instances. And although you can select an area and use something such as **Curves**, many find it to be a counter-intuitive approach.

SEE ALSO

➤*For more details on using Levels, see page 513*

➤*For more details on using Curves, see page 520*

The Dodge tool lightens an area as it is applied to a color image. In the darkroom, photographers would cut out a disk of cardboard and attach it to a stick or piece of stiff wire. When the enlarger was exposing the image, they would wave the tool over the area they wanted to lighten, restricting the light to the desired area. The reduced exposure resulted in a lighter image.

The Dodge tool offers a pair of tool controls in the Options dialog box, which is accessed by double-clicking the Dodge tool in the Toolbox. The **Exposure** control determines how quickly the area is affected. A higher setting lightens the area quickly, whereas a lower setting builds it up gradually. It is usually a better idea to start with a lower setting, which gives more control over the final result, as shown in Figure 15.2.

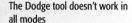

The Dodge tool doesn't work in all modes

The Dodge tool does not work on Index color and Bitmap files. To use the tool on these file types, first convert them to RGB by selecting the **Image** menu and choosing **Mode** and **RGB**. After you finish with the tool, you can convert back to Index or Bitmap by selecting it in the **Mode** submenu.

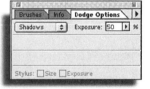

FIGURE 15.2
The Dodge tool Options palette.

In addition to the **Exposure** control, there is also a tonal range pop-up menu that offers a choice between **Highlights**, **Midtones**, and **Shadows**. This setting determines the tonal range in the image that is affected by the Dodge tool. Set it for shadows to lighten only the shadows, ignoring the highlights and midtones.

The step-by-step lessons that follow illustrate how you can use these tools.

Using the Dodge tool

1. Double-click the Dodge tool to select it and open the Options palette.

2. Select **Highlights** from the Options palette pop-up menu and set the **Exposure** to 10.

3. With an appropriate sized brush selected, brush in circles over the light areas in the image, creating a bleached effect (see Figure 15.3).

FIGURE 15.3

Lighten the foreground of the image with the Dodge tool.

If the tool doesn't seem to be working…

If using the Dodge or Burn tool seems to have no effect on your image, check the **Exposure** and tonal range settings in the Options dialog box. If the pop-up menu is set to **Shadows** and you're working on a light area, the tool will have no effect. In addition, if the **Exposure** setting is set very low, the effect could be very slight and gradual, giving the appearance of having no effect at all.

The Burn tool works in the opposite way of the Dodge tool, making the image darker rather than lighter. In the darkroom, photographers would take a piece of cardboard, poke a rough hole in it, and shine the light of the enlarger only on the areas that needed to be darkened. The Burn tool operates in the same way (minus the cardboard and the enlarger of course).

The Options palette for the Burn tool shows the same controls as the Dodge tool, offering the ability to control the **Exposure** and specify a tonal range to be effected.

Using the Burn tool

1. Select the Burn tool from the **Dodge/Burn/Sponge** pop-up menu and double-click the Burn tool to open the Options palette.

2. Select **Shadows** from the Options palette pop-up menu, and set the **Exposure** to 10.

3. With an appropriate sized brush selected, brush in circles over the dark areas in the image, toning down the shadows (see Figure 15.4).

FIGURE 15.4

Use the Burn tool to darken and saturate the shoes.

The Sponge Tool

The Sponge tool breaks with the nice photography metaphor we've been using to this point. To my knowledge, photographers don't sit in the darkroom and dab sponges on their photos. They do however, use them in Photoshop.

The Sponge tool controls the *saturation* in a color image and the contrast in a black-and-white image. Saturation refers to the intensity and purity of the color in an image. Scenes such as

Keep the tools moving

In the darkroom, photographers dodge and burn using a constant circular motion, keeping the tool moving the entire time. This is to avoid any sharp edges around the area being modified. The same is true for the Dodge and Burn tool in Photoshop. Use a feathered brush, a low exposure, and build up the effect with a repetitive circular motion.

sunsets, bright summer days, and night photography tend to be overly saturated. When you modify saturation, you need to be careful, in that too much saturation can make an image look unnatural. In select spots, or for more of a graphic effect, saturation can be a powerful tool.

In the Sponge tool Options palette, the tonal range pop-up menu has been replaced by the **Saturate/Desaturate** pop-up menu (Figure 15.5). Select one or the other to increase or decrease the color intensity. Although the name on the other control has been changed from Exposure to **Opacity**, the result is still the same; increase the value and the effect is applied faster.

FIGURE 15.5

The Sponge tool Options palette.

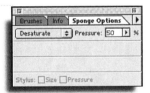

Using the Saturation tool

1. Select the Sponge tool from the **Dodge/Burn/Sponge** pop-out menu, and double-click the Sponge tool to launch the Options palette.

2. Select **Desaturate** from the Options palette pop-up menu and set the **Opacity** to 20.

3. With an appropriate-sized brush selected, brush in circles over the midtone areas in the image to soften and tone down the color values (Figure 15.6).

SEE ALSO

➤ *For more details on using Levels, see page 513*

➤ *For more details on using Curves, see page 520*

FIGURE 15.6

Desaturate the background to emphasize the subject matter.

Cloning and Pattern Creation with the Rubber Stamp

An Introduction to the Rubber Stamp

When I started using Photoshop in the late eighties, I have to confess that the Rubber Stamp tool confused me a bit. I mean, I could understand the paintbrush, eraser, and pencil analogies well enough, but what was this rubber stamp thing? Was I supposed to stamp crude line drawings of hearts and unicorns across my image? (Okay, so I'm going overboard a bit, but I still maintain that the description was a bit lacking).

After I figured out that you could clone image data from one area to another, I was much more impressed. The Rubber Stamp was a great solution for image and pattern creation, and the next best thing to a multiple undo feature. In my estimation, it was one of the main reasons for Photoshop's early popularity, and one of the tools that set it apart.

With Photoshop 5, the Rubber Stamp tool has changed. Adobe has taken out the Paint From Saved, and Snapshot options, replacing them with the more flexible option of painting from the History palette. History allows for multiple Snapshots, as well as painting from any available iteration of the image. In short, it does the job better than the Rubber Stamp options did in the past.

SEE ALSO

➤ *For more information on the History brush and palette controls, see page 36*

The areas where the Rubber Stamp is still the best choice are *cloning* and pattern creation. These are the tasks we explore in this chapter. Although the tasks themselves are pretty straightforward, the usefulness of this tool is still second to none.

Where to Find the Rubber Stamp

The Rubber Stamp is found in the Tools palette. In Photoshop 4, the pattern controls were selected from the Options palette, but with 5.0, Adobe has created a completely separate Rubber Stamp tool with which to create patterns. To select the Pattern Stamp tool, click and hold the Rubber Stamp tool icon and select the Pattern Stamp tool from the pop-out menu that appears (Figure 16.1). Adobe still delivers significant controls in the Options palette, including Apply modes and the opacity slider, aligned controls, and layers sampling boxes. We'll get into more detail on these later.

Need Toolbox help?

If you want a quick reference to all the tools on the Toolbox, look for the tear card in the front of the book. All the tools are visually depicted for your convenience.

FIGURE 16.1
Select the Pattern Stamp tool from the pop-out menu in the Tool palette.

How the Rubber Stamp Works

Whether it's cloning or patterning, the Rubber Stamp tool is referencing pixel data from one place and painting it in another. In the case of a pattern, it is referencing a four-sided area that has been saved as a pattern. The brush paints the same patterned square, over and over again. In the case of a clone, the information is painted based on a reference point in an image. Set the reference point on a man's face, and the brush will paint that face wherever you want it; anywhere in the image, in another layer, or even in a new file.

Cloning Effects

When looking at Photoshop's cloning capabilities, first consider the cloning options themselves. These options include alignment, opacity, and Apply mode options, which can dramatically change the effect as it's applied.

When the various options are understood, you should think about where you are getting the data from, and where it's going. You can capture data from a specific layer, or channel, or even a separate file. And of course, you can move it from any one of these variables to another. If this seems confusing, it'll all make sense as this section unfolds.

To start with, we'll do some basic cloning, which involves selecting the source point where the pixels will come from, and a destination point where they will be painted.

Cloning an image area

1. Select The Rubber Stamp tool from the Toolbox.

2. Determine the source point where the cloning data will come from. In this case, I decided to copy the leaf at the bottom of the image. Place your cursor at the desired *source point*, hold down the (Option) [Alt] key and click to set it. The cursor changes to a crosshair symbol (see Figure 16.2).

FIGURE 16.2

Hold down the (Option) [Alt] key to set the source point for the Rubber Stamp tool.

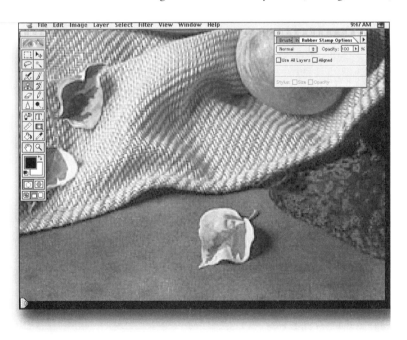

3. Double-click on the Rubber Stamp icon in the Toolbox to open the Options palette; then make the mode **Normal** and enter a value of 100% Opacity.

4. Move the cursor to another area in the image where you want to paint the leaf. Click and drag to clone the image (see Figure 16.3).

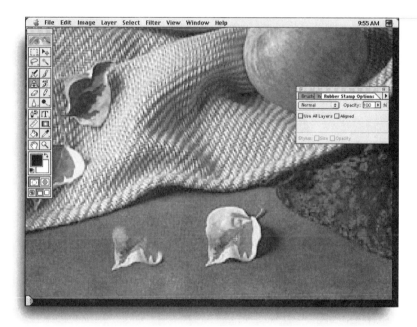

FIGURE 16.3
Paint to clone the image.

The Align Options

When you understand how data moves between one point and another, you can begin to take advantage of the align and non-align options. These two options are controlled by the **Aligned** check box in the Options palette.

When the **Aligned** check box is deselected, the source point snaps back to its original position whenever the mouse is released. This means that you could paint a whole pile of leaves in different areas of the image, by releasing the mouse each time you were finished painting (Figure 16.4). As long as the mouse button is held down, the tool will continue sampling, but when it is released, it reverts back to its starting point.

FIGURE 16.4

Leave the **Aligned** box deselected to repeatedly paint the same part of the image.

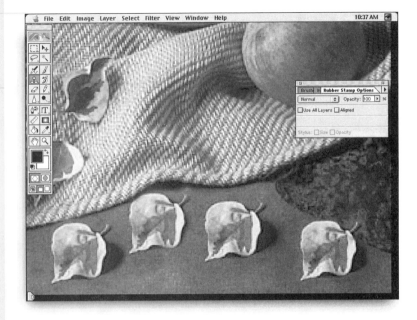

Don't forget Opacity and Apply modes

When you use the Rubber Stamp tool, remember that you can create some interesting effects and gain additional control with the opacity slider and the Apply modes, both of which are located in the Options palette.

By adding transparency with the opacity slider, you can mask any hard edges and create a more seamless integration between the objects and the image. This can be especially effective when painting into a dark background, where you might choose to paint the same object several times using varying degrees of opacity. This builds up of the image and creates a smooth and convincing effect.

Painting with the Apply modes is even more interesting in that the dramatic effects of Difference mode and Color Dodge can be applied selectively, and with more control. Try combining Opacity and Apply modes for even more variation and control.

Checking the **Aligned** check box activates the align option and allows the source point to move as the cursor moves. The relationship between the source point and the cursor is determined by the first brush stroke created after the source is set. For example, if you set the source point and then paint with the cursor an inch to the right, the source point will always be an inch to the right of the cursor. This traveling source point is useful for cleaning up dust and scratches, or for shifting large portions of the image.

SEE ALSO

➤ *For more details on Blending modes, see page 137*

Cloning Between Layers

There will be times when you will want to take information from one layer and move it to another. It might be to add a component to a layer that already has information, or it might be that you want to create a new layer and populate it with the information you're cloning.

When cloning with multiple layers, you need to consider whether your source point is reading one layer or all layers. By default, when you place your source point, it reads only the data on one layer, ignoring any other layers. You can set it to read the data from all layers in a stack by checking the **Use All Layers** check box in the Options palette. This samples any information present at the source point, regardless of what layer it's in.

Cloning between layers

1. Select the Rubber Stamp tool from the Toolbox.

2. From the **Window** menu, choose **Show Layers** to open the Layers palette. Click in the bar of the layer you want to place the source point. This activates the layer.

3. (Option+click) or [Alt+click] to set the source point at the desired spot.

4. With the Rubber Stamp tool active, activate the destination layer in the Layers palette and paint in the effect.

Cloning Between Files

In the same way that the Rubber Stamp lets you move data between layers, you can also move information between two different image files. This is a great way to place specific portions of an image into another file, without dragging an entire layer or pasting from the Clipboard.

Cloning between files

1. Select the Rubber Stamp tool from the Toolbox.

2. Open the Source file and (Option+click) [Alt+click] to set the source point at the desired spot.

3. Open the destination file or create a new file by selecting (Command+N) or [Control+N].

4. Select the Rubber Stamp tool and apply the effect (see Figure 16.5).

FIGURE 16.5

Using the Rubber Stamp
tool to paint between files.

Pattern Effects

The Pattern Stamp tool is similar to the Rubber Stamp tool in that it takes data from one location and moves it to another. The difference is that the Rubber Stamp references image data, and the Pattern Stamp references a rectangular pattern that is repeated over and over again, as shown in Figure 16.6. The pattern is created from image data but generally is abstracted as it is repeated across the image.

Before using the Pattern Stamp tool, you first have to define the pattern itself. When defined, this pattern can be used with the Paint Bucket tool or the **Fill** command, in addition to the Pattern Stamp tool. To select an area for a pattern, you must use a rectangular selection. Circular or abstract selections will not be recognized.

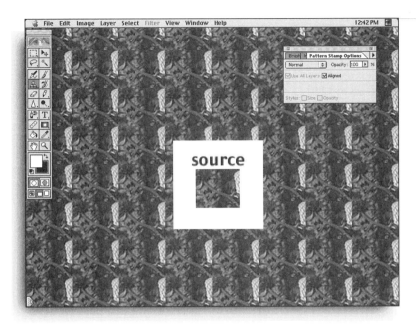

FIGURE 16.6

This repeating pattern was
brushed in with the Pattern
Stamp tool, using the rectangular section as a source.

Defining a pattern

1. Create a rectangular selection in the image using the rectangular Marquee tool.

2. From the **Edit** menu, choose **Define Pattern**.

After a pattern has been defined, it can be applied using any tool
that will reference the pattern design. The pattern will remain as
an active pattern source for the duration of the session, until
Photoshop is closed or another pattern is saved in its place.

Applying a pattern with the Pattern Stamp tool

1. Deselect the area used to define the pattern and select the
Pattern Stamp tool.

2. Select a brush size that is suited to the area being painted
and brush the pattern into the image.

SEE ALSO
➤ *For more information on the History brush and palette controls, see page 36*

Saving multiple patterns

If you need to create and recall
multiple pattern designs, save
each pattern selection as it is
created and paste it into a new
layer. You can then toggle the
layer visibility off to hide it from
view, or turn it back on and
select it to redefine the desired
pattern.

Working with Select Areas of an Image

Creating Paths to Define a Clipping Region

Using Paths

Paths are one of the best ways to define and edit areas of an image. They enable you to define specific areas with precision and save the results for repeated use. When used correctly, paths add almost no extra size to a file and can be freely shared between files and even other applications.

With all this power, paths are still one of the most underused features of Photoshop, especially for the beginning or intermediate user. Much of this is due to the fact that casual users don't understand how paths work. When they do understand, they are faced with the task of mastering Bezier tools, which can be challenging when just starting. The result is that people choose to bypass paths for more simplistic options.

This chapter shows how paths work and explains how to master the tools. Adobe has improved the paths options in Photoshop 5 to help those who don't like the traditional Bezier tools, although we will see that the original is still the best option.

Defining Bezier Tools

The Bezier Pen tool (pronounced "beh-zee-ay") is familiar to most graphic designers, especially those who use vector-based illustration programs such as Adobe Illustrator. The Bezier tool enables you to define an outline shape by clicking to set up anchor points, which are automatically linked with a straight line as the points are placed. Because paths always define an area, you always have to circle back to the starting point to close the path, completing the process. (If you don't close a path, Photoshop closes it for you when you convert to a selection, drawing a straight line between the two open end points.)

Creating and saving a simple path

1. Select the Pen tool from the Tools palette. If it is not visible, click and hold the path's tile and select it from the pop-up menu. Alternatively, you can also press the P key on the keyboard.

2. Click once to place the starting *anchor point* for the path.

3. Continue clicking to place anchor points as desired, creating a simple geometric shape.

4. Close the *path* by clicking on the original anchor point where you started. Notice that a small circle appears next to the Pen tool icon when the mouse is over the starting anchor, showing that the path can be closed (see Figure 17.1).

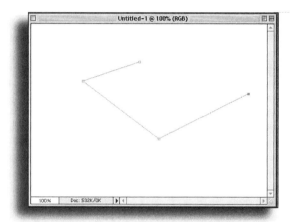

FIGURE 17.1

A small circle appears on the Pen tool icon when the tool is over the closing anchor.

Creating Curved Paths

Defining linear geometric shapes such as squares and rectangles is easy with paths because the lines between the anchors are straight and precise. It's when the shape curves that things get a bit complex. Bezier tools are popular because of the control they give when defining curved shapes. To curve the line segment between two anchor points, click and drag the mouse, which will drag out a pair of handles on each side of the anchor (see Figure 17.2).

The *handles* are linked together by a straight line and move in tandem, controlling the curve and slope of the line segment itself. When you move a single handle, two-line segments move, one on each side of the anchor. (This does not happen with corner points, discussed later in this chapter.) Although some might find this frustrating, it is actually a good thing in that it keeps the line flowing smoothly, allowing you to create convincing circles and ovals.

Restricting the Pen tool

When drawing paths, hold down the Shift key to keep line segments perpendicular. All other Pen tool shortcuts operate exactly as they do in Adobe Illustrator.

FIGURE 17.2

Drag the mouse while placing
an anchor point to reveal handles for creating a curved line
segment.

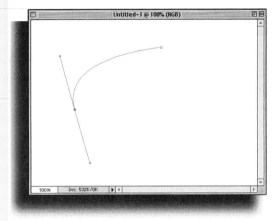

FIGURE 17.2

Drag the mouse while placing
an anchor point to reveal handles for creating a curved line
segment.

Creating curved paths

1. With the Pen tool selected, click once to place the starting anchor point for the path.

2. Position the Pen tool at approximately 3:00 from the initial anchor point, and click and drag to draw a curved segment. Keep the handles vertical for a perfect 45 degree arc, or vary them as needed, as shown in Figure 17.3.

FIGURE 17.3

Place the next anchor at 3:00.

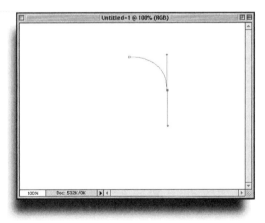

3. Place the next anchor point at approximately 6:00, clicking and dragging horizontally to maintain a smooth arc. This time a perfect horizontal handle set results in a balanced 45-degree arc (see Figure 17.4).

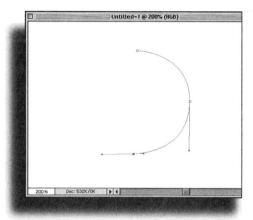

FIGURE 17.4
Place the next anchor at 6:00.

4. Draw additional anchor points at 9:00 and back at the starting point, dragging vertically and horizontally to close the shape. Keeping all four handle sets perfectly vertical and horizontal results in a balanced circle or oval.

So far this is still pretty manageable: we click once for straight line segments and click and drag for curved segments. The next challenge is how to combine curved and straight segments in a single path. Creating a curved line with abrupt direction changes and 45-degree angles would be virtually impossible were it not for the ability to add corner points. Corner points allow the line segments on opposite sides of an anchor point to operate independently. This enables you to create things such as stylized waves, word balloons, or any other linear object with complete control (see Figure 17.5).

You can create corner points within a series of curves by clicking without dragging when placing anchor points. This approach works for some things, but eventually you will need to drag an anchor for one part of a line, while keeping the adjoining segment unaffected. The best way to do this is to complete the path

FIGURE 17.5

Corner points enable you to combine curved and straight line segments for more complex shapes.

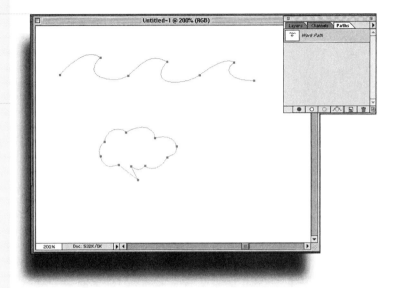

with the curved segments and go back to change the anchor points later. The following step by step shows how to change regular points to corner points in creating a complex shape. The first four steps create a nice, smooth word balloon using curved and straight segments. The last two steps show how to modify the anchor points for a different directional effect.

Converting corner points in a path

1. With the Pen tool selected, click once to place the starting anchor point for the path.

2. Draw an oval, clicking and dragging four additional anchor points to create the basic shape. Click the last anchor point without dragging, placing it next to the original point (Figure 17.6).

3. Position the tool down and to the right and click (don't drag) to place an anchor.

4. Close the path on the original anchor (Figure 17.7).

5. Select the Corner tool from the Path tool pop-up menu in the Toolbox.

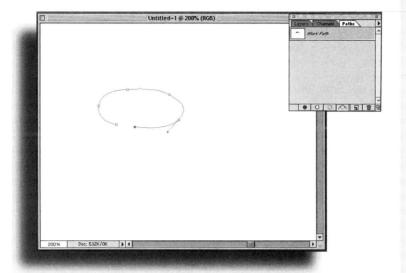

FIGURE 17.6
Draw an open oval, using a
series of curved path segments.

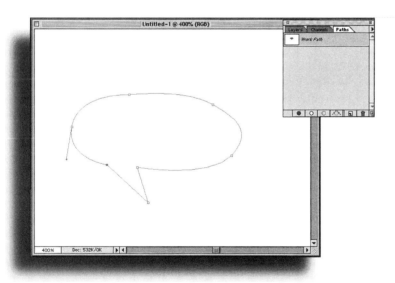

FIGURE 17.7
The closed path shape, before
the Corner tool is applied.

6. Position the pointer over a curved anchor point and click
and drag. Although the handles move in tandem, they are
actually independent of each other. Select them one at a
time and move them into the desired positions as shown in
Figure 17.8.

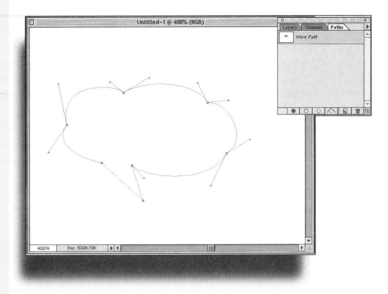

Reworking an Existing Path

Two additional tools that can help in reworking paths are the Add Point and Subtract Point tools. To use the Add Point tool, position the Tool icon over a line segment in an existing path and click the mouse. You can, of course, click and drag to create a curved line segment. This can be part of an effective strategy where you quickly block in the basic path and fine-tune it later, adding more points as needed.

The Subtract Point tool does the opposite of the Add Point tool. Position and click the tool over a point and the point is removed; the next two points are joined by a line segment. This tool works well in cleaning up some of the free-form path options discussed in the next section.

The Freehand Pen Tools

As mentioned before, the precision of the Bezier Pen tool is not for everyone. Some people just don't have the patience or need for defining paths in this way. In a gesture to these people, Adobe has added two new Pen tools to Photoshop 5: the Magnetic Pen tool and the Freeform Pen tool.

Changing the Pen tool to the Selection tool

The Command key (Mac) or Control key (Win) converts the Pen tool to the Selection tool, allowing you to place anchor points and reposition them quickly.

The Freeform Pen tool enables you to draw just as you would with the Photoshop Pencil or Brush tool. This approach creates more expressive and casual shapes, although it does create a ton of anchor points. This usually requires you to go back and clean things up, deleting points and reshaping things with curved segments. The reason for this is that the Freeform Pen tool does not know when to use a curve, so it just draws lots of small segments to define a curving shape. Where the Bezier tool can define a smooth arc with 2 anchors and a line segment, the Freeform Pen tool might use 50 anchors and segments.

The Freeform Pen approach can create problems because the numerous points can create larger files and can confuse some RIPs if they are to be used as *clipping paths*. (Clipping paths will be discussed later in this chapter.)

Drawing a freeform pen

1. With the Options palette open, select the Freeform Pen tool from the Tools palette. In the Options palette, enter an appropriate **Curve Fit** value, understanding that a lower value makes the tool more sensitive to direction changes (see Figure 17.9).

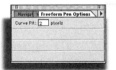

2. Click and drag the tool to define the path shape.

3. To close the path, position the tool cursor over the starting anchor and click to close. A small circle appears next to the tool to indicate that the path might be closed.

What kind of images work well with paths?

Paths are not a selection panacea to be used in all situations. Sometimes they are the perfect solution, and other times you are better off using the Masking or Magic Wand tools.

Use paths when you want to select objects with clearly defined edges, featuring any manner of complex geometric shapes. This implies circles and ovals but also includes cars, toasters, and a cityscape. All these objects feature a combination of curves, lines, and proportions that lend themselves to the strengths of the Bezier Pen tool.

In contrast, you would never think of using paths to define abstract or organic objects such as trees, smoke, or a waterfall. The Pen tool is not sensitive and reactive enough to capture these objects well. You are better off selecting these objects in other ways and converting the selection to a path, as described in the sidebar on page 325

FIGURE 17.9
The options palette enables you to control the smoothness of the Freeform Pen tool.

Constraining movement

When using the Freeform and Magnetic Pen tools, hold down the Spacebar to constrain the movement to the vertical or horizontal directions.

Draw smoothly

Remember that the Freeform Pen tool is speed sensitive and will lay down more points if you draw slowly. Try to draw with smooth, deliberate strokes to minimize excess points.

The Magnetic Pen Tool

The Magnetic Pen tool is a variation on the Freeform tool previously mentioned. It also allows you to drag random path shapes, with one little twist. The tool is sensitive to contrasting pixels, which makes the anchor points adhere to a shape as you draw it. A click places an absolute anchor point, as does a clear change of direction.

Although this sounds like a great idea, it's important to realize that the tool cannot read you mind or your image. You need to analyze your image in terms of contrast and shape complexity and configure the tool accordingly. Photoshop enables you to specify a number of parameters for this tool, which are accessed in the Magnetic Pen Options palette. The Magnetic Pen tool enables you to modify the curve fit, pen width, frequency, and edge contrast sensitivity (Figure 17.10). These parameters are briefly described in the following list:

FIGURE 17.10

The Magnetic Pen Tool Options palette

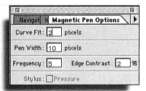

Do you draw slowly?

If you tend to draw slowly, set the pixel frequency in the Options palette to a lower value, and specify a higher **Curve Fit** value.

- **Curve fit**. Refers to the way the curve describes the curve of the path. A lower value makes the path more exact, although it adds more points in the process.
- **Pen width**. Controls the active area on either side of the line, where the tool looks for contrast in the image.
- **Frequency**. Controls how often points are placed on the path.
- **Edge Contrast**. Defines how sensitive the tool should be as it looks for contrast across the active area. Low contrast images should use lower percentage values.

The Magnetic Pen tool suffers from many of the same problems as the Freeform Pen tool. It creates too many points and still does not describe a smooth curving line with any real precision. It is also a bit harder to close magnetic paths, and they can get messy pretty fast. I suppose that these limitations can be over-come with practice, but if you're going to spend time practicing something, make sure you have the Bezier tool down first.

Naming and Saving Paths

When you have the perfect path, you want to be sure and save it so you can use it over and over again. The great thing about paths is that they do not increase file size very much, and it is always better to use paths than to save selections to *channels*.

SEE ALSO

➤ *For information on saving selections, see page 212*

After a path is drawn, it appears in the Paths palette with the title **Work Path**. Saving a path is as simple as double-clicking on the **Work Path** tile and entering a name in the dialog box that appears (see Figure 17.11).

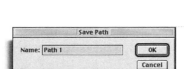

FIGURE 17.11
Enter the layer name in the Save Path dialog box.

Converting Paths to a Selection

When you have a path defined, you will probably want to con-vert it to a selection so that you can edit the image. Paths them-selves are not applied to the image directly; they sit on top of it, tracing an outline of the desired area.

Converting a path to a selection

1. In the Paths palette, click on the desired path to activate it.

Converting selections to paths

Although you usually create a path to make a *selection*, you will sometimes want to go the other way, converting a selec-tion to a path. This can be a good idea if you want to save a selection for later use without ballooning your file size. To convert a selection to a path, select **Make Work Path** from the Paths palette pop-up menu, set the tolerance, and click **OK**. It's then a simple matter to save the path as described elsewhere in this chapter, completing the process.

The only word of caution is to be careful about using a selec-tion that is too complex or that creates excessive points. Too many points can create printing problems, postscript errors, or paths that do not work at all. However, with a little common sense, you can select areas any way you want and convert them with ease.

Multiple shapes in a path

Remember that even if you draw multiple closed path shapes, Photoshop still consid-ers them to be part of the same path. This can be convenient for complex shapes and areas, but it can be confusing if you don't manage it and pay attention to where your paths are being drawn.

2. Select **Make Selection** from the Paths palette pop-up menu.

3. Set the **Feather Radius** in the dialog box that follows, depending on the desired softness of the image.

4. Click **OK** to activate the selection.

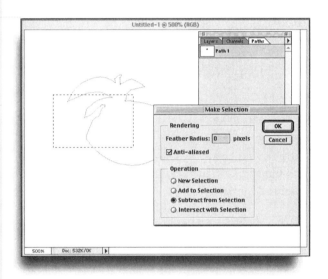

Using selection modifiers

If another selection is active as you create a path selection, you have the option of adding, subtracting, or intersecting the new selection with the current one. You can select these options in the **Operations** section of the Make Selection dialog box that appears in step 3 of the previous step by step (see Figure 17.12). Selecting New Selection deselects the current one.

Importing or Exporting Paths

After a path is saved, you can make a copy of it by selecting **Duplicate Path** from the Paths palette pop-up menu. Give the path a new name in the dialog box that appears and click **OK** to complete the operation. To share paths between files, follow this step by step.

Sharing paths between files

1. Open both image files.

2. In the Paths palette, select and highlight the path to be copied.

3. Drag the path tile to the open window of the destination file to copy the path.

Stroking and Filling Paths

Photoshop provides several options for filling and stroking paths. You can trace a path with color using any of the Photoshop tools, and you can fill it with selected colors, patterns, or even a previous iteration of the History palette.

SEE ALSO

➤ *For information on the History palette, see page 35*

When you stroke a path, the effect is applied to the current active layer, or the background, depending how the file is set up. This might sound obvious, but it's easy to lose track of layers and paths as you work, and you might find that you applied the effect to the wrong layer by mistake.

Stroking a path

1. Highlight the path to be used in the Paths palette.

FIGURE 17.13

Photoshop enables you to designate the tool used to stroke a path.

2. Determine which Photoshop paint tool you want to use for the stroke and double-click it in the Tools palette, opening the Options palette. Set the desired parameters for the tool at this time because Photoshop uses the current options settings at the time the stroke command is executed.

3. Select **Stroke Path** from the Paths palette pop-up menu and select the desired tool from the pop-up menu of the dialog box that appears. Click **OK** to apply the effect (see Figure 17.13).

Filling a path allows its own set of possibilities. Paths can be filled with colors or patterns, and applied using various opacity settings or apply modes. Follow the steps to fill a path.

Filling a path

1. Highlight the path to be used in the Paths palette.

2. Select **Fill Path** from the Paths palette pop-up menu.

3. Determine the contents of the fill in the **Contents** section of the Fill Path dialog box that appears. The pop-up menu allows you to choose from foreground or background colors, patterns and image history iterations, and black-and-white options.

4. Set the desired mode and **Opacity** setting in the **Blending** section.

5. Set the softness of the path by setting the **Feather Radius** and **Anti-Aliased** controls in the **Rendering** section (see Figure 17.14).

FIGURE 17.14
The Fill Path dialog box.

6. Click **OK** to apply the effect.

Creating Clipping Paths

When Photoshop creates an image, it creates a square or rectangle that it fills with pixels. Unlike vector images that can exist as freeform shapes, bitmap images are always confined to the square or rectangular format. When these rectangular images are placed in a page layout, things can get boring fast. Designers don't like to place boxes all over the page; they prefer to *silhouette* images from time to time, creating a more interesting and organic composition. This is where clipping paths come in.

Clipping paths enable you to save a file as a silhouette, sidestepping the standard Photoshop restriction of the rectangle or square.

The approach to creating clipping paths is simple:

- Create a path to define the area or shape.
- Save the path as a clipping path.
- Save the image as an *EPS file*.
- Place the image into your page layout application.

The following steps outline the complete process for setting and using clipping paths.

Setting clipping paths

1. Create a path for the image and save it in the Paths palette.

2. Select **Clipping Path** from the Paths palette pop-up menu.

3. In the dialog box that appears, select the desired path from the **Path** pop-up menu and click **OK**. The name of the path in the Paths palette should appear in outline form, showing that it is an active clipping path.

4. From the **File** menu, choose **Save as** and select **Photoshop EPS** from the **File type** pop-up menu. Save the file to complete the operation. Placing this file in any layout or EPS-based program silhouettes the path, blocking out the background of the image.

SEE ALSO
➤ *For information on saving selections, see page 212*
➤ *For information on the History palette, see page 35*

Using Masks

An Introduction to Quick Masking in Photoshop

One of Photoshop's greatest strengths is its capability to conform to the relative strengths of each individual user. Some people like to use curves, for example, whereas others prefer levels, and still others might prefer brightness or contrast. Photoshop gives you a range of tool options, enabling you to choose which one you like best.

In this chapter, we look at one unique way in which Photoshop enables you to select certain areas of your image. Oh sure, you have the Magic Wand tool, the Lasso, and the Marquee tool, and each of those work very well in defining a selection by its edges. The Photoshop Quick Mask feature lets you define a selection by painting an area, brushing in the selection using the full gamut of Photoshop's tool set. If you tend to think in terms of painted areas rather than outlines and paths, you might find Quick Mask selections to be a more intuitive way of defining an area.

Quick Mask is a special mode in Photoshop that is completely devoted to defining a selection. While in Quick Mask mode, every Photoshop function, tool result, and menu command is related to defining the selected area. When you paint or draw, you are painting a selected area. When you use the Blur tool, you are blurring a selected area, and when you apply a filter, you are actually filtering a selected area. We will look at how to use all these effects in this chapter, along with other masking and selection options.

Quick Mask gets its name from the fact that as you create your selection area, Photoshop masks that area off, tinting it with a colored mask to show what has been selected. When you finish making the selection, you exit Quick Mask mode, and Photoshop automatically converts the mask to a standard selection so that you can edit the image. Quick Mask is a visual, painterly way to make a selection, and if it's handled correctly, it can make unique selections that are impossible to re-create in any other way.

Before we start creating Quick Mask selections, we need to set up the parameters for how Quick Mask will work. The following steps set up the way the painted mask looks as it is applied, along with some other relevant selection parameters.

Setting up the Quick Mask parameters

1. Double-click the Quick Mask icon just below the color swatches in the Tool palette (Figure 18.1).

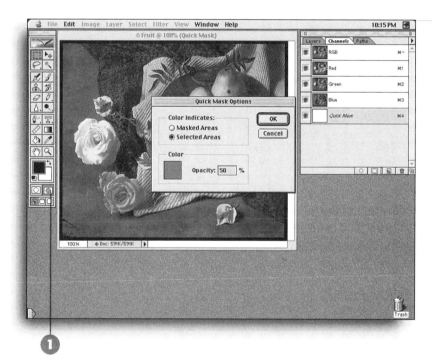

2. Select **Color Indicates** option. Choosing **Masked Areas** means that any colored areas will not be selected when you exit Quick Mask mode. The **Selected Areas** check box means that colored areas will be selected when you exit Quick Mask.

3. Click on the color swatch to launch the Photoshop Color Picker and select the color for your mask. This is especially important if the current color is similar to the color of your selected area.

4. Enter an **Opacity** percentage value to indicate how much of the transparency shows through as you paint it and click **OK**.

Because you already choose a mask color in step 2, you don't need to worry about color anymore while in Quick Mask mode. In fact, Photoshop doesn't even let you work with color in this mode; it converts everything to *grayscale*. To see what I mean, try to select a foreground color in the Color palette; it automatically converts to its grayscale equivalent.

The reason for this is that Photoshop uses grayscale values to control the relative intensity of the mask you are painting. With black as the active color, the paint tools paint the mask at 100% intensity. If white is the *active* color, the mask is erased, and any shades of gray will paint the mask in relative degrees of opacity. In summary, black lays down the mask color; white erases it. And if you make a mask or selection with an 80% gray, any editing done through that selection will be applied at 80%. Paint into that selection and it goes on at 80%; delete that selection and it's deleted to 80%.

With the parameters set, it's time to create your first Quick Mask selection.

Creating a basic Quick Mask selection

1. Click on the Quick Mask icon to enter the Quick Mask mode.

2. Select the Paintbrush tool from the Toolbox, choose a brush size appropriate for the area to be selected, and select black as the foreground color.

3. Begin painting the area to be selected. Notice that Photoshop paints the mask over the area as you paint, as shown in Figure 18.2.

4. To erase any of the mask, select white as the foreground color and paint over the area to be deleted. You will notice that the mask disappears as you do this. To toggle between black and white, press the X key.

Mask opacities

Even though you set the visible transparency of the mask in the previous step by step, the actual transparency of the selection is determined by the grayscale value set as the foreground color while you paint the mask. The **Opacity** value set in the Quick Mask Options dialog box only controls how the mask looks as you're painting it; it does not effect the intensity of the mask or the resulting selection.

FIGURE 18.2
Applying a mask in Quick Mask mode.

5. When the mask covers the appropriate area, click the Standard Mode icon to convert the masked area to a selection. (Please note that all areas except the mask will be selected in this step if you selected **Color Indicates Masked Areas** in the set up procedure.)

Rather than painting a large or complex area from scratch, you might find it beneficial to select part of an area with Photoshop's conventional selection tools to start with, fine-tuning things with Quick Mask later.

To do this, you simply make a selection and click the Quick Mask mode button to enter Quick Mask mode. The current selection will be converted to a mask. The Magic Wand tool is an excellent selection tool to start with, as the proper tolerance setting can select much of the desired area if it's set right. Another approach is to use the Marquee tool and Shift+select large blocks of a selection before entering Quick Mask mode.

SEE ALSO

➤ *For more information on the Magic Wand tool and making selections, see page 206*

Creating Translucent Masks and Selections

We generally think of masks and selections as either activating an area or excluding it from any editing. But it is possible to make a selection that affects only an area partially. For example, if an area is partially selected, painting with black results in a gray stroke that is lighter or darker, depending on how much it is selected. The effect is similar to when a selection edge is *feathered*, and the effect is faded out toward the edges.

I refer to them as translucent selections in the context of Quick Masks because these partial selections are painted on using a gray color rather than straight black. The darker the gray, the more the area shows the effect, whereas masks painted with a lighter gray let the effect show through more slightly. Translucent masks allow areas and layers to fade into one another, creating smooth transition effects. The following steps shows how to set up these transition areas easily using Quick Mask.

Creating a translucent selection

1. Enter Quick Mask by selecting the Quick Mask mode button.

2. Select black as the foreground color and white as the background; select the Gradient tool from the Toolbox. Make sure that foreground to background is selected as the gradient type in the Gradient tool Options palette.

3. Beginning where you want the selection to have its strongest effect, click and drag a gradient across the image (see Figure 18.3).

4. To adjust the fade of the gradient, select **Image**, **Adjust**, **Curves**, and raise or lower the curve to increase or decrease the speed of the fade.

5. Exit Quick Mask mode to activate the selection.

After a translucent selection is created, it's a simple matter to delete it to the background color or to reveal a lower layer (Figure 18.4). You can also fill the selection with a color, pattern, or even a pasted image.

FIGURE 18.3
While in Quick Mask mode, drag a black to white gradient across the image.

FIGURE 18.4
After creating a translucent selection, delete to the background for a fadeout effect.

Sharpen or Blur a Quick Mask

There is more to creating a Quick Mask than simply painting an area and converting it to a selection. Remember that Photoshop enables you to use all its tools on the painted mask you created. This means that you can apply local or global sharpen or blur effects, further modifying the selection you created. After you have a basic Quick Mask area defined, you can use the following methods to further modify the mask:

- Use the Sharpen, Blur, or Smudge tool.

Starting a Quick Mask

Remember that you can start a Quick Mask from any standard selection approach. Try creating a color-based selection and converting that to a Quick Mask for further selection modification.

- Use the Dodge or Burn tool.
- Use the **Curves** controls.
- Use **Edge** effects (**Invert, Equalize, Threshold, Posterize**).
- Use **Filters** to add patterns and distortion.

Use the Sharpen, Blur, and Smudge Tools

The Sharpen, Blur, and Smudge tools are an effective way to modify local edge areas of a selection. For example, if you want to have the edge of a selection fade out on one side but be crisp and sharp on the other, use the Sharpen and Blur tools as needed. In the same way, selecting the Smudge tool enables you to smear and distort selection edges in varying degrees (see Figure 18.5).

FIGURE 18.5

The effects of the Sharpen, Blur, and Smudge tools on a Quick Mask.

The key differentiation between these approaches and selecting feather edges or a distort filter, for example, is that these commands apply their effects globally to the entire selection, whereas the Sharpen, Blur, and Smudge tools enable you to modify local areas of the mask. Quick Mask allows you to use individual tools on specific areas of a selection as needed.

Use the Dodge or Burn Tool

The Dodge or Burn tool provides another way to modify a mask by making the mask value darker or lighter. This approach enables you to darken an edge, which sharpens it and eliminates any anti-aliased or feather effects that might be applied there. Conversely, the Dodge tool lets you soften an edge, creating more of a feathered selection. In this respect, the Dodge or Burn tool modifies a mask in the same way as the Sharpen/Blur tools but does go one step further.

The Dodge or Burn tool also lets you modify the translucency of a mask, making it more opaque or transparent. You can use the Burn tool to darken and solidify a selection area, whereas the Dodge tool lightens and feathers an area. This lets you move beyond modifying only the edges, letting you modify internal areas of a mask and selection as well (see Figure 18.6).

FIGURE 18.6
The Dodge or Burn tool can create or delete transparent sections of an existing Quick Mask.

Use the Curves Controls

When you start a translucent mask, either with a gradient or any of the tools previously listed, you can modify the relative translucency with curves. It's as simple as selecting the **Image** menu and choosing **Adjust**, **Curves** while in Quick Mask mode and moving the curve up or down to lighten or darken the current mask. You can make similar modifications with the Brightness, Contrast, or Levels controls.

Use Edge Effects—Invert, Equalize, Threshold, and Posterize

It is also possible to modify a mask using the four edge effects controls found at the bottom of the **Adjust** submenu in the **Image** menu. These controls can deliver quick shortcuts to various mask editing requirements:

- **Invert** turns the current mask inside out, switching the selected and deselected areas.

- **Equalize** sharpens the mask globally, while adding a slight degree of feather, depending on whether it was present in the original selection.

- **Threshold** eliminates all feather, defining an absolute edge between the selected and deselected areas. You can control where this break occurs by moving the threshold slider in the dialog box that appears when you select this command, as shown in Figure 18.7.

FIGURE 18.7

The Threshold slider controls the edge and area covered by the Quick Mask.

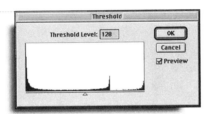

- **Posterize** divides the mask into distinct levels of opacity, which in turn create distinct levels of translucent selections. Simply select the **Posterize** command and enter the number of levels desired in your mask, and Photoshop divides the mask into distinct sections. Be sure the **Preview** box is checked so that you can preview the effect from the dialog box.

Use Filters to Add Patterns and Distortion

One of the most exciting ways to modify a Quick Mask is by using *filters*. Filters affect an active mask in the same way that they affect a standard set of pixel values (excluding color modifications). This means that you can apply a texture or pattern to a mask, which in turn can become a texture selection for you to fill with a color or another image, or to simply delete to the background. Here are the general range of effects that can be applied to a mask:

- **Sharpen or Blur filters**. Apply special Sharpen or **Blur** effects to a mask, such as motion or radial blur filters. Explore the Sharpen /Blur submenus to appreciate the full range of options.

- **Texture effects**. Apply textures or patterns with any of the filters found in the **Artistic**, **Brush Stroke**, **Noise**, **Sketch**, or **Texture** submenus.

- **Distortion effects**. You can apply twirl or wave patterns to a mask using the filters found in the **Distort**, **Render**, and **Other** submenus.

The following step by step applies multiple filters to a Quick Mask. It shows the basic procedure for filtering a mask, as well as giving an indication of how filters can be combined for more complex results.

Filtering a Quick Mask

1. Enter Quick Mask mode by selecting the Quick Mask mode button.

2. From the **Filter** menu, choose **Noise** and **Add Noise**. With the **Preview** button selected, you see the noise mask effect that results (Figure 18.8). Adjust the various noise controls until the desired noise effect is achieved, and click **OK**.

FIGURE 18.8

Apply the **Add Noise** filter to a Quick Mask.

3. From the **Filter** menu, choose **Artistic** and **Palette Knife** and modify the settings to create a random speckle effect. I had to lower the stroke size and increase the softness to create the effect shown in Figure 18.9. Click **OK** to apply the effect.

FIGURE 18.9

The settings and preview for applying the **Palette Knife** filter.

4. From the **Filter** menu, choose **Distort**, **Wave** and modify the settings to distort the pattern (Figure 18.10). Click **OK** to apply the effect.

FIGURE 18.10

The results of the **Wave** filter.

5. Exit Quick Mask mode to convert the mask to a selection.

From Quick Masks to Alpha Channels

Having spent so much time creating these artistic selections, the last thing you want to do is deselect them and have all your work disappear forever. To avoid this, you can save the selection using Photoshop's **Save Selection** command. This ensures that your selection is securely archived, ready to be reactivated whenever you need it.

Saving a selection

1. With the desired selection still active, choose **Select** and **Save Selection**.

2. Enter a name for the selection channel in the dialog box that appears.

3. Make sure that the current document's name is showing in the **Document** pop-up menu, and select **New Selection** from the **Channel** pop-up menu (Figure 18.11).

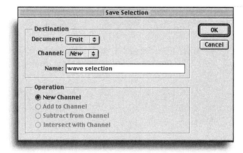

FIGURE 18.11
The Save Selection dialog box.

4. Click **OK** to complete the process.

When Photoshop saves your selection, it actually creates a new channel, called an *Alpha channel*, that records the selection information. Found in the Channels palette next to the RGB or CMYK channels, the Alpha channel shows you the grayscale information used to reactivate the selection. Open the Channels palette to see that the selection was saved and named as you requested. This channel contains the same selection information that you created in the Quick Mask mode; it's just archived for future use.

After a selection is saved, you can reload it at any time. Follow these steps to reload a saved selection from an Alpha channel.

Loading a selection

1. From the **Select** menu, choose **Load Selection**.

2. Select the desired Alpha channel from the **Channel** pop-up menu. If you have just one selection saved for this document, it appears in the menu automatically.

Multiple selections

If you have a selection active as you load another one, you can add, subtract, or intersect the new channel from the current selection, using the **Operations** section of the Load Selection dialog box.

3. Check the **Invert** check box if you want to select everything except the Alpha channel's contents.

4. Click **OK** to load the selection.

SEE ALSO

➤ *For more information on the Magic Wand tool and making selections, see page 206*

Working with Layers

An Introduction to Layers

Although masks and selections present a solid way to isolate parts of an image for editing, they still fall short of the power and flexibility offered by layers. Layers enable you to isolate individual image components, keeping them separate from each other, yet modifying them as needed. Think of layer information as sitting on separate sheets of acetate. They stack on top of each other, allowing you to view the entire image at once, while still making corrections to individual areas.

Type, images, and color adjustments can all be entered in a layer. In fact, Photoshop creates a unique layer type for each, which supports their unique requirements. One other layer type is the **Background** layer, which is automatically created with each new image. The **Background** layer serves as the universal backdrop that the rest of the image is built upon. Each of these layer types is explained in complete detail in the pages that follow (Figure 19.1).

FIGURE 19.1

Photoshop creates four different layer types.

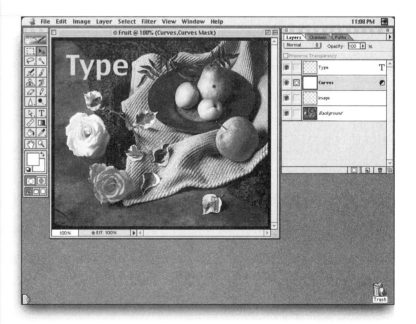

Creating a Layer

You can create a layer in Photoshop in many ways. In addition to straightforward creating a command, some activities automatically generate a layer as they are activated. For example, Photoshop creates a new layer each time you paste materials into an image or create a block of type. Any of the procedures listed here results in the creation of a new layer.

- From the **Layer** menu, select **New Layer** and click **OK** in the dialog box that follows.
- From the Layers palette **Options** menu, select **New Layer** (or **New Adjustment Layer**).
- Click the New Layer icon from the Layers palette.
- Paste information into the image from the Clipboard.
- Create type with the Type tool.
- Drag a layer from one document to another.
- Drag a layer from the Layers palette to another document.

Creating a layer is simple enough, but the reasons for doing so are diverse and sometimes complex. Keeping in mind that the basic function of a layer is to isolate an image component from its surroundings, some of the uses for a layer are as follows:

- To create movable type that can be repositioned within an image
- To create a montage of image components for an illustration
- To create a box or blank area to serve as a backdrop for text insertion.
- To make dynamic, adjustable color corrections (using an adjustment layer)
- To sharpen one part of an image (on one layer), while blurring another
- To create a freehand drawing over an image without editing the image itself
- To preserve a pristine copy of the original image on one layer, while modifying a duplicate on another

Layers increase file size

Additional layers increase the overall file size in an image, so use layers carefully and be prepared to flatten the image if your system has trouble handling the file.

Layer Palette and Menu Controls

All layer functions are controlled from the **Layers** menu or the Layers palette. To interject just a bit of redundancy and confusion into working with layers, Adobe built most of the same commands into both the **Layers** menu and palette. The **Layers** menu does offer the **Effects**, **Type**, and **Align** controls, but otherwise the feature set is the same. Look at the Layers palette controls first, and the remaining menu commands will be covered as we work our way through the chapter.

You open the Layers palette from the **Window** menu by selecting **Show Layers**. The palette shows Apply **Mode** and **Opacity** controls at the top, and the individual layers cascading below it. Each layer is comprised of a Visibility icon at the far left, an Activity icon next to it, and the layer name bar featuring a thumbnail of the layer contents. Click on the Visibility icon to toggle the layer's visibility on and off. When the icon is absent, it indicates that a layer is hidden, whereas an open eye represents a visible layer. The next column is blank, or shows a Paintbrush or Link icon. The Paintbrush indicates that this is the active layer for editing, and the Link icon indicates any layers linked to the active layer.

There are three icons in the lower-right part of the palette: Add Layer Mask, New Layer, and Trash. The Trash Can is for discarding layers and layer masks only, whereas the other two icons are pretty self-explanatory (see Figure 19.2).

FIGURE 19.2
The Layers palette.

SEE ALSO

➤ *For more information on layer masks, see page 364*

Whenever you open an image or create a new file, Photoshop creates a background layer, which appears in the layers palette titled **Background**. Each layer includes a thumbnail icon that reflects the contents of the layer itself.

Because the background layer is meant to act as the solid backdrop to the entire image, many of the layer adjustment cannot be applied to it. Features such as **Layer Effects**, **Layer Options**, and grouping options are not possible with a background image. In order to apply these effects, you must duplicate the background layer or convert it from a background layer to a regular layer.

Converting a background layer to a normal layer

1. Double-click the **Background** layer title bar to open the Make Layer dialog box, as shown in Figure 19.3.

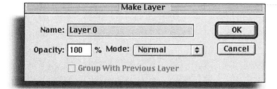

FIGURE 19.3
The Make Layer dialog box.

2. Enter a layer name in the **Name** field.

3. Set the Apply **Mode** and **Opacity** percentage as desired and click **OK**.

Managing Layer Placement and Visibility

The reason layers are so powerful is that they give so much flexibility and control over every aspect of your image. They enable you to hide and reveal image components, edit and preserve information, and apply color corrections independent of the layers beneath them.

Arranging, Duplicating, and Merging Layers

Photoshop only lets you edit one layer at a time. To target a layer as the active editing layer, click in its title section, which will highlight the entire layer bar. At the same time, a Paintbrush appears in the active layer section to show that it is active. When a layer is active, any modifications applied to the image will be applied only to that layer. This means that any color corrections, painting, or filter application will affect only the active layer, leaving the other layers untouched.

Arranging layers in the layer stack is as simple as clicking the layers title section and dragging it to the desired position. You cannot drag any layers below the **Background** layer, and the **Background** layer itself cannot be moved out of its position as the first layer in the stack.

A common approach to working with layers is to duplicate a layer, creating an exact copy. The advantages of this approach are numerous. In addition to creating a backup of the image that you can always go back to, you can also duplicate a layer and erase all but a specific object or section, which you can edit or enhance in some way. This enables you to freely modify the one area without worrying about selections and paths, and the area is always available in its own layer whenever you want to go back and modify it further.

Duplicating a layer

1. Click the title bar of the layer to be copied, highlighting it as the active layer. Make sure that the Paintbrush icon is visible and associated with the active layer.

2. Select **Duplicate Layer** from the Layers palette **Options** pop-up menu, or select **Layer** and **Duplicate Layer**.

3. Enter the name of the new layer in the **As:** name field. Photoshop lists the original layer name followed by the word **Copy** as a default naming scheme, but you can enter anything you like, as shown in Figure 19.4.

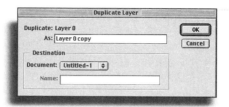

FIGURE 19.4
The Duplicate Layer dialog box.

4. Make sure that the current document name is shown in the **Document** pop-up menu and click **OK**.

As the layers in a file increase, the ability to manage them becomes more important. Sometimes you will want to combine two layers into one, hide a series of layers, or get rid of a layer altogether.

Deleting a layer is as easy as selecting **Delete Layer** from the **Layers** menu or **Layers** palette. You can also drag the layer to the Trash icon at the bottom-right area of the Layers palette.

Four merge commands appear in both the **Layers** menu or the **Layers** palette pop-up menu: **Merge Down**, **Merge Visible**, **Merge Linked**, and **Flatten Image**. **Merge Down** combines the current active layer with the layer just below it in the layer stack. **Merge Visible** merges all layers that are visible as the command is applied. This is a good way to clean up an image and streamline file size. It's as simple as turning off the visibility of any layer you still want separate and selecting **Merge Visible** to combine the rest. **Merge Linked** does just what it say, as it combines multiple linked layers into a single layer. This command is available only when linked layers are present. **Flatten Image** does just what it says; it takes all layers, visible or not, and combines them into one flat, nonlayers image. If any layers are not visible at the time you select the command, Photoshop asks you if you want to discard the hidden layers. Press **Cancel** if you want to go back and add them to the image or duplicate them to another file.

Saving a layer to a new file

You can duplicate a layer to a new file by selecting **New** from the **Document** pop-up menu in step 4. Photoshop creates a new file comprised of the layer's contents.

Saving in other formats

Files with layers can be saved only in the native Photoshop file format. In order to save them in any other format, flatten the image and select **Save As**, choosing the desired file format from the pop-up menu in the dialog box.

Combining Layers by Linking

Photoshop lets you drag the contents of a layer around the screen by selecting the layer in the Layers palette and dragging it with the Move tool. After you align multiple layers just the way you want them, you can link them together so that they move on the screen as a single unit.

This is different from the merge or flatten commands in that the layers remain separate and can be edited and changed independently of each other. The only thing that is linked is the relative pixel positioning between the layers.

To link two layers, highlight one as the active layer, making sure that the Paintbrush is showing in the second column of the Layers palette. Click in the second column of the other layer to be linked and the Link icon appears, showing that it is linked to the active layer (Figure 19.5).

FIGURE 19.5

Click to link layers together.

Altering Layers with Opacity and Apply Modes

Although linking layers enables you to control the vertical and horizontal alignment between two layers, the real fun begins when you use the **Opacity** controls and apply modes. This approach moves away from an emphasis on just the x and y axes and looks at the z axis of how layers can interact with each other as they overlap.

The easiest way to get layers to interact is to change their opacity, making them transparent. Follow the steps here to create a transparent layer.

Creating a transparent layer

1. Select the target layer in the Layers palette, highlighting it to make it active.

2. Click on the **Opacity** pop-up control.

3. Drag the slider right or left, increasing or decreasing the transparency of the layer, as shown in Figure 19.6.

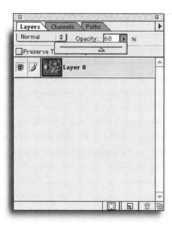

FIGURE 19.6
Drag the Opacity slider to create a transparent layer.

Another way to get layers to interact is to use them with apply modes. As you previously learned, apply modes control the way two different sets of pixel data interact with each other. In the case of layers, apply modes control the way an upper layer interacts with the layer just below it.

To assign an apply mode to a layer, highlight the layer, click on the **Apply Mode** pop-up menu in the Layers palette, and drag down to select the desired mode.

Mask Effects with Clipping Groups

One last layer option is the ability to create clipping groups within a layer stack. A clipping group enables you to designate the lowest layer in a grouped stack as a sort of mask that all the upper layers in the group are seen through.

The areas in the lower layer that determine whether it is a mask are its transparency. If the layer is opaque in all areas, everything in all layers is visible, and the clipping group looks no different than a standard layer stack. However, if transparency is in the

Using the **Preserve Transparency** option

Whenever you have a layer that is partially erased, you can select the **Preserve Transparency** check box in the Layers palette. This enables you to preserve the current transparency status of the layer while still editing it further. This might sound confusing, so let me explain with an example.

Say you have a layer that is empty except for some text you just added. If you select the Paintbrush and begin painting, you modify the entire layer, obliterating the text and filling in what was a transparent background. By selecting **Preserve Transparency** before painting, you only modify areas with pixel values, in this case, inside the text. The text outlines remain clean and crisp, and the transparent areas remain as they were…in a word, preserved.

layer, as in text on a transparent background, the upper layers in the group are visible only through the opaque areas of the lower layer. It's kind of like using the **Preserve Transparency** command across multiple layers.

The exercise below combines many of the layer effects considered so far, within the overall framework of creating a clipping group between multiple layers.

Creating a clipping group

1. From the **File** menu, select **New** and create a file that is 2 inches high and 2 inches wide, with a resolution of 72 pixels/inch.

2. From the **Window** menu, choose **Show Layers** to open the Layers palette and double-click the **Background** layer. Click **OK** in the dialog box that appears, accepting **Layer 0** as the title for the layer.

3. Make two new layers by selecting **New Layer** from the Layers Options palette twice, clicking **OK** in the dialog box each time it appears. At this point, you have three layers, numbered Layer **0–2** (see Figure 19.7).

FIGURE 19.7
Create three layers numbered **0–2**.

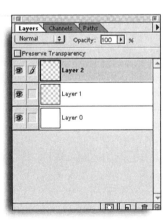

4. Click **Layer 2** to activate it. Select the paint bucket, and with a red color active as the foreground color, click to fill the layer with red. Set the **Opacity** slider to 8% and set the **Apply Mode** pop-up menu to **Dissolve** (see Figure 19.9).

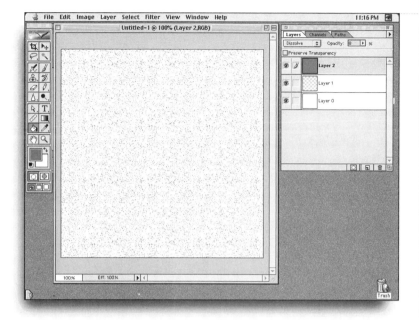

FIGURE 19.8
Fill **Layer 2** with an 8% red dissolve pattern.

5. Click **Layer 1** to activate it. Select blue as the foreground color and white as the background color; then from the **Filter** menu choose **Render** and select **Clouds** (Figure 19.9).

6. Now select **Layer 1** and select the Type tool. Click in the middle of the image and press the letter G, setting the font size to 100 and clicking **OK**. At this point, you should see a red speckle pattern over a blue and white cloud pattern. Turn off the Visibility icons in **Layer 1** and you see the type you just created in its own layer, called **A**.

7. With the top three layers populated, it's time to make your clipping groups. Hold down the Option key (Mac) or the Alt key (Win) and click the black line dividing layer **G** from **Layer 1**. The cloud pattern thumbnail indents slightly to show that it is part of the clipping group, and the cloud pattern is forced into the letter **G** (Figure 19.10).

FIGURE 19.9
Fill **Layer 1** with a blue and white clouds pattern.

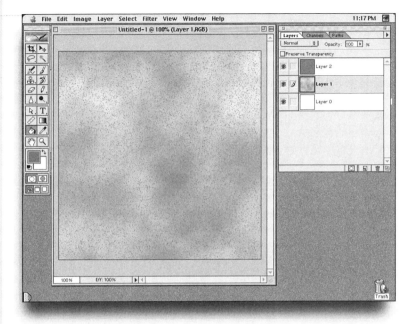

FIGURE 19.10
Option-click above the base layer to add to the clipping group.

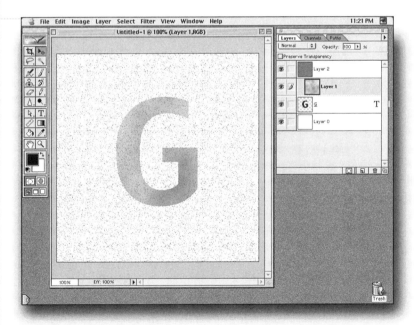

8. Hold down the Option key again (Mac) or the Alt key (Win), and click the black line between **Layer 2** and **Layer 1**, adding the top layer to the clipping group. Again, the thumbnail indents and the red speckle pattern is forced into the letter form (Figure 19.11).

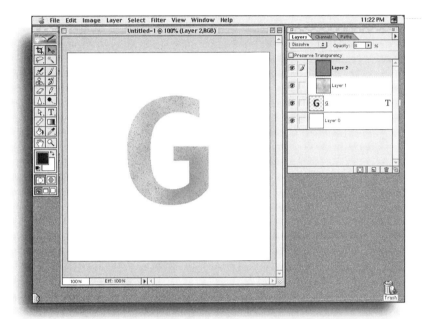

FIGURE 19.11
The results of the clipping group.

9. To understand the space you just created, activate the lowest **Layer 0**, select the Paintbrush, and draw across the layer to see how an layer that is not grouped interacts with the clipping group.

The Layer Effects Controls

New to Photoshop 5 are the Layer Effects commands, a submenu nestled about half way down the **Layer** menu. These effects apply bevel, emboss, and drop shadow effects, with the various apply mode options added into the controls.

There are some important distinctions regarding these layer effects that you need to keep in mind as you begin to explore them. First, you need to understand that the effect is defined by the edge of the pixel data within the layer. In other words, if no transparency exists, the bevel or drop shadow is applied to the whole layer, ignoring any selections. If the layer has transparency, the effect is applied around the edges of what is visible.

The next thing to understand is that the effect is inherent in the entire layer, not to a selection or group of pixels. After an effect is assigned to a layer, any other shapes created in that layer assume the same effect characteristics. This exposes the intended use for this toolset, which as far as I can tell is the creation of display type and buttons for Web pages.

The specific layer effects are listed here, accompanied by a brief description of each effect:

- **Drop Shadow**. Creates an offset drop shadow around the edges of all visible areas in the layer.
- **Inner Shadow**. Creates an inner shadow cutout effect inside the edges of all visible areas of an image.
- **Outer Glow**. Creates a diffuse glow, radiating around the outside of all the visible areas in the layer.
- **Inner Glow**. Creates a diffuse glow, radiating around the inside of all the visible edges in the layer.
- **Bevel and Emboss**. Creates a raised emboss or bevel effect around the visible areas of a layer. Options within this layer are to create a bevel on the inside or outside of the visible areas or to create an emboss or pillow emboss.

When to use emboss

Use an emboss layer effect when you want more of a directional emphasis to the effect. The pillow emboss creates more of a global, halo effect.

Each of these effects works its magic by offsetting the basic layer shape by a certain number of pixels. It fills the offset area with a specified color and lets you choose an apply mode that dictates how the offset pixels overlap other areas. The angle of offset and the opacity of the effect itself also have controls.

Because these effects are applied to the inside and outside of a layer area, it is possible to apply more than one at a time. You can apply a bevel effect, for example, and then add a drop shadow around it. It is also possible to select a global angle for the image itself, so that all angles selected in different layers and effects all go the same way. To do this, from the **Layer** menu, choose **Effects** and select **Global Angle** and set the angle in the dialog box that appears.

All effects are controlled by the Effects dialog box, which you access from the **Layer** menu by choosing **Effects** and selecting **Drop Shadow**. The Effects dialog box shows the name of the effect in a pop-up menu, along with the apply mode, opacity. angle, distance, blur amount, and intensity controls. There is also a color swatch to select the color of the offset pixels, a check box to use or ignore the global angle, and an **Apply** check box that applies or ignores the effect itself (see Figure 19.12).

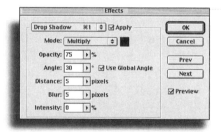

FIGURE 19.12
The Layer Effects dialog box.

You can click **OK** to apply the effect, but you can also click the **Next** button to go through the other effects' options. Combine as many as you like, and click **OK** when you finish to apply all the effects. When you click **OK**, the effect is actually resident in the layer and does not modify the pixel data in the layer itself. It is an algorithm, calculating edge effects similar to the way an Adjustment layer calculates color adjustments. You can convert the effect to tangible pixels by selecting the **Layer** menu and choosing **Effects** and **Create Layers**, which will render the various shadow or bevel effects to a separate layer for you to work with.

Creating Type and Adjustment Layers

Earlier in this chapter, you learned about the three types of layers: image layers, type layers, and adjustment layers. Well, we've gotten this far having looked at only the image layer. Not to worry though, everything mentioned applies to all three. The type and adjustment layers just have a few extra features that need to be considered.

Clicking with the Type tool in an image opens the Type dialog box, allowing you to type the text and set font sizes, parameters, and other formatting details. When you click **OK** to accept the settings, Photoshop automatically creates a new type layer. You can spot a type layer because Photoshop places a large T in the layer bar in the Layers palette.

Type layers are unique in that they create a transparent layer, except for the type itself, that overlays the layers beneath it. A new feature to Photoshop 5.0 is that type layers remain editable at all times, rather than rasterizing the text to pixels as soon as you click **OK**. This means that you can go back into the layer and correct misspellings or add additional text. To do this, double-click the layer bar, which opens the Type dialog box. Make any necessary changes, including color and apply modes, and click **OK**. Another terrific 5.0 addition is the **Preview** check box, which instantly places the type in the image window as you type it in the dialog box. This is a great way to get the type to the exact size before you okay the effect.

SEE ALSO

➤ *For more information on using the Type tool, see page 239*

Tonal Changes with Adjustment Layers

An adjustment layer applies color or tonal changes to all the layers beneath it, while preserving the original data in each of the layers. In other words, the adjustment layer acts like a filter, projecting a cast over the layers below. Discard or turn off the adjustment layer, and the layers below revert to their previous color and contrast levels. This lets you try various tonal options without casting them in stone.

Creating an adjustment layer

1. Open the Layers palette by selecting **Window** and **Show Layers**.

2. Select **New Adjustment Layer** from the Layers palette **Options** menu.

3. In the dialog box that appears, name the layer and select the **Adjustment** option from the **Type** pop-up menu. If no name is specified, the layer will be named for the type of adjustment layer selected from the pop-up menu. Click **OK** to accept the settings, as shown in Figure 19.13. This automatically opens a dialog box associated with the adjustment type.

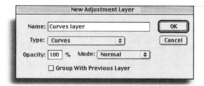

FIGURE **19.13**

Name the layer in the New Adjustment Layer dialog box.

4. Make any desired adjustments and click **OK** to create the layer.

You can create an adjustment layer based on any of the options listed in the **Adjust** submenu of the **Image** menu. When an adjustment layer has been created, you can modify the settings by double-clicking the layer bar in the Layers palette. This opens the dialog box for that particular adjustment layer, showing the last settings used for the layer effect.

Controlling Layer Visibility and Transparency

Layer masks enable you to create absolute magic between the various layers; you can blend, combine, and modify layer content at will, without losing or erasing a single pixel. After you create multiple layers, you need to find a reliable way to combine them.

For example, if your top image layer covers the entire canvas, you will not see any of the layers below. At that point, you have four options: create transparencies, use apply modes, use layer options, or create a layer mask. I will briefly touch on the first two; then we'll jump into options and layer masks.

Using Apply Modes with Layers

Apply modes combine layers using the standard apply mode set. To apply modes, highlight the target layer in the Layers palette and select the desired mode from the **Apply Mode** pop-up menu. This approach affects the layer globally and has limitations for maintaining any specific characteristics of one particular layer.

The apply modes control how overlapping image data interacts with each other. In a normal world (and in **Normal Mode**), the top (blend) layer simply covers the lower (base) layer. Therefore, an opaque upper layer, Paint tool stroke, image calculation, or filter obliterates what is beneath it. It's when anything other than **Normal** is selected that things get interesting.

What the apply mode actually does is compare the values of the top and bottom pixels as they overlap, and it makes a decision about the value that it makes visible. A mode might specify that the lighter or darker pixels show through, or even that the difference of two pixels show through. The exact functionality of each apply mode is as follows:

- **Normal**. Shows the top value completely, covering the lower layers at 100% opacity.
- **Multiply**. Darkens the image in a cumulative effect, creating high contrast in high chrome areas.
- **Screen**. Always lightens the image in a washed out, bleached effect, unless black is selected as a new value.
- **Overlay**. Lightens or darkens the image depending on what is being blended. Primarily modifies the 1/4 and 3/4 tone areas.
- **Soft Light**. Softly applies the blend image to the base image. **Soft Light** does not obliterate any of the base image;

it simply tints it with the hue or value of the blend pixel value.

- **Hard Light**. Creates high contrast, washing out light areas of the blend image and toning down the dark areas.

- **Color Dodge**. Lightens and bleaches the entire image, except for pure RGB/CMYK values.

- **Color Burn**. Darkens the entire image down, providing deep saturation in the pure RGB/CMYK values.

- **Darken**. Darkens the image by comparing the blend and base pixel values, always choosing the darker of the two.

- **Lighten**. Lightens the image by comparing the blend and base pixel values, always choosing the lighter of the two.

- **Difference**. Generally darkens and inverts the image in terms of color and tone.

- **Exclusion**. Reverses the color and tonality in the same way as **Difference**, except that darker blend values desaturate the underlying image as they maintain tonal values.

- **Hue**. Adds the hue of the blend color, while maintaining the tone and saturation of what's underneath.

- **Saturation**. Saturates the base image more or less, depending on the saturation values of the blend color. This mode does not alter the tone or hue of the base image.

- **Color**. Tints the base value of the image with the hue and saturation of the blend image. The contrast and tonality of the base image is untouched.

- **Luminosity**. The opposite of **Color**, in that the hue and saturation of the base image are unchanged as the tonality of the blend image is applied.

Changing Layer Transparency

You can create transparency for the entire layer by lowering the transparency slider, super-imposing one layer upon the other. To do this, click on the **Opacity** arrow in the Layers palette to pop up the opacity slider. Move the slider back and forth until the desired level of opacity is attained. This is good for certain effects but not acceptable for general uses.

Another more viable option is to erase the parts of the layer you don't want, which lets the lower layers show through. An effective approach is to vary the eraser pressure or opacity, which enables you to erase the varying levels of transparency. In this way, you can eliminate all of one section, while fading out and feathering other sections as you go. This works very well, except that after you erase part of a layer, you can't bring it back.

Creating Layer Masks

Convert the background layer to make changes

You cannot apply a layer mask to the background layer. Convert the background layer to a normal layer by double-clicking the **Background** layer in the Layers palette and clicking **OK** in the dialog box that follows.

Layer masks enable you to have your cake and eat it too. You can erase all or part of a layer as previously described, and you can bring the erased portion back whenever you need to. With layer masks, you actually create a mask that sits on top of the layer, hiding some portions and letting other parts show through. When you want to bring back a hidden part, you just go back and erase the mask. This approach is similar to creating a Quick Mask in that you click an icon to activate the mask, and you paint over the image to define the mask area. Unlike Quick Mask, you do not see a tinted area that defines your selection; rather the layer below is either revealed or concealed.

SEE ALSO

➤ *For more information on Quick Mask, see page 332*

Paint a layer mask with white to reveal it and with black to conceal it. To create a translucent mask, paint with shades of gray, with 50% gray creating a 50% transparency, and so on. The Airbrush is a very effective tool for creating soft transitions within a layer mask. If you select the Eraser, remember that the tone sensitivity is reversed to the background color rather than to the foreground color because the Eraser reveals the background color whenever it works.

Creating a layer mask

1. Highlight the layer to be masked and click on the Layer Mask icon at the bottom of the Layers palette. A Layer Mask Thumbnail icon is added next to the layer thumbnail, and the Layer Mask icon appears in the second column of the layer bar (Figure 19.14).

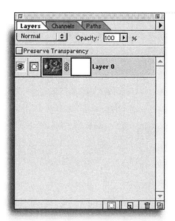

FIGURE 19.14
Adding a layer mask.

2. Select a Paint tool from the tool bar, and select black as the foreground color. (Use black as the background color if you're using the Eraser).

3. Paint into the layer with the tool; the image disappears as you paint. To replace a transparent section, press the X key to change the foreground color to white, and paint the image back.

4. To modify the layers image, click on the thumbnail icon of the image, highlighting it with a black outline. Click back on the Mask icon to alter the mask again.

The Layer Options Palette

On a basic level, layer options deliver control over layer parameters such as the name, opacity, and apply modes, just as the Layers palette does. On a more complex level, they are a hybrid between the transparency slider in the Layers palette, and actual layer masks described in the previous section. The idea is that you can specify transparency in a layer based on tonal values. For example, all pixels lighter or darker than a certain value can be made transparent, allowing underlying layers to show through. Layer options effects can be applied to an entire layer or to a single channel of a layer.

Central to the options' controls are the **This Layer** and **Underlying Layer** sliders. These controls dictate which pixels are visible and which are hidden within the active layer and those below it. The **This Layer** slider controls the active layer, and the **Underlying** slider controls all the layers beneath it. The numeric value of the slider corresponds to the tonal range of the layer or image, with 255 equaling white and 0 equaling black. By moving the slider in from the endpoint of either 0 or 255, the pixels in the layer or underlying image become transparent. For example, moving the slider from 255 to 240 hides all pixels with values from 241 to 255. The same goes for pixels at the darker end of the spectrum as well. To modify pixels in a single channel, click on the **Blend If** pop-up menu and select the target channel to be modified.

Modifying layer options

1. Begin by selecting **Layer Options** from the Layers palette **Options** menu, which opens the Layer Options dialog box (Figure 19.15).

2. With the **Preview** box checked, apply the transparency effects by modifying the sliders in the **Blend If** section. Hide pixels in the current layer by moving the **This Layer** slider. Hide pixels in the underlying layers by modifying the Underlying slider.

3. Modify the **Opacity** and **Mode** controls if necessary, and click **OK** to apply the effect.

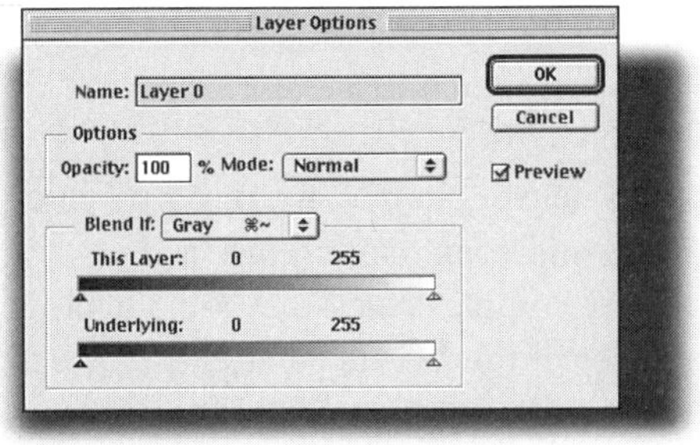

FIGURE 19.15

The Layer Options dialog box.

SEE ALSO

➤ *For more information on layer masks, see page 364*

➤ *For more information on using the Type tool, see page 239*

➤ *For more information on Quick Mask, see page 332*

Using Channels

What Is a Channel?

A common source of confusion for intermediate and even advanced Photoshop users is understanding exactly what a channel is, and how it differs from a layer. In this chapter, we will explore exactly how channels work and then look at how to put that knowledge to use. Keep in mind that Photoshop offers so many different ways to modify colors and selections, so if this process is too detailed for your tastes, you can use other ways to achieve similar results. Having said that, modifying color and selections through channels is a very powerful approach that more than repays the time spent learning it.

Channels contain 8-bit grayscale information used to determine the value for each pixel in the image. When the pixel values from each channel are combined, they create color variations that add up to the continuous tone color image you see on the screen. The exact system for how this works is ultimately determined by which Color mode you're working in. The main thing to understand is that the grayscale values in each channel overlap each other, and Photoshop adds them up and arrives at a color value for that pixel.

To see this system at work, open the channels palette by selecting the **Window** menu and choosing **Show Channels**. The Channels palette looks very similar to the Layers palette, in that each channel appears as a bar across the palette, with a Visibility icon that lets you turn the channel on and off (see Figure 20.1). The top channel in the stack is the composite channel, which represents the entire image. All images must have the requisite channels to create the Color mode specified for the image; they cannot be deleted, although their contents can be altered. For example, you cannot delete the **Green** channel in an RGB image, although you can erase part of it or modify the data.

FIGURE 20.1

The Channels palette is layed out similar to the Layers palette.

RGB Channels

RGB files are comprised of three channels: red, green, and blue. The RGB color space offers a wide range of color combinations, second only to LAB color in brightness and intensity. Because most scanners and digital cameras capture images in RGB mode, it is a good idea to leave the image in this format for as long as possible. If you are going to print, do so at the very last minute, after you make any color or image corrections. If the image is to remain in its electronic format, leave it in RGB permanently.

When you look at an RGB channel, understand that dark tones represent an absence of color and that light tones reveal its presence. In other words, a red channel that is light shows a lot of red through the image, whereas a dark channel has an absence of red, showing its inverse color cyan. This is an important point: when you want to increase a channel's color, lighten the channel; to decrease the color, darken the channel.

CMYK Channels

CMYK files consist of cyan, magenta, yellow, and black channels. Because there are four channels instead of three, CMYK files are 25% larger than their RGB or LAB counterparts. CMYK files have a restricted color range compared to RGB or LAB. This is due more to the imperfections of putting ink on paper than the actual color combinations themselves. Because printed images require light to bounce off them rather than shine through them, they loose the luminous qualities of other systems. This loss results in dull colors, primarily in the high chroma spectrum of bright blues and greens.

Additive and subtractive color

RGB is called an additive model; adding all the color channels at 100% equals white. CMYK is a subtractive model; subtracting all four channels equals white, as dictated by the color of the paper.

In a CMYK channel, dark areas represent the presence of color. This is the exact opposite of RGB, meaning that a light cyan channel shows very little cyan, revealing a lot of red, it's inverse color, in the image. The important point for CMYK is the opposite of the RGB approach: when you want to increase a channel's color, darken the channel; to decrease the color, lighten the channel.

LAB Channels

LAB color is a completely different animal from the other two examples discussed so far. Rather than consider a separate channel for each individual color, LAB color operates on a combination of color polarities and black-and-white tonalities. Specifically, LAB offers three channels:

- The A channel that represents the polarities between green and red
- The B channel that represents the polarities between blue and yellow
- The Lightness channel that represents the light and dark densities of the image

LAB makes you consider the image differently, going straight to the Lightness channel to lighten and darken, and tweaking color from the A or B channels. Don't let the polarity of the various channels throw you either; all color models have a polarity factor. As mentioned before, when you decrease the red channel in an RGB image, it goes cyan— a polarity exists between these two colors in the red channel. The polarity is reversed in CMYK, in that decreasing the cyan channel increases the red. Rather than calling it the red/cyan channel, it just goes by red or cyan, depending on the Color mode. The other polarities are green/magenta and blue/yellow. Like the LAB model, CMYK adds a black channel that handles most of the lights and darks.

Follow the guidelines below when correcting LAB images:

- To make it darker, darken the lightness channel.
- To make it lighter, lighten the lightness channel.

- To make it more green, darken the A channel.
- To make it more red, lighten the A channel.
- To make it more blue, darken the B channel.
- To make it more yellow, lighten the B channel.

Selection Channels

It is also possible to use channels to define and reload various selections within the image. These channels are like Quick Masks in the way they define a selection by their area. In fact, if you go to the Channels palette while you have a Quick Mask active, you will see a temporary channel created for the mask (see Figure 20.2).

FIGURE 20.2

When you create a Quick Mask, Photoshop automatically creates a temporary Alpha channel.

A selection channel is a grayscale channel that represents a selection or mask in the image. Black in an Alpha channel represents a deselected area, and white represents a selected area. We saw in Chapter 18 on Quick Masks that you can create a transparent selection that allows the image to be modified incrementally. In an Alpha channel, selection transparency is represented by shades of gray that stretch between the white and black parameters described above. A light gray is a mostly selected area, and a dark gray is a slightly selected area.

SEE ALSO

➤ *For complete information on Quick Masks, see page 332*

You can create an Alpha channel in three ways:

- Select New Channel from the Options pop-up menu in the Channels palette.
- From the **Select** menu, choose **Save Selection**.
- From the **Image** menu, choose **Calculations** and use the Calculations dialog box.

Image Editing with Channels

Now that you have a basic idea of how channels work, you need to understand what you can do with them. Generally speaking, you can exploit three tasks with channels: global image changes, local image changes, and selection manipulation.

Global Changes

When editing channels, it's important to make subtle or gradual changes in order to maintain a naturalistic look to the image. An easy way to do this is to change the entire channel globally. This applies the effect across the entire layer, keeping everything smooth and consistent.

Global changes are especially effective for color corrections. If an image has a color cast or is lit by an unnatural light source, globally correcting an entire channel can bring things back in line. When making global color corrections to a channel, choices are more limited that if you were editing the whole image. You can choose to use Curves, Levels, or the Brightness/Contrast tools to get the job done. I recommend Curves due to the control and flexibility it gives you in modifying all or part of the tonal range in the channel.

Using curves on a channel

1. From the **Window** menu, choose **Show Channels** to open the Channels palette.

2. Click on the channel to be modified so it is highlighted. Then click the Visibility icon next to the top composite channel. This enables you to modify the channel you want as it shows the entire image (see Figure 20.3).

FIGURE 20.3
Select the channel to be modified, while viewing the entire
composite image.

3. From the **Image** menu, choose **Adjust**, **Curves** to open the
Curves dialog box.

4. Place various data points on the curve as needed and drag up
or down to lighten or darken the channel.

5. Click **OK** to apply the effect.

SEE ALSO

➤ *For more details on Curves, see page 520*

A simple alternative to using curves to modify a channel is to use
the **Brightness** contrast controls. This enables you to change
just two parameters, while creating a surprisingly wide range of
combinations. The **Brightness** slider tends to make more subtle
and gradual changes to the entire image, whereas the **Contrast**
slider pushes more dramatic color shifts into the highlights or
shadows of the image.

Using Brightness/Contrast on a channel

1. From the **Window** menu, choose **Show Channels** to open
the Channels palette.

2. Click on the channel to be modified so it is highlighted. Then click the Visibility icon next to the top composite channel. This enables you to modify the channel you want as it shows the entire image.

3. From the **Image** menu, select **Adjust** and choose **Brightness/Contrast** to open the Brightness/Contrast dialog box.

4. Modify the **Brightness** or contrast sliders as needed to color correct the image.

5. Click **OK** to apply the effect.

If you want to stay busy for days or maybe weeks, try exploring the possibilities offered by filtering channels. In the same way that you can color correct a single channel, you can also add patterns or textures. This offsets the color polarities within that channel, creating a wide range of effects.

To filter a channel, follow the previous steps, selecting a filter option instead of the **Brightness/Contrast** controls in step 3.

Local Corrections

The power of channels comes into its own when you start to modify sections of a channel on a local level. Maybe you just want to punch up the flesh tones in a face or the color of a flower. For the times when a global correction just won't work, local corrections can be very effective.

When I say local corrections, I'm simply referring to selecting any of Photoshop's paint tools and brushing corrections directly into the channel. When making these kinds of changes, use a soft feathered brush and build up the effect gradually by using a low **Opacity** or **Pressure** setting. This helps the changes blend in with the surroundings, maintaining a naturalistic look to the image.

Remember that all you want to do with the paint tool is lighten or darken the channel. Although you can use the Airbrush or Paintbrush tools, you will find that the best tool for natural channel corrections is the Dodge or Burn tool. All the Dodge or

Burn tool does is make things lighter or darker, which is all you need for a channel. This means that you can increase the red or cyan, for example, by using this tool to paint into an area. Dodge/Burn is especially effective because it maintains the image integrity as you work with it. If you use the Airbrush tool to paint a black or white section of a channel, you see a colored fog gradually replacing the image data. All your detail is swept away by a flat area of color. The Dodge or Burn tool lets you maintain full detail as you change the color balance for the local area.

Dodge/Burn a channel

1. From the **Window** menu, choose **Show Channels** to open the Channels palette.

2. Click on the channel you want to modify to highlight it. Then click the Visibility icon next to the top composite channel. This enables you to modify the channel you want as it shows the entire image.

3. Click and hold on the Dodge/Burn tool and select the desired tool from the pop-out menu that appears. (Please note that because channels are already black and white, the Sponge tool has no effect in this process.)

4. Double-click the Dodge or Burn tool to open the Options palette. Set the **Exposure** and shadow/midtone/highlight range for the tool.

5. Paint into the channel as desired. Switch from the Dodge tool to the Burn tool to add or subtract color (see Figure 20.4).

6. Click **OK** to apply the effect.

Selection Controls

On a simplistic level, channels enable you to save selections to reload at a later time. To save a selection you, from the **Select** menu, choose **Save Selection** and click **OK** in the dialog box that appears (see Figure 20.5). In fact you can go along saving and reloading selections without ever grasping the role channels play in the process.

FIGURE 20.4

Use the Dodge or Burn tool to add or subtract color from the image.

FIGURE 20.5

From the **Select** menu, choose **Save Selection** to save the current selection to an Alpha channel.

A nuance of working with channels is in how they allow you to combine an existing selection with a new selection. For example, perhaps you want to deselect an object against a selected skyline area. If you have the object selected and saved to a channel, you can load the object selection and subtract it from the existing selection. Photoshop enables you to combine selections in the following ways:

- **New Selection**: Creates a completely new selection based on the information in the channel specified. This is the only available option if nothing else is selected when you load the channel.

- **Add To Selection:** Adds the channel-based selection to an existing selection.

- **Subtract From Selection:** Subtracts the channel-based selection from an existing selection.

- **Intersect With Selection:** Selects only the area where the existing selection and the channel-based selection overlap.

When you **Choose Select**, **Load Selection** the Load Selection dialog appears, which gives you full control over how the selection is to be loaded (see Figure 20.6). Choose the selection to be loaded from the channel pop-up menu and click the **Invert** check box if you want to load the inverse of the channel-based selection. Select the loading method from the **Operation** sections, choosing from one of the options previously mentioned.

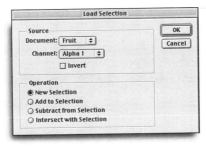

FIGURE 20.6

In the Load Selection dialog box, you can add, subtract, or intersect selections.

Combining Channels

As mentioned before, if you look at a channel by itself, it looks like a regular black-and-white image. But if you look at all your channels next to each other, you see that they are not identical black-and-white images. The red channel is lighter in the red areas, the blue channel is lighter in the blue areas, and they are all darker where their respective colors are absent.

Sometimes it can be to your advantage to combine these grayscale images in varying degrees to either create a new selection or to apply a color cast in select areas of an image.

Photoshop gives you two direct ways to combine channels, and we will spend the remainder of this chapter looking at them.

Using the Channel Mixer

New to Photoshop 5.0 is the Channel Mixer. The Channel Mixer modifies a target channel by allowing you to incrementally blend in the other channels.

Open the Channel Mixer from the Image menu, by choosing **Adjust** and **Channel Mixer**, which opens the Channel Mixer dialog box (see Figure 20,7). At the very top of the box is the Output Channel pop-up menu, which allows you to select the channel to be modified. The Channel Mixer only works on color channels, so if you have any selection-based Alpha channels in your image, they will not be available in the pop-up.

FIGURE 20.7

The Channel Mixer dialog box.

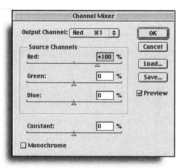

Below **Output Channel** is the **Source Channels** section, with sliders representing all the color channels in your image. This section provides the information that changes the output channel. At the bottom of the dialog box is the **Constant** slider. The **Constant** slider proportionately decreases the black point in the channel as you drag the slider from left to right. The result of this action adds a global color cast to the entire image of either the channel color or its polar opposite.

At the very bottom of the dialog box is the **Monochrome** check box. Clicking it combines all channel values into one black-and-white composite image. The interesting thing is that although

Photoshop averages the channel values and renders a black-and-white image, the file structure remains in RGB, CMYK, or whatever the previous mode might have been.

The main thing to remember when using the Channel Mixer is that you are only modifying the one target output channel. When you see the color sliders in the source channels sections, you will expect them to add that color to your image. Photoshop has conditioned us to expect to add blue to our image when we increase a slider labeled Blue. Because we are only modifying the one output channel, we will add or subtract only the colors associated with that output channel. This means that if I have green selected in the output channel pop-up menu, the changes to the source channels section will only result in adding green or magenta to the image. Each source channel adds green or magenta in different ways and to different sections of the image, depending on the grayscale values of the source channel itself.

Channel Calculations

The Channel Mixer combines channels by adding the value of other channels directly to a target channel. Channel calculations use the Apply modes to combine channels into a composite result. The calculations controls offer more flexibility and control than any other option considered thus far.

In addition to straight channels, Calculations also allow you to combine the contents of individual layers, using the entire layer contents or their individual color channels. All these layers and channels are combined using Photoshop's Apply modes, with the result of the calculation being written to a selection, new channel, or a new document.

SEE ALSO
➤ *For more information on Photoshop's Apply Modes, see page 137*

From the **Image** menu, choose **Calculations** and the Calculations dialog box appears. The controls show two source sections that enable you to choose the layer and channel from the active document, along with a check box that enables you invert the source material (see Figure 20.8). The Layers pop-up menu lets you choose from any existing layers in the document and also has a merged option that selects all the layers as a single merged source. It's also worth noting that the Channels pop-up includes all existing channels, including any selection-based Alpha channels.

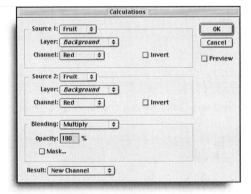

FIGURE 20.8
The Channels Calculations dialog box.

At the bottom of the dialog box is the **Blending** section that determines how the source materials is combined. Rather than calculating a simple sum, Photoshop lets you use any Apply mode to add the two sources together. The **Blending** section also lets you determine the opacity or the result and it you convert the calculation as a mask. The final option in this dialog is the **Result** pop-up menu that writes the result to a selection, new channel, or a new document.

SEE ALSO

➤ *For complete information on Quick Masks, see page 332*
➤ *For more details on Curves, see page 520*
➤ *For more information on Photoshop's Apply Modes, see page 137*

Using Filters and Creating Special Effects

Applying Photoshop Native Filters

Apply blur filters

Add noise

Remove dust and scratches

Use the sharpen filters

Apply artistic filters

Use filters for special effects

Organizing Photoshop's Filters

Photoshop includes ninety-nine different filters in all, sorted into thirteen different categories. You can find them on the **Filter** menu. Here are the categories, in alphabetical order:

- **Artistic**
- **Blur**
- **Brush Strokes**
- **Distort**
- **Noise**
- **Pixelate**
- **Render**
- **Sharpen**
- **Sketch**
- **Stylize**
- **Texture**
- **Video**
- **Other**

However, these categories don't really give you much of a sense of what the filters within them can do, so I prefer to group them differently. We'll look at these filters as belonging to one of four groups:

- Filters that improve the image quality
- Filters that add artistic effects
- Filters that add special effects
- Filters that perform technical corrections

Some new terms for you

Native, with regard to filters, simply means those that come with your copy of Photoshop 5, as opposed to third-party plug-in filters such Eye Candy or Kai's Power Tools that you buy elsewhere and plug-in yourself. You'll probably come across the word *plug-in* as many times as you do filter, but they refer to the same thing. They're mini-applications that plug into Photoshop to provide additional functions.

Image-Quality Filters

The Image-Quality filter sets are Blur, Noise, and Sharpen. These are the real workhorses of the Photoshop filter collection. You will use at least some of them on virtually every picture you work on.

Blur

Most of us work hard at taking "sharp" photos and making "sharp" scans. Pictures *should* be in focus and not blurred, right? Right, most of the time. Sometimes, though, a selectively applied blur is exactly what a picture needs. For instance, suppose I have a picture with a very messy background that detracts from the subject. I can select just the background and blur it, which will help hide it. Figure 21.1 shows before and after views. Pretty cool, huh?

FIGURE 21.1

Before and after blurring the background.

1 Before

2 After

Applying blur filter

1. Use whatever combination of selection tools and tricks necessary to isolate the area you want to blur. (In the previous figure, I used the magic wand to select the central flower, pressed Shift, and used the Lasso to select the lower two-thirds of the picture. Then I inverted, so only the top back area was selected.)

2. Choose **Filter, Blur** to apply a slight, overall blur. If that's not enough, you can apply it again, as many times as needed. Or you can try **Blur More**.

3. If this still isn't sufficient, choose **Filter, Gaussian Blur**. Figure 21.2 shows the Gaussian Blur dialog box. The window inside the box enables you to preview the amount of blur you apply. (Drag the image inside the window so you can see the part you're working on.)

FIGURE 21.2

Set the amount of blur by moving the slider or typing a number.

4. Higher numbers increase the amount of blur. In Figure 21.3, I set the blur factor so that background details disappear.

5. When you achieve the effect you want, click **OK** to apply the blur to the picture. It might take several seconds, depending on the speed of the computer and the size of the area being blurred. Finally, deselect the area.

As you can clearly see in the previous before and after pictures, blurring the background not only removes annoying detail but adds greater depth to the picture.

FIGURE 21.3

Set the amount of blur by moving the slider or typing a number.

1 Slider

Gaussian Blur

The **Gaussian Blur** filter is especially useful because you can set a precise amount of blurring from .1 to 255 pixels, and because you can see what you're doing while you are doing it. You can even use the **Gaussian Blur** filter to anti-alias edges or to smooth a drop shadow. The **Blur** and **Blur More** filters, which lack dialog boxes, simply apply a one pixel or two pixel width blur to the image by repeating the adjacent pixels at half intensity on top of the original image.

Motion Blur

Under the **Blur** filter category, there are three more filters that are occasionally useful. **Motion Blur** suggests movement by blurring the picture along a line. You can set the length of the blur and the precise angle in the Motion Blur dialog box. It's not a very realistic-looking blur, however. It looks more like you moved the camera than as if the subject moved. Still, it has some uses. It's nice for use with type, as in Figure 21.4. You might also experiment with it to create a brushed metal effect for a background or to put a curtain of rain over your picture.

FIGURE 21.4

Enter an amount to blur and a direction.

Radial Blur

The **Radial Blur** filter gives you two choices: **Spin** and **Zoom**. **Spin** mode gives you a blur that looks as if the image is spinning around its center point. **Zoom** mode theoretically gives you the effect of zooming the camera into or away from the image. In Figure 21.5, I applied **Spin** to a flower that was centered on the page, and in Figure 21.6, I am applying **Zoom** to the same flower. The dialog box for these filters doesn't enable you to preview the effect, but you can get a general idea of the dimension of the effect by looking at the diagram in the box. Drag inside it to relocate the center point for the effect. Changing the amount of blur changes the length of the blur lines in the diagram.

As you can see in Figure 21.6, this dialog box enables you to choose the quality level of the blur. The setting determines how the blur is calculated, with little apparent difference between **Draft** and **Best**. Where the difference shows up is in the amount of time it takes for your computer to do the math and apply the blur to your picture.

In a hurry?

If you're not patient or if your computer isn't the most powerful model available, stick with **Good** quality, and forget **Best**. You'll never notice the difference.

FIGURE 21.5
This example used a blur amount of 10.

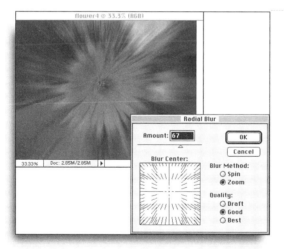

Smart Blur

The **Smart Blur** filter (**Filter, Blur, Smart blur**) is probably the most useful one of all, especially for image editing and photo repair. It blurs everything in the image, or selection, except the edges. **Smart Blur** calculates the differences between color regions to determine boundaries and maintains these boundaries while blurring everything within them. **Smart Blur** is the perfect filter when you need to take 10 years off a portrait subject's face, smooth out teenage skin, or get rid of the texture in a piece of cloth without losing the folds. Figure 21.7 shows the **Smart Blur** filter being applied to a rather grainy portrait. See how it smoothes out the uneven skin tones and removes small imperfections. Be careful using this filter. If you overcorrect, you might make the surface too smooth, and your subject will look as if he has been dipped in liquid plastic.

FIGURE 21.7
Experiment with the settings until the blur looks right.

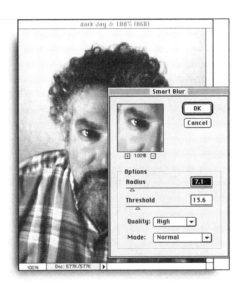

To choose the right **Blur** filter, follow these guidelines:

Blur	Very slight general blur.
Blur More	Slightly stronger blur, same as applying **Blur** twice.
Gaussian Blur	Variable blur, distributed by mathematical formula.
Motion Blur	Moves everything by variable distance in a straight line.
Radial Blur	**Spin** blurs in a circle around central point; **Zoom** blurs out from central point.
Smart Blur	Detects and avoids blurring edges of objects; blurs centers.

Noise

Noise seems like a strange word to use in conjunction with pictures. It actually comes from the world of television. Video noise, which is what we're really talking about here, is essentially the same stuff you hear as background on a tape recording—a sort of generalized hiss. It translates to the picture as a random sprinkling of graininess. In general, it's something you want to eliminate as much as possible in both picture and sound. But, like everything else, it has its uses. On a soundtrack, you might add some noise to disguise a different kind of noise. In a picture, you might add noise to a too smooth background, or use it as an overall speckled effect.

Add Noise

Photoshop groups filters that both add and remove noise under the general heading **Filter**, **Noise**. The first of these, **Add Noise**, does exactly what it says. In Figure 21.8, I'm applying the **Add Noise** filter to the same portrait. The dialog box lets you set the amount of noise, and whether it's applied evenly or by Gaussian distribution. If you select **Gaussian**, you see that the noise is more dense in darker parts of the picture. You can also opt for **Monochromatic** noise, which means that all the added noise pixels appear gray or black—otherwise, they appear colored.

FIGURE 21.8
Noise settings range from 1 to 999.

Despeckle, as you might expect, has the opposite effect. Instead of adding noise, it removes it. This filter looks for individual pixels that contrast sharply with those around them and blurs them so they don't stand out. If you have a grainy scan or digital photo, using the **Despeckle** filter will smooth it out without blurring the image. The **Despeckle** filter has no adjustable settings. If applying it once doesn't remove enough of the spots, apply it again, or move on to the **Dust** and **Scratches** filter.

Applying Despeckle or any other nonadjustable filter

1. Select the area to which you want to apply the filter. If no area is selected it will apply to the entire picture.

2. Choose **Filter, Noise, Despeckle**. The filter is applied.

Dust & Scratches

Dust and scratches are a very common problem, especially on scanned photographs. The **Dust & Scratches** filter, shown in Figure 21.9, removes them. There are two parameters to set in the dialog box. The **Radius** setting varies from 1 to 16 and controls how many pixels are included in the area that the filter "looks at" when smoothing a scratch or dust spot. A radius of 16 blurs a very large area. **Threshold** can vary from 0 to 255 and affects the amount of difference required between a pixel and its surroundings before the filter recognizes it as a spot. Most dust and grain will be at the low end of the **Threshold** scale. After you get past 10–12, you won't notice much dust removal.

Median

The **Median** filter is a less flexible version of the **Dust & Scratches** filter. It's one of the original Photoshop filters and is included mostly for users who go back to the early days of Photoshop. It selects the average or "median" color for the distance of the **Radius** you set in its dialog box (see Figure 21.10).

Sharpen

The first three filters in the **Sharpen** category work by enhancing the contrast between adjacent pixels to give the appearance of a better focused picture.

The ellipsis means "there's more…"

Whenever you see an ellipsis (those three little dots…) after a menu item, it means that a dialog box will open when you select that item.

A neat filter trick

For a cool special effect, try the **Dust & Scratches** filter with a **Radius** of 16 and a **Threshold** of 0. It reduces your picture to abstract light and dark areas.

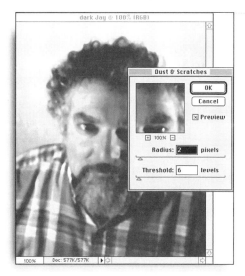

FIGURE 21.9

Keeping the **Radius** setting low removes more small dust specks.

FIGURE 21.10

Larger **Radius** settings produce blurrier images.

Sharpen, Sharpen Edges, Sharpen More

The **Sharpen** and **Sharpen More** filters apply themselves to every pixel in the picture or selected area, whereas the **Sharpen Edges** filter seeks out edges of objects by evaluating the differences in color and contrast between adjacent pixels. It then enhances these differences, producing an apparent edge sharpening. In reality, none of these filters can actually bring back an out-of-focus photograph. As good as Photoshop is, it can't render an image that's just not there. But it *can* create the illusion of sharpness. The effect of these filters is sometimes quite subtle. Figure 21.11 shows a slightly soft photo, with the Sharpen filters applied.

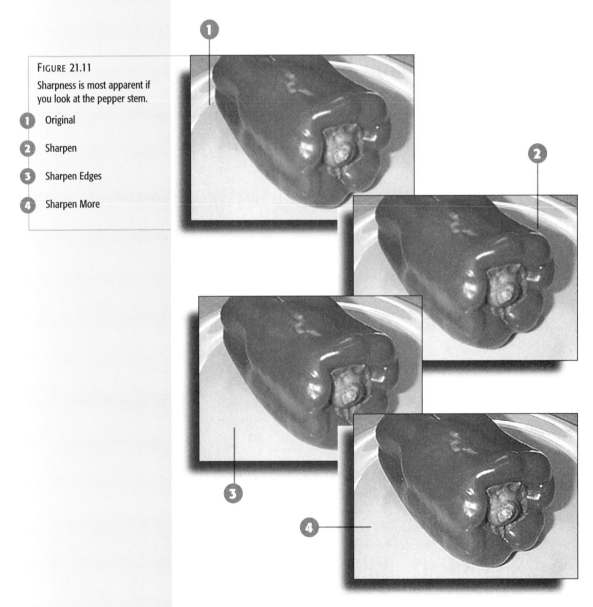

FIGURE 21.11

Sharpness is most apparent if you look at the pepper stem.

1 Original

2 Sharpen

3 Sharpen Edges

4 Sharpen More

Unsharp Mask

The final filter in this set is the most useful of all: **Unsharp Mask**. Many professionals use this filter on every image they process. Photos inevitably lose some sharpness during scanning. Even digital photos transferred directly into the computer might not be as sharp as we want. **Unsharp Mask** can restore the appearance of sharp focus to a soft picture. The **Unsharp Mask** filter has three variables: **Amount**, **Radius**, and **Threshold**.

Applying the Unsharp Mask filter

1. Select **Filter, Sharpen, Unsharp Mask** to open its dialog box, shown in Figure 21.12.

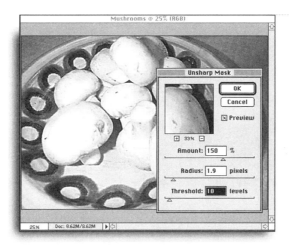

FIGURE 21.12
Be sure to check **Preview** so you can see your changes.

2. Drag the **Amount** to about 150%. This setting, which can vary from 1–500 determines how much sharpening is applied. The way to decide where to set it is to start at 500% and back off until the image looks sharp but not overly so. If you see visible halos around the edges of objects, you have oversharpened them.

3. Drag the **Radius** to the middle of its scale and back it down again until you don't see halos around the edges. The **Radius** determines how far from each pixel the effect is applied. Although it can vary all the way from .1 to 150, the most useful settings are between 1 and 4. A higher setting will again oversharpen the image, whereas a setting of less than .6 isn't enough to notice.

4. Finally, set the **Threshold** to some number greater than 5 but less than 20. Threshold settings range anywhere from 0–255, but numbers smaller than 5 will sharpen any noise or dust in the picture, whereas higher numbers sharpen only pixels that are very similar in value.

5. Click **OK** when you finish to apply the **Unsharp Mask**. Figure 21.13 shows the photo with and without it.

FIGURE 21.13

The example on the left is not sharpened. The one on the right has **Unsharp Mask** applied.

1 Without Unsharp Mask

2 With Unsharp Mask

Filters for Art's Sake

The next sets of figures are grouped together because they are all in one way or another artistic. They imitate a style of painting or a particular medium or tool. The filters in this category include not only those that Photoshop has designated **Artistic**, but also the **Brush Stroke** and **Sketch** filters.

Artistic Filters

There are fifteen filters that Photoshop considers "artistic." We'll apply them all to a rather uninspired photo of a pepper, so you can see how even an ordinary picture can be made into a work of art with the right filter. The "raw" photo is shown in Figure 21.14.

FIGURE 21.14

The original photo, before adding filters.

Colored Pencil

The **Colored Pencil** filter makes your picture look as if it has been rendered in colored pencils or very thin chalks. Depending on how you set the **Paper Brightness** in its dialog box, shown in Figure 21.15, you'll see either gray or white highlights. The preview window lets you see the effect of changing the settings.

FIGURE 21.15

Greater stroke pressure retains more of the image.

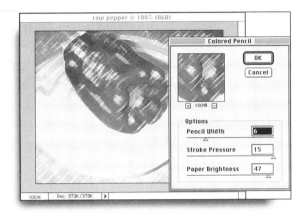

Help! There's no preview box!

Some Photoshop filters don't give you a full screen preview. The reason for this is that they require a lot of calculation, and it would take an unreasonably long time to set up the preview and then redo it when you click the button to apply the filter. If you want to see more of your image in the small preview window, click the minus symbol to the right of the window to reduce the image to 50% or 33%.

Cutout

The **Cutout** filter does what's called posterization. In effect, it makes the picture look as if it had been cut out of several pieces of colored paper. The dialog box, which you can see in Figure 21.16, enables you to choose a number of levels to which the image will be reduced—the number of pieces of colored paper available. **Edge Simplicity** and **Edge Fidelity** determine how closely the "cut" edges will resemble the original object. Too much simplicity reduces the picture to a few abstract geometric shapes. High contrast subjects give the best results with this filter.

FIGURE 21.16

Be careful not to oversimplify the levels or edges.

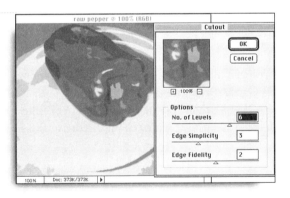

Dry Brush

The **Dry Brush** filter imitates a technique much beloved by watercolor and tempera artists. It's one of the few filters that looks good with almost any kind of image. Figure 21.17 shows the effects of the filter and its dialog box. Keeping the settings low (**Brush Size**: 0; **Image Detail**: 0; **Texture**: 1) gives you a delicate lacy edge around shapes, whereas setting **Image Detail** to 10 produces a very realistic "painting" from your photo. I love this filter, and I use it a lot.

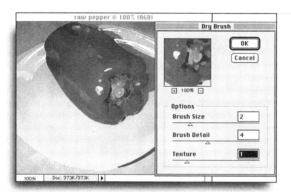

FIGURE 21.17
Greater brush detail eliminates blobs of "paint."

Film Grain

Photographers hate it. Avant-garde filmmakers love it. It's film grain—those little dots of emulsion that give blown-up photos that blobby look. Photoshop's **Film Grain** filter adds little gray specks to your picture, concentrated in the darker areas, just like the real thing. Essentially, it's another noise filter, but you can control the amount and size of the noise. Figure 21.18 shows an example, along with the Film Grain dialog box. It has limited usefulness but might be helpful as a first step in multifiltered pictures.

FIGURE 21.18

Graininess is more pronounced in shadow areas.

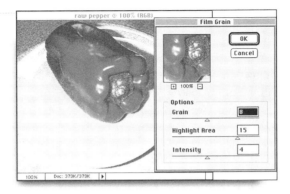

FIGURE 21.18

Graininess is more pronounced in shadow areas.

Fading a filter

You think you chose the right filter but the effect is just too much? That's when you need to use the **Fade Filter** command. Open **Filter, Fade** or press (Shift+Command) [Ctrl+F) to open the Fade Filter dialog box. Enter an **Opacity** percentage or click the **Preview** check box and drag the Opacity slider until the image looks just the way you want it to.

Fresco

Fresco is Italian for "fresh" and refers to the painting technique of applying pigments of fresh, wet plaster to paint murals. Why Adobe chose this name for this filter is beyond me. The settings are like those of the **Dry Brush** filter, but the effects are much more intense. This filter darkens your picture, possibly more than you want. Consider fading the effect after you apply it. (See SideNote.) Figure 21.19 shows the filter and its dialog box.

SEE ALSO
➤ *To fade filters with Blending modes, see Chapter 137*

FIGURE 21.19

This filter adds too much black to many pictures.

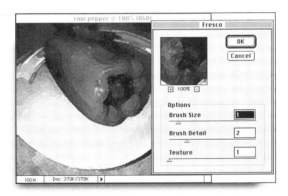

Neon Glow

The **Neon Glow** filter does some strange things. It uses the background and foreground colors you set in the toolbar, plus a third color that you can set in its dialog box. **Neon Glow** produces a strange other-worldly effect—but not really much of a neon effect. It is extremely color-dependent, so make sure to choose contrasting colors for best results. The filter and its dialog box are seen in Figure 21.20.

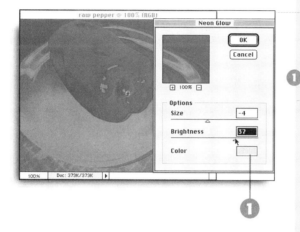

FIGURE 21.20
Click the small color block to open the Color Picker.

1   Opens Color Picker

Paint Daubs

The **Paint Daubs** filter is quite a lot like the **Dry Brush** filter in appearance. It's another one that works well with most pictures. You can set **Brush Size** and **Sharpness**, and choose among several brushes. Shown in Figure 21.21 is the **Light Rough** brush. Experiment with the settings on this filter. You can use it to render the subject as a smooth-edged abstraction or a spotty, heavily textured object.

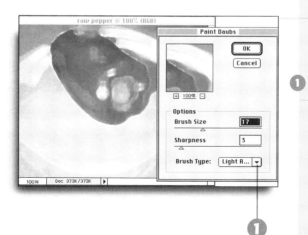

FIGURE 21.21
There are six brushes in the set, including **Sparkle** and **Simple**.

1   Select to change brush type

Palette Knife

When a painter uses a palette knife, the result is large areas of smudged color blending interestingly at the edges. Ideally, that's what this filter would do, too. Instead it reduces the picture to blocks of color by grouping similar pixels and averaging them. The **Palette Knife** filter produces a soft patchwork effect that's neither interesting nor useful.

Plastic Wrap

Plastic Wrap is another filter that probably should have been thrown back into the bit bucket (the programmer's trash can). It places a gray film over the whole picture and then adds white "highlights" around large objects. The result, as seen in Figure 21.22, is a picture that looks as if the subject had been shrink-wrapped in very thick plastic or dunked in liquid latex. You can vary the thickness of the plastic and how well it "fits" by experimenting with the settings.

FIGURE 21.22
Not a very useful filter.

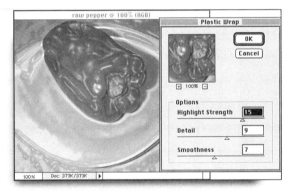

Poster Edges

The **Poster Edges** filter actually posterizes the whole picture, not just the edges, but then it adds a black line around the edges of objects. It gives the picture a sort of pseudo-woodcut look. Within the dialog box, shown in Figure 21.23, you can set the degree of **Posterization** as well as the **Edge Thickness** and **Edge Intensity** of the edge lines. This is a good filter to use with still life photos, but seldom successful with portraits.

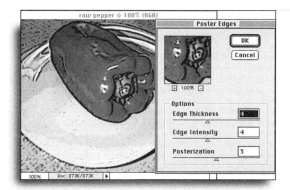

FIGURE 21.23

Be careful about applying this filter to textured backgrounds; it might make more of the texture than you intend.

Rough Pastels

The **Rough Pastels** filter is one of my favorites. It looks good with any image and has saved many otherwise uninteresting ones. It simulates a pastel drawing on a heavily textured surface, using diagonal strokes that contrast nicely with the horizontal grain of the texture. As you can see in Figure 21.24, it has a larger and more comprehensive dialog box that enables you to select from several preset textures or to load your own. (See the SideNote.) Within this dialog box, and others that employ Textures, you can adjust the size of the texture, the apparent height of "bumps," and the direction that light theoretically hits the texture, creating the highlight and shadow that define it. These parameters have no optimum setting. Just experiment with your picture until it looks right to you.

Adding textures

You're not stuck with Photoshop's texture options. You can create your own textures and import them into any of the filters that use a Texture setting. One way is to start with a photograph. Another is to start with a blank canvas, add noise, and then filter the noise. Simply save the textures as Photoshop documents; then you can open them and apply them as textures through the dialog box, using the **Scaling**, **Relief**, and **Light Direction** options for even more control.

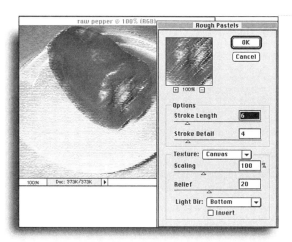

FIGURE 21.24

Lower stroke length and detail settings allow more of the subject to show through the effect.

Smudge Stick

The **Smudge Stick** filter can be very effective if used at its lowest **Stroke Length** and **Intensity** settings. It gives the appearance of dragging a soft cloth across a pastel or chalk drawing—gently smudging and muddying the colors. At higher settings, it adds too much black to most pictures. Figure 21.25 shows the filter and its dialog box.

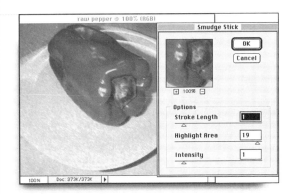

Sponge

People who teach children's art classes are always searching for new ways for the kids to apply paint. One of the more successful is sponge painting—dabbing the paper with a torn sponge dipped in poster paint. Settings using a small **Brush Size** and low **Smoothness** seem to work best. Flat areas might take on a mottled appearance, as in Figure 21.26, so you might want to mask the background before you apply the filter.

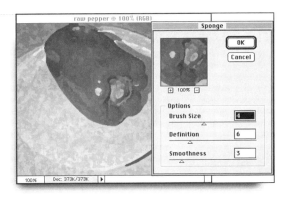

Underpainting

When artists start a painting, they usually begin by sketching out the main shapes and forms in the picture and then roughing these in with a big flat brush and thin paint. This is called underpainting, and Photoshop's **Underpainting** filter gives a very good imitation of the effect. This filter, like the **Rough Pastels**, uses Texture settings, so you can paint on canvas, burlap, or any texture you like. Like real underpainting, the **Underpainting** filter leaves a rather vague and undefined image. I like to use it as a first step in creating an imitation oil painting, going back over the picture with brushes to add highlights and define shapes. Figure 21.27 shows the **Underpainting** filter and its dialog box. Figure 21.28 shows the picture with brush strokes added.

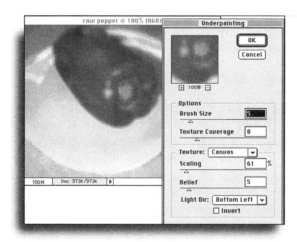

FIGURE 21.27
Underpainting is a good beginning for a picture.

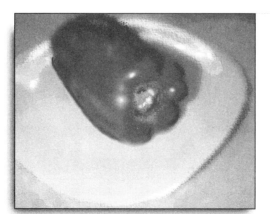

FIGURE 21.28
Use a brush to add back lost highlights and edges.

Watercolor

After the success of the **Underpainting** filter, the **Watercolor** filter is a major disappointment. Even on low settings, it turns the picture dark and looks almost nothing like a watercolor. Figure 21.29 shows an example.

FIGURE 21.29

The **Watercolor** filter has very limited usefulness.

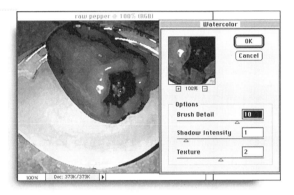

Brush Stroke Filters

The **Brush Stroke** filters all attempt to imitate one or another kind of paintbrush. Some are more successful than others. We'll apply them to a desert landscape from Red Rock Canyon, Nevada. The "raw" picture is shown in Figure 21.30.

FIGURE 21.30

Unfiltered landscape.

Accented Edges

The **Accented Edges** filter seeks out the edges of shapes in the picture and intensifies them. It looks best when the **Edge Width** setting is kept small. **Edge Brightness** ranges from 1 to 50. Settings greater than 25 turn the edges light colored, whereas lower numbers darken them. Figure 21.31 shows the filter applied to the sample picture.

FIGURE 21.31
At low **Smoothness** settings, the filter finds and enhances many small edges.

Angled Strokes

If I were in charge of Photoshop, the **Angled Strokes** filter would be found under the **Sketch** category, instead of with **Brushstrokes**. It turns your picture into something that looks like a crosshatched pencil sketch (see Figure 21.32). It's a nice-looking filter, though, and seems to work well with most pictures. The **Direction Balance** settings range from 0–100, with 50 giving you an even balance of left and right strokes.

Crosshatch

Crosshatch is very similar to **Angled Strokes** but more pronounced. It, too, looks good with most pictures. At intermediate settings, it looks like a very carefully rendered drawing. Figure 21.33 shows the filter applied, with its dialog box.

FIGURE 21.32

The **Angled Strokes** filter seems to work most effectively with higher **Sharpness** settings.

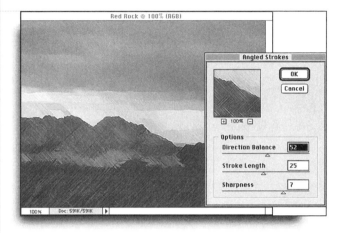

FIGURE 21.33

The **Strength** setting controls the embossed texture that accompanies each stroke.

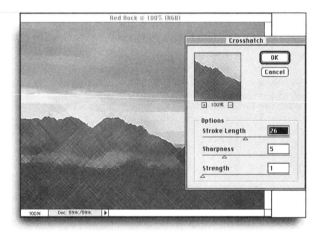

Dark Strokes

There aren't many situations where I'd choose this filter. One would be if I had a very light picture that needed some intensifying. The **Dark Strokes** filter tends to make everything become quite dark. You can adjust the balance of lights and darks and the intensity of Dark and Light strokes in the filter's dialog box, shown in Figure 21.34.

FIGURE 21.34
This filter is quite similar to
Angled Strokes.

Ink Outlines

Ink Outlines is another filter that's quite similar to **Dark Strokes** and **Angled Strokes**. It places first a white line and then a black line around every edge that it identifies. Applied to a still life or landscape, the **Ink Outlines** filter can give you the look of an old woodcut or steel engraving. If you use it on a portrait, however, it adds warts, blobs, and other potentially undesirable effects. In Figure 21.35, you can see the **Ink Outlines** filter applied to the desert landscape.

FIGURE 21.35
This filter is quite similar to
Angled Strokes.

Spatter

The **Spatter** filter gives you a stippled effect, as if you dabbed a very stiff brush full of oil paint directly on the canvas. Again, I wouldn't try this on a portrait or a delicate still life, but it's very effective on a landscape, especially if you have first applied a less well-defined filter, such as **Underpainting**. The Spatter dialog box, shown in Figure 21.36 enables you to set the **Spray Radius** for the spatter effect, and the **Smoothness** of the spray. Smaller numbers for **Smoothness** provide a misty effect, with small dots of paint, whereas larger numbers give you larger dots, in effect a heavier spray.

FIGURE 21.36

Try the **Spatter** filter on text, for an interesting look.

Sprayed Strokes

The **Sprayed Strokes** filter is very similar to **Spatter**, except that it's directional. In Figure 21.37, **Sprayed Strokes** is applied with the direction set to **Left Diagonal**. The other options are Right **Diagonal**, **Horizontal**, and **Vertical**. The filter works best if the **Stroke** Radius is kept small.

Combining filters

Remember that you're not restricted to using just one filter per image. You can layer one filter over another, or apply a second filter directly on top of the first. You can also apply the same filter several times for a more intense effect or, depending on the filter, a more abstract one. If a picture has too little detail to be interesting with some of the edge enhancing filters, try adding noise first or applying the edge filter several times.

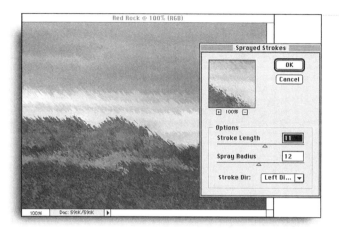

FIGURE 21.37
Try masking the sky and spraying it in the opposite direction.

Sumi-e

Sumi-e is Japanese for brush painting, but the results of the **Sumi-e** filter look more like the brushwork of a berserk Sumo wrestler than a Zen master. This filter turns any area with any sort of detail almost completely black, even at the lowest settings. It's relatively useless on most pictures. You can see what it did to our sample landscape in Figure 21.38. However, the **Sumi-e** filter works very nicely with type, adding texture to it. Apply it and then fade the filter until the type becomes legible. Figure 21.39 shows the effect.

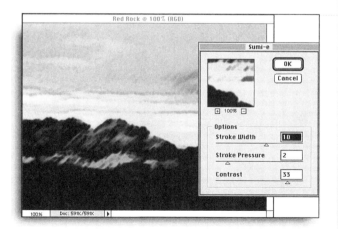

FIGURE 21.38
Not great for art…

FIGURE 21.39
…but nice for type.

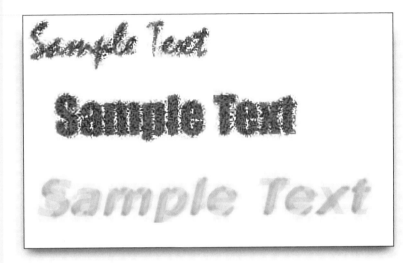

Sketch Filters

The fourteen **Sketch** filters mostly use the foreground and back-ground colors you set in the Toolbox as the main colors in your image. Experiment with placing the darker tone in the fore-ground color and in the background color. You might find that some of these effects work better if the foreground color is dark. We'll apply these filters to the flower shown in Figure 21.40.

FIGURE 21.40
Unfiltered daisy.

Bas Relief

The **Bas Relief** filter uses the foreground and background colors
to create a low relief rendering of your picture. If you choose
colors carefully, it can look like copper foil, hammered metal, or
carved stone. You can set the depth and smoothness of the relief
in the filter's dialog box (see Figure 21.41), and also the direction
in which light is presumed to strike it.

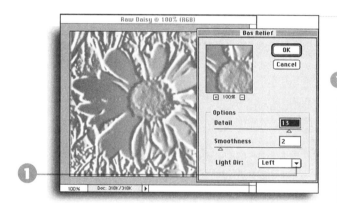

FIGURE 21.41

Try the light in different directions to see which works best.

1   Select to change light direction

Chalk and Charcoal

With the **Chalk and Charcoal** filter, which reduces the image
to three tones, you need to set the foreground to a dark color
and the background to a light one. The third color, by default, is
a medium gray, so choose colors that work with it. I am most
satisfied simply using black and white. This filter can produce
beautiful drawings. Figure 21.42 shows the filter and its dialog
box.

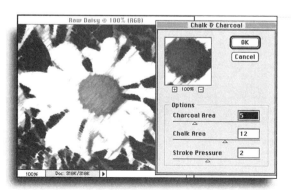

FIGURE 21.42

Remember that **Charcoal** uses
the foreground color and
Chalk the background.

Charcoal

The **Charcoal** filter does much the same thing as **Chalk and Charcoal** but uses only the foreground and background colors. It's more difficult to control because there are only two colors. Experiment until you are satisfied. In Figure 21.43, you can see the effect of the Charcoal filter on the sample image.

FIGURE **21.43**

Be careful not to let your picture get too dark.

Chrome

The **Chrome** filter is actually one of the more successful ones. It manages to make the image look as if it's been chrome plated, by rendering it in patterns of black, white, and gray lines. Of course, as you can see in Figure 21.44 in the process you lose a lot of detail.

FIGURE **21.44**

You can use the **Chrome** filter as a separate, semitransparent layer over the original image, if you want to keep the colors.

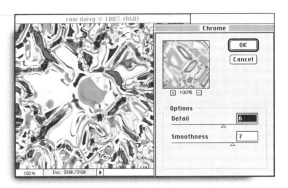

Conté Crayon

Conté Crayon is my favorite medium for drawing, so it's no surprise that I love this filter. The "crayons" are actually very compressed chalk and come in black, gray, and several shades of reddish-brown. The filter looks most natural if you restrain your foreground and background colors to browns and white. Photoshop adds the grays for you. This filter uses background **Textures**, which you can also adjust in its dialog box, shown in Figure 21.45.

FIGURE 21.45
This filter might look better with the texture size reduced.

Graphic Pen

I never liked the **Graphic Pen** filter until I tried it on this picture. It reduces the image to an ink sketch composed of lines and dots. It's not successful on pictures with a lot of detail but works nicely when the subject has plenty of contrast and is distinct enough to accept being "scratched over." Figure 21.46 shows the filter in use.

Halftone Pattern

The **Halftone** filter does a sort of imitation halftone conversion of your image into a pattern of circles, lines, or dots. It makes a strong graphic statement but is of limited usefulness.

FIGURE 21.46

Larger shapes work best with this filter—detail gets lost.

Note Paper, Plaster

These two filters are very similar, except that **Plaster** has a smooth surface, and **Note Paper** is heavily textured. They look best with large, uncomplicated shapes. Figure 21.47 shows the **Note Paper** filter. Remember that the foreground color should be the darker one, unless you want your image to appear as a negative.

FIGURE 21.47

This looks more like flocked wallpaper than note paper.

Photocopy

Photocopy is another filter that has very limited usefulness. Why would you *want* to make your picture look like a poor-quality photocopy of itself?

Reticulation

Reticulation is a photographer's trick, actually a mistake that happens in the darkroom when one of the processing chemicals is too cold. It causes the grains of emulsion to clump together, producing a very spotty image. The **Reticulation** filter, as you can see in Figure 21.48, does the same thing.

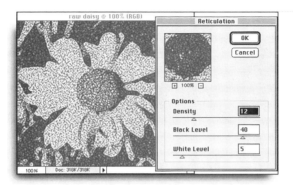

FIGURE 21.48
The **Reticulation** filter transforms the image to dots.

Stamp

The **Stamp** filter is much like **Note Paper**, but without the texture. It works very well with pictures that have large flat areas with plenty of contrast, making them look like rubber stamps. You can adjust the smoothness and balance of dark and light in the dialog box, shown in Figure 21.49.

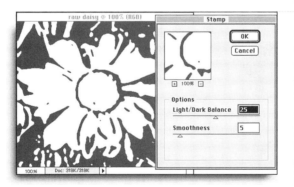

FIGURE 21.49
The **Stamp** filters looks especially good, with the daisy picture.

Torn Edges

The **Torn Edges** filter applies the same kind of treatment to the picture as the **Stamp** filter, except that lines are fuzzy rather than well-defined. It doesn't really look like torn paper, although that was most likely the intent. Instead it looks as if you used very wet paint on blotting paper. You can see it applied in Figure 21.50.

Water Paper

The **Water Paper** filter is a strange one. Photoshop's authors intended to create a filter to look as if the image were dunked in a pail of water, with the paper fibers absorbing some of the paint. Instead, the picture looks in some cases as if it were woven or like it had a window screen placed over it. The filter, which is shown in Figure 21.51, is worth experimenting with.

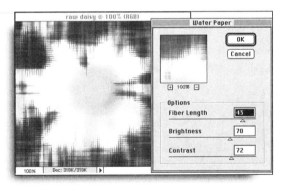

Special Effects Filters

The sets of filters that can be lumped as special effects are **Distort**, **Pixelate**, **Stylize**, and **Texture**. Some of them are terrific and do wonderful things to a mediocre picture. Others go too far and are virtually useless for most applications. We'll apply them to the picture shown unfiltered in Figure 21.52.

FIGURE 21.52
Box of apples, unfiltered.

Distort

Most of the **Distort** filters warp the image in one way or another. Some make it bulge in or out, some twist it, and some cover it with water or glass. The first filter on the list, however, simply adds a glow.

Diffuse Glow

You can use the **Diffuse Glow** filter, as it is in Figure 21.53, to put a light dusting of powdered sugar on the apples or to put a colored glow on almost anything. The color of the glow is whatever you have set as a background color. This filter also looks good when used on text.

FIGURE 21.53

A white glow could be snow, sugar, mist in the trees…

Displacement

The **Displacement** filter remaps the image according to the values in a second image, called a **Displacement Map**. Photoshop comes with a collection of displacement maps, and you can also save other images in the .psd format to use as displacement maps. This is a difficult filter to predict an outcome for; you have to try various settings and maps until you get an effect you like. In Figure 21.54, I applied a **Displacement Map** called **Schnable Effect**.

FIGURE 21.54

Displacement Maps are in the Photoshop, Plug-Ins folder.

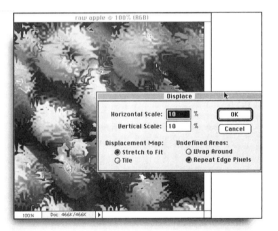

Glass, Ocean Ripple, Ripple

These three filters are so similar they can be considered as different degrees of the same basic filter. They all impart a glassy, bumpy, apparently reflective surface by adding patterns of black and white lines or spots to the picture. Figure 21.55 shows the **Glass** filter, which is the most adjustable of the three.

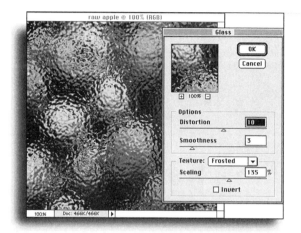

FIGURE 21.55
Ripple and **Ocean Ripple** produce bigger bumps.

Pinch, Spherize, ZigZag

Like the Ripple filters, these are three variations on the same theme. These filters make the image appear to be sitting on a convex, concave, or otherwise bumpy surface. In Figure 21.56, I applied the **Spherize** filter, making the apples appear to be reflected in a convex mirror.

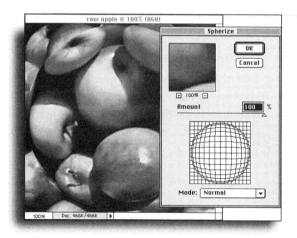

FIGURE 21.56
Drag on the map in the dialog box to adjust the degree of curve in the picture.

Polar Coordinates, Shear, Twirl, Wave

The final group of distortion filters remaps the image along an axis, or in a specific pattern such as **Twirl**. These haven't much practical use but are fun to play with. Figure 21.57 shows the **Twirl** filter.

FIGURE 21.57

Drag the slider to increase or decrease the effect.

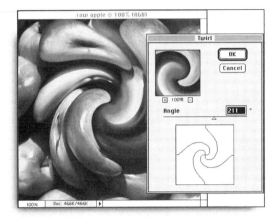

Pixelate

All the pixelate filters work by breaking the image into clumps of pixels: square blocks, dots, irregular blocks, and so on. There aren't many useful filters in this group. Unless applied at their smallest settings, these filters will make most images unrecognizable.

Color Halftone, Mezzotint

These two filters attempt to replicate printing techniques. Neither is especially successful. **Halftone** looks like an enlargement of a cheap comic book, whereas **Mezzotint**, seen in Figure 21.58, simply adds black dots or lines and posterizes the image.

FIGURE 21.58

Choose dots, lines, or strokes, (which are lines of random thickness).

Crystallize, Facet, Fragment, Mosaic

These filters break up the image by color into blocks. **Mosaic's** blocks are square, the others odd-shaped. At best, they make good patchwork quilt designs. At worst, they remind me of the way TV "real-life" shows sometimes hide the faces of alleged perpetrators. Figure 21.59 shows the **Crystallize** filter applied to the apples.

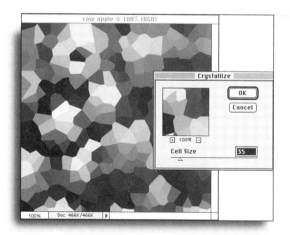

FIGURE 21.59

Drag the slider to increase or decrease the effect.

Pointillize

Pointillize is the only filter I like in this set. If you're a fan of the French Impressionist painter Georges Seurat, you're already familiar with Pointillism, the technique he introduced of creating paintings with small dots of color that the eye blends into shapes. The **Pointillize** filter does more or less the same thing, as long as you keep the cell size small. Figure 21.60 shows the result.

FIGURE 21.60

Settings range from 3–300. Numbers greater than 10 are useless.

Stylize

Within this category are some of Photoshop's best filters—and a few that you'll probably never use.

Diffuse

The **Diffuse** filter simply puts fuzzy edges on everything. It's great for making out-of-focus pictures look as if they meant to be that way. The dialog box, shown in Figure 21.61, lets you choose to fuzz all edges, dark ones, or light ones.

FIGURE 21.61

If your picture isn't soft enough, apply the filter a second time.

Emboss

This filter works like the **Bas Relief** and **Plaster** filters described earlier, with one notable exception. The dialog box enables you to set the angle at which the light appears to strike the picture. Edges reflect in color and it's generally more adaptable, hence more successful than the others. Figure 21.62 shows an example.

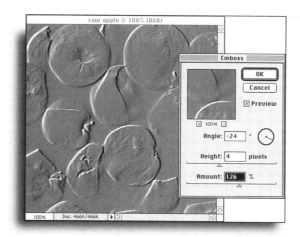

FIGURE 21.62

Heights between 4 and 6 pixels work best with most subjects.

Extrude, Tiles

If you were to cover your picture with plastic blocks, you'd get something like the result of the **Extrude** filter. This is one of the less successful efforts and really not worth wasting time on. **Tiles** is similar but less three-dimensional. Unless you want your picture chopped up into white edged blocks, forget it.

Find Edges , Glowing Edges, Trace Contour

All these filters actually trace contours rather than edges. The **Find Edges** filter can produce some truly stunning effects. It has nothing to set and no dialog box. Applying it transforms your image into a rainbow-colored drawing, with thin lines tracing the contours of the objects. Figure 21.63 shows how our sample picture came out. If you ever wanted to design neon signs, you'll love the **Glowing Edges** filter. This is more or less the same as the **Find Edges** filter, except that the lines it draws are thicker and brighter. The result, which is almost impossible to show in black and white, is a picture that appears to be made from spaghetti-like clumps of neon. It's a nifty effect and would be nice on a Web page because it reduces to only a handful of colors. **Trace Contours** is a more delicate version of **Find Edges**, usually giving you only a few lines instead of many. It's the least useful of these filters.

FIGURE 21.63

Nothing to adjust; it just finds and traces the contours.

Solarize

Another essentially useless filter, **Solarize** functions by inverting the Curves of the image so that values lighter than 50% become black. It has no adjustments and tends to make most pictures too dark to reproduce well.

Wind

Wind is kind of fun. The effect is as if a strong wind is blowing the colors off the picture. You can set the wind to blow from left or right, and whether it's a steady wind, a heavier blast, or a staggered wind. Figure 21.64 shows the **Wind** filter applied.

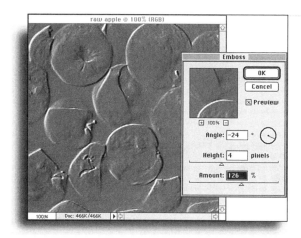

FIGURE 21.64

If you want the wind to blow from some other direction, rotate the picture.

Texture

The six filters in the Texture category are really fun to play with, even though they might not have much practical use beyond making interesting backgrounds for other art.

Cracquelure

Suppose your image was painted onto something with some thickness, such as a layer of plaster on a board. Then suppose that part of the plaster cracked and fell off, taking the paint with it. The result is **Craquelure**. You can see an example in Figure 21.65. The dialog box lets you set the distance between cracks and the depth.

FIGURE 21.65
It's a strange effect, but possibly useful.

FIGURE 21.65
It's a strange effect, but possibly useful.

Grain

Grain is a lot like **Film Grain**, described earlier. **Grain** type and size offer more choices but all it really does is to add noise to the picture.

Mosaic Tiles, Patchwork

The **Mosaic Tile** filter is a disappointment to me. I hoped for something that would look a little more realistic, more like Fractal Painter's mosaics—or at least a nice square-cornered tile. But, what you see in Figure 21.66 is what you get, wavy edges and gray grout. The **Patchwork** filter looks more like what I usually think of as mosaic tiles. It divides the image into same size squares, but not very realistically.

Stained Glass

The **Stained Glass** filter makes real-looking stained glass. The only difficulty is that it tends to turn the picture abstract at anything other than the very smallest cell size. The border thickness, or what in real stained glass would be lead strips, takes on the foreground color from the toolbar, so be sure to set it to something appropriate. Figure 21.67 shows the filter applied.

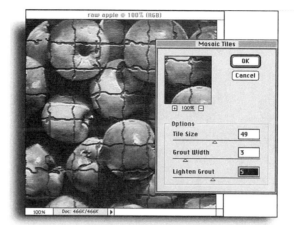

FIGURE 21.66
Floor tiles, maybe?

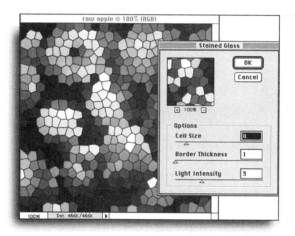

FIGURE 21.67
These could also be mosaic tiles.

Texturizer

Remember the **Texture** component of the **Rough Pastels** filter and some of the other "artistic" filters? Here it is on its own, so you can turn your surface texture to canvas, sandstone, burlap, or what have you without also turning the picture into something else. The **Texturizer** filter is ideal when your picture needs texture but you don't want to sacrifice realism. Figure 21.68 shows the filter applied.

FIGURE 21.68

FIGURE 21.68
The effect is as if the photo-graph were printed on sand-stone.

Technical Filters

These filters include the Render filters that can create clouds and add lens flares and lighting effects to your picture, plus the **Video** and **Other** filter sets that serve specific functions for video conversion.

Render

All the Render filters create special effects with light. They can add clouds to a cloudless sky or simulate fog, smoke, or unearth-ly glows depending on the colors you use. The **Lighting Effects** filter is particularly useful when you need to emphasize or de-emphasize part of a picture. Random filters are also the most mathematically intensive filters in Photoshop and may take a long time to apply.

3D Transform

The 3D Transform filter lets you apply your picture as a surface texture on a cube, sphere, or cylinder. The pan and tilt controls enable you to change your perspective on the object.

Clouds, Difference Clouds

Clouds are created from the foreground and background colors. They're always thin, wispy cirrus clouds, but they look quite realistic. **Clouds** are not affected by the image that's already on the screen, if any, and can (and should) be applied to an empty layer and then placed into the scene. **Difference Clouds** gives you a similar, but not identical, result because it uses a different algorithm to create the cloud shapes.

Lens Flare

Lens Flare is an "effect" that photographers usually try to avoid. It's caused by sunlight or a spotlight reflecting off one or more of the glass elements in a camera lens and produces a blob of light on the picture. Figure 21.69 shows the effect and its dialog box.

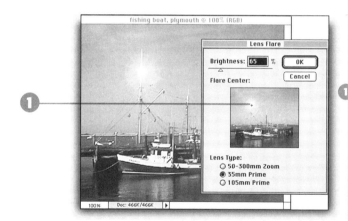

FIGURE 21.69

Use the thumbnail to position the flare exactly where you want it.

1   Positioned flare

Lighting Effects

The **Lighting Effects** filter is one of the most complicated filters Photoshop has and probably the most useful—when you figure it out. It can simulate all kinds of lighting effects from a flashlight to multiple spotlights to colored lights. Figure 21.70 shows its dialog box. Use the **Lighting Effects** filter to emphasize part of a picture or to hide undesirable parts by putting them in shadow.

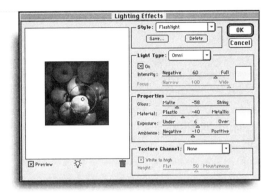

FIGURE 21.70
Experiment with the settings.

Video

These filters are used when you're going to or from videotape.

De-Interlace

Video images are interlaced, which means that the odd lines and even lines alternate scanning onto the TV screen or monitor. This produces a jittery, jumpy image. **De-Interlacing** restores "normal" order to the scan lines and removes jitter from images you are importing to the computer.

NTSC Colors

This filter removes "illegal" colors that can't display on ordinary video monitors. It does so by converting them to the nearest "legal" color.

SEE ALSO

➤ *To fade filters with Blending modes, see page 137*

Finding and Installing
More Filters

Find commercial, shareware, and freeware filters

Install filters

Use Kai's Power Tools

Use Alien Skin Eye Candy

Learn about Extensis PhotoTools

Commercial Filters

Installing third-party filters

Nothing can be much easier than installing an individual filter. Simply drag it into the Photoshop Plug-Ins folder, if you use a Mac. Windows users, place it in the folder Photoshop\Plug-Ins\Filters. When you restart your computer and open Photoshop, the new filter appears in the list under the Filter menu. If you purchase a set of filters, such as Alien Skin's Eye Candy or Extensis PhotoTools, an installer is included that automatically places the filters where they belong. Installed third-party filters appear in the filter list after Photoshop's native filters.

Look in any good software store or mail-order catalog. In the same general area where Photoshop appears, you can find a good selection of third-party plug-in filters. These are filters that you add to the Plug-Ins folder in your copy of Photoshop. They show up on the filter menu underneath Photoshop's own filters and work more or less the same way. Some, notably Kai's Power Tools, have unique interfaces but nothing you can't figure out.

There are basically two kinds of third-party filters: those that make you more productive by simplifying some task such as color correction or masking, and those that make you more creative, by giving you additional tools and tricks. Let's look first at productivity tools.

Extensis Intellihance

Download a demo

You can download a demo version of Intellihance from Extensis from http://www.extensis.com/products/Intellihance/

Try it for free and then buy it online if you like the results. You can also order it from your favorite mail-order software vendor for less than $100 or as part of a bundle with two other Extensis plug-in sets.

Photoshop has some very awesome color correction tools, as you learned in earlier chapters of this book. But they're only as good as the person using them. You can spend all day tweaking the colors in your picture and still not get quite what you want. Or you can install Intellihance and let the plug-in do the tweaking for you. Intellihance is a "smart" filter. You have only to tell it how you want your pictures corrected: how much contrast, saturation, and so on. This is done in the window shown in Figure 22.1. After you set preferences, you can simply click a button and it will make corrections according to the preferences you established. In just a couple of seconds, the job is done.

You can then go in and fine-tune the corrections using the Intellihance dialog box and sliders, which are a little easier to use than Photoshop's own. In Figure 22.2, I'm fine-tuning the Sharpness and getting instant feedback from the large preview window at the right of the dialog box.

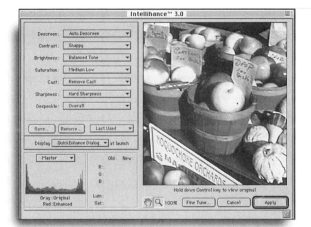

FIGURE 22.1
Use the pop-ups to set your preferences.

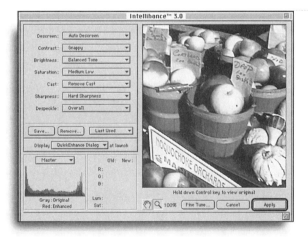

FIGURE 22.2
Press Control to see the original picture.

Apply Intellihance to an image

1. Select **Filter, Extensis, Intellihance**. If this is the first time you're using the filter, open the Intellihance Preferences dialog box.

2. Set your preferences for how Intellihance will correct the picture. Click **Apply** when done.

3. If you have previously set preferences, simply click the Enhance Image button (shown in Figure 22.3) to enhance the image.

FIGURE 22.3

If you press (Command+F) [Control+F] after selecting the filter, you can skip the dialog box.

Vivid Details TestStrip

If you have any experience with old-fashioned, nondigital dark-rooms, you know the importance of making a test strip before you burn through many sheets of expensive color paper. Vivid Details has created a plug-in that makes digital test strips, so you can see on your screen and as printer output, precisely what difference your color adjustments make.

The Test Strip window, shown in Figure 22.4, enables you to look at variations, as Photoshop's own Variations dialog box does. The main difference is that you have much more precise control with TestStrip. And you can print your test strips to see how closely your printer and screen match each other. In the example in the figure, I'm adjusting the color balance by looking at my original, surrounded by thumbnails that each add 15% of red, green, blue, magenta, cyan, or yellow. By dragging the slider, I can increase or decrease the percentage of color added. I can also click on the image to take a color sample and read out precisely how it's described in RGB or CMYK mode.

Limited free trial

Download a trial version of TestStrip 2.0 at www.vividdetails.com.

It's limited to fifteen uses, but that's enough to tell you whether or not it will make your color correction tasks easier. Own it for less than $150.

FIGURE 22.4
TestStrip can show you variations on Exposure, Saturation, Color Balance, and single color adjustments.

In addition to Color Balance, you can use Test Strip to adjust a single color, or to adjust saturation or exposure. Simply click on the appropriate icon at the top-right area of the window to see the controls for other modes. TestStrip can even be automated, either by using Photoshop's Actions and recording your changes, or by saving and applying TestStrip's settings file to similar pictures.

Chroma Graphics

The original ChromaGraphics plug-in, Chromatica, is still popular. Parts of it, notably the MagicMasking and Edge Wizard tools, have also been released as separate plug-ins.

Chromatica

Chromatica consists of several tools that enable you to make selections and masks more easily, blend edges, and do some spectacular color change effects while keeping all the image detail intact. ChromaColor is the mask and color change tool. Figure 22.5 shows it in use.

FIGURE 22.5

Drag across a color to select it.

Where to find it...

Chromatica, MagicMask, and
EdgeWizard are all available from
your favorite software vendors, for
under $100 each. I didn't find online
demo versions, but you can get
more information about the products from their Web site:
www.chromagraphics.com

If I want to change the red baskets in this picture of a farm stand
to green ones, ChromaColor is the right tool for the job. In
Figure 22.6, I selected several of the red baskets, by holding
down the Shift key to allow multiple selections and dragging the
ChromaMask selection tool across the red areas. The piece of
spectrum at the left of the window shows what colors have been
selected. (Use the Eraser tool to clean up your mask before you
go on.) To make the change, click the tab for **ChromaColor**
(see Figure 22.6).

FIGURE 22.6

Click to switch between
ChromaMask and
ChromaColor.

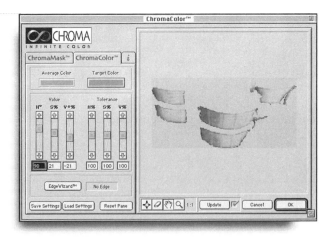

As you can see, there are two color swatches. The one on the left shows the average color of all pixels selected. The right-hand target swatch shows what the colors will change to. Clicking on it opens the Photoshop Color Picker, so you can choose the color to change to. The new color will be applied transparently, keeping the same detail and values as the previous color. EdgeWizard blends the edges of the new color so it eases directly into the picture.

Using Chromatica to replace a single color

1. Choose **Filter, Chromatica, ChromaColor**. Click the **ChromaMask** tab if ChromaMask isn't already active. Set the preview to **Masked In**.

2. Click the Selection tool and click-drag over the color you want to remove. Press Shift and repeat the click-drag to select more of the color.

3. Click the **ChromaColor** tab. Click on the **Target** color swatch to open the Color Picker. Select a color to replace the color you masked.

4. If you want to experiment, use the **HSV Value** sliders to change the **Target** color. Be sure **Update** is checked so you can see the effect of your changes.

5. Use the **HSV Tolerance** sliders underneath the **Target** color swatch to fine-tune your color selection. Click **OK** when done to return to Photoshop with the color change made.

ChromaPalette

If you want to make more drastic changes, perhaps remapping all the colors, open **ChromaPalette**. Figure 22.7 shows the ChromaPalette window. On the left, I built a palette of the colors in the original photograph. On the right, I opened **Cabernet Grapes**, one of the saved palettes that comes with the program. (The CD-ROM version includes 1,000 different palettes!) ChromaPalette remaps the colors in the picture to use the colors from the saved palette. If I want, I can also save the palette I have created with the original colors, by clicking the **Save Palette** button and giving it a name.

FIGURE 22.7

If Update is checked, you can see the results as soon as you load a palette.

Kai's Power Tools

Kai Krause is the guiding genius behind a huge number of computer graphics applications and plug-ins, including Kai's Power Tools, Bryce, Convolver, Vector Effects, Final Effects, Goo, Soap, and probably many goodies yet to be announced. Power Tools (also known as KPT) 3, the current edition, comes with an *Explorer Guide* rather than a manual. There's much to explore, but you can discover it just as easily by clicking your way through the odd, but intuitive, interface. There are excellent help screens available within each filter. (Look for a question mark and click it.) The goal of these filters, along with doing interesting things to your photos, is to do interesting things to the way you relate to the computer. They will make you think, laugh, and occasionally cheer.

To say the KPT set has nineteen tools is to greatly understate the case. Yes, nineteen items appear on the submenu, but each of these items is really a set of multipurpose tools rather than a single filter. Think of a Swiss Army Knife or the Leatherman 30-in-1 folding toolkit, and you're getting close to the way KPT tools work.

KPT Gradient Designer

Figure 22.8 shows the Gradient designer, which is fairly typical of the KPT interface. When you use most of the KPT filters, you won't see anything else on the screen. This is so you're not distracted while you "play" with the filter. Experimentation is the best way to figure out what these tools can do for you.

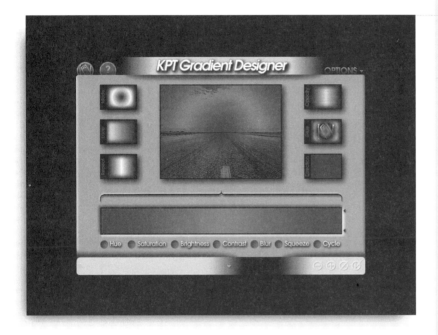

FIGURE 22.8

You can create blends of up to 512 colors.

The central preview window shows what you're doing as you make changes, and you can adjust the opacity to see the gradient in position on your picture. "Glue," found in most KPT filters, is similar to blending modes and determines how the filter is applied to the underlying picture.

KPT Interform

KPT Interform creates textures, but in a peculiar way, by merging other textures. In this filter, you start with two "parent" textures, selected from lists of presets with names such as "cracked blue lava," "Dragon tattoo," "neon bunny," and "Seussian

Clues for the clueless

Clicking on the question mark on any of the KPT filters brings up a very comprehensive help system, with many tips and "secret" commands for using the filter. Be sure to read the help screens, even if the filter seems to be doing what you want it to. You'll learn additional tricks.

Fribbldigniggets," The Mother and Father textures create a genetically-related Child texture, not simply overlaying one texture on the other but mathematically merging them. Figure 22.9 shows the Interform screen. Because the textures are also capable of moving, you can create texture "movies" to use for moving Web backgrounds or for whatever purposes you want to apply them.

FIGURE 22.9

Dot Field plus Zebra Fire = Zebradotfirefield?

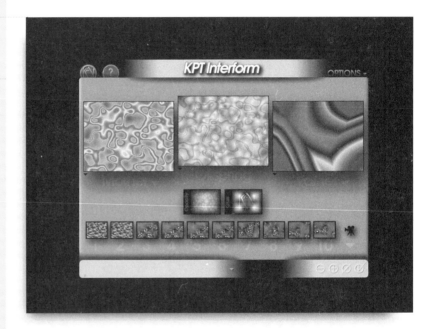

KPT Texture Explorer

Texture Explorer also creates textures, but according to different mathematical rules. In the Texture Explorer window, shown in Figure 22.10, you can see one large square of "source" texture, and arranged around it, sixteen squares of different derivative textures. In this case, the source is a photograph I opened in Photoshop. Clicking on any of the derivative textures gives you another sixteen, based on that one's particular mathematical formula. The balls at the left of the window, with the tree branch etched behind them, are the mutation tree. Clicking the balls determines the level of mutation that will be applied each time derivative textures are figured. The color gradient below the mutation tree also affects the derivative textures. To change color gradients, click and hold on the color strip to open a very long list of saved gradients.

FIGURE 22.10
Adjust the opacity to see the derivative texture applied to the source.

KPT Spheroid Designer

The Spheroid Designer, seen in Figure 22.11, has an interface that Kai says is based on an old, stale brownie. The sample sphere at the center shows the work in progress. It's the equivalent of a Preview window. The four smaller clusters of spheres around it are the light sources you can apply to your sphere. Click once on the larger ones to turn them on and use the small, marble-sized ones to control the color, position, intensity, and highlight intensity of each light source. As with any of Kai's tools, clicking the logo lets you see the effect in full screen form.

FIGURE 22.11

Your Sphere can be concave or convex by adjusting the Sphere Curvature to a positive or negative number.

The three balls at the lower-left area of the screen control the curvature of the sphere, the glossiness and amount of ambient light around it, and the opacity. Clicking and dragging on these balls changes their settings.

There are many more dots and balls and other goodies to click on in this interface. The clustered balls determine how many spheres you'll generate. The Mutation Tree in the upper-left corner of the screen, as in the Texture Generator, gives you random variations on your sphere. You can set bump polarity, height, rotation, and zoom with the four small dots below and to the right of the Bump map panel. The best way to figure out what the various buttons and dots actually do is to experiment. You won't get bored with this tool, and even if you do nothing else for a week, you won't discover all its possibilities. Figure 22.12 shows the filter applied.

KPT Glass Lens

You can get the effect of a single bubble on your picture with even less effort by using the KPT Glass Lens. This filter, shown in Figure 22.13, has fewer choices and is therefore easier to apply. Choose **Soft**, **Normal**, or **Bright** mode. Adjust the highlight by dragging on the preview window. When you are ready to apply the filter, click the green button.

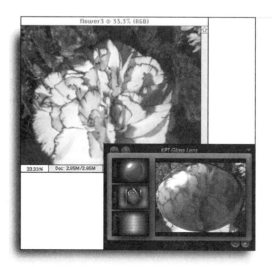

FIGURE 22.13

If you don't like the effect, the red button cancels it.

No free lunch

You can find out more about KPT 3 and other MetaTools products at its Web site `http://www.meta-tools.com`

What you won't find is a demo version of KPT; You have to go to your local software store or software mail-order house. It'll cost you approximately $129. for the full set of toys.

KPT Page Curl

This effect is a KPT classic, going back to an early release of Kai's tools. It's shown applied to a photo in Figure 22.14. The interface is very simple because you can't change the curling corner. (Sure you can, unofficially. Rotate the image before you apply the curl.)

FIGURE 22.14

The page appears to be printed on curling silver foil.

If you want to apply it a *second* time, in a different direction, press and hold 7 on the keypad, while pressing (Command+F) [Control+F] to reapply the filter from upper-left area. Holding 9 applies the filter from the upper-right area, and 1 from the lower-left area. (It makes more sense if you look at the keypad as representing the corners of the picture.) This only works if you have already applied the filter once to its original (lower-right) corner.

KPT Twirl

This filter isn't much more useful than Photoshop's own Twirl filter, but it's lots of fun to play with because it creates a great kaleidoscope effect. Figure 22.15 shows an example. Choose **Twirl** or **Kaleida** from the Mode selector and drag across the preview window to change the pattern. **Vortex Tile** is a somewhat similar effect that can make wonderful lacy patterns.

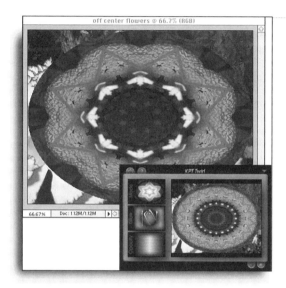

FIGURE 22.15

Remember that you can apply these filters to selected parts of the image, as well as to the whole page.

KPT MetaToys Lens f/x

One of the coolest, if not the most useful, of Kai's tools is the MetaToys Lens. You can think of it as a magnifying glass that does tricks (see Figure 22.16). Each of the lines and bumps and buttons on it does something. Clicking the words **Lens f/x**, for instance, opens the menu of effects available with this tool, allowing you to switch without going back to the Photoshop screen. Effects that the Lens applies are **Pixel**, **Gaussian**, **Noise**, **Edge**, **Intensity**, **Smudge**, **Glass Lens**, and **Twirl**.

FIGURE 22.16

You can spend hours learning this tool.

The gray marks along the left side, along with the two red balls on either end of them, control the intensity and opacity of the effect you apply. The left side handles intensity and the right opacity. Clicking either ball and dragging up increases the percentage, whereas dragging down decreases it. The third ball, when present, controls the directionality of the effect. Clicking and dragging this third one applies that direction to the effect, if it's an effect that can be directional. In the figure, we're using the **Edges** effect, which is similar to Photoshop's Find Edges, but does a better job.

The top button is the **Preview** button. It toggles your view through the lens between the center of the image and whatever the lens happens to be on top of. You can drag it all over the image to preview the effect on different areas. You can also drag it across the rest of the screen to see what your menu bars, trash can, or recycle bin look like with the effect applied.

The lower button is the **Reset** button. It returns all the settings to their defaults. The gauge directly below the **Reset** button is the **Options** gauge. Pressing it opens the **Glue** menu listing options for applying the effect. You have, generally speaking, the same options you have when applying any other Photoshop effects: **Normal**, **Darken**, **Lighten**, **Multiply**, and so on. Remember that after you apply a KPT effect, you can still go back and fade it using Photoshop's **Fade** settings.

After you adjust the effect the way you want it, click the small green dot at the bottom-right area of the lens to apply it. If you decide you don't want it, click the red dot instead to cancel and return to the regular Photoshop screen.

Convolver

The most powerful of all Kai's tools is the **Convolver**. What is a Convolver? **Convolver** has two functions: corrective and creative. If you use it only for one of these, you'll be glad to have it, but you'll be missing half the fun. In **Tweak** mode, it applies the same sort of saturation, brightness, and color corrections as Photoshop's own tools. But it applies them through an interface that encourages you to experiment, not just to try to achieve something sort of realistic. Figure 22.17 shows **Convolver** in **Tweak** mode. The central preview window shows you a before and after view.

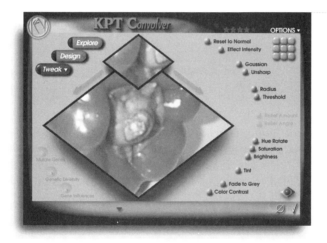

FIGURE 22.17

You make adjustments by dragging on the little round balls.

Along the right side of the screen are the **Image** controls. To apply one, click its button and drag right or left. Numbers appear in the bar below the preview window to tell you what settings you're using. You can apply most of these tools as a negative as well as a positive. **Saturation**, for instance, starts at 100% when you first click the button. Dragging left lowers the saturation to amounts less than 100%, while dragging right raises it. How high? I stopped after 3,200%.

Design mode uses the Image controls in pairs, taking the central diamond and breaking it into 15 windows, each representing a combination of two **Image** control effects in a sort of cross-matrix. It sounds complicated, but it's not, as you can see in Figure 22.18. The effects are applied in steps downward and merged in the middle of the matrix.

FIGURE 22.18

Drag the arrows to set the degree of difference in the steps.

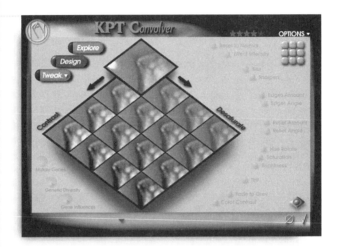

It's good to see stars

Exploration is its own reward with **Convolver**, but there are more tangible ones as well. To encourage you to poke around, the program includes some hidden tools. After you try each of the modes, you earn your first star–and a new tool along with it. As you go further, you earn more stars. Each one adds a new tool when you're ready to apply it. It takes a while to work up to all five stars. (The fifth and final star gives you **Animation**!)

You'll notice an arrow along each axis of the diamond and a label denoting one of the effects. Each axis has nine different options and considering that they can go positive or negative, that makes 18 possible settings for each axis. Multiply that by 15 tiles of variations and 10 degrees of intensity for each setting, and you end up with a lot of options. **Design** mode and **Explore** mode use the same matrix of windows, but **Explore** mode takes the variations even further, by adding "genetic diversity." The mind boggles....

The best thing about **Convolver** is not so much what it does, although it's extremely powerful and definitely useful, but its biggest feature is that it brings all the tools together. When you tweak an image, you don't have to keep going back to the menu to get new tools. Everything's right there. If changing the saturation affects something else, you don't have to go very far to fix it.

There are still more filters in the KPT set. You can spend many hours playing, experimenting, having fun with them—and you should. These filters are designed to tweak your creativity, as well as your photos. I try to spend at least a couple of hours every week experimenting. It's playtime, but it also teaches me a lot.

Alien Skin Eye Candy

Kai's not the only one who invents interesting plug-ins for Photoshop. The folks at Alien Skin have come up with a set of goodies called Eye Candy. It comes in both Mac and Windows flavors and can be found at your local software store or mail-order source for approximately $125. Some of the Eye Candy effects are probably not for everyday use, unless your day job is designing covers for a science fiction magazine. Others, however, such as drop shadow and perspective shadow, can be very useful.

The Alien Skin interface changes according to the effect you're applying, but the basic screen, shown in Figure 22.19, remains the same. The large square in the lower-right area gives you a preview of the effect being applied, and the sliders adjust the parameters.

Try it out!!!

Those nice folks at AlienSkin have put up a demo version of Eye Candy. Download it from http://www.alienskin.com/eyecandy/ec_man.htm

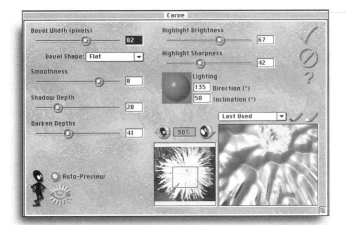

FIGURE 22.19
Eye Candy's **Carve** filter makes a selected area appear to be carved or chiseled into the image.

Carve, seen here, is one of the 21 Eye Candy effects, along with fur, smoke, fire, jiggle, squint, swirl, and a lot more. You can adjust all possible parameters of each of these effects, making the fur wavy, long, or shiny, the smoke dense or wispy, or the flames as high and wide as you like.

Applying many of these effects requires first selecting an area to which the effect will be applied, or adding a layer for it. A few, such as **Antimatter**, simply do their thing. Antimatter inverts the brightness without affecting the colors or saturation value. Darks become light and lights go dark. Figure 22.20 shows **Antimatter** applied.

FIGURE **22.20**

The white flower petals turn black but the background colors simply get lighter.

Water Drops is a typical Eye Candy Filter, shown in Figure 22.21.

Apply the Water Drops (or any similar) filter

1. Select the part of the picture to which you want to apply water drops. Choose **Filter, EyeCandy, Water Drops**.

2. Be sure Auto Preview is checked so you can see your changes.

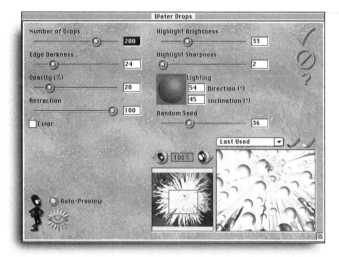

FIGURE 22.21
The **Water Drops** filter can also make jewels, buttons, or jujubes.

3. Drag the top slider to set the number of drops. As the number increases, the size decreases.

4. Set the **Edge Darkness** slider to control the edge shadows that define the water droplets' hemispherical shape. Some settings look better than others, depending on what the drops are applied to. Try a lower value on a dark background or a high one against a light background.

5. Set the **Opacity** of the drops. If they're plain water, they won't be opaque. If your drops are motor oil, or some other similar substance, set the **Opacity** high.

6. Drag the **Refraction** slider to control the amount the background is "warped" by the lens action of the water drops.

7. Drag on the **Lighting** ball and enter amounts for **Direction** and **Inclination** to adjust the way light hits the water drops. Set the **Highlight Brightness** and **Highlight Sharpness** as desired.

8. If the drops are something other than clear water, adjust their color by clicking on the color swatch to open the Color Picker.

9. **Random Seed** adds a randomness factor to the placement of the drops. Experiment with it until you achieve an effect you like.

10. Click the check mark to accept the filter or the "no" symbol to cancel.

Several of the Eye Candy filters do really nice things for type. I particularly like the **Outer Bevel**, shown in Figure 22.22, or for raised type on a flat surface, the **Inner Bevel**.

FIGURE 22.22
Try the other filters on type, too.

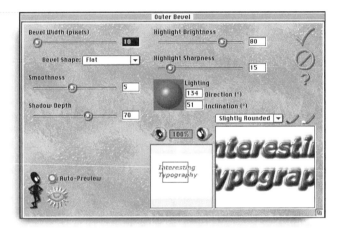

As a final note, Eye Candy's filters can also be used to create background patterns and textures for use with graphics or on Web pages. In Figure 22.23, I've used the Weave filter on a blank canvas to make a nice basket weave effect.

FIGURE 22.23
You can also apply other filters to this basic pattern.

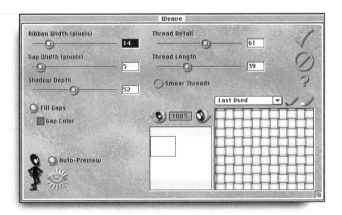

Extensis PhotoTools

PhotoTools is a comprehensive set of plug-ins that makes working with Photoshop easier and more pleasant. (Find it at the usual software sources for approximately $125.) It includes a version of Intellihance, which you learned about earlier in this chapter, and it has lots of other goodies as well. There are tools to bevel and build buttons, to cast shadows and glows, and even to work with type.

PhotoText

PhotoText, the type tool, is the one I use most. Even with the improved type handling capability in Photoshop 5, PhotoText remains a much better way to set type. The PhotoText dialog box, shown in Figure 22.24, gives you access to more type styles than Photoshop itself, as well as auto leading, automatic anti-aliasing, and even style sheets. Imagine—you can create and save type styles you use often, just as in your favorite word processor.

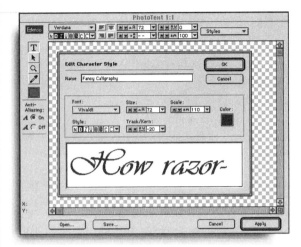

Most generous demo

You can download limited-time, full-working versions of all the Extensis plug-ins on the World Wide Web. Go to **www.extensis.com** and check out the Photoshop plug-ins for Mac or Windows. They're good for 30 days in demo mode, and then you can register by phone with a credit card.

Figure 22.25 shows the Styles dialog box. To save a new style, simply give it a name and set its parameters. Next time you want to use it, it will be waiting in the pop-up menus under Styles. You can also save blocks of text that you enter in PhotoTools. Click the **Save** button, and they'll be saved in a format that PhotoTools can recognize and reopen.

You can change type attributes on individual characters by selecting them with the Type tool, or on the entire text block by selecting it. Because the type is set on a new layer, you can easily apply Photoshop's Type Paths tool to turn it into a selection and use it for special effects. Headlines set in this way, because they can be properly kerned and letter-spaced, look better than those done directly in Photoshop.

PhotoGlow

Want to put a glow around your type? It's a cinch if you have PhotoTools installed. Select the type or object to glow, open the **PhotoGlow** box, as shown in Figure 22.26, and set up exactly as much glow as you want. PhotoGlow works on any selection, making it even more versatile than Photoshop's own Glow tool.

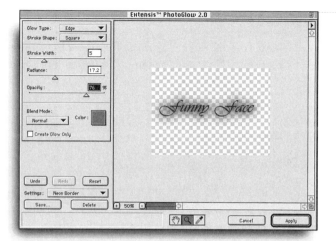

FIGURE 22.26
Change the glow color by click-ing on the swatch to open the Color Picker.

The other tools in the PhotoTool set use a similar interface and are just as easy and effective.

PhotoFrame

The newest Extensis package adds border and edge effects to your pictures. Its interface, shown in Figure 22.27, is easy to use and very close to that of PhotoTools. Select a frame from the accompanying CD-ROMs, adjust the color, width, orientation, and blur, and there it is. PhotoFrame comes with over 300 dif-ferent frame styles to use with Web pages and print and multi-media projects.

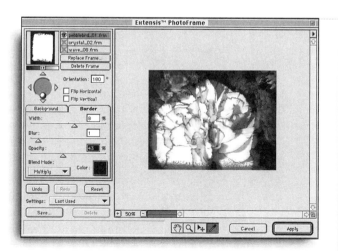

FIGURE 22.27
Frames can be positioned off-center, if you want. Just drag on the preview or use the "joystick."

Total Xaos

To my mind, total chaos would be to *not* have these excellent tools available. Paint Alchemy, Terrazzo, and TypeCaster are sold separately or as a package, called Total Xaos, which also includes Fresco, a set of 80 digital backgrounds—and a T-shirt.

Paint Alchemy

Paint Alchemy is magic. It lets you transform your pictures into painter-like masterpieces. Paint Alchemy comes with 101 prein-stalled styles for your immediate use, including Cubist, Granite, Oil Canvas, and Vortex. You can imitate Picasso, VanGogh, or simply create your own unique special effects. The results range from subtle to bold, traditional to highly abstract. The interface, shown in Figure 22.28, is completely intuitive. Choose a brush shape, click on the palettes to apply variations, roll the dice to **Randomize**, and click **Preview** to see the changes. When you're happy with the preview screen, click **Apply**, step back, and wait for the oohs and ahhs.

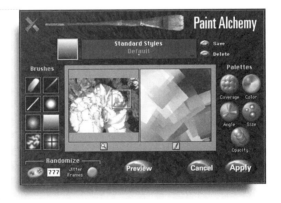

FIGURE 22.28

The preview window doesn't update until you click **Preview**.

Terrazzo

Have you ever wondered where top Web designers get those beautiful tiled backgrounds? They create them, with Photoshop and Terrazzo. It makes any image into a Web-ready tile and cre-ates breath-taking tiled effects for print and multimedia. In Figure 22.29, I've turned the flowers into a stunning stained glass or quilt pattern. By simply dragging the mouse across the source picture, I can preview an infinite number of variations.

TypeCaster

Use TypeCaster to create 3D type in Photoshop for headlines and logos. You can drag and drop any of the 50 included textures or create your own. TypeCaster scales, rotates, and extrudes type with precision. Although the PhotoTools Bevel is a little easier to work with, TypeCaster can do a few tricks that Bevel can't. Figure 22.30 shows the TypeCaster screen. I applied both bevel and extrude to the letters, and adjusted the lighting to make an effectively 3D image.

Shareware and Freeware Filters

Generally speaking, you get your money's worth when you invest in commercial programs. The ones we previewed here are all worth owning. But if you just can't afford to spend a lot of money on plug-ins, that doesn't mean you can't use any. There are literally hundreds of useful and fun filters for both Mac and Windows that are either freeware or inexpensive shareware.

Start your search for shareware at Photoshop Paradise:
`http://desktopPublishing.com/photoshop.html`

Windows users, try PC Resources for Photoshop. It's a comprehensive site with filters, how-to's, and much more:
`http://www.netins.net/showcase/wolf359/plugcomm.htm`

The ultimate plug-ins source for commercial demos as well as shareware is called, appropriately, Pluginhead. They also have pointers to custom brushes, displacement maps, and more sites with more stuff. Check it out at `http://pluginhead.i-us.com/`

Creating Special Image Effects

Shadows and Highlights

If you want an object to look "real," it can't just float in space, evenly lit from all sides at once. Life's not like that. Light is directional, whether you're outdoors in sunshine or indoors with overhead fluorescents, working under the glow of a desk lamp, or in a room romantically lit by a single candle. If you apply light to an object, two things happen. One, the object probably (unless it's a remarkably dull surface) has a highlight. Two, behind the object there's a shadow.

Adding shadows and highlights

1. Use the round marquee to draw a circle, pressing the Shift key to assure that the circle stays round.

2. Set the foreground color to something that contrasts with the background. (I happen to like blue.) Open the **Edit** menu and choose **Fill**, using the foreground color. The selected shape fills with the color. Your screen should look something like Figure 23.1.

FIGURE 23.1
This makes the basic ball.

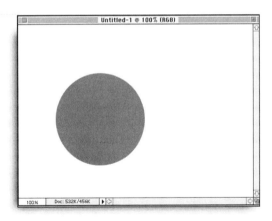

3. The next step is to use the **Add Noise** filter, to give the ball some texture. Select the ball with the **Magic Wand**. Select **Filter,** Noise, **Add Noise**. Set the amount to about 120 and apply it with Gaussian distribution.

4. Now, we'll make it round. Select **Filter, Distort, Spherize**. Set the amount to 100% and apply the filter. Notice, in Figure 23.2, how the texture helps to emphasize the shape.

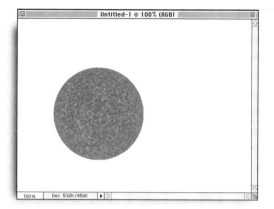

FIGURE 23.2
It's looking rounder.

5. Now, for a little light. (The ball should still be selected. If not, select the background and invert.) Open **Filter, Render, Lighting Effects**. Use the settings shown in Figure 23.3. Drag the highlight to the upper-left quarter of the ball. Click **OK** to apply the light.

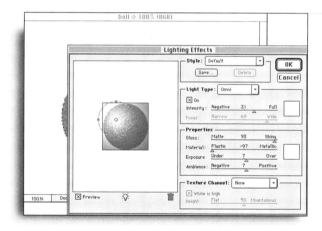

FIGURE 23.3
The light emphasizes the shape even more.

6. And finally, add the shadow. Open **Layer, Effect, Drop Shadow**. (see Figure 23.4). Be sure Preview is checked so you can see what you are doing. Set the **Mode** to **Normal**, the **Opacity** to about 75%. Set the shadow distance to about 40 pixels, and the **Blur** to about 25 pixels. (The spotlight we're using isn't very strong or very well focused.) Adjust the angle by dragging on the clock dial until the shadow is opposite the highlight.

Shedding some light on shadows

You can use two dozen, or more, different ways to create shadow effects. You can copy the shape of an object, fill it with black on a separate layer, and sneak that in behind the object as its shadow. You can use Photoshop's shadow effect, or if you have either Eye Candy or PhotoTools plug-ins, you can use their excellent drop shadow filters—no one way is right. Experiment with different kinds of shadows. Sooner or later, you'll find the way that's easiest for you.

FIGURE 23.4

These effects are new in
Photoshop 5.

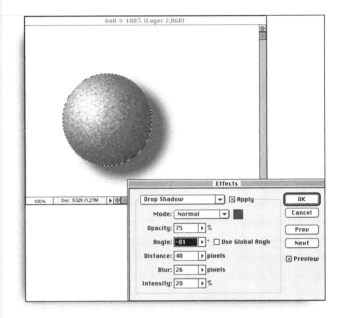

7. Set the **Intensity** to 20%. If the shadow looks too dark,
click on the black swatch to open the Color Picker and
choose a lighter gray for the shadow. Because I used blue as
a base color for the ball, I chose a gray with some blue in it.
The finished ball is shown in Figure 23.5.

FIGURE 23.5

You can create something
from nothing.

Reflections

There are actually two kinds of reflections. The first is a mirror image and the second an "incomplete" reflection that you see, for instance, if you place an object on a shiny surface. Both kinds are surprisingly easy to create.

Mirror Images

Mirror images are, of course, most commonly seen in mirrors. However, mirrors aren't necessarily hung on the wall. You can put an imaginary mirror anywhere. I have a cat who likes to watch things come out of the printer. After I shot the picture in Figure 23.6, I thought how much more fun it would be if Ari was watching himself print. So, I created Figure 23.7.

FIGURE 23.6
Cat on a printer.

FIGURE 23.7

Cat on printer watching cat in printer.

Adding a mirror image

1. First, I selected and copied the entire picture. Then, I pasted it onto a new layer. I used the Measuring tool to find out how wide the page in the printer appeared to be and then used **Edit, Transform, Scale** to shrink the picture down so it would fit. Figure 23.8 shows this stage.

FIGURE 23.8
The scaled cat is on layer 1.

2. Next, I rotated the image and then used **Edit, Transform, Skew** to drag the corners out so it appears to be lying flat. At this point, it looked like Figure 23.9

FIGURE 23.9
Not quite right.

3. It didn't fit the printer as well as it could. So I used **Edit, Transform, Distort** to push it down into the tray. I enlarged the view in Figure 23.10 so you can see the **Skew** box and how I placed the picture into the printer tray.

FIGURE 23.10
Now it's flat.

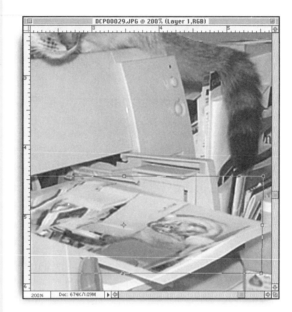

4. Finally, I copied and pasted the edge of the printer tray over the picture. I used the **Magnetic Lasso** to select the printer and pasted it into a new layer, which I dragged on top of the picture layer. The final step is to merge the layers so no one can backtrack to see how it was done. Go back and study the final picture in Figure 23.7. Pretty cool, huh?

Reflective Surfaces

Black velvet is the least reflective surface I could find as a background to photograph the flower in Figure 23.11. Suppose we'd rather see it on black marble. Not at all difficult to do.

FIGURE 23.11
I think it's a daisy.

Creating a reflective surface

1. The first step is to select the flower. It's easier to select the background and then invert the selection. Then copy the flower, using (Command+C) [Control+C]and (Command+P) [Control+P] to paste it onto a new layer. (When you copy and paste, the pasted image automatically appears on a new layer.)

2. Mirrors show things reversed from the way we see them, so the second step is to flip the copy vertically, by opening the **Edit** menu and choosing **Transform, Flip Vertical**.

3. Drag the copy so that it lines up with the part of the object that's reflected (see Figure 23.12).

4. On the Layers palette, set the opacity for this layer to about 50%. Because the reflection shouldn't look *too* perfect, open the **Filter** menu; choose **Blur** and apply **Gaussian Blur**. I used a radius of 4 pixels.

FIGURE 23.12

If you press the Shift key, you can drag straight down.

5. It's still too perfect. Next, open the **Edit** menu. Choose **Transform** and then **Distort**. Now drag the corners of the box to scrunch the reflection a little. Figure 23.13 shows this step.

FIGURE 23.13

Reflections depend on the thickness of the reflecting material.

6. To get rid of the overlapping parts of the reflected flower, make the original flower active again, select it, and make a layer mask, masking out the selection. (Open the **Layer** menu and select **Add Layer Mask**.) When you drag this on top of the reflected flower, as in Figure 23.14, you can see exactly what parts need to be removed.

FIGURE 23.14

The mask shows what needs to come out.

7. After erasing the pieces of flower that are visible in the unmasked area, return to the masked layer and remove the mask, which gives you the flower without overlapping refec-tion. As a final step, to give the background a more mar-bleized look, set the background color to black and the foreground to dark gray; then select the black from the orig-inal flower later. Choose **Filter, Render**, **Clouds**. Because the difference in the two colors is slight, the clouds aren't overwhelming. The final result is shown in Figure 23.15.

FIGURE 23.15

You can even draw in veins in the marble if you want to get that detailed.

Glows

Glows are mainly used behind text, but they can also add interest to a picture. In Figure 23.16, I have a bunch of grapes on a white background. To put a glow behind them, use the following steps.

Making things glow

1. Select the grapes. Copy and paste them to a new layer.

2. Open the **Layer** menu and then choose **Effects, Outer Glow**.

3. Click on the color swatch to open the Color Picker. Choose a nice bright glow color.

4. Drag the sliders to set the parameters for the glow, as shown in Figure 23.17.

5. Click **OK** to apply the glow. Merge the layers by opening the **Layer** menu and selecting **Merge Visible**. Figure 23.18 shows the final result.

FIGURE 23.16
I want these grapes to light up.

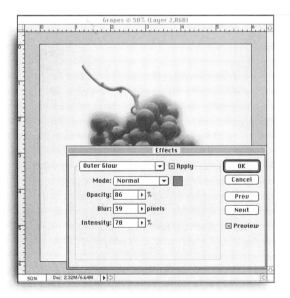

FIGURE 23.17
Intensity can go as high as 600%.

FIGURE 23.18

These grapes are more interesting.

Neon Glows

One of the neat things about Las Vegas is all the amazing neon signs. I really like the look of neon tubing for certain kinds of lettering or logos, and sometimes just as a fun way to draw. You can do a neat imitation of neon in Photoshop using the path tools. Here's how.

Using Neon Glow

1. Start with a fairly dark background. Neon looks best against black or deep blue. (You can also put your "neon" over a dark photo background.)

2. Use the Freeform path tool to draw your basic neon shape(s). Figure 23.19 shows this step.

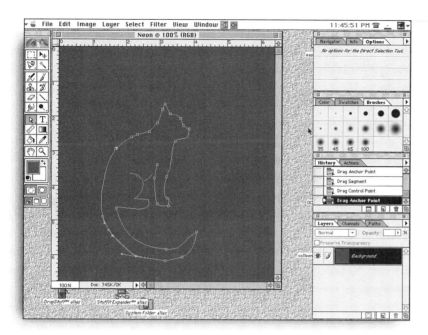

FIGURE 23.19
Keep shapes simple.

3. Now we'll add some color. Choose a very light version of the color you want for your neon. Select the Airbrush tool and a wide, soft brush. Set the pressure to about 25%. On the **Paths** pop-out menu, choose **Stroke Path**, or **Stroke Sub-Paths**, if you have drawn more than one path (see Figure 23.20). This creates the glow behind the neon.

4. The next step is to add the neon tubing. Choose a bright, neon-type color. For instance, if your glow is a soft pink, choose a related bright pink. Set the airbrush pressure to about 75%, and choose a small hard-edged brush. Again choose **Stroke Path** or **Stroke Sub-Paths**. This adds the neon tubing, as in Figure 23.21.

5. Finally, we'll add a highlight. Set the foreground color to white, and choose the next to smallest brush. Set the airbrush pressure to about 30%, and stroke the paths again. Turn off the paths, and your result will look something like Figure 23.22 (if you happen to have drawn a pink cat).

FIGURE 23.20

The neon glow.

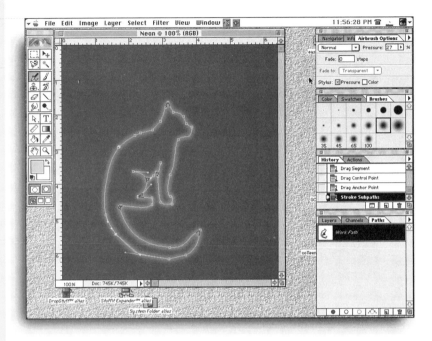

FIGURE 23.21

Now you can see the neon.

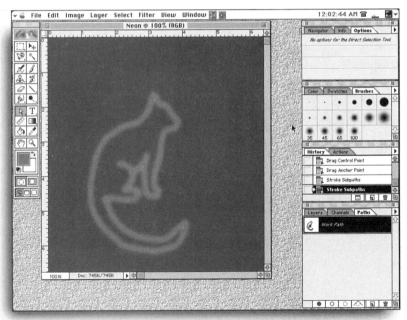

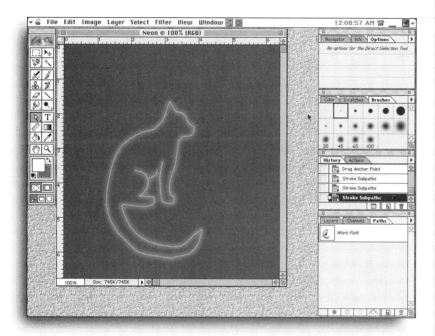

FIGURE 23.22
The highlight makes it look real.

6. You can go back in and add more colors of neon and more shapes, if you want. My finished neon picture appears in Figure 23.23.

FIGURE 23.23
Don't get too complex. Neon has its limits.

You can create a similar neon effect without drawing the shapes, if you start with a fairly simple image. In Figure 23.24, I have selected the flower and chosen **Make Workpath** from the **Paths** menu.

Following the preceding steps, I turned the path into neon.

FIGURE 23.25

The flower, edged in neon.

Now, here's the tricky part. I poured some of my background color into the flower with the Paint Bucket tool. It filled in the similar colored areas but left the highlights and some of the petal lines unfilled. I selected these, and again, made them into work-paths, and applied the neon. I selected the middle of the flower separately and made it yellow neon. Then I went back with the black paint and filled in around the neon lines. The result is a better flower shape than I could have drawn, rendered in neon (see Figure 23.26).

FIGURE 23.26
Neon chrysanthemum.

Imitating "Art"

One of the things Photoshop does especially well is to translate photos into a good imitation of other media. If you have ever wanted the skills to paint with oils or watercolors, this section is for you.

Oil Paintings

Claude Monet (1840-1926)

Claude Monet had little or no formal training in art but became one of the masters of what we today know as French Impressionism. To learn more about Monet, visit `http://www.claudemonet.com/`

There are as many different styles of painting as there are painters. My own preference is for the French Impressionists. I like Monet's soft, misty landscapes, but I can't help wondering what he'd have painted if he'd been in the United States instead of France. Suppose, instead of a lily pond, we'd plunked him down in the Valley of Fire, Nevada. Figure 23.27 shows what he'd have seen.

FIGURE 23.27
Desert and sky, Nevada.

Creating a Monet-like impressionist oil painting

1. Artists use a technique called Underpainting as a first step in creating a painting. They use a coarse brush and thinned out paint to apply the basic colors and shapes of the picture. Photoshop's Underpainting filter (choose **Filter, Artistic, Underpainting**) mimics this step very well. Figure 23.38

shows the photo with the filter applied. Locate the file Nevada. tif in the Goodies/Samples folder on the Photoshop 5 CD.

FIGURE 23.28
Underpainting is typically soft edged and lacks detail.

2. Now you need to add back the details. The impressionsists would typically do this by using a stiff brush and adding small strokes of color. If you set the blending mode to **Dissolve**, the paintbrush tool works very much like a stiff brush, putting color down in bits (see Figure 23.29).

FIGURE 23.29
The right side has been worked on; the left side has not.

3. As a final touch, we'll go over it with a light application of **Smudge Stick**. (Choose **Filter, Artistic, SmudgeStick**.) I set **Stroke Length** and **Highlight Area** to 1 and **Intensity** to 0 because I didn't want too much smudging or the picture to turn too dark. Figure 23.30 shows the final result.

FIGURE 23.30
Smudge Stick applied.

My paintbox

When I work on a painting and change colors frequently, I find it much easier to use the Swatches palette as a paintbox, rather than to go to the Color Picker each time I want to dip my brush in a new color. If you drag on the **Swatch** tab, you can "tear off" the palette and put it anywhere on your desktop that's convenient. You can also sample colors from the picture with the Eyedropper tool and add them to your palette. Click the Eyedropper tool on a color to add, and click an empty space on the palette. The Eyedropper tool becomes a bucket and pours a sample into the palette.

Watercolor

Artists generally agree that watercolor is the most difficult medium to master. It demands a steady hand and because it's transparent, it doesn't let you cover up mistakes very successfully. When you choose an image to convert to a watercolor, look for one without too many dark tones. Watercolors are usually quite light and emit an airy feeling. Flowers and still lifes generally make good watercolors. However, Photoshop's Watercolor filter isn't always the best tool for the job.

Figure 23.31 shows a photo converted with the Dry Brush filter. Notice that the background stayed light and that the flowers have a nice, lacy edge.

FIGURE 23.31

Daffodils with **DryBrush** applied. (Open the **Filter** menu; choose **Artistic** and **DryBrush**.)

Figure 23.32 shows the same photo converted with the Watercolor filter. It's dark, blobby, and doesn't look much like a watercolor. It could have been a woodblock print or possibly painted with poster paints, but that wasn't what we were trying to do. The point is, always choose your filters by what they actually do, not by what they're called.

Charcoal Drawings

It's seldom enough to just apply a filter to a picture. Most of the time, you need to apply the filter and then go back into your picture with a brush or perhaps an eraser to clean up and restore some of the details that the filter either lost or overemphasized. Here's an example. In Figure 23.33, I used the Chalk and Charcoal filter on a picture of a white dog. The shadowed areas are too dark, and some of the finer detail of the face is lost.

By going over the drawing with a brush, I can put back a lot of the detail. But to really restore delicate areas such as the eyes, it's easier to copy them from the original, paste them on a new layer, and blend them in by decreasing the opacity. After some brushwork, and copying and merging the parts I couldn't redraw, here's the finished picture (see Figure 23.34).

FIGURE 23.32

Daffodils with **Watercolor** applied. (Open the **Filter** menu; choose **Artistic** and **Watercolor**.)

FIGURE 23.33

White husky, rendered in Chalk and Charcoal.

FIGURE 23.34
White husky, retouched.

Creating Special Type Effects

Create Gaussian blur shadows

Cut letters from images

Use the Photoshop Drop Shadow effect

Create metallic letters

Drop Shadows

The most common effect behind type is a drop shadow. It adds a 3D quality, making the type stand out from the rest of the page. Drop shadows can be created in any of several different ways. The easiest way is to use Photoshop 5's new drop shadow effect, but you can also do a very simple drop shadow just by copying the text to a separate layer and adding a Gaussian Blur. Let's look at this step by step.

Gaussian Blur Shadows

Creating Gaussian Blur shadows

The key to special effects

The key to using special effects with type is to remember that the goal is to enhance the communication, not to obscure it. Use effects that add emphasis to type, not ones that make it harder to read.

1. Put the type on the page. Figure 24.1 shows some plain type on a plain white background. If you don't remember how to place type, please review Chapter 11.

FIGURE 24.1
Nothing fancy....

The
Shadow
Knew...

2. Copy the type and paste it onto a new layer. Move it a little bit so it's not right on top of the original type layer (see Figure 24.2). Note: The copy will be the same color as your original type. If you want a dark shadow, open the **Image** menu; then choose **Adjust, Replace Color** to turn the copied type black. (I prefer colored shadows with colored type.)

3. Choose **Filter, Blur, Gaussian Blur** as shown in Figure 24.3, with a radius of approximately 3 pixels. (If your shadow is black, blurring will turn it gray. If it's in color, blurring will lighten it appropriately.)

FIGURE 24.2

Looks more like a misprint than a shadow.

1 Text

2 Shadow

FIGURE 24.3

Blurring gives us the shadowy effect.

4. Now, slide the shadow around until it's where you want it. The further offset it is, the more your type appears to float over the page. Rearrange the layers so the type layer is on top of the shadow layer. Merge downward to combine the layers. Figure 24.4 shows the shadowed type.

FIGURE 24.4

I set the shadow fairly close to keep my type near the surface of the page.

Shadows fall on whatever is behind them. If you want your type to appear even more three dimensional, you can move the shadow from behind to beneath the type.

Making shadows even more three dimensional

1. Be sure your shadow layer is the active layer. If your type is on separate lines, as the example is, select one line at a time with the rectangular marquee. Open the **Edit** menu; then choose **Transform, Skew**. Then drag the top of the boundary box so the shadow spreads to the appropriate angle. Repeat this step for each line, as in Figure 24.5.

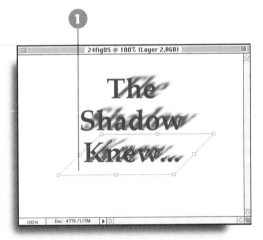

FIGURE 24.5

1 Be sure you skew the shadows to approximately the same angle.

2. Be sure that the bottom of the shadows remains aligned with the bottom of the letters if you want to make them appear vertical on a flat surface, as in Figure 24.6. If you leave space between the shadow and the letters, they seem to hover above the flat background.

Photoshop Effects Drop Shadow

The easiest way to create a drop shadow, especially when you're not sure what kind of shadow you want or how big, dense, dark, or blurry it should be, is to choose **Layer, Effects, Drop Shadow**. The Effects dialog box appears, as in Figure 24.7. To design a drop shadow using this tool, follow these steps.

FIGURE 24.6

If the shadow seems too dark, reduce its opacity before you merge the layers.

Using the drop shadow effect

1. Set the type. Open the **Layer** menu; choose **Effects, Drop Shadow**. Check the **Preview** and **Apply** boxes to see your changes.

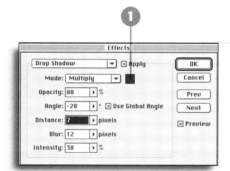

FIGURE 24.7

Click on the square to change the shadow color.

1 Drop Shadow color

2. Set the mode to **Normal**. Start with the **Opacity** at approximately 75%. Change it if necessary.

3. Click the arrow to the right of the **Angle** window to open a clock face for setting the shadow angle, or type a number into the box if you know what the angle should be.

4. Distance determines how far away the shadow is from the text. Start with a setting of 5 pixels and experiment.

5. **Blur** determines how diffuse the shadow is. If you want the shadow to be distant, keep it between 4–6 pixels. Otherwise, 10–11 gives a nice soft shadow.

6. **Intensity** sets the darkness of the shadow. Settings of 0%–25% are usual.

7. Click **OK** when the shadow looks the way you want it to.

Bevel and Emboss

Shadows are one way of separating the text from the background and giving it a somewhat 3D feel. Beveled edges and embossing are other ways. What they do, in effect, is to raise the front surface of the letter. Figure 24.8 shows examples of Photoshop's **Bevel** and **Emboss** effects.

Photoshop's Effects

Photoshop's **Outer Bevel** effect (choose **Layer, Effect, Outer Bevel**) gives you a flat-faced raised letter, with some thickness behind it. You need to look carefully to see that it's not just a drop shadow.

The **Outer Bevel** (choose **Layer, Effect, Inner Bevel**) produces letters that are flush against the background at their edges but raised in the middle, so they appear to be slightly rounded.

The **Emboss** effect (choose **Layer, Effect, Emboss**) combines the outer and inner bevel to produce letters that are both raised and rounded.

The **Emboss** effect (choose **Layer**, **Effect**, **Pillow**) rounds the space around the letters as well as the letters themselves, so they appear to be rounded letters outlined on a puffy surface.

You can combine several different effects to put raised lettering on a beveled edge plaque or nameplate as in Figure 24.9. It's especially effective if you color the letters gold.

Extensis PhotoBevel

If you have the Extensis PhotoTools Plug-ins, you can make elegantly framed and embossed letters very easily.

Using Extensis PhotoBevel

1. Start a new page. Drag a selection marquee the size you want your frame to be. Open the **Filter** menu; choose **PhotoTools, PhotoBevel** (see Figure 24.10). Experiment with the settings until you have a frame style that you like.

2. Next, set the type inside the frame. Because you're using PhotoTools, you might as well set the type in PhotoText. Figure 24.11 shows this step. PhotoText is better than Photoshop's own Text tool for this purpose because it lets you set any kind of type as bold. When you apply textures, embossing, or other effects to type, it's best to use a bold face so the effect shows up better.

FIGURE 24.10

Dark and pale gold set as background and foreground colors to produce a gilded frame.

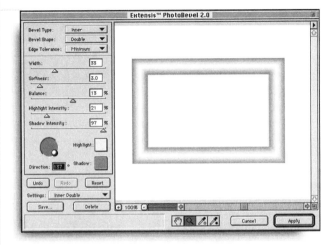

FIGURE 24.11

You can see the type in position with PhotoText.

3. Select just the letters and apply **PhotoBevel** (see Figure 24.12). Here again, the colors are set to a light and dark gold to make colored letters. Experiment with the settings until the type looks the way you want it to; then click **Apply** when you're satisfied.

FIGURE 24.12
Now we have raised letters.

4. As a final step, to make the letters stand out a little more, use **Photo CastShadow** to put just a little bit of shadow to the right of the letters. Figure 24.13 shows the effect of this step. Note the settings for the x and y axis. They control the position of the shadow.

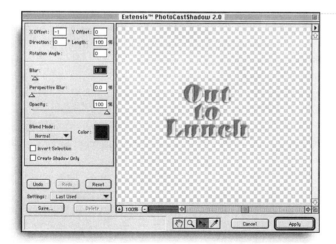

FIGURE 24.13

We don't want much shadow here—just enough to darken the edges of the letters.

One final graphic embellishment is added, and Figure 24.14 shows the final sign.

FIGURE 24.14

Of course, we only eat healthy lunches.

Glows

Out of memory errors

The deeper you get into Photoshop, the more likely you are to get messages to the effect that "Sorry. There's not enough memory to do that." That's if you're lucky. Sometimes, the computer will simply freeze. If it does, you can only start over. If it warns you that it's running out of memory, immediately stop and save your work. Quitting and restarting Photoshop will usually free up enough memory so that you can return to the task at hand. If not, you can increase the amount of memory allocated to the application.

A glow is essentially a shadow applied in color, frequently over rather than behind an object or piece of type. Putting a glow behind type can have the same effect as a drop shadow—to emphasize the words. You can often use a glow in situations where a drop shadow won't look right. Figure 24.15 shows a typical use of type over a photo. But the type doesn't really stand out as much as it could. A drop shadow would get lost with the shadows already in the picture, but a glow might be just what it needs.

Because the type is on a separate layer, it's simple to apply the **Outer Glow** effect (choose **Layer, Effects, Outer Glow**). I chose a broad glow, and set the color to a light yellow to pick up one of the predominant colors in the apple picture. The type itself is red. The yellow glow gives it just enough contrast so it doesn't get lost (see Figure 24.16).

Figure 24.15
A is for almost legible.

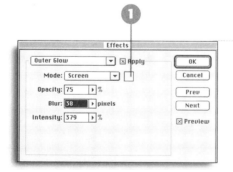

FIGURE 24.16
A is for applying a glow.

1 Glow color

Neon

Putting a neon effect on lettering is similar to putting neon on a drawing, as we did in the previous chapter. You can start by drawing your letters as paths. Then stroking them first with a wide airbrush spray, then with a hard edged smaller brush in a brighter color, and finally with a thin white highlight. Figure 24.17 shows how this kind of neon effect might be used.

FIGURE 24.17

Hand drawn neon lettering.

Metallic Letters

Metallic letter effects are a cinch with Photoshop 5's gradients. Here's how to make nice chrome or gold letters that look beveled, without using any special effects other than the Gradient tool.

Using gradients to create metallic letters

1. Start with a plain dark background or with a dark photo over which you'll place the type. Make a new layer.

2. Select the type Outline tool. Choose a large bold font and enter the first line of your text (see Figure 24.18). Click **OK** to place the outline.

3. For chrome letters, set the background color to white and the foreground color to black. Select the straight Gradient tool shown in Figure 24.19 and draw a gradient from the bottom to the top of one of the letters.

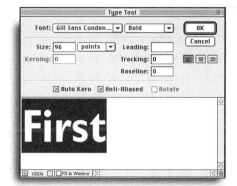

FIGURE 24.18

Make sure the letters are big enough.

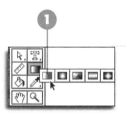

FIGURE 24.19

Draw the first gradient from the bottom up.

1 Linear gradient

4. At this stage, your letters should look like the ones in Figure 24.20. Do not deselect the letters.

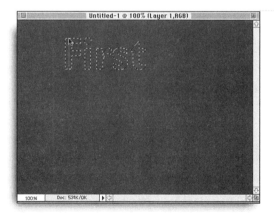

FIGURE 24.20

Letters with a dark gradient applied.

5. Choose **Select, Modify, Contract**. Then shrink the selection by 3 pixels, as in Figure 24.21.

FIGURE 24.21

This creates the beveled edge.

6. Set the foreground color to medium gray, keeping the background color white.

7. Draw a gradient inside the letters from top to bottom. Figure 24.22 shows the result of this step.

FIGURE 24.22

Be sure you draw the inner gradient in the opposite direction.

8. To create a bronze or gold letter, follow the same steps, but set your first gradient to a dark yellow or yellow brown for its dark tone. Set the second gradient to a medium gold or bronze for its dark tone, grading to a very light yellow or pale bronze.

9. Create additional depth in the letters by shifting the cutout after you first fill it. Figure 24.23 shows some variations on this technique.

Cut-Out Letters and Filled Letters

One of the things Photoshop can do easily that ordinary graphics programs can't handle very well is to apply photos and textures to lettering. You can go two ways with Photoshop's type Path tool. You can cut letters out of a background and use them as the type, or you can use the cutout background and fill it in with something else. Figure 24.24 shows examples of both. The letters were cut out of a picture of a plate of pasta, and placed at random angles in a puddle of sauce. The same sauce color was poured into the cut-out shapes and accented with airbrushed yellow to simulate grated cheese. Finally, a glow was applied behind the letters to separate them just a little bit from the noodles.

FIGURE 24.23

Vary the size of the bevel by contracting the selection more or less.

FIGURE 24.24

Two ways to use cut out letters.

Cutting Letters Out of a Photo

Suppose you need to create an eye-stopping title for a magazine spread on breads. Why not make the letters out of bread? We can start with a stock photo of a piece of whole wheat toast and cut the letters out of it.

Cutting letters from photos

1. Locate a suitable photo. Select the type Outline tool and choose an appropriate **Font** and **Size** (see Figure 24.25).

2. Enter the text. Click **OK** to apply it.

3. You see the letters outlined with a selection marquee. If you press the Delete key, you cut the letters out of the picture, as in Figure 24.26.

4. Or you can invert the selection and delete, leaving you with the toasted letters, as in Figure 24.27.

5. But suppose now that you have the letters in basic bread, you want to add crust to them. Begin by moving them apart, as in Figure 24.28. Choose **Layer, Type, Render Type**. This, in effect, paints the letters on the page. Now, using the Select and Move tools, cut the letters apart, one by one, and drag them so there's more space in between.

FIGURE 24.26
Better than you can do with a knife.

FIGURE 24.27
Just the letters.

FIGURE 24.28
This is to give the bread room to rise.

6. Select the type. It's easiest if you use the **Magic Wand** to select the background and then invert. (Be sure, whenever you use this trick, that you also select the insides of letters such as B, O, and so on.)

7. The bread crust should be a little bit uneven, but not too much so. Open the **Filter** menu; choose **Distort, Ripple**, using small ripples and moving the slider until you can just begin to see the effect. Figure 24.29 shows this step.

FIGURE 24.29
Don't overdo the ripples.

8. Choose **Select, Modify, Expand** to expand the selection by 4 pixels. This places an additional 4 pixels around the selection, and it gives the bread a nice thick crust. Then, set the foreground color to dark brown and choose **Edit, Stroke** for 2 pixels, to create a dark edge for the crust.

9. Select the letters again and cut them to a separate layer. Turn off this layer, so you see only the crust. Select the background, delete it, and invert, so the letters are active. Use a lighter brown and the Airbrush tool to paint in some crust. Don't worry about making it even. In Figure 24.30, you can see my airbrushed crust.

FIGURE 24.30
Try to stay within the lines.

10. Turn the bread layer on again and slide it until it fits inside the crust. You may need to touch up the insides of the letters, if they filled in.

11. As a final touch, add a drop shadow behind the letters. Figure 24.32 shows the finished lettering.

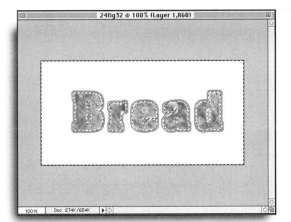

FIGURE 24.31
Almost done.

FIGURE 24.32
The drop shadow adds some depth and emphasis to the type.

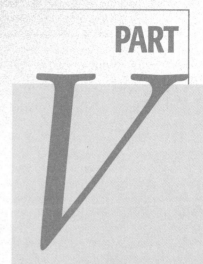

PART

V

Repairing, Retouching, and Enhancing Images

Correcting Image Color

Using Shadows, Midtones, and Highlights

The capability to make color adjustments to scanned imagery is an important part of the pre-layout process. A *color cast* can be introduced when an image is scanned, especially on flatbed scanners. Local color changes are often necessary to correct for color shifts that take place when an RGB image is converted to CMYK. Color adjustment techniques are also used for special effects or to pump up color in parts of an image. Good tonal balance is the key to producing accurate color, balancing the shadows, midtones, and highlights to best represent the scanned image.

When we examine and later correct images, we are first concerned with the *gray balance* of the image. The three primary indicators for gray balance are the shadow, midtone, and highlight areas of an image. These three are often further broken down to include 1/4 tones and 3/4 tones. The first step in evaluating an image is to identify these areas of the image and observe how well-balanced the overall image is. Is it weighted too heavily in the shadow areas? Is it mostly midtone values with little shadow and highlight detail? Of course, the composition of the image itself is a deciding factor in whether a tonal adjustment is necessary as well.

- The **shadows** of an image are the image's darkest areas. When the shadow areas of an image are too dark, detail is often lost. If the shadow areas of an image are too bright, the image appears flat in the shadow areas and lacks definition. What you should be looking for in the shadow areas of your image are values that are dark enough to create contrast and enhance the sharpness of the image.

- The **highlights** of an image are the brightest areas of the image. When the highlight values are too high, areas of the image can appear blown out (white) and subtle detail is lost. When the highlights of an image are too low, the image appears foggy and likely appears flat in the midtone regions.

- The *midtones* of an image are the areas in the image that fill in the gap between highlights and shadows. A well-balanced image contains a large number of pixels that fall in the mid-tone range. The thing to look for here is how the midtones are weighted throughout the image. If the midtone values are weighted too closely to the shadows of the image, the image appears dark with little transition between the high-light and the shadow. When the midtones are weighted too heavily toward the highlight areas, the shadows in the image increase to accommodate this.

To become expert at color correction and adjustment, you should learn as much as possible about the color theory behind RGB and CMYK. Because scanners and computer monitors deal in RGB only, understanding the relationship between the RGB colors and CMYK printing ink colors helps you get the color adjustment right the first time and removes some of the guess-work. The finer points of color theory and the CMYK printing process are outside the scope of this book, although a plethora of books have been written on these subjects from this publisher and others.

Adjusting with Levels

When adjusting a grayscale image, the following are three par-ticular areas of importance in regards to gray balance:

- *Black point.* The darkest area on your image. Theoretically, the part of the image that prints solid black.
- *White point.* The brightest point in the image; the part of the image that prints white.
- *Midtones.* The middle grays of the image that often consti-tute the largest area on normal key images.

In the following example, the final product for the image we adjust is an offset printed piece. To make judgments about tonal balance and adjustment for offset printing, you must know the following:

■ *Screen frequency.* To scan the grayscale image at the correct resolution, you must know the screen frequency (line screen) the piece will be printed with. The only people who can tell you what line screen to use are the folks at the printing company. After you know the screen frequency, multiply the screen frequency by two to arrive at the target resolution for your image.

■ *Dot gain.* Dot gain is specified in percentage and is the amount of growth a 50% halftone dot experiences when printed. Dot gain varies greatly from printing press to printing press and is affected by such things as ink properties, plating procedures, paper type, and the type of printing press used. Always ask your printer about dot gain when discussing a print job.

■ *Textured or colored paper.* Textured and colored paper do not reflect as much light as white coated paper. Therefore, it might be necessary to compensate on the image by increasing contrast and brightness.

In this example, we are using a CMYK image because the photograph is going to be placed in a business magazine that prints CMYK color on white coated paper. The magazine prints on a Web printing press that gets 15% dot gain and is printed at a screen frequency of 150 lpi (lines per inch). Now that we know the parameters of our target image, we can make the proper adjustments to the gray balance of the photograph.

Adjust Gray Balance

1. The original image is too dark in the shadows, too bright in the highlights, and somewhat flat in the midtones (see Figure 25.1). To correct this image, we need to bring out and enhance the detail while maintaining an even balance of gray levels.

2. Choose **Show Info** from the **Window** menu to display the Info palette (see Figure 25.2). Make sure the "K" values are displayed in one of the upper sections of the Info palette. Click the tiny triangle next to one of the Eyedropper icons in the Info palette to change the color to Actual Color if the "K" value is not displayed.

FIGURE 25.1

An image that is weighted too heavily in the shadows and highlights with too little detail in the midtones.

FIGURE 25.2

The Info palette.

3. Choose **Histogram** from the **Image** menu to display the histogram for this image (see Figure 25.3).

4. Click **OK** after you have evaluated the histogram for this image. The histogram is simply a tool to view the distribution of the pixels and does not change the image in any way.

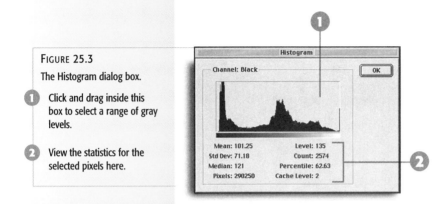

FIGURE 25.3

The Histogram dialog box.

1 Click and drag inside this box to select a range of gray levels.

2 View the statistics for the selected pixels here.

Reading a Histogram

The *histogram* is a graphical depiction of the pixel distribution in the image. The darkest pixels (shadow) are on the left and the brightest pixels (highlights) on the right. The pixels are represented in gray levels from 0 on the left to 255 on the right. You can see this value in the Info palette by choosing RGB from one of the Eyedropper menus in the Info palette. Position the cursor in the histogram to get information about the distribution of the pixels, or click and drag to select a range of pixels. Notice the large peak on the left side of the histogram, indicating that there are a significant number of dark pixels. The values in the Histogram dialog box represent the following data about the image:

- **Mean.** The mean represents the average brightness level of the entire image. This value is a good indicator of whether the image is too bright or too dark. The mean value of image is 101.25, which means that most of the image resides in the midtone range (around 128 gray level).

- **Standard Deviation.** Standard deviation (Std Dev) indicates how widely the pixel values vary from the mean.

- **Median.** The median value is the middle value within the total range of values for the image or selected area. A good median value for this image is around 128 (halfway between 0 and 255). The median value of 121 indicates that the image is pretty well-balanced around the midtones.

- *Pixels.* The pixels field displays the total number of pixels in the entire image or selected area. The mean, standard deviation, and median statistics are derived from this value. There are 290,250 total pixels in the image.

- *Level.* The level field displays the gray level of a specific point or range of values (0–255) in the histogram. To view the information for a specific point, position the cursor over a point in the histogram, or click and drag to display a range of values.

- *Count.* When selecting a specific point or range of values in the histogram, the count field displays the total number of pixels with these values.

- *Percentile.* The percentile field displays the percentage of pixels below (darker than) the value displayed in the level field.

Using the Levels Dialog Box

The histogram indicates that the image may be too heavily weighted in the shadow areas. Looking at the image onscreen, some detail will likely be revealed if we adjust the shadow areas. Move the cursor over the image and observe the values in the Info palette to get a feel for where gray levels are distributed in your image. In this example, the highlight areas in the hair are entirely blown out to 255 (0% K) and the shadow areas are pretty flat, showing little detail.

Defining the Shadows and Highlights

1. Choose **Adjust** from the **Image** menu and then select **Levels** or type (**Ctrl+L**) [**Command+L**] to display the Levels dialog box (see Figure 25.4). The Levels dialog box contains the same histogram displayed when viewing the histogram of the image.

2. The first thing you need to do is define the black point (darkest shadow) and white point (brightest highlight) of your image. Double-click the white Eyedropper in the Levels dialog box to display the Color Picker.

FIGURE 25.4

The Levels dialog box.

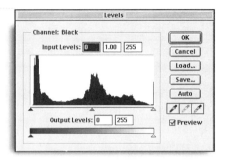

3. Enter 96% in the **Brightness** value box and set the **Hue (H)** and **Saturation (S)** to 0. This means that the brightest pixels in our image will be a 4% printable dot. Keep in mind that some dot gain will occur, though not as much as indicated for the 50% dot. Basically we are telling Photoshop that when we specify the white point, the value will be 245 gray (4% K) instead of 255 gray (0% K). Click **OK** in the Color Picker after you enter the value for the highlight pixels.

4. With the Levels dialog box still open, click the highlight area in your image with the white Eyedropper tool. Look for the brightest highlight in the image. The value of the highlight pixels you clicked are set to 245 gray level (4% ink) and the values of the pixels in the entire image are proportionately adjusted to accommodate this new highlight level. Any pixels with values greater than the pixels you clicked with the white Eyedropper tool become specular whites (no gray value).

5. Without closing the Levels dialog box, drag around in the image to find the shadow pixels. Take care not to click in the image area yet. View the values of the pixels in the Info palette.

6. Double-click the black Eyedropper tool in the Levels dialog box and enter 10% in the **Brightness** value box and set the **Hue** and **Saturation** to 0. A 10% Brightness value results in a 91% printable dot, the desired shadow value. Again keep in mind that some dot gain will occur, making the 91% dot print closer to 100%. Click **OK** in the Color Picker after you enter value for the shadows.

Checking the before and after values

The RGB values in the Info palette display the before and after values if you position your cursor over pixels in the image while the Levels dialog box is open.

Resetting dialog boxes

If you make a mistake in selecting the pixels for the highlight value, you can reset the Levels dialog box by (**Alt+clicking**)[**Option+clicking**] the Reset button. When holding down the (**Alt**) [**Option**] key, the **Cancel** button becomes the **Reset** button. This resetting method applies to most of Photoshop's dialog boxes.

7. With the Levels dialog box still open, locate the darkest area in the image and click the image with the black Eyedropper tool. The darkest area on the image now prints a 91% dot. The values of the pixels in the entire image are proportionately adjusted to accommodate this new shadow level. Any pixels with values lower than the pixels you clicked with the black Eyedropper tool now have a gray level of 0 (100% black). The Info palette displays the before and after values for the pixels in the image while the Levels dialog box is open.

8. Now that we have set the black and white points of the image, let's adjust the gamma (midtones) of the image. Click and drag the middle triangle slider under the histogram to the left to brighten the midtone areas or to the right to darken them. In my example, dragging the middle triangle slightly to the left reveals a lot of shadow detail in the subject's jacket and sweater that was not visible before.

9. Finally, drag the left triangle slider under the histogram to the right until it is under where the histogram begins. Drag the right triangle slider to the left until it is under the last column of pixels in the histogram. The **Input Levels** adjust the distribution of the pixels in the image, while the **Output Levels** adjust the white point and black point (see Figure 25.5). Click **OK** to save the changes to the image.

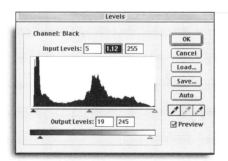

FIGURE 25.5

The Levels dialog box with changes to the Input and Output levels.

10. Choose **Histogram** from the **Image** menu to display the histogram for the image and compare this histogram to the original values (see Figure 25.6).

FIGURE 25.6

Note the difference in the shadow areas of the histogram on the corrected image compared to the original histogram.

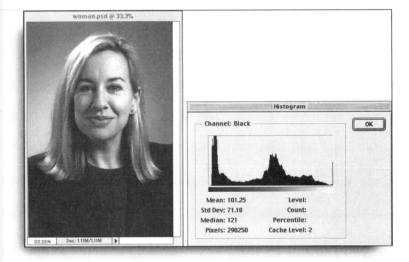

Adjusting RGB with Curves

When working in RGB, think of the RGB values as intensities of colored light. Colors are darker when the level of light is lower and brighter when the levels are higher. A dim red light, for example, appears darker than a bright red light. RGB values are indicated on a scale of 0–255, representing the 256 gray levels (levels of light). A value of 0 represents the absence of color, whereas a value of 255 is the maximum amount of color.

Looking for Color Cast

Neutral gray colors have red, green, and blue values that are the same or close. If two of the colors are relatively the same and the third is different by more than 10 levels in a neutral colored area, the image probably has a color cast. Color casts are evidenced by a dominant color tint to a photograph when it is proofed or printed. Color cast is easier to correct when the image is scanned using a *gray wedge* that is scanned with the image. When you do not have the benefit of a gray wedge, you have to evaluate the colors in the image to determine if a color cast is present. Color casts are introduced into an image during scanning and may not be apparent at first glance when you do no have the original photograph to compare to the screen representation.

Adjusting Color Cast

1. Open any RGB color image to try these steps to adjust color with the Levels dialog box.

2. Choose **Show Info** from the **Window** menu to display the Info palette. Click the triangle next to one of the Eyedropper icons in the Info palette and choose RGB Color.

3. Select the Marquee tool so the cursor is represented by a crosshair icon. You could also press the **Caps Lock** key to make any tool display a crosshair cursor.

4. Shadows are good places to look for color cast. Position the cursor over the shadow areas of your image and observe the RGB values in the Info palette. Identify the areas that should be black or shades of gray. If any one of the RGB values is significantly higher than the other two values, you probably have a color cast problem. For example, if the Green and Blue values are relatively close in value to each other and the Red value is significantly higher, the image has a red cast to it.

5. The white areas in the image should contain RGB values that are close in value and close to 255. We do not want any areas that are 255 Red, 255 Green, and 255 Blue because these areas will be blown out, lacking a printed halftone dot. The white areas, however, should have RGB values between 245 and 250. Position the cursor over the white areas of your image to evaluate the balance for the whites in the image. If, for example, the Red and Green values are relatively close, but the Blue value is somewhat lower, we'll probably have to add some blue to the highlights because blue helps to make whites whiter.

Adjusting Highlight and Shadow with Curves

Now that we've evaluated the values in the image, we use the Curves dialog box to make adjustments to the images. We start off by adjusting the white (highlight) and black (shadow) points because defining the shadows and highlights will help us make accurate adjustments to the midtones of the image.

Using Curves to Adjust Highlight and Shadow

1. Before we make any color changes, let's adjust the highlight and shadow areas. Choose **Adjust** from the **Image** menu, then select **Curves** or type (**Ctrl+M**) [**Command+M**] to display the Curves dialog box (see Figure 25.7).

FIGURE 25.7
The Curves dialog box.

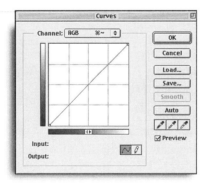

2. The grayscale of the image is represented in the Curves dialog box. The blend bar under the grid depicts the values of the grayscale. All the gray values in the image are plotted along the linear curve displayed in the grid. These are the input values—the values currently in the image. Notice that the Curves dialog box also has Eyedropper tools to specify the black point and white point, as well as an Eyedropper to specify the 50% gray value. For now, we are going to define only the black and white points.

3. You can adjust the curve for the composite RGB image or for each individual RGB channel. Make sure RGB is selected in the Channel drop-down menu at the top of the Curves dialog box.

4. Double-click the white Eyedropper in the Curves dialog box to display the Color Picker.

5. Enter 245 for the Red, Green, and Blue values in the Color Picker, and then click OK.

6. With the Curves dialog box still open, click the highlight area in the image with the white Eyedropper tool. Look for the brightest highlight (whites) in the image. The value of the highlight pixels you clicked is set to 245 gray level, and the values of the pixels in the entire image are proportionately adjusted to accommodate this new highlight level. Any pixels with values greater than the pixels you clicked with the white Eyedropper tool become specular whites (no gray value). Observe that the RGB values in the Info palette display the before and after values if you position your cursor over pixels in the image while the Curves dialog box is open.

7. Double-click the black Eyedropper tool in the Curves dialog box and enter 10 for the Red, Green, and Blue values. Click **OK**.

8. With the Curves dialog box still open, locate the darkest area in the image and click the image with the black Eyedropper tool. The darkest area on the image should have RGB values of 0 or close to 0. The values of the pixels in the entire image are proportionately adjusted to accommodate this new shadow level. Any pixels with values lower than the pixels you clicked with the black Eyedropper tool now have a gray level of 0. The Info palette displays the before and after values for the pixels in the image while the Curves dialog box is open. Click OK when you are happy with the black and white point settings. Remember you can hold down the (**Alt**) [**Option**] key to change the Cancel button into the Reset button and reset the Curves dialog box.

Adjusting Midtone Values with Curves

Now that we have set the black and white points of the image, let's adjust the gamma (midtones) of the image. You may have noticed that any color cast problems you detected while evaluating your RGB image have diminished after adjusting the black and white points. This is because setting the black and white point values to neutral values adjusted all the pixels in the image to correspond to these changes. In other words, setting the white and black points to equivalent values adjusts the overall color balance of the image.

Making Midtone Adjustments

1. Choose **Adjust** from the **Image** menu and then select **Curves** or type (**Ctrl+M**) [**Command+M**] to display the Curves dialog box again. Make sure that none of the Eyedroppers in the Curves dialog box are selected. If one is selected, click it again to deselect it. To identify the midtone values in your image, position the cursor over the image and click. Hold down the mouse button and note the floating circle in the Curves dialog box. The circle shows you where the values you are clicking are located on the curve (see Figure 25.8).

2. To adjust the midtones of the image, click in the center of the grid in the Curves dialog box and drag towards the lower-right corner to darken the midtones or toward the upper-right corner to brighten the midtones. Note the input and output values under the grid when you are dragging the midpoint of the curve. Drag the center point of the curve

until the midtone values are acceptable to you (see Figure 25.9). You can also type the input and output values directly into their respective boxes in the Curves dialog box. Click **OK** when you're happy with your adjustment.

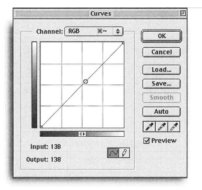

FIGURE 25.8

With the Curves dialog box open, click and drag in the image window to find the place on the curve for the area you are clicking.

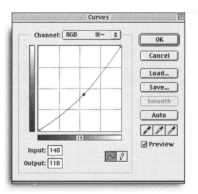

FIGURE 25.9

Click and drag the curve to adjust the midtone values.

Correcting Color Cast with Color Balance

If you detect a color cast in your image, use the Color Balance dialog box to adjust the overall color balance. Choose **Adjust** from the **Image** menu; then select **Color Balance** or type (**Ctrl+B**) [**Command+B**] to display the Color Balance dialog box (see Figure 25.10).

FIGURE 25.10

The Color Balance dialog box.

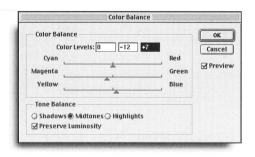

Click and drag the triangle sliders in the Color Balance section of this dialog box to adjust overall color cast. Color cast adjustments are usually made in the midtone section of images, so click the **Midtones** radio button in the Tone Balance section of the dialog box. In this dialog box, the subtractive primary colors (Cyan, Magenta, and Yellow) are on the left and the additive primaries on the right (Red, Green, Blue). If, for example, you determine that there is too much yellow in the midtones of your image, click and drag the bottom triangle slider to the right away from yellow, adding more blue.

- Check the **Preview** check box to preview the changes you make in the image window on your image.

- Check the **Preserve Luminosity** check box to preserve the gray balance of the image. If you do not check this box, the color adjustments you make to your image may alter the image contrast.

- Select the **Shadows** radio button in the **Tone Balance** section to adjust the colors in the shadow areas of the image. You will notice some adjustment to the midtones as well because colors are adjusted along the gamma curve of the image.

- Select the **Highlights** radio button in the **Tone Balance** section to adjust the colors in the highlight areas of the image. You will also notice a slight adjustment to midtones and shadows to accommodate any changes you make.

- Select the **Midtones** radio button in the **Tone Balance** section to adjust the midtone colors of the image. Adjusting the midtone values has the largest overall affect on your image color balance.

- The **Color Levels** boxes indicate the percent of change made for each of the three respective Color sliders.

Remember to use the Info palette to view the before and after values of pixels in your image when making changes in the Color Balance dialog box (see Figure 25.11). Position your cursor over areas of the image that are indicative of the color balance problem you perceive. Take care to make small changes to adjust for color cast because making a change that is too great introduces another color cast.

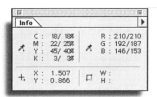

FIGURE 25.11
The input and output values are indicated in the Info palette separated by a slash.

Adjusting CMYK Values

The CMYK values are percentages of printing inks. After an image has been converted to CMYK mode, it is best to work on the image in CMYK rather than converting it back to RGB, because the colors shift with each conversion. In this example, we are going to use the Curves dialog box to adjust the color of an image. The method for adjusting the image is the same as previously explained for RGB images, although with CMYK images we are dealing with color inks.

Reading the CMYK Values

1. Open a CMYK image or convert an RGB image to CMYK Mode by choosing **Mode** from the **Image** menu and then selecting **CMYK Color**.

2. Choose **Show Info** from the **Window** menu to display the Info palette. Click the triangle next to one of the Eyedropper icons in the Info palette. Then choose CMYK Color or Actual Color to display the CMYK values in a section of the palette.

3. Select the Marquee in the toolbox so that the cursor is represented by a crosshair icon. You can also press the **Caps Lock** key to make other tools display the crosshair cursor.

4. Move the cursor around the image and observe the CMYK values in the Info palette. Note the areas of the image that contain high percentages of ink as well as those with low percentages. Use what you know about color mixing to check the color balance of your image. For instance, you probably know that yellow and cyan produce green, while magenta and yellow produce red and orange tones. Try to pinpoint any trouble spots. You may want to use the **Color Sampler Tool** (explained in the next section) to record some pixel values for later comparison.

Using the Color Sampler Tool

The **Color Sampler tool** enables you to click up to four points on your image and store the values in the Info palette (see Figure 25.12). I usually sample one highlight, one shadow, one neutral gray area, if there is one, and one skin tone, if there is one. If you're identifying trouble spots relating to color balance, click these pixels to do a comparison after you have made color changes. The **Color Sampler tool** is located in the toolbox with the **Eyedropper tool**.

Defining Color Samples

1. Double-click the **Color Sampler tool** in the toolbox to display the Color Sampler Tool Options palette and choose the way you want the tool to behave.

2. Click the image with this tool to store color samples in the Info palette.

3. Click and drag the crosshair icons to reposition them on the image.

4. (**Alt+Click**) [**Option+Click**] the crosshair icons to remove them and define new color samples.

5. Choose **Hide Color Samplers** from the Info palette menu by clicking the triangle in the upper-right corner of the Info palette. When the color samplers are hidden, you can choose **Show Color Samplers** from the Info palette menu to display them on the image and in the Info palette.

FIGURE 25.12
The four sampled values are stored in the Info palette and depicted on the image itself.

The Color Sampler Tool Options

Double-click the Color Sampler tool in the toolbox to display the Color Sampler Options palette. Click the pull-down menu to specify the behavior of the Color Sampler tool.

- Select **Point Sample** to sample the value of a single pixel when you click the image with the **Color Sampler tool**. If you use this method, which is the default method, be careful not to select a pixel value that is not representative of the overall color you're trying to sample.

- Select **3 by 3 Average** to sample the average value of a three-pixel by three-pixel area when you click the image with the **Color Sampler tool**. This method works best for most images and helps avoid the chance of selecting a pixel that is not representative of the color you're seeing in a particular area of the image.

- Select **5 by 5 Average** to sample the average value of a five-pixel by five-pixel area when you click the image with the **Color Sampler tool**. This is a good choice for very high resolution images and when you just want to average a larger number of pixels for a sample value.

Defining CMYK Highlights and Shadows

Now that you have evaluated the image and identified the trouble spots to keep an eye on when making color adjustments, use the Curves dialog box to make adjustments to the color balance of the image. Start by defining the highlight and shadow values of your image.

Setting the White Point and Black Point of CMYK Images

1. Choose **Adjust** from the **Image** menu. Then select **Curves** or type (**Ctrl+M**) [**Command+M**] to display the Curves dialog box.

2. The grayscale of the image is represented in the CMYK channel of the Curves dialog box. The blend bar under the grid depicts the values of the grayscale. All the gray values in the image are plotted along the linear curve displayed in the grid. These are the input values—the values currently in the image.

3. Make sure CMYK is selected in the Channel drop-down menu at the top of the Curves dialog box.

4. Double-click the white Eyedropper in the Curves dialog box to display the Color Picker.

5. Enter **5, 3, 3, 0** for the CMYK values in the Color Picker to define the ink percentages that will be used for the whitest points in the image, and then click **OK**.

6. With the Curves dialog box still open, click the highlight area in the image with the white Eyedropper tool. Look for the brightest highlight (white) in the image. The value of the highlight pixels you clicked is set to those you specified for the white point color. Any pixels with values greater than the pixels you clicked with the white Eyedropper tool become specular whites (no color value). Observe that the CMYK values in the Info palette display the before and after values if you position your cursor over pixels in the image while the Curves dialog box is open.

7. Double-click the black Eyedropper tool in the Curves dialog box and enter **65, 50, 50, 95** for the CMYK values respectively. These values give a black that has total ink density of

260%, which is safe for most printing projects. Total ink density is the maximum amount of ink that can safely be printed in one spot on the printing press. Ask your printer about total ink density for your printing projects. Click **OK**.

8. With the Curves dialog box still open, locate the darkest area in the image and click the image with the black Eyedropper tool. The values of the pixels in the entire image are proportionately adjusted to accommodate this new shadow level. Any pixels with values lower than the pixels you clicked with the black Eyedropper tool now have the value specified for the black Eyedropper tool.

Adjusting CMYK Midtone Values

Once you have defined the highlight and shadow values in the image you can adjust the midtone values between these two settings. When you adjust the midtone values in the Curves dialog box, all the values in the image are adjusted to some degree along the arc of the curve. Color adjustments are made to the individual color channels using the Curves dialog box.

Adjusting Midtones with Curves

1. Click the center of the line in the grid of the Curves dialog box to adjust the midtone brightness of the image. Drag the center of the curve until the Input value under the grid is the original value you want to change and the Output value is the target value.

2. Select the individual color channels from the **Channel** drop-down menu at the top of the Curves dialog box to display the curves for those colors. Click and drag these curves to correct color cast in the image. You can click your image in the image window when you have a specific color channel selected to display a circle along the curve, indicating where to adjust the color. Click along the curve in the Curves dialog box to add anchor points to make more specific adjustments (see Figure 25.13).

Changing the Grid Size in the Curves Dialog Box

(**Alt+Click**) [**Option+Click**] the grid inside the Curves dialog box to toggle it between a four-by-four grid and a 10-by-10 grid. The 10-by-10 grid helps to pinpoint ink percentages in 10% increments.

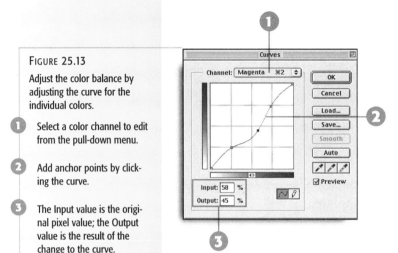

FIGURE 25.13

Adjust the color balance by adjusting the curve for the individual colors.

1. Select a color channel to edit from the pull-down menu.

2. Add anchor points by clicking the curve.

3. The Input value is the original pixel value; the Output value is the result of the change to the curve.

Adjusting Color with the Channel Mixer

The Channel Mixer enables you to adjust the amount of color that is added to individual channels based on the other color channels. Choose **Adjust** from the **Image** menu and then select **Channel Mixer** to display the Channel Mixer dialog box. As with all color adjustments, the color percentages added to the channels are dependent on the shape of the gamma curve for that channel.

For example, in Figure 25.14, Cyan is selected as the Output channel. This means that cyan ink will be increased or decreased when it is combined with the corresponding Source channel. In this case, dragging the Magenta slider to +45% adds 45% cyan to places in the image where there is 100% magenta (see Figure 25.14).

If we drag the Magenta slider to -45%, then 45% cyan is subtracted from the places where there is 100% magenta combined with some percentage of cyan. The Channel Mixer can be a powerful tool for making color adjustments to your image, though you should keep things like total ink density in mind. Adding ink percentages throughout your image could increase the *total ink density* beyond the limit recommended by your printer. If you check the **Monochrome** check box, all the color information is moved to the Black channel of the image based on how you adjust the Color sliders.

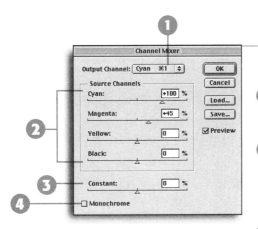

Figure 25.14

The Channel Mixer dialog box.

1 The Output channel determines what color is added to the image.

2 The Source Channels are where you choose how much of the Output Channel color to mix for each Source channel.

3 Add the same amount of the Output channel color to all Color channels.

4 Monochrome puts all values on the Black channel and enables you to add the color values to adjust the grayscale image.

At first glance, the Channel Mixer is a bit daunting. I suggest creating a very simple image that includes overlapping boxes of the process colors. Use the Info palette to view the color changes that take place as you make adjustments in the Channel Mixer to see exactly what's happening to your image. I made a series of boxes, each filled with 100% of each of the process colors and overlapped them. I then made another set of four boxes, each filled with 50% of the process colors and overlapped them. With the Channel Mixer dialog box onscreen, along with the Info palette, I made changes and read the color values of my image in the Info palette.

Judging Variations

Using the Variations dialog box you can make color corrections based on proxy images simply by clicking. Choose **Adjust** from the **Image** menu, and then select **Variations** to display the Variations dialog box (see Figure 25.15). The original image in the upper-left corner of this dialog box is the way the image looked when you started. The **Current Pick** displays the image with the changes applied.

FIGURE 25.15

The Variations dialog box. Click
the image thumbnails to adjust
the image.

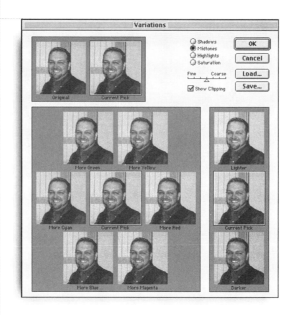

- Select the radio button for the part of the image you want to modify. Choose to adjust the **Shadows**, **Midtones**, **Highlights**, or **Saturation**. If you choose **Saturation** here, you can choose to increase or decrease the saturation of color in the image.

- Drag the triangle to the left toward **Fine** to make subtle changes. Drag the triangle to the right toward **Coarse** to make bigger changes.

- Check the **Show Clipping** check box to display a color mask over the areas that will be out of gamut. If the image is in CMYK mode already, these masked areas cannot be changed any further.

- Click the **Lighter** and **Darker** pictures to increase or decrease the overall gamma of the interest. Keep in mind that these choices affect the contrast of the image.

- Click the **Save** button to save the settings in this dialog box so you can apply them to other images using the **Load** button.

Colorizing Images

Using Hue and Saturation to adjust color

Using Replace Color to selectively change colors

Using Selective Color to make intelligent selections

Painting to affect Hue and Saturation

Using Adjustment layers to make color changes

Adjusting Hue and Saturation

Colorizing in Photoshop is relatively simple once you get the basic rules down. When colorizing an image in Photoshop, it is important to preserve the luminosity (grayscale) of the image whether you're colorizing a grayscale image or a full-color RGB or CMYK image. For this reason, the *Hue* and *Saturation* component of the colors you use to colorize is applied to the image leaving the *Lightness* value (luminosity) intact.

There are a number of ways to affect the Hue and Saturation component of pixels in your image. These adjustments can be applied to selected areas, entire images, individual layers, and even painted onto images using the Painting tools. The best place to start to understand the way colors are adjusted using hue and saturation is in the Hue/Saturation dialog box.

Working with the Hue/Saturation Dialog Box

1. Open an RGB color image.

2. Choose **Adjust** from the **Image** menu and then select **Hue Saturation** or type (Ctrl+U) [Command+U] to display the Hue/Saturation dialog box (see Figure 26.1).

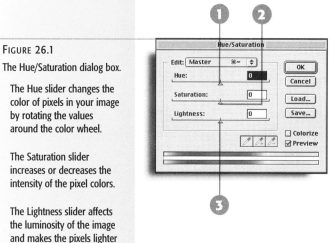

FIGURE 26.1

The Hue/Saturation dialog box.

1 The Hue slider changes the color of pixels in your image by rotating the values around the color wheel.

2 The Saturation slider increases or decreases the intensity of the pixel colors.

3 The Lightness slider affects the luminosity of the image and makes the pixels lighter or darker.

3. Be sure **Master** is selected in the pull-down menu at the top of the dialog box. Drag the Hue, Saturation, and Lightness triangle sliders to observe the effect in your image. Notice that adjusting the Lightness value can adversely change the image. If you drag the Lightness slider too far to the right, the image becomes foggy looking, losing much of the detail in the midtones and highlights. If you drag the Lightness slider too far to the left, the image becomes too dark, losing *contrast* and absorbing shadow detail. When colorizing, it is best to leave the Lightness setting alone or make very small changes if necessary.

4. Select a color range to affect by clicking the **Edit** pull-down menu at the top of the Hue/Saturation dialog box (see Figure 26.2).

5. When you select a color from the **Edit** pull-down menu, a set of range sliders are displayed between the two blend bars at the bottom of the **Hue/Saturation** dialog box. Click and drag these range sliders to increase or decrease the range of colors affected by changes you make to the Hue, Saturation, and Lightness (see Figure 26.3).

6. When one of the colors is selected in the **Edit** pull-down menu, the Eyedropper buttons are activated. Use the Eyedropper to click your image to specify the colors in the image to affect. Hold down the **Shift** key and click your image with the Eyedropper to expand the range of colors affected. Hold down the (Alt) [Option] key and click the image to remove colors from the target range. You can also use the Eyedropper buttons with the plus and minus signs to add and remove colors from the range respectively.

Picturing Hue and Saturation

In order to understand what happens when you adjust the Hue and Saturation values in your image, it helps to visualize the Hue, Saturation, and Brightness (HSB) color model. The HSB color model is depicted as a cylinder. The Hues (colors) are represented around the cylinder and are specified as degrees. The Brightness values are depicted on the cylinder from top to bottom, 100% brightness at the top and 0% at the bottom. If we were to slice the cylinder into 100 pieces, each representing one of the brightness values, the saturation values would be depicted from the center of each disc (0% saturation) out to the edges (100% saturation).

Now envision the pixels in your image, each of them represented on the HSB color model. When we adjust Hue, Saturation, and Brightness via the Hue/Saturation dialog box, the triangle sliders start out in the center of each component and represents the current position of the pixels in the image. If, for example, we drag the Hue slider +10 to the right, all the pixels in the image are changed to the Hue values that are 10 steps to the right of their respective values. The same applies to Saturation and Brightness.

Sampling colors from the image

When you have the Hue/Saturation dialog box open, move your cursor over the image, click with the Eyedropper cursor to sample a color from the image, and display it in the foreground color swatch in the Toolbox. When you make adjustments using Hue, Saturation, and Lightness, the foreground color swatch changes to display the effect on the sampled color.

FIGURE 26.2

Select a color from the **Edit** pull-down menu to restrict your adjustments to specific color ranges in the image.

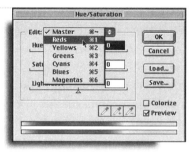

FIGURE 26.3

Drag the range sliders to control the range of color affected in your image.

1   Drag the range sliders to select the color range you want to affect with the Hue, Saturation, and Lightness sliders.

2   Use the Eyedroppers to click color areas of your image to select the colors you want to affect. Use the Eyedropper with the plus sign to add to the range and the Eyedropper with the minus sign to reduce the range.

3   Check the Colorize check box to make all the pixels in the image the same Hue.

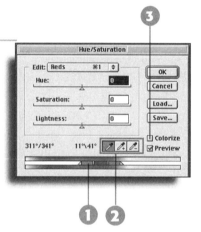

7. Check the **Colorize** check box to make all the pixels in the image the same Hue value. You can then drag the Hue slider to change the color of the pixels. You will probably want to drag the Saturation slider to the left because it is automatically set to 100% when Colorize is checked.

8. If you want to save the color adjustments made in the Hue/Saturation dialog box and apply them to another image, click the **Save** button and save the settings on your hard disk. Click the **Load** button to restore settings for the Hue/Saturation dialog box that you previously saved.

Colorizing a Grayscale Image

You can create a color-toned image from a grayscale image using the **Hue/Saturation** dialog box. Unlike a monotone image, which is made of only one ink color, this method produces a full-range color image that appears to be made of only two colors. If you do not change the Lightness value in the Hue/Saturation dialog box, the *luminosity* of the image is maintained and only the color values of the pixels are affected.

To colorize a grayscale image:

1. Open any grayscale image in Photoshop. Choose **Mode** from the **Image** menu; then select **RGB Color** to convert the grayscale image into an RGB image. Because we created the RGB pixels from grayscale values, all the pixels contain equal amounts of red, green, and blue. Therefore, the Hues of the pixels are all the same value.

2. Choose **Adjust** from the **Image** menu; then select **Hue/Saturation** or type (Ctrl+U) [Command+U] to display the Hue/Saturation dialog box.

3. Check the **Colorize** check box and then adjust the Hue and Saturation values of the image to apply color to the grayscale image. Notice that you cannot affect the color of the pixels unless you check the **Colorize** check box. The Hue and Saturation value that is initially displayed when you check the **Colorize** check box is the hue and saturation of the current **Foreground** color. The range of color values in the image are displayed in the Blend bar at the bottom of the Hue/Saturation dialog box.

Using the Painting Tools to Tint Grayscale Images

When colorizing a grayscale image with the Painting tools, the object is to achieve a tinted effect, much like the color-tinted black and white photographs before color photography was available. All the Painting tools contain *Blending modes* for adjusting the Hue and Saturation values of pixels in the image. Keep in mind that your grayscale image, even after converting to

RGB, is made of pixels that all contain the same Hue value. Therefore, adjusting only the Saturation of the pixels does not change their color.

Hand-tinting a grayscale image

1. Open any grayscale image and convert it to RGB by choosing **Mode** from the **Image** menu and then selecting **RGB Color.**

2. Choose **Show Layers** from the **Window** menu to display the Layers palette. We are going to paint our changes on layers so we can adjust them and correct overpainting with a layer mask.

3. Choose **Show Color** from the **Window** menu to display the Color palette.

4. Choose **Show Brushes** from the **Window** menu to display the Brushes palette.

5. Double-click the Paintbrush tool in the Toolbox to display the Paintbrush Options palette (see Figure 26.4). The Paintbrush Options are grouped with the Navigator palette. If you plan on using the Navigator palette, drag its tab out of the group to separate it from the Options palette.

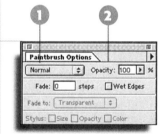

FIGURE 26.4

The Paintbrush Options palette.

1 Choose **Blending modes** from this pull-down menu.

2 Set Opacity by typing a value here or by clicking the triangle.

6. Mix a color in the Color palette that you want to use as your painting color.

7. In the Paintbrush Options palette, choose **Color** as the Blending mode from the pull-down menu if you want to make the color changes without using layers.

8. In the Paintbrush Options palette, you may want to set the Opacity for the Paintbrush to a relatively low percentage to maintain a washed-out, tinted effect.

9. Select a brush size for your Paintbrush from the Brushes palette. A brush with a soft edge usually works best for tinting an image.

10. If you want to paint directly on the image, be sure **Color** is set as the Blending mode in the Paintbrush Options palette; then paint on the image. Try not to stop (let go of the mouse button) and paint over the same area again because this adds another application of the foreground color to the existing color. The next section explains how to apply tints to your image using layers.

Tinting Your Image on Layers

In the previous steps, you learned how to tint your image using the Paintbrush tool with the Color Blending mode set in the Paintbrush Options palette. In the following steps, we'll apply the color tints to individual layers. Painting on layers provides many more options for affecting the blending of color tints with the existing image, not to mention the forgiveness factor, because we can add and remove layers at will.

Applying color to layers

1. Choose **New** from the **Layer** menu; then select **Layer** to create a new layer in the Layers palette. Give this palette a name that reflects the color you are painting with or the part of the image you plan on painting. For example, if you are going to paint the shirt light blue, name the layer "Shirt" or "Light Blue."

2. Set the Blending mode for this layer to **Color** by clicking the pull-down menu at the top of the Layers palette (see Figure 26.5).

Setting Opacity from the keyboard

To change the Opacity in the Paintbrush palette or any palette that offers this option, you can type single-digit numbers on the numeric keypad to set the Opacity in increments of 10. For example: type 2 for 20% and 0 for 100%. Type two digits on the numeric keypad to set a specific opacity like 23%.

FIGURE 26.5

The Layers palette.

1. Select the Blending modes from this pull-down menu.

2. Set the Opacity for the layer here.

3. You can click this icon to create a new layer, but you have to double-click the layer to give it a name.

Selecting brush size via the Context menu

To switch to the next or previous brush in the Brushes palette when a Painting tool is selected, (click with the right mouse button) [Ctrl+Click] the image to display the context menu.

3. Paint over the areas of the image you want to colorize. Try not to stop and paint over the same area again because this adds another application of the foreground color to the existing color. Don't worry if you overpaint because you can fix that later using a layer mask.

4. Make a new layer for each color and name those layers accordingly. If you don't like your results, simply delete the layer and add a new one.

5. Set the Blending mode for your layers to **Multiply** to create a realistic-looking colorization.

6. Play around with the **Opacity** setting for the layers until you're happy with the way the color tints look.

7. Choose **Add Layer Mask** from the **Layer** menu; then select **Reveal All** to add a *layer mask* to your layer. The layer mask enables you to mask out the overpainting that may have occurred when you applied the paintbrush. The layer mask *thumbnail* is added to the Layers palette and automatically selected (see Figure 26.6). You can choose to paint on the layer by clicking the layer thumbnail or on the layer mask by clicking the layer mask thumbnail.

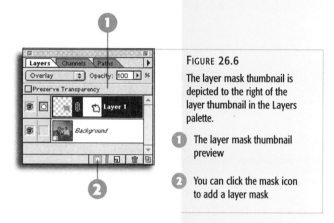

FIGURE 26.6

The layer mask thumbnail is depicted to the right of the layer thumbnail in the Layers palette.

1 The layer mask thumbnail preview

2 You can click the mask icon to add a layer mask

8. Set the foreground color to black and be sure the layer mask is selected in the Layers palette. You can easily set the foreground color to black by typing the letter D to set the default foreground and background colors of black and white respectively.

9. Select the Paintbrush tool in the Toolbox and be sure the Blending mode is set to Normal and the Opacity to 100% in the Paintbrush Options palette. Paint on the layer mask with black as the foreground color to remove any overpainting that occurred when you painted the tint on the layer. Paint on the layer mask with White as the foreground color to restore the layer contents to the original values. If your background color is set to White, type the letter X to swap the foreground and background colors.

10. When you're happy with the adjustments made using the layer mask, choose **Remove Layer Mask** from the **Layer** menu. A dialog box appears prompting you to apply the layer mask or discard it. Choose **Apply** if you want to change your layer to include the corrections you made on the layer mask.

11. Once you have tinted the entire image, choose **Flatten Image** from the **Layer** menu to flatten the image down to a single **Background** layer. I suggest saving a version of the file with the layers intact so you can make further changes if necessary.

Tinting with Adjustment Layers

To tint an image that is already in color, we can paint with the Hue of a color, the Saturation of a color, or a combination of both. In this example, we add some color to a color image using a combination of layers and Adjustment layers.

Adding color with an Adjustment layer

1. Open an RGB or CMYK color image in Photoshop.

2. Choose **Show Layers** from the **Window** menu to display the Layers palette. We'll put our adjustments on layers so we can remove them if we want and start again.

3. We are going to create an Adjustment layer to modify the color of specific parts of our image. Adjustment Layers are mask layers that enable us to make color adjustments to the underlying layers. To automatically create a mask for an adjustment layer, select the part of your image that you want to change using the Selection tools, like the Lasso tools or the Marquee tools.

4. Once you have made a selection on your image, choose **New** from the **Layer** menu; then select **Adjustment Layer** to display the **New Adjustment Layer** dialog box (see Figure 26.7).

5. Select **Hue/Saturation** from the **Type** pull-down menu in the New Adjustment Layer dialog box.

6. Choose **Overlay** from the **Mode** pull-down menu in the New Adjustment dialog box and click **OK** to display the **Hue/Saturation Layer** dialog box (see Figure 26.8).

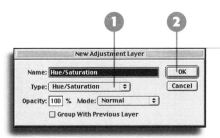

FIGURE 26.7

The New Adjustment Layer dialog box.

① Select the type of adjustment you want to make from the **Type** pull-down menu.

② When you click **OK**, the dialog box for the choice you made in the **Type** pull-down menu is displayed.

FIGURE 26.8

The **Hue/Saturation Layer** dialog box.

7. Check the **Colorize** check box in the **Hue/Saturation Layer** dialog box. Set the Hue and Saturation values to tint the color image. The initial settings for these two sliders are determined by the foreground color. Click **OK** to create the Adjustment layer. The Adjustment layer automatically has a mask that protects the parts of the image outside the area you selected before creating the Adjustment layer.

8. Adjust the opacity of the Adjustment layer to further affect the way the layer interacts with the underlying layers. Double-click the Adjustment Layer to modify the color adjustment.

The previous steps outline a method to tint an existing color image. We set the Blending mode for the Adjustment layer to **Overlay** to apply our color changes in combination with the existing colors of the image. Experiment with the Blending modes in the Layers palette. When you choose **Normal** as the Blending mode, you can shift the hues of the underlying layers using the Hue/Saturation Adjustment Layer.

SEE ALSO

➤ *For more information on Blending modes, see "Specifying Blending Mode and Opacity" page 137*

Painting with Hue

To make subtle color changes to an image, we can adjust only the Hue component of the color. The Hue is the color component. When we paint with Hue, the Saturation and Brightness levels of the pixels are left unchanged.

Shifting the Hues of pixels with the Paintbrush

1. Open an RGB or CMYK image in Photoshop.

2. Double-click the Paintbrush tool in the Toolbox to display the Paintbrush Options palette.

3. Set the Blending mode for the Paintbrush tool to Hue.

4. Select a brush size from the Brushes palette and mix a foreground color in the Color palette. When you paint with the Hue Blending mode set in the Paintbrush Options palette, you paint with only the Hue component of the foreground color.

5. Paint the image to change the Hue value of the painted pixels to the Hue value of the foreground color.

Using Replace Color

The Replace Color command enables you to select parts of the image based on color and adjust the Hue, Saturation, and Lightness of the selected areas.

Changing the Hue, Saturation and Lightness of select areas

1. Open an RGB or CMYK color image in Photoshop.

2. Choose **Adjust** from the **Image** menu; then select **Replace Color** to display the Replace Color dialog box (see Figure 26.9).

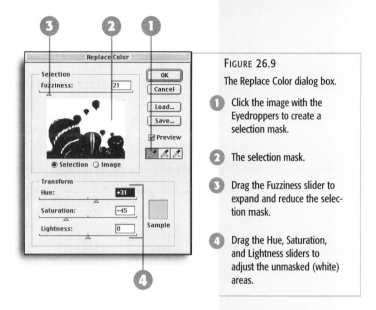

3. Check the **Preview** check box if it is not already checked.

4. Click the **Selection** radio button to display a selection mask in the image preview window.

5. Click a color area on the image with the Eyedropper tool. The selection mask reflects the selected colors.

6. Hold down the **Shift** key and drag on the image to enlarge the selection area.

7. Drag the **Fuzziness** triangle slider to the right to increase the selection or to the left to decrease the selection.

8. Adjust the Hue, Saturation, and Lightness values to change the selected areas of the image.

Using Selective Color

The Selective Color dialog box enables you to make color adjustments to CMYK images based on the primary colors in an image. The Selective Color dialog box also enables you to make color adjustments to the black, white, and *neutral values* in the image.

Shifting the primary colors of an image

1. Open a CMYK color image in Photoshop.

2. Choose **Adjust** from the **Image** menu; then select **Selective Color** to display the Selective Color dialog box (see Figure 26.10).

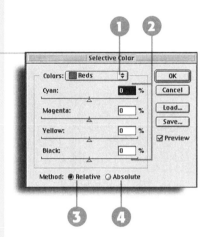

FIGURE 26.10

The Selective Color dialog box.

1 Choose the colors you want to affect from the **Colors** pull-down menu.

2 Drag the color sliders to add and remove color.

3 Choose **Relative** to adjust colors only when they are present.

4 Choose **Absolute** to add color even if the color component is not originally present.

3. Check the **Preview** check box to see the changes to your image as you make them.

4. Select **Relative** as the Method at the bottom of the Selective Color dialog box. Relative makes changes to the ink percentages based on the value of the color. If we increase cyan 20% in the Selective Color dialog box, for example, a 50% cyan value in our image increases by 10% (20% of 50%), resulting in 60% cyan. When the **Absolute** method is used, the 20% cyan is added to the 50% cyan, resulting in 70% cyan.

5. Choose **Neutrals** from the **Colors** pull-down menu at the top of the **Selective Color** dialog box. To decrease the amount of magenta, for example, in the neutral areas of the image, drag the triangle slider under Magenta to the left.

6. Choose a color from the **Colors** pull-down menu at the top of the Selective Color dialog box. Drag the triangle sliders to add or remove percentages of Cyan, Magenta, Yellow, or Black.

SEE ALSO

➤ *For more information on Blending Modes, see "Specifying Blending Mode and Opacity" page 137*

Using Light and Shadows

Creating Drop Shadows

The most effective way to create drop shadows in Photoshop is by utilizing the layer effects. There are five layer effects available in Photoshop: **Drop Shadow**, **Inner Shadow**, **Outer Glow**, **Inner Glow**, and **Bevel and Emboss**. The beauty of these five effects is that they are attached to the working layer and automatically adjust to the shape of the layer's contents. In the following example, you need a background image and a layer containing a silhouetted image. I'm using a *silhouette* of a guitar on a textured background.

Applying layer effects

1. Create a Photoshop file that contains a background layer and a silhouetted layer (see Figure 27.1).

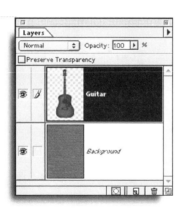

FIGURE 27.1

Create a file that contains a layer with a silhouetted image on a layer that contains some background image.

2. Select the layer that contains the silhouette because this is the layer we are going to apply the drop shadow to.

3. Choose **Effects** from the **Layer** menu and then select **Drop Shadow** to display the Effects dialog box (see Figure 27.2). On the MacOS, hold down the **Control** key and click on the layer in the Layers palette to display the context menu; then select **Effects** to display the Effects dialog box. Windows users must click on the layer bar (the area with the layer's name) in the Layers palette with the right mouse button to display the context menu.

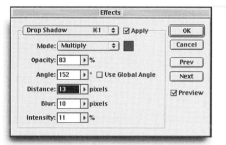

FIGURE 27.2
The Effects dialog box.

4. Check the **Preview** check box and make adjustments to the settings in the Effects dialog box for the **Drop Shadow**.

- The **Mode** pull-down menu is where you choose the Blending mode for the drop shadow. The most effective Blending mode for creating drop shadows is **Multiply** (the default **Mode**). You might want to experiment with other Blending modes to achieve other effects. For example, select **Color Dodge** here to create a backlit effect.

- To the right of the **Mode** pull-down menu is a color swatch. Click this swatch to display the **Color Picker** and select a color for your drop shadow. The default color is black, but I like to set it around 80% black to achieve a more realistic looking shadow.

- The **Opacity** setting controls how much of the underlying imagery is visible in the shadow and helps to further adjust the shade of the shadow. Type a value here, or click on the triangle and drag the slider to select opacity.

- The **Angle** setting determines the direction of the offset of the shadow. Type a value here, or click on the triangle and drag the slider to select an angle for the shadow. If you check the **Use Global Angle** check box, the global angle specified in the Effects menu will be applied.

- The **Distance** setting determines the offset of the shadow in pixels—how large the shadow is. Type a value here, or click on the triangle and drag the slider to select a distance value.

- The **Blur** setting determines how much of a blur effect to apply to the drop shadow. You can set this value to zero to achieve a hard shadow, though most drop shadows look more realistic with a blur applied. Type a value here, or click on the triangle and drag the slider to select a blur amount.

- The **Intensity** setting determines how dark the shadow is and has a counter-effect on the blur of the shadow—higher values decreasing the blur effect. Type a value here, or click on the triangle and drag the slider to set intensity.

5. Click **OK** when you're happy with the drop shadow. The drop shadow effect is applied to the layer and the **Effect** icon appears to the right of the layer's name (see Figure 27.3). **Double-click** on the **Effect** icon in the Layers palette to modify the settings in the Effects dialog box.

FIGURE 27.3

The Effect icon is added to the layer when an effect is applied to that layer. Double-click the icon to modify the effect settings.

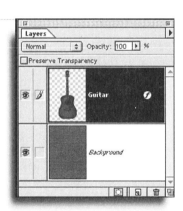

6. If you want to create an independent layer of the drop shadow effect, choose **Layer, Effects, Create Layer**. The drop shadow appears on its own layer enabling you to further modify it (see Figure 27.4).

7. If you want to remove a layer effect, choose **Layer, Effects, Clear Effects**. If you choose **Copy Effects** from this same menu, you can apply the same effect on another layer by choosing **Paste Effects**.

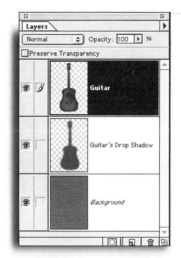

FIGURE 27.4

Use the **Create Layer** option in the **Effects** menu to put the drop shadow effect on its own layer. Now you can modify the shadow separately from the image.

Creating a Shadow from Scratch

It is often necessary to create cast shadows when *compositing* images from different sources. In this example, I am going to take a jet airplane and composite it with a background of the Rocky Mountains. It's a good idea when compositing images to examine the background image for clues as to where the light source is and what type of shadows it creates in the images. This gives you a good idea of how you should create your shadows for any images you incorporate with the background. In my example, simply dropping in the jet plane without creating some sort of cast shadow would create an unrealistic effect, especially because of the existing shadows in the background and on the jet itself.

Making a realistic shadow

1. Start off by creating a drop shadow using the drop shadow layer effect explained in the previous section. This gives us a good starting point to create the cast shadow (see Figure 27.5). In my example, I need to create a shadow that looks like the underside of the jet, so I'll need to be a little creative here.

2. Choose **Effects** from the **Layer** menu and then select **Create Layer** to put the newly created drop shadow on its own layer (see Figure 27.6).

FIGURE 27.5

Start off by creating a drop shadow so you'll have a basic shape to work with.

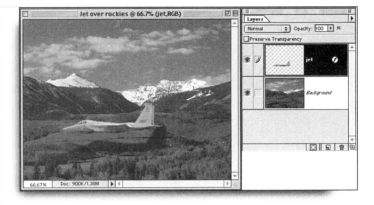

FIGURE 27.6

With the drop shadow on its own layer, we can modify the shadow to suit our needs.

3. Select the layer that contains the drop shadow and choose **Transform** from the **Edit** menu; then select **Scale** to reduce the size of the shadow to create the illusion of distance. Hold down the **Shift** key and drag the corners of the scaling rectangle to resize the image (see Figure 27.7). Double-click inside the scaling rectangle to apply the changes to scale you made.

4. We will use a combination of painting on the actual shadow layer to add more shadow and painting on a layer mask to remove shadow areas to create the shape we need. To add a layer mask to the shadow layer, click on the Mask icon at the bottom of the Layers palette (see Figure 27.8).

FIGURE 27.7
Use the Scale transformation to reduce the size of the shadow and create the illusion of distance.

5. Select the Paintbrush tool from the Toolbox and select a brush size from the Brushes palette. A soft brush works best here because we want to maintain a soft edge to the shadow. With black as your foreground color, paint on the layer mask to remove parts of the shadow. If you remove too much, make your foreground color white and paint on the layer mask to restore the image. In my example, I removed the tail fins and made the fuselage a bit narrower (see Figure 27.8).

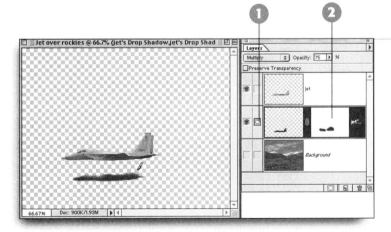

FIGURE 27.8

Click on the Mask icon to create a layer mask for the shadow layer.

1 The Mask icon

2 The layer mask thumbnail in the Layers palette

6. When you're done making adjustments to the layer mask of the shadow layer, apply the mask to the layer by choosing the **Layer** menu and selecting **Remove Layer Mask**. We need to apply the layer mask to the layer at this point because we will likely want to paint some new shadow in areas that we masked.

7. Now we're ready to paint in some more shadow detail. With the Paintbrush tool selected, hold down the (Alt) [Option] key to display the Eyedropper cursor and click in the existing shadow on the shadow layer to set the foreground color. Paint in the changes necessary to make the shadow conform to your idea of what the shadow should look like. In my example, I added some wings and other detail to the tail section to approximate what I think the shadow of this jet will look like with an overhead light source (see Figure 27.9).

FIGURE 27.9

Paint with Paintbrush tool and a soft brush to create more shadow detail.

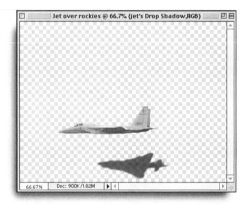

8. Use the Move tool to position the shadow over the background image and in relation to the object on the layer (the jet in my example) (see Figure 27.10).

FIGURE 27.10
The final image with the newly created shadow.

Using the Lighting Effects Filter

The **Lighting Effects** filter is a powerful filter that enables you to create an infinite number of lighting effects—from spotlights to footlights to directional lighting. In order to use the **Lighting Effects** filter, your image must be in RGB Color mode. From the **Filter** menu, choose **Render** and then select **Lighting Effects** to display the Lighting Effects dialog box (see Figure 27.11).

Experiment with lighting effects

1. Choose a lighting style from the **Style** pull-down menu. Experiment with some of these lighting effects to see how they work.

2. Choose the type of light to use from the pull-down menu for **Light Type**, and then set the **Intensity** and **Focus** of the light using the triangle sliders.

3. Set the properties of the light by dragging the triangle sliders in the **Properties** section.

4. Choose a color for the **Light Type** and **Properties** by clicking the color swatch to the right of these sections.

5. If you include an alpha channel with a texture, choose the alpha channel from the **Texture Channel** pull-down menu. You can also use the Red, Green, or Blue channels as texture channels.

6. Click the **Save** button to save your lighting effects settings for future use.

Memory requirements for the **Lighting Effects** filter

The **Lighting Effects** filter requires a significant amount of RAM (memory). If you are unable to launch the filter because of low memory conditions, assign more RAM to the Photoshop application. If you are using MacOS, try turning on Virtual Memory in the **Memory Control Panel**. The **Lighting Effects** filter also requires a computer with an FPU (floating point math coprocessor), standard on many computers. Windows users can set the amount of RAM allocated to Photoshop in the Memory and Image Cache Preferences dialog box. Increasing the Virtual Memory for Windows does not improve the performance of Photoshop. Refer to the Windows documentation for information on setting Virtual Memory.

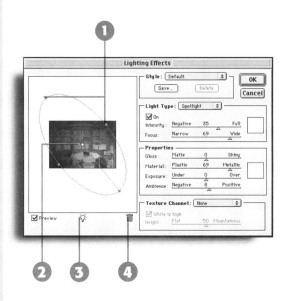

FIGURE 27.11

The Lighting Effects dialog box.

1. Drag the handles around the lighting effect in the preview window to adjust the amount of light.

2. Click the handle in the center of the lighting effect to move the lighting effect in the preview window.

3. Drag the Light Bulb icon under the preview window onto the preview image to add additional lighting effects. Each of these additional lighting effects can have separate and independent settings from each other.

4. Delete additional lighting effects by clicking the center handle and dragging the lighting effect to the Trash Can under the preview window. Note that one lighting effect must be present at all times.

Creating 3D Effects

You can easily create the illusion of dimension by applying light and shadow to objects. All objects that appear to dwell in 3D space are created using light colors to depict the object and dark colors to create shadow effects.

Creating a three-dimensional globe

1. Create a new file that is 5 inches by 7 inches and 150 pixels per inch. The color mode can be RGB or CMYK and the background should be filled with white.

2. We'll start off by creating a horizon to use as our background image. Select the Linear Gradient tool in the Toolbox by pressing the letter G. Double-click the Linear Gradient tool to display the Linear Gradient Options palette (see Figure 27.12).

FIGURE 27.12

The Linear Gradient Options palette.

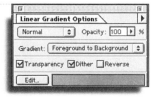

3. Select **Foreground to Background** from the pull-down menu in the **Linear Gradient Options**. The Blending mode should be **Normal** and the **Opacity** 100%.

4. We're going to create a horizon line that combines a color for the sky and a color for the ground. Set the foreground color to light blue or any color you want to use as the sky color. Set the background color to light brown or any color you want to use as the ground.

5. Click and drag a short vertical line with the Linear Gradient tool in the image window to create a horizon line (see Figure 27.13).

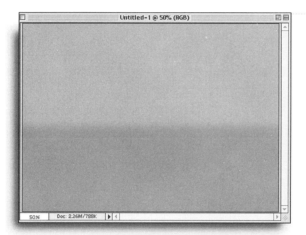

6. From the **Window** menu, choose **Show Layers** to display the Layers palette. From the **Layer** menu, Choose **New** and then select **Layer** to create a new layer in the Layers palette or type (Ctrl+Shift+N) [Command+Shift+N].

7. Select the Elliptical Marquee tool in the Toolbox and create a circular selection in the middle of your document on the new layer you created in the previous step (see Figure 27.14).

Making a circular selection

To create an exact circle using the Elliptical Marquee tool, hold down the Shift key while dragging. You will find it much easier to create a circle if you create it from the center out. Hold down the (Alt) [Option] key to create a selection from the center out.

FIGURE 27.14

Create a circular selection on
the empty layer.

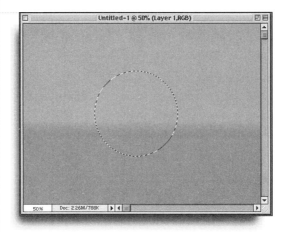

8. Select the Radial Gradient tool in the Toolbox. Double-click
   the Radial Gradient tool to display the Radial Gradient
   Options palette and be sure **foreground to background** is
   selected in the pull-down menu.

9. Press the letter D to restore the default foreground and
   background colors of black and white respectively. Press the
   letter X to swap the foreground colors so the foreground
   color is white and the background color is black.

10. Click and drag with the Radial Gradient tool inside the cir-
    cular selection. Start about 1/4 of the way in from the left
    and top of the circle and drag down and to the right, extend-
    ing the gradient just beyond the edge of the circular selec-
    tion (see Figure 27.15). Type (Ctrl+D) [Command+D] to
    deselect the circular selection.

Now that we have our globe on its own layer, we should add a
cast shadow to position the globe spatially over our background
layer.

Casting a shadow for the globe

1. Create a new layer and place it between the layer that contains the globe and the Background layer.

2. Create an oval selection with the Elliptical Marquee tool on
   the new layer (see Figure 27.16).

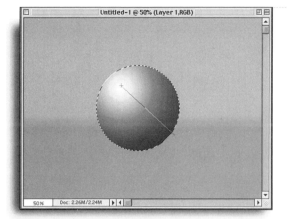

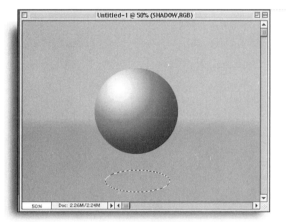

FIGURE 27.16
Create an oval selection to make the shadow.

3. From the **Edit** menu, choose **Fill** or type (Shift+Backspace) [Shift+Delete] to display the Fill dialog box (see Figure 27.17). Select **50% Gray** from the **Contents** pull-down menu. Leave the Blending mode set to **Normal** and the **Opacity** to 100%. Click **OK** to fill the oval selection with 50% gray.

4. Type (Ctrl+D) [Command+D] to deselect the oval selection.

5. In the Layers palette, set the Blending mode for the layer containing the shadow to **Multiply** to create a realistic looking shadow (see Figure 27.17). If you want your shadow to have a softer edge, choose one of the **Blur** filters from the **Filter** menu.

FIGURE 27.17

The Multiply Blending mode creates a realistic looking shadow.

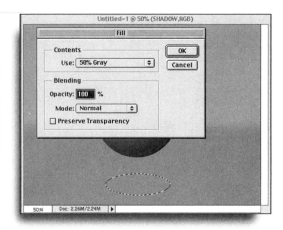

SEE ALSO

➤ *For more information on working in layers, see page 141*

➤ *For more information on using the Gradient tools, see page 253*

Creating Vignettes, Borders, and Backgrounds

Create a textured background

Frame your image with special effects

Use Actions to create borders and frames

Paint a vignette

Create feathered edges

Creating Vignettes

Vignettes are images with softly blended edges, usually in some geometric shape, such as a circle, oval, or square. In this section, we examine the vignette action in the Actions palette and then perform the same effect using fewer steps. You can use a variety of methods to create Vignettes, Borders, and Backgrounds in Photoshop. In many cases, you can utilize the built-in functions of Photoshop as well as some of the Actions included in the Extras folder within the Photoshop folder. Because Photoshop has so many built-in ways to create these effects, I suggest exploring these possibilities before you invest a lot of time and effort "reinventing the wheel." You can use the techniques described here on a file with a single Background layer or on an individual layer to create composite images.

Creating Vignettes with Actions

The **Vignette (selection)** action in the Actions palette is pretty much all you need to create effective *vignettes*, though you must learn some techniques if you want to create vignettes with variable edge effects, covered a little later in this chapter. The steps to creating a simple vignette are just two: Make a selection and then play the **Vignette (selection)** action.

Using the Vignette (selection) Action

1. Open any image in Photoshop.

2. Choose **Show Actions** from the **Window** menu to display the Actions palette and click the triangle for the **Default Actions** set (see Figure 28.1).

Restoring the Default Actions

The **Default Actions** are included with Photoshop when you first install it. You can, however, delete the **Default Actions** set from the Actions palette by dragging it onto the **Trash Can** icon or by clicking the **Trash Can** icon when the set is selected. If the **Default Actions** are not present in your Actions palette, or if some of the actions in the set are missing, choose **Reset Actions** from the Actions palette menu to restore the default actions.

FIGURE 28.1

The Actions palette with the **Default Actions** displayed.

3. Set the Actions palette to **Button Mode** by clicking the arrow in the upper-right corner of the Actions palette to choose **Button Mode** from the pull-down menu. In **Button Mode,** all the actions in the Actions palette are depicted as buttons enabling you to play an action simply by clicking a button (see Figure 28.2).

FIGURE 28.2

Button Mode enables you to play actions by clicking a button.

4. Use one of the selection tools in the Toolbox to create a selection on your image. I used the **Lasso** tool to create a cloud-shaped selection on my image (see Figure 28.3).

FIGURE 28.3

Create a selection in the shape of the vignette you want to create.

5. Click on the **Vignette (selection)** button in the Actions palette. When the **Feather** dialog box appears, enter a feather value (I used 20 pixels) and then press **OK** to continue the action. Voilà! This actions creates some new layers, so choose **Show Layers** from the **Window** menu to display the Layers palette (see Figure 28.4).

FIGURE 28.4

The vignette is created on a transparent layer with an additional layer added for the background color. Notice that the original image is still intact on the Background layer.

The resulting image is a decent vignette, although you didn't really have much control over the process. If you want to see how the vignette was created, switch out of **Button Mode** by choosing **Button Mode** again from the Actions palette menu.

Click the triangle to the left of **Vignette (selection)** to display the parts of the action. Click the triangle next to the parts to display the steps for each part (see Figure 28.5).

FIGURE 28.5

Evaluate an action by clicking the triangles next to the actions.

Creating a Vignette in Five Easy Steps

Sometimes, all I want to do is open a file, create a simple vignette, and save the file. Open any file to perform these five simple steps.

Steps to creating a vignette

1. Use a selection tool to make a selection on your image. (I'm using the Elliptical Marquee tool.) Take care to inset the selection far enough from the edges of the image so the *feather* effect will not be squared off.

2. Choose **Inverse** from the **Select** menu to create an inverse selection.

3. Set the foreground or background color to the color you want to use as the background of the image. (I used white.)

4. Choose **Feather** from the **Select** menu and specify the feather radius. (I used 14 pixels.)

5. Press the (Backspace) [delete] key to fill with the background color or (Alt+Backspace) [Option+Delete] to fill with the foreground color. Filling the inverse selection area creates the vignette (see Figure 28.6).

FIGURE 28.6
A simple oval shaped vignette.

Creating Vignettes with the Painting Tools

You can use a freeform approach to creating vignettes by painting on a layer mask with big soft brushes. This means that we'll need to have the image we want to vignette on a transparent layer. You can apply the following effects using two images: one for the background and one to create the vignette effect. I'm going to create the vignette on a solid white background for illustration purposes.

Painting a vignette with the Paintbrush

1. Open any image in Photoshop. If the image is on the Background layer in the Layers palette, double-click the Background layer to convert it to a transparent layer.

2. Choose **Add Layer Mask** form the **Layer** menu and then select **Reveal All** to add a layer mask to the layer in the Layers palette (see Figure 28.7).

FIGURE 28.7

The layer mask is depicted to the right of the layer's thumbnail picture.

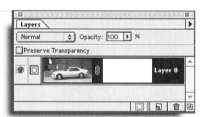

3. Select a large soft brush from the Brushes palette.

4. Use the Paintbrush or Airbrush tool and paint on the layer mask with black as the Foreground color. The painted areas disappear from the image because painting with black masks those areas (see Figure 28.8).

FIGURE 28.8

The layer mask aids in creating the vignette effect by masking the painted areas.

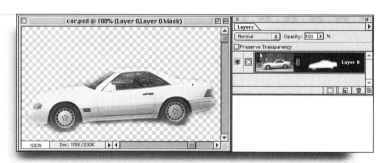

5. When you are happy with the vignette effect you created, choose the **Layer** menu; then select **Remove Layer Mask** and **Apply** the layer mask to the layer.

6. Create a new layer in the Layers palette and fill that entire layer with a solid color. Drag this layer beneath the layer that contains the vignette. You can also use the Move tool to drag this layer onto another image that you want to use a background.

Creating Vignettes with the Gradient Tools

Another way to create vignette effects is to use the Gradient tools on a layer mask. The layer mask offers optimal flexibility in this case because we can continually modify the layer mask until we're happy with the results.

Applying gradients to layer masks

1. Open any image in Photoshop. If the image is on the Background layer in the Layers palette, double-click the Background layer to convert it to a transparent layer.

2. From the **Layer** menu, choose **Add Layer Mask** and then select **Reveal All** to add a layer mask to the layer in the Layers palette.

3. Select one of the **Gradient** tools from the Toolbox. (I used the Linear Gradient Tool.) Double-click the Gradient tool to display the Gradient Tool Options palette. Because we'll be painting on the layer mask, we need to paint with black and white. Choose **Foreground to Background** from the Gradient Tool Options palette and set the foreground color to white and the background color to black. You can easily accomplish this by pressing the letter D to set the default foreground and background colors. Simply press the letter X to swap the foreground and background colors if necessary.

4. Click and drag over the image in the image window to create a gradient on the layer mask. I suppose you can call the effect created with the Linear Gradient Tool a fade, though I like to think of it as a vignette on one side of my image (see Figure 28.9). Experiment with the other Gradient tools and edit the Gradient in the Gradient Tool Options palette to fine-tune the effect.

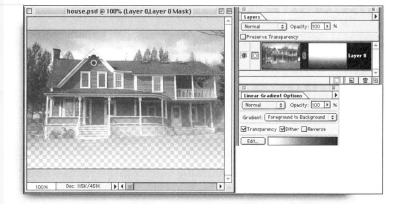

5. When you are happy with the vignette effect you created, from the **Layer** menu, choose **Remove Layer Mask** and **Apply** the layer mask to the layer.

6. Create a new layer in the Layers palette and fill that entire layer with a solid color. Drag this layer beneath the layer that contains the vignette. You can also use the Move tool to drag this layer onto another image that you want to use as a background.

Creating Borders and Edge Effects

You can create an infinite number of borders and edge effects on your images by following a few simple steps to select the area to change and then applying filters or color adjustments to the selected area. This section involves the use of some special effects filters available under the **Filter** menu. For the most part, filters are selected and applied based on their visual effect that will vary from image to image. Experimenting with the variety of available filters can give you an idea of how they work and when they are applicable to the job at hand. Many of the special effects filters are only available in RGB mode, something to keep in mind if you want to use these edge effects on your own images.

Creating a Border Selection

In order to create border and edge effects, you must first acquire a technique to select the border region of an image. In the following example, we will first create a border selection and then apply a filter effect to the selected border region to frame the image.

Steps to creating a border selection

1. Open an RGB image in Photoshop.

2. From the **Select** menu, choose **All** or type (Ctrl+A) [Command+A] to select the entire image.

3. From the **Select** menu, choose **Modify.** Then select **Border** to display the Border dialog box and type 64 for pixel width; 64 is the maximum pixel width allowed here. Click **OK**. The selection marquee changes to display a selected area that is 32 pixels wide around the edges of the image (see Figure 28.10). The **Border** command creates a selection border that is built by adding 32 pixels to the outside of the marquee and 32 pixels to the inside of the marquee (64 pixels) in our example. Because the selection marquee was right out to the edge of the image, only 32 pixels were added to the inside of the marquee to create the border.

FIGURE 28.10
The border selection.

4. You can expand the border selection beyond the maximum limit of 64 pixels. From the **Select** menu, choose **Modify** and then select **Expand** to display the Expand Selection dialog box. Enter the number of pixels you want to expand the border by. (I added 10 pixels for a total border of 42 pixels.) The maximum value for this dialog box is 16 pixels, but you can apply it multiple times to further expand the selection.

5. Press the letter D to set the background color to white. Type (Backspace) [delete] to fill the selected area with white. Note that the border has a feather effect automatically applied to it creating a frame effect (see Figure 28.11).

FIGURE 28.11

The frame effect is created by the border selection.

6. From the **Filter** menu, choose **Texture** and then select **Mosaic Tiles** to display the Mosaic Tiles dialog box (see Figure 28.12). Specify the settings for the **Mosaic Tiles** filter and click **OK** to apply the filter to the selected border of the image (see Figure 28.13).

7. From the **Filter** menu, choose **Fade Mosaic Tiles** to further adjust the way the filter interacts with the image.

FIGURE 28.12
The Mosaic Tiles dialog box.

FIGURE 28.13
The **Mosaic Tiles** filter applied to the border selection.

Experiment with other fill colors and filter effects. A limitless number of edge effects are possible using the previous steps.

Creating Frames with Actions

Photoshop comes with a number of Actions to create frame effects. In the following example, we will apply one of these frame effects and explore ways to modify the Actions to suit our needs.

Creating a wood frame

1. Open any color image that is at least 100 pixels X 100 pixels, in Photoshop.

2. From the **Window** menu, choose **Show Actions** to display the Actions palette if it is not already onscreen.

3. Click on the triangle next to the **Default Actions** set in the Actions palette to display the actions contained therein.

4. Click on the **Wood Frame - 50 pixel** action; then click the **Play** button at the bottom of the Actions palette. The **Play** button is the white triangle pointing to the right.his action creates a wood frame that is 50 pixels wide around your image, but you're not stuck with a 50-pixel-wide frame or one in this color for that matter. Let's change some of the action items.

Changing a Default Action

Modifying the steps of an Action

1. Click on the triangle to the left of the **Wood Frame - 50 pixel** action to display the items recorded for the Action. Notice that the first thing this action does is play another action called **Frame Channel - 50 pixel**. That Action is the one that actually creates the 50-pixel frame used to make the wood frame.

2. Click on the triangle to the left of **Frame Channel - 50 pixel** to display its contents.

3. Locate the four occurrences of the **Transform Current Layer** action. Click inside the embossed box to the left of these four Actions to turn on their dialog boxes (see Figure 28.14). This means that when the Action plays, the Transformation dialog box will wait for your input before continuing.

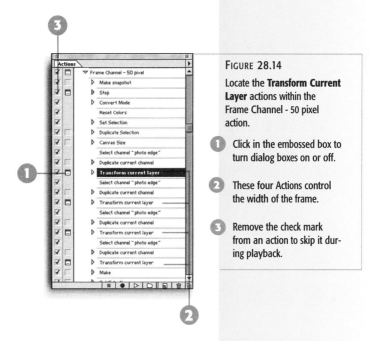

FIGURE 28.14

Locate the **Transform Current Layer** actions within the Frame Channel - 50 pixel action.

1 Click in the embossed box to turn dialog boxes on or off.

2 These four Actions control the width of the frame.

3 Remove the check mark from an action to skip it during playback.

4. Open another image in Photoshop or choose **Revert** from the **File** menu to revert the current image to its original state.

5. Select the **Wood Frame - 50 pixel** action in the Actions palette and click the **Play** button.

6. The action pauses and displays the **Transformation** dialog box four times during the playback of the action (see Figure 28.15). Each time we will enter the x and y values in the **Position** section of the dialog box. The first time it appears, enter (**30x**, **30y**). The second time, enter (-**30x**, -**30y**). The third time, enter (**30x**, -**30y**). Finally, for the fourth dialog box, enter (-**30x**, **30y**). When the action finishes, you will have a 30-pixel frame around your image.

Using the History palette to revert

You can revert to any previous state for your image using the History palette. Choose **Show History** from the **Window** menu to display the History palette and click on the topmost snapshot to revert to the image's original state. You can delete the history items by choosing **Clear History** from the History palette menu.

FIGURE 28.15
The Transformation dialog box.

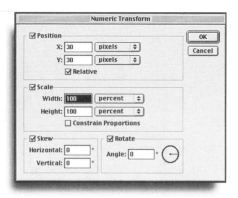

Rerecording Action Items

In some cases, you have to rerecord an action item to change the action to suit your needs. Using the **Wood Frame - 50 pixel** action example, let's change the color of the wood frame.

Redefining steps in an Action

1. Open an image or revert the open image to its original state.

2. Click on the triangle to the left of the **Wood Frame - 50 pixel** action in the **Default Actions** set to display the contents of the action.

3. Click on the **Set Foreground Color** action item to select it; then click the **Trash Can** icon at the bottom of the Actions palette to delete it.

4. Click on the **Record** button at the bottom of the Actions palette to record a new foreground color. The **Record** button is the round button, which turns red while recording.

5. Mix a new foreground color using the Color palette or **Color Picker**.

6. Click on the **Stop** button at the bottom of the Actions palette to stop recording. The **Stop** button is the square button to the left of the **Record** button.

When you play the **Wood Frame - 50 pixel** action, the wood frame will be created in the color you selected as the foreground color. In cases where an action item displays a dialog box, you can choose **Record Again** from the Action palette menu to specify the settings for that action item's dialog box.

Photoshop's extra frame actions

Photoshop comes with a number of Actions located in the Extras folder within the Photoshop folder on your hard drive. There are a number of frame actions contained in a set called Frames. Choose **Load Actions** from the Actions palette menu to load these actions into the Actions palette.

Creating Backgrounds

You can create backgrounds in Photoshop in numerous ways. In this section, we'll examine some methods of creating backgrounds from scratch. In reality, any image that you place on the bottom-most layer in the Layers palette is a background image, so we'll concentrate on creating textured and patterned backgrounds here.

Creating a textured background

1. From the **File** menu, choose **New** to create a new file. Let's make this file 7 inches X 5 inches, RGB, 72 pixels per inch. Click **OK** to create the new file.

2. Click on the foreground color swatch in the Toolbox and create a color using the **Color Picker** or mix a color using the Color palette.

3. Type (Alt+Backspace) [Option+Delete] to fill the entire image area with the foreground color.

4. From the **Filter** menu, choose **Noise** and then select **Add Noise** to display the Add Noise dialog box (see Figure 28.16). Set the **Amount** to **75**, click the **Gaussian** radio button, check the **Monochromatic** check box, and then click **OK.**

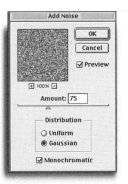

FIGURE 28.16
The Add Noise filter dialog box.

5. We could stop right here and call this our background, but let's apply a few more filters. Choose **Distort** from the **Filter** menu and then select **Ripple** to display the Ripple

dialog box (see Figure 28.17). Set the **Amount** to **300%** and select **Medium** from the **Size** pull-down menu. Click **OK** to apply the Ripple filter.

FIGURE 28.17

The Ripple dialog box.

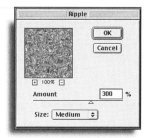

6. From the **Filter** menu, choose **Artistic** and then select **Dry Brush** to display the Dry Brush dialog box (see Figure 28.18). Set the **Brush Size** to **2**, the **Brush Detail** to **8**, and the **Texture** to **1.** Click **OK** to apply the Dry Brush filter.

FIGURE 28.18

The Dry Brush dialog box.

Photoshop's extra texture actions

The Extras folder inside the Photoshop folder on your hard drive contains a number of Action Sets that can be loaded into the Actions palette. Among these is the **Texture** Actions set that enables you to create a wide variety of background textures. Choose **Load Actions** from the Actions palette menu and navigate to the Actions folder inside the Extras folder within the Photoshop folder on your hard drive.

7. If you want to change the color of the texture you created, choose **Adjust** from the **Image** menu and then select **Hue/Saturation** to display the Hue/Saturation dialog box. Click on the **Colorize** check box and adjust the **Hue** and **Saturation** values.

As you can see, creating textured backgrounds is relatively simple. The **Add Noise** filter is the crucial step in creating a noisy enough background color so the other filters have something to work with.

Retouching and Repairing

Cloning to repair images

Removing dust and scratches

Creating missing image detail

Repairing creases and torn areas

Retouching with the Rubber Stamp Tool

The Rubber Stamp is a *cloning* tool that enables you to pick up one part of an image and apply it to another. Using the Rubber Stamp tool, you can fill in the empty spaces, remove dirt and scratches, and invent some image data to rebuild missing pieces of an image.

Cloning with the Rubber Stamp tool

1. You can use the Rubber Stamp tool on an image in any of the available color modes. Open an image that contains some areas that are in need of repair. Perform any color correction or sharpening before using the Rubber Stamp tool to repair the image. It is especially important that the mage is sharpened beforehand, because sharpening makes scratches and creases more apparent.

2. Crop the image before you start repairing it to avoid spending time retouching areas that you will end up cropping off.

3. Double-click on the Rubber Stamp tool in the Toolbox to display the Rubber Stamp Options palette (see Figure 29.1).

FIGURE 29.1

The Rubber Stamp Options palette.

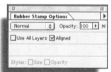

4. Set the Blending mode to **Normal**, the **Opacity** to 100% and be sure the **Aligned** check box is checked. You can leave the **Use All Layers** check box deselected unless your file contains more than one layer that you want to clone from.

5. From the **File** menu, choose **Preferences** and then select **Display & Cursors** to display the Preferences dialog box. Select **Brush Size** for the **Painting Cursors** option (see Figure 29.2) and then click on **OK**. This preference displays the cursor in the size and shape of the brush to help make the correct brush selection.

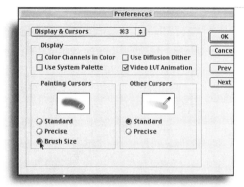

FIGURE 29.2

Choose **Brush Size** for the **Painting Cursors** option to make the cursor display in the brush size and shape when painting.

6. From the **Window** menu, choose **Show Brushes** to display the Brushes palette and select a brush. It's okay to use a brush with a soft edge as long as the brush isn't too big because the soft edge blurs parts of the image. I like to use a soft brush so the cloning blends smoothly with the existing image.

7. Zoom in close to an area in need of repair. You might want to use the Navigator palette to help move around the image when you're zoomed in close. From the **Window** menu, choose **Show Navigator** to display the Navigator palette, as shown in Figure 29.3.

Selecting a brush from the **Context** menu

Display the **Context** menu (click the right mouse button) [Control+click] on the image when you have a painting tool or the Rubber Stamp tool selected. Select from **Next Brush**, **Previous Brush**, **First Brush**, or **Last Brush**.

FIGURE 29.3.

The Navigator palette.

1 Drag this box to choose what appears in the image window.

2 Drag the triangle slider to zoom in and out.

3 Resize the Navigator palette by dragging from the lower-right corner.

8. (Alt+click) [Option+click] on the image to select the point you want to start cloning from. The Cursor changes to display the Rubber Stamp cursor with a white triangle when you hold down the (Alt) [Option] key. Choose an area close the part of the image you want to fix.

9. Position your cursor over the part of the image you want to begin cloning onto and click one time (no keys held down). Note that the place you click is replaced with the part of the image you (Alt+clicked) [Option+clicked]. You can (Alt+click) [Option+click] an origin point and then click and drag with the Rubber Stamp tool, but the dragging often creates a secondary pattern that is undesirable. The most effective way to use the Rubber Stamp tool in most instances is to select the origin point ((Alt+click) [Option+click]) and then click the destination point, tapping in changes gradually (see Figure 29.4). It's time consuming, but the results are worth it.

FIGURE 29.4

The before and after depiction of cloning with the Rubber Stamp tool.

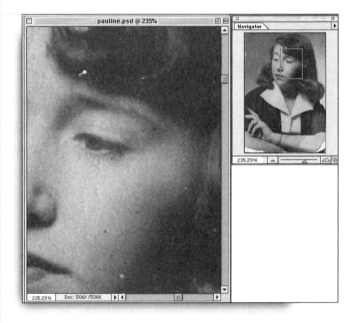

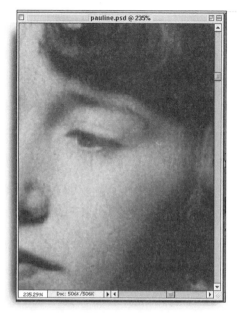

FIGURE 29.4b
The after depiction of cloning with the Rubber Stamp.

10. Use this technique to repair the entire image. You will have to invent the parts of the image that are missing by using parts of the image you already have. Concentrate on the larger imperfections; then read on for techniques to repair the specks, dust, and scratches in the image.

Retouching with the History Brush

If you make mistakes when using the Rubber Stamp tool, you can easily repair them by painting back parts of the image from anywhere in the history of the changes you made so far. It is also a good idea to periodically take *snapshots* of your image at different stages, so you can return to that state at a future time. The History palette records every step you make and provides a means to take snapshots of your image as you work.

Reverting to previous states with the History Brush

1. From the **Window** menu, choose **Show History** to display the History palette (see Figure 29.5).

FIGURE 29.5

The History palette.

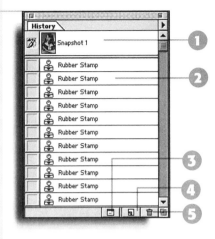

1 Snapshots are recorded at the top of the History palette.

2 Return to any previous image state by clicking the history state.

3 Click here to create a new document from the current history state.

4 Click here to take a snapshot of the image in its current state.

5 Click here to delete snapshots and history states.

2. Select the History Brush in the Toolbox. Double-click the History Brush icon in the Toolbox to display the History Brush options palette (see Figure 29.6). Ensure that the Blending mode is set to **Normal** and the **Opacity** to 100%. Do not check the **Impressionist** check box unless you want to paint using the impressionist effect.

FIGURE 29.6

The History Brush options palette.

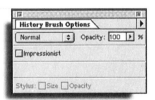

3. Click inside the embossed box to the left of either the Snapshot or a history state to select the history state you want to paint from with the History brush (see Figure 29.7).

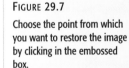

FIGURE 29.7

Choose the point from which you want to restore the image by clicking in the embossed box.

1 The History brush icon appears here when you click to select the point you want to restore from.

4. Position the cursor over the part of the image you want to restore and begin painting. The act of painting with the History brush is recorded in the History palette as well.

Using the Dust & Scratches Filter

You can use the **Dust & Scratches** filter to a limited extent to eliminate some of the artifacts that result from sharpening the image and to remove small creases and scratches. This filter works best on large areas and blurs the image somewhat to achieve the effect of removing the dust and scratches. In the following example, we use the **Dust & Scratches** filter to smooth the background of an image that contains creases, scratches, and dust specks.

Removing dust and scratches

1. Use any of the selection tools to select the part of the image you want to apply the **Dust & Scratches** filter effect to. I selected the background of the image with the Lasso tool (see Figure 29.8).

FIGURE 29.8

Create a selection to isolate the part of the image you want to affect.

2. From the **Filter** menu, choose **Noise** and then select **Dust & Scratches** to display the Dust & Scratches dialog box (see Figure 29.9).

FIGURE 29.9

The Dust & Scratches dialog box.

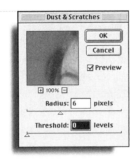

3. Drag the triangle slider for **Radius** until the dust and scratches in your image disappear. Click the **Preview** check box to see the effect of your settings on the image. You might have to wait a few seconds for the screen to redraw depending on the file size and resolution. The **Threshold** value limits the parts of the image affected based on grayscale value. Leave the **Threshold** value at 0 (zero) so all the pixels in the image are affected.

4. Click outside the Dust & Scratches dialog box and on the image to change the picture preview in the dialog box. Or click inside the preview box and drag with the Hand icon. Note that clicking in the preview box with the Hand icon toggles a before and after preview. You can also click off the **Preview** check box to see the before and after effect on the whole image.

5. Click **OK** to apply the **Dust & Scratches** filter.

Retouching with the Pattern Stamp Tool

The Pattern Stamp tool enables you to select a rectangular part of an image and define it as a pattern. You can then paint with the Pattern Stamp tool to apply the pattern to the image. The following example uses the Pattern Stamp tool to paint the background of the image with a pattern picked up from the image.

Retouching with the Pattern Stamp tool

1. Use the rectangular Marquee tool to select a part of your image that contains a consistent pattern. Take care to avoid selecting patterns that will be apparent when repeated. In my example, I did some minor retouching on a small area with the Rubber Stamp tool and then made a rectangular selection of the area (see Figure 29.10).

FIGURE 29.10

Select an area devoid of obvious internal artifacts that will make the painted pattern appear repetitious.

2. From the **Edit** menu, choose **Define Pattern** to store the selected pixels as a pattern.

3. Type (Ctrl+D) [Command+D] to deselect the area you used to define the pattern.

4. Select the Pattern Stamp tool from the Toolbox. It is located in the same place as the Rubber Stamp tool in the Tool menu. Double-click the Pattern Stamp tool to display the Pattern Stamp Options palette, as shown in Figure 29.11.

FIGURE 29.11

The Pattern Stamp Options palette.

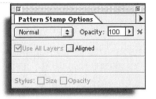

5. If the **Align** option in the Pattern Stamp Options palette is checked, deselect it. This helps to avoid a repeating pattern because every time we let go of the mouse and start painting again with the Pattern Stamp tool, the pattern starts from the upper-left corner of the original rectangular selection instead of completing the defined pattern.

6. Choose **Lighten** as the Blending mode from the pull-down menu in the Pattern Stamp Options palette. The Lighten blending mode only affects the pixels with values lighter than the ones I'm painting with, which will further ensure that a repeating pattern does not appear.

7. Paint with the Pattern Stamp tool using a relatively large brush. (I used a 45-pixel brush.) Apply the pattern in small circular strokes to retouch the image (the background in my image), as shown in see Figure 29.12.

FIGURE 29.12

The pattern applied to the background of the image using the Lighten Blending mode.

8. If you notice any apparent repeating patterns, use the Rubber Stamp tool to eliminate them.

Combining Image Elements

Adding and removing image elements

Creating a montage

Using the layer mask

Adding Image Elements

Photoshop always offers two ways to combine imagery. The first method entails creating individual layers for each element that gives you the most flexibility. The second method is to work on a single layer, painting or cutting and pasting changes. In most cases, the most sensible method is the first, to create layers for each image element. True, the History palette enables you go back and undo virtually any steps performed on the image, but using layers enables you to save a working copy that can be further modified in the future. In the following example, remove a subject from one background and place him on another.

Combining two image elements

1. The first things to consider when combining two images are the resolution of each image and the color mode. In my example, both images are RGB color and 300 pixels per inch. I can scale an image when I bring it into the background image, though I prefer to have the resolutions of the two images as close as possible to avoid interpolation when enlarging or the loss of color data and image detail when reducing.

2. Select the image you want to combine with the selection tools. You can use the rectangular Marquee tool here, though I like to use the Lasso tool so that I have less work in the combined image (see Figure 30.1).

3. Select the Move tool in the Toolbox and drag the selected image onto the background image, creating a new layer in the process (see Figure 30.2).

4. Click on the Layer Mask icon at the bottom of the Layers palette to create a layer mask for the image you just dragged onto the background. Use the layer mask to erase the unwanted areas of the layered image, as shown in Figure 30.3.

5. Set the foreground color to black and the background color to white. You can accomplish this by simply typing the letter D for the default colors.

FIGURE 30.1

Make a selection of the image you want to combine with some background image.

FIGURE 30.2

A new layer is automatically created when you drag one image onto another.

6. Select the Paintbrush tool in the Toolbox. Double-click the Paintbrush Tool icon in the Toolbox to display the Paintbrush Options palette. Be sure the **Opacity** is set to 100% and the Blending mode to **Normal** in the Paintbrush Options palette.

FIGURE 30.3

Create a layer mask.

1 Click the Layer Mask icon to create a layer mask.

2 The layer mask is depicted to the right of the image thumbnail.

7. Select a relatively small brush size with a soft edge. (I used a 9-pixel brush.)

8. Click once on the layer mask thumbnail to be sure it is selected. Paint on the layer mask with black to remove (mask) the edges around our image (see Figure 30.4). You might want to hide the background image by clicking the Eyeball icon for that layer, to make it easier to see the edges of the image. If you make a mistake while painting the mask, change the foreground color to white and paint to restore the image. If your background color is set to white, press the letter X to swap the foreground and background colors.

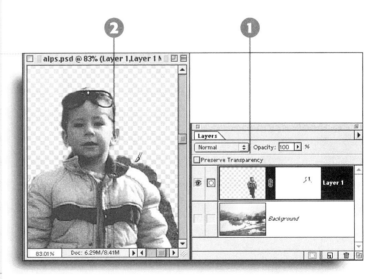

FIGURE 30.4

Paint with black over the image when the layer mask is selected in the Layers palette to remove unwanted image data.

1 The layer mask thumbnail depicts the changes made by painting with black.

2 Paint with black to remove (mask) the image. Paint with white to restore (unmask) the image.

9. Continue painting with gradually smaller brushes until the image is silhouetted to your liking. I recommend saving the layered image in Photoshop format so you can make changes in the future if necessary.

10. Drag the layer mask to the trash in the Layers palette to apply or discard the layer mask.

SEE ALSO

➤ *For more information on the Layers palette, see page 22.*

➤ *To learn more about layer masks, see page 141.*

Shadow and Lighting Concerns When Combining Images

In the previous example, we took a subject from one environment and placed him into another. Each environment has its own set of shadow and lighting conditions that must be rectified if the combined image is to look realistic. In the following example, we add a cast shadow and darken the background image to some degree to make the composited images look realistic.

Casting a shadow

1. If you have not already done so, remove or apply the layer mask for the layer on which you want to create a cast shadow.

2. Select the layer on which you want to create a shadow (the layer with the boy on it in my example).

3. From the **Layer** menu, choose **Effects** and then select **Drop Shadow** to display the Effects dialog box (see Figure 30.5).

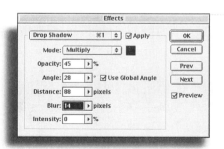

FIGURE 30.5

The Effects dialog box with the Drop Shadow Effect selected.

4. Set the distance to a value that enables you to see the drop shadow on the image when the **Preview** box is checked. Set the **Opacity** to a value that you think represents the kind of shadow that would be cast based on the ambient light in the image. In my example, the light is somewhat diffused by clouds, so I'm going to use a 45% **Opacity** for my shadow. Click **OK** to create the drop shadow.

5. The drop shadow layer effect is currently attached to the layer it was created from. From the **Layer** menu, choose **Effects** and then select **Create Layer** to put the drop shadow on its own layer (see Figure 30.6).

FIGURE 30.6

When the drop shadow is on its own layer, we can manipulate it.

6. Select the layer that contains the drop shadow in the Layers palette.

7. From the **Edit** menu, choose **Transform** and then select **Distort** to display the transformation box around the drop shadow in the image window (see Figure 30.7).

8. Click and drag the boxes along the transformation box's path to reshape the drop shadow and create a cast shadow (see Figure 30.8).

9. Double-click inside the transformation box or press Return to apply the transformation. Press the Esc key to dismiss the transformation box and leave the image unchanged.

FIGURE 30.7

The transformation box enables you reshape the shadow by dragging the anchor boxes.

FIGURE 30.8

Pull the shadow down onto the ground to create a cast shadow.

Using Dodge and Burn to Change Lighting

The Dodge and Burn tools can be quite effective in creating subtle changes to light and shadow in an image. The Dodge tool lightens the luminosity value of pixels whereas the Burn tool darkens this value.

Dodging and burning areas of an image

1. The trick to using Dodge and Burn effectively is to use a very low **Exposure** setting and apply the changes gradually to the image. Select the Burn tool from the Toolbox. Double-click the Burn tool icon in the Toolbox to display the Burn Options palette (see Figure 30.9).

FIGURE 30.9
The Burn Options palette.

2. Select the gray values you want to affect from the pull-down menu in the Burn Options palette. Set the **Exposure** to control the amount of change painting with the Burn tool has on the image. For my example, I want to affect the midtone values with a low exposure (12%).

3. Use a medium to large brush size with a soft edge to paint on the image. Keep in mind that each application of the Burn tool darkens the image. In my example, I burned the ground at the feet of the boy to create a shadow more in line with the shadows of the boy's body.

4. The Dodge tool works in much the same way, except the pixels' values will be lightened to create a lighting effect. Use the Dodge tool with a low **Exposure** setting to increase the brightness of an area. Take care not to overexpose an area resulting in loss of detail. In my example, I used the Dodge tool to lighten the jacket and face of the boy with subtlety (see Figure 30.10).

FIGURE 30.10

The final image with the Dodge and Burn tool applied.

Creating a Montage

A montage is simply a collection of images overlayed with various compositing effects. In Photoshop, creating a *montage* is a relatively simple matter of putting a bunch of images on individual layers and using the Blending modes and layer mask to combine them. In my example, I used a solid black background and overlayed three images to create a composite image.

Creating blends on layer masks

1. Create a new file. I created a 7-inch by 5-inch, 300-pixel-per-inch image in the RGB color mode. Fill the background of this image with black.

2. Open an image to add to the montage. I used an image of some colorful fall leaves. Use the Move tool to drag the image onto your background, creating a new layer (see Figure 30.11).

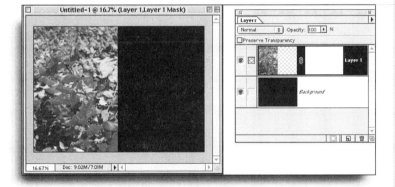

Figure 30.11

Drag an image onto your background to create a new layer.

3. Create a layer mask for the image on the new layer by clicking on the Layer Mask icon at the bottom of the Layers palette.

4. Select the Linear Gradient tool in the Toolbox. Double-click the Linear Gradient tool icon in the Toolbox to display the Linear Gradient Tool Options palette and select **Foreground to Background** as the **Gradient** type from the pull-down menu.

5. Set the Foreground color to White and the Background color to Black.

6. Be sure the layer mask is selected in the Layers palette and create a linear gradient that starts from the middle of your image and ends just short of the edge of the image to create a vignette edge (see Figure 30.12).

FIGURE 30.12

Create vignette edges by using the Gradient tool on the layer mask.

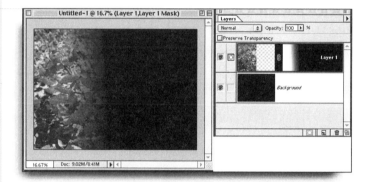

SEE ALSO

➤ *For more information on how to use the Gradient tool, see page 257.*

Creating silhouettes on layer masks

1. Open another image to add to your composite montage and drag it into the composite image to create a new layer. I used a photo of a woman's face.

2. Add a layer mask to this image by clicking on the Mask icon at the bottom of the Layers palette.

3. Select the Paintbrush or Airbrush tool from the Toolbox.

4. Choose a large brush size. (I used a 200-pixel brush with a soft edge.)

5. Set the Foreground color to black and paint on the layer mask to silhouette the image creating a soft blending effect (see Figure 30.13).

6. Bring in other images and use these effect to composite them onto a background image. My final contains four layers (see Figure 30.14).

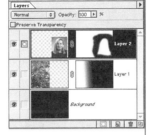

FIGURE 30.13
Paint on the layer mask with
black to create soft brush
effects.

FIGURE 30.14
The final montage with three
images and a type layer composited.

Removing Image Elements

It is sometimes necessary to remove a subject or object from an image. The challenge here is to invent the data that would otherwise appear behind the person or object you're removing. In many cases, however, the background imagery is consistent enough or ambiguous enough to accomplish this task. In my example, I will remove an overhead light and a table centerpiece from an image of a patio, as shown in Figure 30.15.

FIGURE 30.15

Examine the original image to determine what parts can be created from existing image areas.

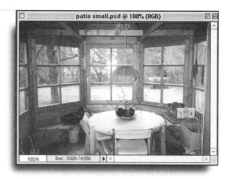

Using the Rubber Stamp to remove image elements

1. Select the Rubber Stamp tool from the Toolbox. Double-click the Rubber Stamp Tool icon in the Toolbox to display the Rubber Stamp Tool Options palette and ensure that the **Aligned** check box is indeed checked.

SEE ALSO

➤ *For more information on the Rubber Stamp tool, see page 304.*

2. Select a brush size for your Rubber Stamp tool. It's best to use small brush sizes here, even though it will take longer to edit the image.

3. Zoom in close to the object you want to remove and examine the surrounding area for places where you can pick up image data to clone in the place of the object you're removing.

4. (Alt+click) [Option+click] the area of the image you want to copy from.

5. Paint with the Rubber Stamp tool (no keys held down) to apply the image area you (Alt+clicked) [Option+clicked]. I suggest tapping in the changes by clicking with the Rubber Stamp tool rather than dragging to paint so you have more control over the editing (see Figure 30.16).

6. From the **Window** menu, choose **Transform** to display the History palette. Use the History palette to go back a few steps if you make a mistake along the way. You might also want to periodically take snapshots using the History palette

FIGURE 30.16

Use a combination of (Alt) [Option] clicking and clicking (no keys held down) to tap in the changes to your image.

so you can restore your image back to a given point. Choose **New Snapshot** from the History Palette menu to take a snapshot of your image at a particular stage while editing.

7. When you are done using the Rubber Stamp tool to clone out areas of the image, examine the image to be sure you haven't created any repeating patterns. See my final image in Figure 30.17.

FIGURE 30.17

The final image with the over-head light and the centerpiece removed.

SEE ALSO

➤ *For more information on the Layers palette, see page 22.*

➤ *To learn more about layer masks, see page 141.*

➤ *For more information on how to use the Gradient tool, see page 257.*

➤ *For more information on the Rubber Stamp tool, see page 304.*

What's New in Photoshop 5

Major New Features

Many people consider Photoshop 5 an evolutionary upgrade to the product. Photoshop 5 introduces several important improvements and new features to extend this already powerful tool. Adobe has added several important enhancements to empower users with more flexibility and control when creating images. Many of the new additions to the program reduce the need for additional plug-ins or multiple-step procedures. Here are a few of the most important changes to Photoshop 5:

- Changes and improvements have been made to all the dialog boxes in the Color Settings preferences.

- Adobe has taken a giant step forward in color management by the support of ICC profiles in Photoshop (see sidenote). Not only can you specify a particular color profile for your image, but you can also attach the ICC color tag to your file so it appears the same way the next time you open it.

- For those using Photoshop for prepress, you can now specify dot gain compensation for each of the CMYK colors using the familiar gamma curves.

- A new Gamma Control Panel makes it much easier to calibrate your monitor and even generates an ICC profile with the settings you select.

What are ICC Profiles?

ICC Profiles are color profiles written in a standard format defined by the ICC (International Color Consortium). These profiles, which are cross-platform and nonproprietary, can be read by all ICC-compatible software applications, which includes Photoshop. Color profiles are created for devices such as scanners, digital cameras, printers, and monitors. Prior to the introduction of ICC Profiles, color profiles in general had to be created for each device relationship. For example: If you had a scanner and two printers, you needed two profiles to relate the color space of the scanner with each of the two printers. If you had two scanners and three printers, you would need six distinct profiles to describe the relationship of color for each pairing of the devices. Add color profiles for your monitor to this mix and they soon become unmanageable.

The beauty of the ICC Profile as opposed to these other color management profiles that deal with profiling one device with another is that the ICC profiles are device-independent. An ICC Profile converts color data from a device (such as a scanner or printer) into one of the CIE color spaces, a neutral color space that is always the same on any platform. Using this method, a single ICC Profile is required for each device rather than a profile for each pairing of devices. At this writing, ICC Profiles are gaining wide support throughout the industry and have been incorporated into virtually all the color management systems currently available.

To learn more about ICC Profiles and color management, visit the International Color Consortium Web page at www.color.org.

- The History palette is Photoshop's answer to multiple undo procedures. You can set the History palette to record up to 100 editing states. This means you can undo the last 100 things you did in Photoshop. You can also save multiple snapshots of your work in the History palette.

- The new 16-bit per channel option provides you with more flexibility when performing color correction. In short, you can store more color information per pixel (twice as much) than you could in previous versions.

- Layer Effects is a new addition to the Layers palette enabling you to apply some of your favorite effects such as drop shadows, bevels, and embossing. Specify your settings in a dialog box and attach them to the layer in one step.

- Type Layers now enable you to edit your text as many times as necessary before committing to a rasterized version. The Type dialog box offers settings for kerning, tracking, and color specification, plus the ability to use multiple fonts on a layer.

- The new Spot Color channels enable you to specify multiple spot colors that can be saved in the DCS 2.0 format. Convert your duotones to Multiple Channel mode and you'll have separate color channels for each color.

- A number of tools have been added to the Tool palette and are explained in detail later in this appendix.

- The Channel Mixer enables you to mix the values of the channels in your image to create special effects. The Channel Mixer is also available as an Adjustment Layer.

- A great improvement has been made on the number of things that can be recorded using the Actions palette, enabling you to record virtually every step you make.

- A new 3D Transform rendering filter enables you select a portion of your image and manipulate it in a 3D space.

- With the new file format additions, you can import and export Flashpix format files and import any PDF file. Special support has been added to import multipage PDF files when using the **Automate** command under the **File** menu.

- Transformation tools are now located under the **Edit** menu instead of the **Layers** menu. A new **Transform** command under the **Select** menu enables you transform selections. You can even transform paths using the same transformation tools under the **Edit** menu.

Color Management

Photoshop 5 has enhanced color management support with several key feature changes and additions. The Monitor Setup dialog box has been eliminated from this version of Photoshop. For the MacOS, Photoshop gets its information about the monitor color space from Apple's ColorSync. The ColorSync Control Panel on the MacOS supports ICC profiles and enables you to specify a monitor setup that can be used by multiple software applications. Under Windows 95/98/NT, the monitor color space is controlled by the Gamma Control Panel provided with Photoshop. The use and implementation of ICC Profiles is the biggest change to color management in Photoshop 5, though you can opt to disable the color management features. I strongly recommend investing some time in learning about color management and ICC Profiles so you can take full advantage of these dynamic features.

Color Settings

Color Settings dialog boxes have been improved throughout Photoshop to improve color management and selection. You now have four choices when you choose **Color Settings** under the **File** menu: **RGB Setup**, **CMYK Setup**, **Grayscale Setup**, and **Profile Setup**. The **RGB Setup** controls the way your monitor displays colors and enables you to specify the conditions you are working in, as well as the type of monitor you are using. The **CMYK Setup** provides the settings for converting to the CMYK color space. The **Grayscale Setup** enables you choose how you want grayscale images to behave (using RGB gray levels or Black Ink percentages).

What is dot gain?

Dot gain is the increase in size of a printed 50% halftone dot. Dot gain can occur due to a variety of factors, but we're primarily concerned with the difference in dot size between the film and the printed piece. Dot gain results in a printed piece appearing darker than the film, typically between 10% and 20% darker. We determine dot gain by measuring the size of the 50% printed halftone dot. If the 50% dot prints as a 70% dot, we know we have 20% dot gain. Dot gain varies from press to press and is affected by the type of paper and ink used. Because dot gain affects the midtone areas of an image more than the highlights and shadows, the best way to compensate for it is using an adjustment curve. In Photoshop, we can compensate for dot gain by reducing the size of the dot on the film so it ends up being the right size on the printed piece. In CMYK printing, the dot gain can vary among the four process colors. In the CMYK Setup dialog box in Photoshop, we can specify dot gain compensation for each of the four process colors independently or apply a single compensation for all four. Be sure you know what you're doing and have spoken to your printer before trying your hand at dot gain compensation.

The RGB and CMYK color spaces can be specified using ICC Profiles. This means you can specify an ICC color profile for the type of monitor you're using as well as the profile for the CMYK printer you're printing to. Using these profiles, you can closely match the color you see on your monitor with the colors that will be printed to a particular printer. Aside from specifying the monitor RGB, you can also specify an RGB model different from that of your particular monitor to help you match the RGB color space of other monitors and other computer platforms.

Images can be saved with ICC tags that will be applied when the image is opened again in Photoshop or other applications that support ICC Profiles. In the Profile Setup dialog box, you choose whether to attach ICC Profile tags to your images. You can further specify how Photoshop handles opening files that contain ICC Profile tags (see Figure A.1). When ICC is not used to define CMYK values, Dot Gain Curves defined in the CMYK setup dialog box are used.

FIGURE **A.1**

The ICC Profile Setup dialog box enables you to specify when and how ICC Profiles are implemented.

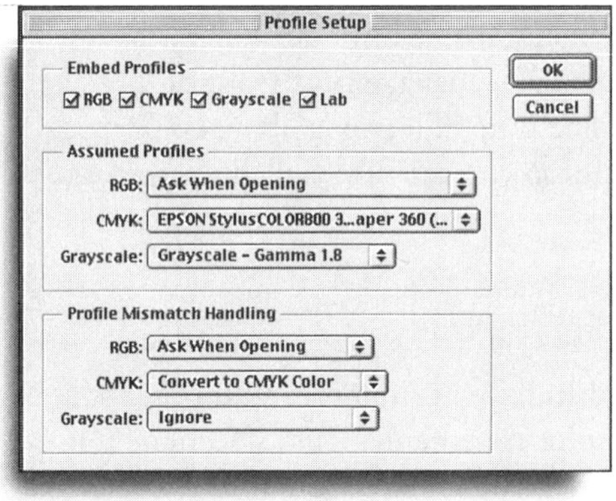

SEE ALSO
➤ *For specific information on color settings, see page 115*

The Gamma Control Panel

The Gamma Control Panel has been improved and in many ways simplified to help you calibrate your monitor and define an ICC Profile for your monitor. You can specify the monitor information using a single dialog box, like you did in previous versions (see Figure A.2). You can also perform the calibration process using a step-by-step (assistant) method that guides you through the necessary steps (see Figure A.3).

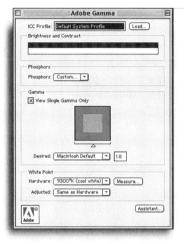

FIGURE A.2

Define your monitor and working environment specifications using the Gamma Control Panel. Click the **Assistant** button in the lower-right corner to use the step-by-step assistant.

FIGURE A.3

If you're not sure how to specify the values in the single Gamma Control Panel, choose the **Step By Step (Assistant)**.

The History Palette

One of the long-standing feature requests for Photoshop was for a multiple undo feature. Adobe bettered the multiple undo option with the new History palette (see Figure A.4).

The History palette keeps track of the changes you make and enables you to go back as many as 100 steps. Note the stored snapshots at the top of the palette.

Why do I need 16-bit color?

The capability to describe each pixels color value with 16 bits of binary data means that an RGB pixel contains 48 bits and a CMYK pixel contains 64 bits of data. Color monitors are capable of displaying only a maximum of 24 bits of data per pixel, so you can't actually see the additional colors provided by the 48 bits. Postscript output devices such as printers and imagesetters can only handle 8 bits of data per pixel per color, so you can't actually print a 64-bit CMYK image. So why, you ask, bother with 16-bit color?

The additional bits per pixel provide you with extra working space when making color corrections and adjustments. In some cases, it can prevent adverse effects such as posterization and flattening of an image while you're making adjustments. In the end, you need an image that contains 8 bits per channel to print, and Photoshop does a nice job of converting the 16-bit data to 8-bit data. Some scanners can capture 16-bit data, enabling you to work on an image with a wide dynamic color range before converting it to 8 bits for printing. Of course, you're scanner plug-in must also support 16 bits.

- As you edit, the History palette displays a listing of the most recent changes you made to the image. You can click on any editing step to revert to that stage of your editing session. You can also drag the slider bar in the palette to move forward or backward.

- You can create snapshots of the image at any state to "store" the image. This snapshot can be used as a fallback for future revisions.

- You can use the History Brush to "paint the history palette." This enables you to create powerful and creative effects melding different states of an image.

16-Bit Channel Support

Photoshop now supports 16-bit channels. This means that each pixel in your image is described by 16 bits of binary data for each color channel instead of the standard 8 bits. Although not many output devices can handle 16-bit color images, the additional color information does offer more flexibility when making color corrections and adjustments. This empowers you with more flexibility with detailed and high-resolution imagery.

- Support for 64-bit CMYK images means that each of the process colors can be described using 16 bits of binary information per pixel. Keep in mind that when you save the image to be printed to a PostScript device, you end up with 8 bits per pixel per color or a 32-bit CMYK image.

- Hue/Saturation, Brightness/Contrast, Color Balance, Equalize, Invert, and the Channel Mixer now also support 16-bit channels in images.

- Images with 16-bit channels can be edited using the Crop, Rubber Stamp, and History Brush tools. You can also resize 16-bit images using the Image Size dialog box and rotate them using the **Arbitrary** setting of the **Rotate Canvas** command, both located under the **Image** menu.

Layer Effects

Layers were the incredible new addition to Photoshop in version 3.0. Photoshop 4.0 enhanced this feature with the inclusion of adjustment layers. Photoshop 5.0 extends layers even further by introducing layer effects. Layer effects give you several "out of the box" effects that you can carry out on a selected layer. These effects are applied dynamically and are attached to the layer. You have the option of keeping the effect attached to the layer or breaking it out onto its own layer for further manipulation and control. It is now a simple matter of entering values in a dialog box to create these special effects. You can also combine the effects into a single effect for a layer. From the **Layer** menu choose **Effects** to specify the layer effects (see Figure A.5). Here are the five layer effects available in Photoshop:

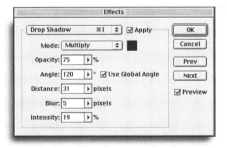

FIGURE A.5
The Layer Effects dialog box.

- **Drop Shadow**
- **Inner Shadow**
- **Outer Glow**

- **Inner Glow**
- **Bevel and Emboss** (including **Inner/Outer Bevel**, **Emboss and Pillow Emboss**)

SEE ALSO

➤ *For more information on layer effects, see page 149*

New Tools

In addition to new features, Photoshop 5 also includes several new and enhanced tools. These tools address frequently requested improvements to Photoshop by users of all backgrounds. Here are the new tools:

- *Color Sampler.* This tool enables you to place up to four samplers in an image to give persistent before and after color readouts in the Info palette for multiple locations in the image.
- *Magnetic Lasso and Magnetic Pen.* The magnetic tools intelligently snap to the edges of an image, allowing you to define new selections or paths as you drag.
- *Freeform Pen.* Creating paths with the Freeform Pen is just like dragging the Lasso tool. You can now create freeform paths in a snap!
- *Measure tool.* The Measure tool acts like a ruler, enabling you to measure distances and angles between points in an image.
- *Vertical Type and Type Mask.* Creating vertical type and vertical type masks is no longer an arduous task. By selecting either of these tools, text is created vertically.
- *Pattern Stamp.* To improve on the Rubber Stamp's "from pattern" setting in previous versions, Photoshop 5.0 introduces the Pattern Stamp that is singularly suited for painting with defined patterns in an image.
- *History Brush.* Using the History Palette as its source, the History Brush paints from a previous edit state to create interesting and powerful effects. This tool replaces the Paint from Saved and Paint from Snapshot options in previous versions of Photoshop.

- *Gradient tool.* This tool has been improved to pop up with the original gradient types, as well as new angular, diamond, and reflected gradient types. Gradients also now have less banding and can reverse the direction of gradient colors.

Type Layers

Photoshop's Type features have drastically changed in 5.0. The Type tools now create re-editable type layers, which enable you to change the contents of the layer at any time. Type layers can be horizontally or vertically oriented and can be "rendered" complete when the layer meets with your approval. The Type Tool dialog box offers many new features, as well as the ability to preview and move the text on your image while the dialog box is open (see Figure A.6):

FIGURE **A.6**
The Type Tool dialog box.

- Photoshop 5 now has powerful support for kerning and tracking, as well as an **Auto Kern** feature. It also has improved handling of leading and has added a baseline shift option.

- Multiple fonts and font styles can be selected in an individual type layer.

- All editing in the Type Tool dialog is previewed live in the image, with the ability to reposition the text with the dialog box open. The dialog box is also resizable and zoomable.

- The orientation of text can be toggled between horizontal and vertical. Vertical type can be rotated.
- Type layers can be free transformed and can take advantage of layer effects. Additional editing on the type can be carried out by rasterizing the text into a regular layer.

SEE ALSO

➤ *For more information on type layers, see page 147*

New Adjustments/Adjustment Layers

Improvements have been made to the adjustment layers as well as to the image adjustment dialog boxes in the **Adjust** submenu under the **Image** menu.

Hue/Saturation Dialog Box Changes

An improved Hue/Saturation dialog box now enables you to specify a range of colors to adjust via an expandable slider between the color bars (see Figure A.7). Color can be selected using the color bar interface or by clicking in the image window.

FIGURE A.7

The Hue/Saturation dialog box depicting the expandable color selection slider between the two color bars.

SEE ALSO

➤ *For more information on Hue/Saturation, see page 536*

The Channel Mixer

The Channel Mixer enables you to mix and balance the available color channels for your image (see Figure A.8). You can, for example, take some of the information on the **Red** channel and put it on the **Blue** channel to create a special effect.

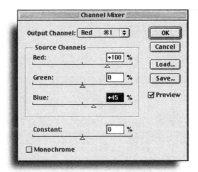

FIGURE A.8
The Channel Mixer dialog box.

SEE ALSO

➤ *For more information on the Channel Mixer, see Page 532*

Spot Color Support

Spot Color channels can be added to an image using the Channels palette. When created, the Spot Color channels can be merged into existing CMYK or RGB channels. If you save a CMYK image that also contains Spot Color channels in the DCS 2.0 file format, the Spot Color channels can be separated to individual plates when printing. When a Monotone, Duotone, Tritone, or Quadtone is converted to Multichannel mode, the colors are represented on individual Spot channels.

Improved Scriptability

Photoshop 4 introduced scriptability to Photoshop with the Actions palette, though with many limitations as to what could be recorded. Photoshop 5 greatly expands the number of record-able actions to include the following:

- Paths palette
- Layers palette
- History palette
- Gradient tool

- Marquee tool
- Crop tool
- Polygon and Lasso tool
- Line tool
- Move tool
- Magic Wand tool
- Paint Bucket tool
- Type tool
- Lighting Effects
- Calculations
- Apply Image
- File Info
- Switching and Selecting documents
- Free Transforms

Aside from the additions listed here, the current measurement units set in the preferences are used when recording actions. When the measurement units are set to the new **Percent** setting, relative positions are recorded in the action. More menu commands are accessible when you choose **Insert Menu Item** from the Actions palette menu.

SEE ALSO

➤ *For more information on Actions, refer to page 162*

Actions Plug-Ins

Support has been added for a new Actions plug-in type that controls the functionality of Photoshop and provides a method to automate complicated tasks and workflow. All Actions plug-ins are located in the **Help** menu or the **Automate** submenu under the **File** menu. The plug-ins provided with Photoshop include the following:

- On the **Help** menu, the **Resize Image** option helps you to resize an image based on the desire output specifications.

- On the **Help** menu, the **Export Image with Transparency** option enables you to export an image in EPS, PNG, or GIF format while specifying a clipping path, Alpha channel, or transparency color to create transparent areas in the image.

- The **Batch** command located in the **Automate** submenu under the **File** menu replaces the **Batch** command formerly located in the Actions palette. Enhancements have been added to include the logging of program errors during a batch.

- From the **File** menu, choose **Automate** and then select **Conditional Mode Change** to change the color mode of the image based on the mode it's already in. This command is handy for changing the color mode as the first step of an action that requires a specific color mode.

- The **Contact Sheet** command located in the **Automate** submenu under the **File** menu creates a thumbnail contact sheet of all the images in a specified folder. You control the size of the thumbnails and number of thumbnails per page.

- From the **File** menu, choose **Automate** and then select **Fit Image** to fit an image into a specific space without changing its aspect ratio.

- From the **File** menu, choose **Automate** and then select **Multi-page PDF to PSD** to convert a PDF file that contains multiple pages into multiple Photoshop files.

3D Transform

Portions of images can now be selected and manipulated as if they were 3D objects. The 3D Transform filter enables you to create clever images from a 2D image source and represent it in three-dimensional form. The resulting image remains two-dimensional and is "rendered" into the image. From the **Filter** menu, choose **Render** and then select **3D Transform** to display the 3D Transform dialog box (see Figure A.9).

SEE ALSO

➤ *For more information on Photoshop Filters, see page 386*

File Format Additions

Adobe continues its support of standard and popular image formats by adding support for the following:

- Importing and exporting Flashpix images.
- Import and rasterization of any Adobe Acrobat (PDF) file. This includes multipage PDF files.
- Saving of PDF files, including control over the JPEG and ZIP compression levels.
- DCS 2.0 support can save separations in a single file and include Alpha/Spot channels. Photoshop 5 now supports DCS 1.0 and 2.0 as separate file formats.

Transformation Improvements

A center point for rotation has now been added to Free Transform. The center point can be moved around to select the anchor point for rotation. The Free Transform option enables you to repeat the last transformation settings, as well as transform selections and paths. All transform commands are now conveniently located in the **Edit** menu, with the exception of the **Transform Selection** command that is located in the **Select** menu.

FIGURE A.10

The movable center point (depicted in lower-left corner of selection) enables you to anchor your transformations anywhere you like.

SEE ALSO

➤ *For more information on transforming selections, see page 268*

Other New Features

Scattered among the new features are several new additions that are not easily categorized.

- From the **View** menu, when you choose **Preview**, separate preview modes for individual CMYK plates as well as CMYK composite preview are available.

- Photoshop 5 has improved the quality of 8-bit RGB to CMYK conversions. When converting to Indexed Color mode, the Adaptive palette choice produces improved results. A **Best Quality** option is now available for indexed color conversions as well.

- Indexed color dithering includes a **Preserve Exact Colors** option. This means that colors in the image that are also in the palette will not be dithered. This preserves fine lines and text for images—ideal for the Web.

- New **Alignment** and **Distribution** options have been added to the **Layers** menu to enable you to align and distribute linked layers. Layers are aligned to or distributed around a selection if one is present.

- From the **Select** menu, choose **Reselect** to restore the previous selection marquee.

- The dialog box for Indexed Color conversion has been improved and now includes a **Preview** check box so you can see the affect your choices will have on the image.

- You can now specify a lowercase three-character extension in the **Saving Files** preference. This is helpful when saving files for UNIX Web servers that require all lowercase letters in file names. Faster saving of large files that include thumbnails has been added, and you can now save MacOS and Windows thumbnails independently.

Improvements and Changes

With all of new features, there comes some change and improvements to some of the previously introduced features and tools. These improvements and changes have been added to accommodate frequently requested suggestions and new features included in this version.

- Improved and more complete Windows help for tools. Tools also now show a **Cancel** sign when they cannot be used. If a canceled tool is used, a single click causes a beep whereas a double-click will tell why.

- Space bar, hand scrolling, and -/+ zoom in/out behavior has been added to all dragging-based selection tools. This includes the Lasso, Polygon Lasso, Magnetic Lasso, Magnetic Pen, and Freeform Pen.

- Enhancements have been made to several menus and dialog boxes to accommodate other changes made in this version.

New and Changed Keyboard Shortcuts

With each new version of Photoshop comes new keyboard shortcuts. Several new shortcuts have been added in this version, in addition to changes to the existing ones.

- *Page Up and Page Down*. Move up and down by screenful.
- *Shift Page Up and Shift Page Down*. Move up and down by 10-unit increments (depends on measurement units).
- (Ctrl)[Command] *Page Up and Cmd/Ctrl Page Down*. Move left and right by screenful.
- *(Shift+Ctrl) [Shift+Command] Page Up and (Shift+Ctrl) [Shift+Command] Page Down*. Move left and right by 10 units.
- (Ctrl+Shift+T) [Command+Shift+T] . Repeat last transformation.
- (Ctrl+Shift+Z) [Command+Shift+Z]. Previous history entry.
- (Ctrl+Alt+Z) [Command+Option+Z]. Next history entry.
- (Ctrl+Alt+D) [Command+Option+D]. Reselect.
- =. Selects the Pen Add Knot tool (the Pen tool with the plus sign).
- -. Selects the Pen Delete Knot tool (the Pen tool with the minus sign).
- *J*. Airbrush tool shortcut (formerly *A*).
- *A*. Direct Selection tool.

The Pen tool shortcut keys are now the same as Adobe Illustrator, for consistency. Tool shortcut keys no longer cycle through the tool slots. You must press the Shift key to cycle through the tools in the Toolbox cells.

SEE ALSO

➤ *For specific information on color settings, see page 115*

➤ *For more information on layer effects, see page 149*

➤ *For more information on type layers, see page 177*

➤ *For more information on Hue/Saturation, see page 536*

➤ *For more information on the Channel Mixer, see Page 532*

➤ *For more information on Spot channels, refer to page 369*

➤ *For more information on Actions, refer to page 162*

➤ *For more information on Photoshop filters, see page 386*

➤ *For more information on transforming selections, see page 268*

Installing and Upgrading

B

The installation process of Photoshop 5.0 is straightforward and uncluttered. It provides you with an opportunity to select the components that will be beneficial to you in your use of Photoshop. Not all users require all features, so you can take advantage of this appendix for information on installing Photoshop to suit your needs. And if you already have an existing Photoshop installation that you want to upgrade to Photoshop 5.0, this appendix also provides information on such a task.

Installing Photoshop 5.0 from Scratch

To begin a clean installation of Photoshop 5.0, you must open the Photoshop 5.0 Setup program. This program installs Photoshop and its related files onto your system.

Install Photoshop 5.0

1. Insert your installation media (presumably CD-ROM) and open the SETUP.EXE program on Windows, the Install Adobe Photoshop application on MacOS.

2. The Adobe Photoshop 5.0 Setup program appears, as shown in Figure B.1. Click **Next** to proceed.

FIGURE B.1

The Photoshop 5.0 Setup program handles the installation process for the software.

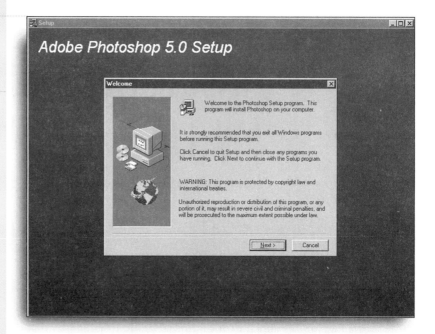

3. The Setup program prompts you to select the country in which you purchased the software from. Select the check box for the country you purchased the software in.

4. Click the **Next** button to proceed. The Software License Agreement dialog box (Figure B.2) appears for you to review the licensing agreement for Photoshop 5.0.

5. Click **Accept** if you agree to the license agreement. If you do not agree to the agreement, click the **Decline** button to cancel the installation. The Setup Type dialog box appears, as shown in Figure B.3.

6. Select the type of installation you want to use for Photoshop. Your options for Windows are: **Typical**, **Compact**, and **Custom**. The MacOS offers two choices: **Easy Install** and **Custom Install**.

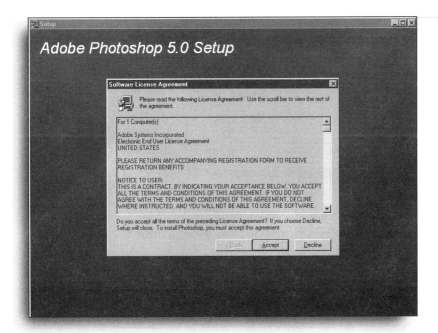

FIGURE B.2

The Software License Agreement states the licensing rules and obligations for Photoshop 5.0.

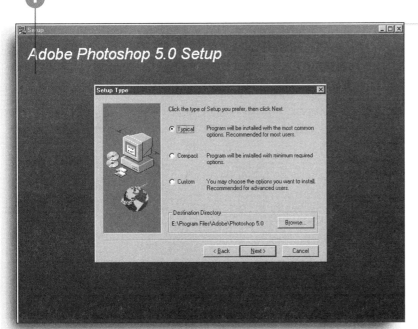

FIGURE B.3

Use the Setup Type dialog box to select the type of installation you want to use for Photoshop 5.0. You can also specify a destination directory at this point.

1 Windows

2 MacOS

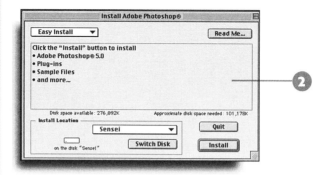

7. Select a destination directory for your Photoshop 5.0 Setup by using the **Browse** button. You might choose to accept the default installation directory of **<System Root>:\Program Files\Adobe\Photoshop 5.0** for Windows or the **Startup Disk** on the MacOS.

8. Click the **Next** button to proceed. If you chose to install either the **Typical** or **Compact** Setup on Windows or the **Easy Install** on MacOS, move to step 11.

9. If you selected a **Custom** installation, you are prompted to select the components you want to install (Figure B.4). Deselect the options you do not want to install. Refer to "Installation Options" later in the Appendix for a description of each option.

10. Click the **Next** button to proceed.

11. The User Information dialog box, shown in Figure B.5, appears and prompts you for your name, company name, and Photoshop 5.0 serial number. Enter the information into this dialog box and click the **Next** button.

12. If an invalid serial number is provided, you receive an error message such as the one shown in Figure B.6. Otherwise, the Setup program proceeds to install the software onto your workstation.

FIGURE B.4

The Select Components dialog box appears when you choose a **Custom** Setup type. This enables you to pick and choose what is installed with Photoshop.

1 Windows

2 MacOS

FIGURE B.5

You must enter a valid serial number for Photoshop 5.0 into the User Information dialog box. Serial numbers for previous versions do not work here!

FIGURE B.6

An incorrect serial number receives a distinctive error.

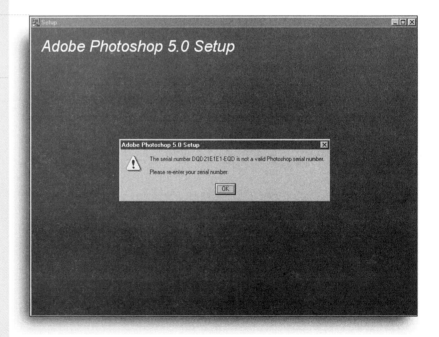

13. After the Setup program is complete, the Setup program informs you that it has completed the installation process. It also gives you the option to read the Read Me file for recent news on Photoshop. On the MacOS, the Read Me file is presented at the start of the installation process at which point you can read it and continue the installation or print it and read it later. The Read Me file is saved on the hard drive as part of the installation for both Windows and MacOS platforms. Click **Finish** to close the Setup program. On the MacOS, after the installation is complete, you are prompted to enter registration information that can be submitted via the Internet or printed to a printer. Click the **Cancel** button here if you want to finish the installation and register later.

Upgrading an Existing Photoshop Installation

Upgrading from a previous version of Photoshop to version 5.0 is simplicity in itself with the Photoshop 5.0 Upgrade Setup program. This program verifies your previous installation or older installation media and proceeds to install Photoshop 5.0 on your workstation.

Upgrade existing installation

1. Insert your upgrade installation media (presumably CD-ROM) and open the SETUP program for Windows or the Install Photoshop 5.0 application for MacOS.

2. The Adobe Photoshop 5.0 Setup program appears. Click **Next** to proceed.

3. The Setup program prompts you on how you want to verify your existing copy of Photoshop on Windows, shown in Figure B.7. From the radio buttons, select how you want to verify your legitimate copy of Photoshop. The MacOS automatically searches all installed hard drives for other versions of Photoshop.

The Upgrade Setup program verifies an existing copy of Photoshop from either a prior installation or the original installation media.

The Photoshop 5.0 Upgrade Setup program for Windows provides you with three different options to verify your ownership of an existing Photoshop version:

- *Search hard drive(s) for prior installation.* This instructs the Setup program to search your local hard disk drives for an existing installation of Photoshop 4.01 or lower.

- *Search a specific folder for prior installation.* This enables you to instruct the Setup program to look in a specific folder for an existing installation of Photoshop 4.01 or lower.

- *Verify original Photoshop diskette or CD.* If you do not have your original Photoshop version installed, you can still install 5.0 by verifying from the original installation media for Photoshop 4.01 or lower.

4. Click **Next** to proceed to the verification of your previous version on Windows. Depending on which method you selected, you might be prompted to either select an existing installation directory or insert the original installation media into your floppy diskette or CD-ROM drive. On the

MacOS, if the installer does not find a valid copy of Photoshop on your hard drive, you are prompted to insert the original installation media for a previous or current version.

5. After verifying your original Photoshop version, the Setup program prompts you to select the country in which you purchased the software from. Select the check box for the country you purchased the software in.

6. Click the **Next** button to proceed. The Software License Agreement dialog box appears for you to review the licensing agreement for Photoshop 5.0.

7. Click **Next** if you agree to the license agreement. If you do not agree to the agreement, click the **Decline** button to cancel the installation. The Setup Type dialog appears, as shown in Figure B.3.

8. Select the type of installation you want to use for Photoshop. Your options for Windows are: **Typical**, **Compact**, and **Custom**. The MacOS offers two options: **Easy Install** and **Custom Install**.

9. Select a destination directory for your Photoshop 5.0 Setup by using the **Browse** button. You might choose to accept the default installation directory of **<System Root>:\Program Files\Adobe\Photoshop 5.0 for Windows** or the **Startup disk on the MacOS**.

10. Click the **Next** button to proceed.

11. If you selected a **Custom** installation, you are prompted to select the components you want to install. Deselect the options you do not want to install. Refer to "Installation Options" later in the Appendix for a description of each option.

12. After you finish deciding what you want to install, click the **Next** button to confirm your selections.

13. The User Information dialog box, shown in Figure B.5, appears and prompts you for your name, company name, and Photoshop 5.0 serial number. Enter the information into this dialog box and click the **Next** button.

14. If an invalid serial number is provided, you receive an error message such as the one shown in Figure B.6. Otherwise, the Setup program proceeds to install the software onto your workstation.

15. After the Setup program is complete, the Setup program informs you that it has completed the installation process. It also gives you the option to read the Read Me file for recent news on Photoshop. Click **Finish** to close the Setup program.

16. The Setup program completes your installation. When finished, you are prompted if you want to read the Photoshop 5.0 Read Me file. On the MacOS, the Read Me file is presented at the start of the installation process at which point you can read it and continue the installation or print it and read it later. The Read Me file is saved on the hard drive as part of the installation for both Windows and MacOS platforms. To finish, click the **Finish** button.

Installation Options

The Photoshop Setup program provides you with several options and different components. These components each represent a different set of files that compliment certain features of Photoshop 5.0:

- *Program Files.* The Photoshop executable file and its related resource files are part of this component. This component must be installed to use Photoshop.

- *ICC Profiles.* The Kodak ICC Color Management modules let you build color separation tables based on the profiles of different color printers and output devices.

- *Samples Files.* The Sample Files component contains several sample images created in Photoshop to showcase its capabilities. You can use these images for inspiration and reference.

- *Duotone Files.* With this component selected, Duotone, Tritone, and Quadtone files are installed for print work to increase the tonal range of a grayscale and monochromatic images.

- *Filter Files*. The full assortment of Adobe Gallery Effects and standard Photoshop filters that can be used to create effects on your images. Filters enable you to enhance your image through automated processes and features.

- *Adobe Online Files*. Photoshop 5.0 has direct links to Adobe Online Web sites related to Photoshop. With these files installed, Photoshop 5.0 can interact with these sites and connect you to their resources, assuming you have access to the Internet from your computer.

- *Brushes Files*. Photoshop provides you with a compliment of custom brushes that you can use in your work.

- *Patterns Files*. As with brushes, the Patterns files give you a variety of different patterns that you can use when creating or modifying images.

- *CMap Files*. Installs the CMap files required for CJK double-byte fonts.

- *Fonts*. Adobe's standard compliment of fonts that are included with Photoshop 5.0. These high-quality fonts can be used in your own work, royalty free.

Troubleshooting

Throughout your time using Photoshop 5.0, you are bound to experience a few problems. This appendix has been created to give you some basic troubleshooting information for a variety of different scenarios. The troubleshooting information has been divided into a few key topics:

- *Installation Issues*. Experiencing problems installing Photoshop onto your workstation? This topic provides information on common installation problems.

- *Problems with Program Operation*. If Photoshop is stubborn and refuses to work properly, this is the topic for you. Program errors and global issues are documented here.

- *Using Tools*. Each Photoshop tool has its own quirks and oddities that might confound you. Here are some tips and troubleshooting notes on using individual tools in the program.

- *Filter Problems*. With the power of filters can come the complexities and issues of add-ons. Familiarize yourself with filter troubleshooting to make sure that you get the result you want.

- *Working through Actions and History*. Actions and History do not always work how we want them to. It is important to understand how to work through problems with these two features.

Access Adobe Online

You can access Adobe Online by pressing the graphic at the top of the toolbar. This service delivers updated information to your computer.

- *Problems with Input Devices.* Mice, tablets, scanners...all varieties of input devices can cause problems in Photoshop. This last topic covers useful information when dealing with different devices.

Installation Issues

Problem: The Photoshop Setup program tells me I entered an Invalid or Incorrect Serial Number.

Solution: It is important that you enter the correct serial number for Photoshop 5.0 when prompted. A serial number for a previous version will not work with version 5.0. Make sure that you enter the number that came with your software.

Problem: The Photoshop Setup program tells me I do not have enough disk space.

Solution: Photoshop requires approximately 67 megabytes for a complete installation. Always make sure that you have sufficient room for the program, for your operating system swap files, and for Photoshop's own swap file.

Problem: The Photoshop Upgrade Setup program tells me that a qualifying version of Photoshop was not detected.

Solution: When upgrading from a previous release of Photoshop, you must either have the previous version (4.01 or lower) installed on your workstation or you must provide your original installation media. Make sure that you either have a working copy of Photoshop 4.01 or lower installed or insert your original installation diskette or CD-ROM when prompted.

Readme!

Be sure to read any information that comes on the Photoshop 5 CD-ROM prior to installing the software.

Problem: **The Photoshop Setup program tells me a file is in use.**

Solution: As with all installation programs, always make sure that you have exited any running programs before proceeding with the installation. If the Photoshop Setup program attempts to copy a file to your workstation that is already in use by another program, the Setup program will not continue properly. Always close all running programs before beginning the installation.

Problems with Program Operation

Problem: **My computer says that it cannot find PHOTOSHP.EXE** (the Photoshop executable file) **when I choose the Photoshop icon from the Start menu. (Windows users)**

Solution: If the Setup program did not properly complete its installation or files have been moved or removed from your workstation, the shortcut to the Photoshop program might not function properly. Make sure that you do indeed have a PHOTOSHP.EXE file on your workstation in the proper directory. You may need to reinstall Photoshop to recreate the necessary files and shortcuts.

Problem: **I'm getting one of the following errors: PHOTOSHP caused a General Protection Fault, PHOTO-SHP caused an Invalid Page Fault, Application Error, Unhandled Exception detected, Illegal**

Instruction, Segment load failure. (Windows users)

Solution: Although a system error might appear to only occur in Photoshop, this does not necessarily mean that Photoshop is to blame. Memory conflicts between device drivers, software, and hardware can cause significant problems in many programs. Photoshop might just be the only application that is memory-or processor-intensive enough to cause the fundamental problem to manifest itself. One of the first things that you should do is exit all other programs and reduce the possibility of contention between resources. This might include disabling certain device drivers or system programs. Always make sure that Photoshop has enough free room with resources (RAM, physical hard disk, CPU) so that it does not have to struggle to perform. Also insure that your system does not have any hardware conflicts that might cause such problems. Finally, you uninstall Photoshop and reinstall it with your system in "Safe mode" to minimize conflicts. This insures that Photoshop is installed correctly.

Problem: **I'm getting a "Scratch disk is full" error.**

Solution: When working with large images, Photoshop uses a scratch disk to temporarily store data. The scratch disk requires suitable space to store this data. Make sure that the scratch disk you specified in the Preferences dialog box has enough free space to complete your action. You may need to clean up some space on the scratch disk or switch the scratch disk to another physical drive if possible.

Problem: **My files of a certain image type are no longer recognized by Photoshop from the Explorer. (Windows users)**

Solution: Often file extensions on Windows machines are shared between different file types. When a program is installed after Photoshop, sometimes these file types are associated with a different program for a different file type. You might need to re-create your file associations.

Problem: **I'm running out of memory. Operations are taking a long time and I'm getting error messages.**

Solution: Photoshop is hardly a friendly beast when it comes to memory consumption. If you run out of memory or the program slows down a lot after working for a certain amount of time, you can do two things: Use the **Edit, Purge** function to clear up Photoshop's RAM storage. Secondly, you can customize Photoshop's memory and scratch disk usage from the **File**, Preferences dialog box. You can also limit the History feature to minimize its rather blatant memory consumption.

Problem: **I'm trying to save an image in a particular format, however the Save As dialog box does not list that file type.**

Solution: File types when saving a file are based on what mode you are working in. If you are working in RGB mode with layers, you will not see all available file types when saving your image. Make sure to flatten images before saving to a format other than Photoshop's own .PSD format. Additionally, make sure that the corresponding file format plug-in is located in the Photoshop Plug-ins directory. If you are in doubt, you might want to reinstall Photoshop to make sure that all required files are present. Also, a file format such as a .GIF must be saved by going through **File**, **Export** as opposed to Save or **Save As**.

Problem: **When I try to open Photoshop, I get a "Could not initialize Photoshop due to a disk error" message.**

Solution: Sometimes Photoshop's preferences file becomes corrupted, particularly with Macintoshes. You might need to delete the Photoshop preference file to get into Photoshop again. Unfortunately, deleting the Photoshop preference file restores Photoshop's default preferences and custom settings. This error might also indicate problems with your hard disk drive. Use disk repair software such as Scandisk under Windows or Norton Disk Doctor on a Macintosh to examine your hard drive and repair any errors.

Problem: **When opening a file, I get an error that says "This document has been damaged by a disk error."**

Solution: In the event of a disk problem, your images might be corrupted and unreadable by Photoshop. Photoshop does typically give the option to open the document anyway, but you might see screen artifacting or unreadable images. This typically happens due to a defective media (disk drive, hard disk drive, and so on), a defective SCSI cable, or incorrect

SCSI termination. Make sure that your media is functioning properly before attempting to re-open the file.

Problem: **Opening an image takes a REALLY long time.**

Solution: Many images are simply too large to be loaded quickly by Photoshop. You can streamline the process by making sure that your images are a reasonable size. If this is not a possibility, make sure that Photoshop has ample resources available to it. Also, you can diminish Photoshop's redraw performance to improve speed in opening images. From the Preferences dialog box, select **Image Cache**. Enter 1 into the **Cache Levels** text box and restart Photoshop. Additionally, some filters and plug-ins might cause extended load times. Consider removing plug-ins through the process of elimination to make sure that they are not causing the problem.

Problem: **Some menu items are missing from the menu bar!**

Solution: On rare occasions, menu items might be missing due to multiple removable drives connected via SCSI on one machine. Remove any extra removable drives and restart Photoshop.

Problem: **When trying to open an image I saved, I get an error "Could not open <filename> because the file-format module cannot parse the file."**

Solution: If you changed an extension on a file but did not change to the corresponding file type when saving, the file is still saved as a Photoshop .PSD file with a different extension. Rename the file to a .PSD extension and try to open the file. It is possible that the file itself is corrupt however.

Problem: **My familiar keyboard shortcuts don't work!**

Solution: There have been changes in the Photoshop 5.0 keyboard shortcuts. Become familiar with the new shortcuts by taking a look at the tear card in the front of the book.

Problem: **Photoshop complains that an existing copy is in use on the network when I try to open it.**

Solution: Photoshop 5.0 only allows one machine on a local area network with the same serial number to operate at one time. To use Photoshop 5.0 simultaneously on more than one machine, you require additional licenses for each copy.

Using Tools

Problem: **My painting tools don't work.**

Solution: When working with painting tools, it is important to remember that they work only on the target layer and inside the current selection. Make sure that you are not painting outside of an active selection and that you are working on the correct layer.

Problem: **I'm trying to use the History Brush, but nothing seems to happen.**

Solution: When painting with the History Brush, make sure that you have made a selection in the History palette.

| Problem: | Not all type styles are available to me as they were in Photoshop 4.0. |

Solution: Photoshop 5.0 has a new type engine and relies on the existing TrueType/ATM fonts installed on your system. Photoshop no longer "creates" the styles of italic or bold for all fonts. If you are looking for a particular style to apply to a font, you need to locate a matching font file.

Filter Problems

Problem: **Plug-in filters are missing or dimmed in the Plug-ins menu.**

Solution: If the plug-in files are not located in the Plug-ins directory, they will not be available to Photoshop. Make sure that all Plug-in files are present in the proper directory. You might also have to change the Plug-ins directory in the **File**, Preferences dialog box. Finally, some filters can be used only on some images when they are in a particular mode (typically RGB). Make sure that you are in the proper mode when trying to apply a filter. On rare occasions, the Photoshop preferences file does become corrupt and prevents Photoshop from using the plug-in files. You might need to delete your Preferences file to correct this problem.

Problem: **When applying a filter, I get an error "Could not complete your request because there is not enough memory (RAM)."**

Whose filter is it?

If you installed a third-party filter and have problems with it, locate the Web site of the company or individual that created it and seek assistance.

Solution: Many filters are resource intensive. They not only require considerable CPU but also a hefty amount of RAM. If your machine or Photoshop itself is low on RAM, you might not be able to carry out some actions. Make sure that you have allocated enough memory to Photoshop and that no other programs are competing with Photoshop for resources.

Problem: **My filter doesn't work like I expected it to.**

Solution: Filters can be stubborn animals, particularly when you are not familiar with them. A steadfast rule when working with filters is to make sure that you have the appropriate region of your image selected. Most filters work within a defined selection. Also take advantage of some filter's capability to real-time display how the effect will appear on your image. Finally, use History or Undo features to experiment with filters until you achieve the effect you desire.

Problem: **Some of my old filters do not work properly with Photoshop 5.0.**

Solution: Many older filters, particularly those from Photoshop 3.0, will not work properly with Photoshop 5.0. Seek out the vendor of the respective filter and see if he has a newer version compatible with Photoshop 5.0.

Problem: **I have filters in several different directories on my hard disk drive. How do I let Photoshop use them all?**

Solution: Unfortunately, all plug-ins must be located in the Photoshop plug-ins directory. You must move your different files to be located in the same physical location.

Working Through Actions and History

Problem: **I ran an action and got an error. I fixed the problem, but now when I rerun the action I don't get the desired result.**

Solution: Typically, if you know that the action in question works, this is because the action has created channels or layers but was stopped before it had a chance to delete them. When the action is run, it then goes to reuse the same layers and channels even though they were not created for that run. Before rerunning any action that has been stopped, always check your Layers and Channels palettes to see if the action has created any new layers or channels. Delete them before continuing. As a general rule, always save before running an action so that you can revert, or use the History palette to step back.

Problem: **My action fails when I try to perform a special effect or layer operation.**

Solution: The most common cause for this is the mode the image is currently in. You might need to be in RGB mode, for example, for the action to be carried out.

Visit Adobe's Web site

Make sure to visit
www.adobe.com for the latest
Photoshop 5 information and
support.

Problem: **When running an action, I get an error that says "the command 'set' is not currently available."**

Solution: Some actions require an active selection. If a selection was not made before running the action, Photoshop does not have a selection to work with and tries to save it to a channel. Before running the action, make a selection.

Problem: **When running an action, I get an error that says "the command 'hue/saturation' is not currently available."**

Solution: Many actions expect you to have an image open in RGB mode. This error occurs when an image is in Grayscale mode and the action expects it to be in RGB.

Problem: **The more I work on an image, the more Photoshop slows down.**

Solution: The History feature in Photoshop 5.0 is a demanding one. The history is recorded in the enormous native Photoshop file format, which can cause considerable slow-down the more you work. Consider setting how far back the history setting goes from the History Options dialog box, found by clicking on the arrow tab of the History palette. The default is 20 steps; however, you might want to reduce that considerably. Also remember to Purge Photoshop's RAM storage, including History, from the **Edit**, **Purge** function.

Problem: **When I delete steps in the History palette, I lose all subsequent steps.**

Solution: This is normal. The History palette is by default linear. If you delete step two out of five steps, steps three through five are removed. However, you do have the option of making the History palette nonlinear in the palette options. This can be incredibly confusing but very powerful. Consider it as more of a set of random image states that can be blended with the History Brush.

Problems with Input Devices

Problem: **My tablet doesn't seem to be working in Photoshop, but it is outside of it.**

Solution: Make sure that you have the stylus Size/Opacity/Color options checked in the Tool Option palette. Remember to turn them off when using a mouse, however, or you will get some strange non-pressure effects. Also keep in mind that some programs leave their tablet options running even after you leave the program, so you might need to restart your computer or reset your drivers for your tablet to work properly.

Problem: **I cannot use my scanner or import from my digital camera directly in Photoshop.**

Solution: Make sure that your scanner or camera software is properly installed and that you have selected the TWAIN source within Photoshop. Without the TWAIN source selected, Photoshop does not know how to speak to your device.

Problem: **I can't get the level of control over my mouse that I'd like when drawing in Photoshop.**

Solution: Keep in mind that not all mice are created equal. Many mice, especially those of the inexpensive variety, have a low resolution. If you want to work in high resolution and detail, consider a higher-quality mouse, trackball, or tablet.

Glossary

Active Color The color currently displayed as the foreground color.

Aliasing The name for the jaggies that are seen when an image doesn't contain enough information to make a smooth transition on angled or rounded edges. Also called stair-stepping because the edge may look more like a series of stairs rather than circular.

Alpha Channels Additional channels listed in the Channels palette that describe selection areas using grayscale information.

Anchor Point A point on a path that defines its shape and allows it to change direction. It is created by clicking the Pen tool.

Anti-aliasing The method of reducing jagged edges by slightly blurring the edges of shapes and text to make them appear smooth.

ASCII American Standard Code for Information Interchange. This is just a fancy way to say "text only." ASCII files can be read in word processing applications and text editors.

Baseline A typographical term describing the imaginary horizontal line that the body of a letter rests upon.

Binary The binary system is a number system comprised of two digits: 1 and 0.

Blending Modes In Photoshop, color filters that affect the blending of colors with underlying colors, typically when using the painting tools or layers.

Browser An application used to view Web pages created using the Hypertext Markup Language (HTML).

Channels Grayscale representations that show color distribution throughout the image. Can also indicate saved selections and Quick Mask areas.

Clipping Paths Paths created using the Pen tools in Photoshop to silhouette an image for inclusion in a page layout program such as PageMaker or QuarkXPress.

Cloning The act of duplicating part of an image by setting a reference point and brushing it into the image.

CLUT Color LookUp Table. A color table used to match colors from one color space to another. In the case of scanners, density values are matched with their corresponding RGB color to create an editable image. CLUT is also used to describe a color table that is saved to disk for future reference.

CMYK An acronym for Cyan, Magenta, Yellow, and Black, the four colors that printers use to create full-color documents and images.

Color Cast The overall change in hue that is created by the usually unintentional addition of another hue.

Color Model The model used to depict a particular set of colors, such as the RGB Color Model that depicts all the colors available using Red, Green, and Blue light.

Color Table A table that contains all of the colors used in an image. Color Tables are primarily used for indexed color images and can contain up to 256 colors.

Compositing Combining multiple images to create a single image.

Contrast The difference in distance between the highlight and shadow values in an image.

Corner Point A point that changes a path direction 90 degrees.

Despeckle A method of removing noise from an image by detecting areas of high-color contrast and blurring the edges between them.

Digital Camera A camera that captures images to a hard disk or memory card inside the camera. The images can then be uploaded to a computer hard disk.

Dot Gain The change in size of a printed dot from film to the printed sheet. Indicated as a percentage and measured on the 50% printed dot.

DPI Dots Per Inch. The resolution of input devices such as scanners and digital cameras, as well as the resolution of output devices such as Laser printers and Imagesetters.

Drop Shadow A shadow placed behind text or other image elements to create the effect of three dimensions.

Duotone An image that is comprised of two colors, each color representing a portion of the image's grayscale values.

EPS File An image file format that stands for Encapsulated Postscript.

Feather The creation of a soft edge along a selection by blending pixels within a defined radius.

Filters An image processing sequence within Photoshop that applies a prescribed effect to all or part of an image.

Freeware Programs or add-ons that are free to use.

Gaussian Blur An adjustable blur produced by applying a weighted average to each pixel. The value is arrived at by using a Gaussian, or bell-shaped curve.

Gray Balance Usually refers to the amount of cyan, magenta, and yellow necessary to create a neutral gray. Also used to represent the balancing of the tonal values throughout an image to produce a full range of image detail.

Gray Wedge A photographic strip that contains percentages of gray usually in ten percent increments and can be purchased at many graphic arts and camera stores.

Grayscale A color mode that uses 8-bit tonal information, rendering the image in 256 shades of gray.

Handles Points and lines connected to an anchor point on a path. Moving the handles curves the line segment associated with the anchor point.

Highlights The brightest points in an image.

Hue Colors described in human terms such as purple, greenish-blue, and so on; the color component of the HSB color space.

JPEG Joint Photographic Experts Group. A *lossy* compression scheme used to compress color image data.

Kerning To increase or decrease the space between pairs of typed characters to visually improve the overall appearance of a word or phrase.

Kilobytes 1,024 bytes of data on a computer.

layer Mask A dynamic mask added to a layer to facilitate masking the layer contents.

lightness The luminosity value (gray values) in the HSB color space.

line Screen The unit of measure used in creating halftone images for print. Higher line screen values reflect finer resolutions.

Lossless Compression A compression scheme, such as that used by the GIF file format, that compresses the image and the file size while maintaining all original data. There's no loss in image quality.

Lossy Compression A compression scheme, such as that used in the JPEG file format, which reduces the file size by removing data from the original file. This results in a lower image quality.

LPI Lines Per Inch. The resolution of an offset printed image reflected as lines of 50% halftone dots per inch.

Luminosity The grayscale values of an image when displayed on a monitor using light intensity to represent gray values.

Megabytes 1,024 kilobytes of data on a computer.

Midtones The middle tonal ranges of an image that fall between the shadows and highlights.

Moiré Pattern An undesirable pattern that becomes apparent when two patterns are overlapped. This happens with halftone dots and creates an undulating secondary pattern on a printed image.

Montage A collection of overlapping images. In Photoshop, a collection of images overlayed with various compositing effects such as Blending modes and layer masks.

Native With regard to filters, this simply means those that come with your copy of Photoshop 5, as opposed to third-party plug-in filters, such as Eye Candy or Kai's Power Tools that you buy elsewhere and plug-in yourself.

Neutral Values Color values that do not contain hues, such as black, grays, and white.

Path A linear outline of an image area or shape.

Pixelate Grouping similarly colored pixels into a variety of shaped cells.

Plug-in Miniapplications that plug into Photoshop to provide additional functions.

PPI Pixels Per Inch. The resolution of an electronic image such as a Photoshop image.

Printer Driver A small file that contains information specific to a particular printer. Printer drivers contain the information used by the Page Setup and Print dialog boxes in software applications.

Quadtone A grayscale image printed with four inks that blend to reproduce tinted grays instead of colors.

QuickTime An Apple extension that controls the playback and compression of video images and sound.

Radial A pattern that emanates outward from a center point, creating a circular shape.

Rasterize The process of creating pixel data from vector elements.

Resolution Refers to the detail within a digital image, as determined by the number of dots or pixels per inch.

RGB Red, Green, and Blue color space; the colors used by monitors.

Sampling Down Reducing the dimensions of an image. Pixels are removed by a process known as sampling, which measures the color value of each pixel and uses that data to remove pixels altogether or averages a group of pixels into one.

Sampling Up Enlarging an image. Extra pixels are added by a process known as sampling, which measures the color value of each pixel and from that data determines what values to assign the new pixels.

Saturation The intensity of a particular hue in the HSB color space; the degree of pure color that is present in an image. Pure color refers to the absence of black or white, which would tint or tone down the color.

Screen Frequency The number of lines (of halftone dots) per inch on a halftone screen; also called screen ruling.

Selection Refers to an active area in an image that can be edited, which is indicated by a flashing dashed line in the image.

Shadows The darkest points in an image.

Shareware Programs or add-ons that are freely available to use and try out but must be paid for after a certain number of uses or days.

Silhouette To isolate an object from its background in a Photoshop image, either by selection or by creating clipping paths.

Snapshot In Photoshop, capturing the state of an image at a particular point during editing; usually to provide a means to return to that state. Snapshots are stored in the History palette.

Source Point The reference point used by the Rubber Stamp tool to apply cloning information to the image.

Thumbnail A small image that is representative of a larger image. In Photoshop, the pictures that appear in the Layers, Channels, History, and Paths palettes.

Total Ink Density The maximum amount of ink, specified as a percentage, that is allowed at any given spot on your image when it is printed on an offset printing press. A total ink density of 300%, for example, means that the combination of cyan, magenta, yellow, and black ink at any given place on your image cannot be higher than 300% total.

Tracking To increase or decrease the space between all characters in a range of text, including word spacing.

Tritone An image that is comprised of three colors, each color representing a portion of the image's grayscale values.

Video CaptureBoard A computer card that extends the capability of a computer to enable it to import and export video from some external source such as a VHS or BETA video camera.

Vignette A feathered edge applied to an image, usually using some sort of geometric shape such as an oval ellipse.

Index

Image-Quality filters